A WOMAN'S JOURNEY
ROUND THE WORLD

BY IDA PFEIFFER

An unabridged translation from the German.

from Vienna to Brazil, Chili, Tahiti, China, Hindostan, Persia, and Asia
Minor.

Table of Contents

3

PREFACE.

I have been called, in many of the public journals, a "professed tourist;" but I am sorry to say that I have no title to the appellation in its usual sense. On the one hand I possess too little wit and humour to render my writings amusing; and, on the other, too little knowledge to judge rightly of what I have gone through. The only gift to which I can lay claim is that of narrating in a simple manner the different scenes in which I have played a part, and the different objects I have beheld; if I ever pronounce an opinion, I do so merely on my own personal experience.

Many will perhaps believe that I undertook so long a journey from vanity. I can only say in answer to this—whoever thinks so should make such a trip himself, in order to gain the conviction, that nothing but a natural wish for travel, a boundless desire of acquiring knowledge, could ever enable a person to overcome the hardships, privations, and dangers to which I have been exposed.

In exactly the same manner as the artist feels an invincible desire to paint, and the poet to give free course to his thoughts, so was I hurried away with an unconquerable wish to see the world. In my youth I dreamed of travelling—in my old age I find amusement in reflecting on what I have beheld.

The public received very favourably my plain unvarnished account of "A Voyage to the Holy Land, and to Iceland and Scandinavia." Emboldened by their kindness, I once more step forward with the journal of my last and most considerable voyage, and I shall feel content if the narration of my adventures procures for my readers only a portion of the immense fund of pleasure derived from the voyage by

THE AUTHORESS.

Vienna, March 16, 1850.

With the hope that we may forward the views of the authoress, and be the means of exciting the public attention to her position and wants, we append the following statement by Mr. A. Petermann, which appeared in the *Athenæum* of the 6th of December, 1851:

"Madame Pfeiffer came to London last April, with the intention of undertaking a fresh journey; her love of travelling appearing not only unabated, but even augmented by the success of her journey round the world. She had planned, as her fourth undertaking, a journey to some of those portions of the globe which she had not yet visited—namely, Australia and the islands of the Asiatic Archipelago; intending to proceed thither by the usual route round the Cape. Her purpose was, however, changed while in London. The recently discovered Lake

Ngami, in Southern Africa, and the interesting region to the north, towards the equator—the reflection how successfully she had travelled among savage tribes, where armed men hesitated to penetrate, how well she had borne alike the cold of Iceland and the heat of Babylonia—and lastly, the suggestion that she might be destined to raise the veil from some of the totally unknown portions of the interior of Africa—made her determine on stopping at the Cape, and trying to proceed thence, if possible, northwards into the equatorial regions of the African Continent.

"Madame Pfeiffer left for the Cape, on the 22nd of May last, in a sailing vessel—her usual mode of travelling by sea, steamboats being too expensive. She arrived safely at Cape Town on the 11th of August, as I learned from a letter which I received from her last week, dated the 20th of August. From that letter the following are extracts:—

"'The impression which this place (Cape Town) made on me, was not an agreeable one. The mountains surrounding the town are bare, the town itself (London being still fresh in my recollection) resembles a village. The houses are of only one story, with terraces instead of roofs. From the deck of the vessel a single tree was visible, standing on a hill. In short, on my arrival I was at once much disappointed, and this disappointment rather increases than otherwise. In the town the European mode of living is entirely prevalent—more so than in any other place abroad that I have seen. I have made a good many inquiries as to travelling into the interior; and have been, throughout, assured that the natives are everywhere kindly disposed to travellers, and that as a woman I should be able to penetrate much farther than a man,—and I have been strongly advised to undertake a journey as far as the unknown lakes, and even beyond. Still, with all these splendid prospects and hopes, I fear I shall travel less in this country than in any other. Here, the first thing you are told is, that you must purchase waggons, oxen, horses, asses,—hire expensive guides, etc., etc. How far should I reach in this way with my £100 sterling? I will give you an example of the charges in this country:—for the carriage of my little luggage to my lodgings I had to pay 10s. 6d.! I had previously landed in what I thought the most expensive places in the world—London, Calcutta, Canton, etc.—had everywhere a much greater distance to go from the vessel to my lodgings, and nowhere had I paid half of what they charged me here. Board and lodging I have also found very dear. Fortunately, I have been very kindly received into the house of Mr. Thaewitzer, the Hamburgh consul, where I live, very agreeably, but do not much advance the object which brought me here. I shall, in the course of the month, undertake a short journey with some Dutch boers to Klein Williams; and I fear that this will form the beginning and the end of my travels in this country.'

"From these extracts it will be seen that the resolute lady has at her command but very slender means for the performance of her journeys. The sum of £100, which was granted to her by the Austrian government, forms the whole of her funds. Private resources she has none. It took her twenty years to save enough money to perform her first journey!—namely, that to the Holy Land. While in London, she received scarcely any encouragement; and her works were not appreciated by the public, or indeed known, till she had left this country. It is to be regretted that the want of a little pecuniary assistance should deter the enterprising lady from carrying out her projected journey in Southern Africa. Though not a scientific traveller, she is a faithful recorder of what she sees and hears; and she is prepared to note the bearings and distances of the journey, make meteorological observations, and keep a careful diary—so that the results of her projected journey would perhaps be of as much interest as those of other travellers of greater pretensions."

CHAPTER I. THE VOYAGE TO THE BRAZILS.

DEPARTURE FROM VIENNA—STAY IN HAMBURGH—STEAMERS AND SAILING VESSELS—DEPARTURE FROM HAMBURGH— CUXHAVEN—THE BRITISH CHANNEL—FLYING-FISH—THE PHISOLIDA—CONSTELLATIONS—PASSING THE LINE—THE "VAMPEROS"—A GALE AND STORM—CAPE FRIO—ARRIVAL IN THE PORT OF RIO JANEIRO.

On the first of May, 1846, I left Vienna, and, with the exception of slight stoppages at Prague, Dresden, and Leipsic, proceeded directly to Hamburgh, there to embark for the Brazils. In Prague I had the pleasure of meeting Count Berchthold, who had accompanied me during a portion of my journey in the East. He informed me that he should like to be my companion in the voyage to the Brazils, and I promised to wait for him in Hamburgh.

I had a second most interesting meeting on the steamer from Prague to Dresden, namely, with the widow of Professor Mikan. In the year 1817, this lady had, on the occasion of the marriage of the Austrian Princess Leopaldine with Don Pedro I., followed her husband to the Brazils, and afterwards made with him a scientific journey into the interior of the country.

I had often heard this lady's name mentioned, and my joy at making her personal acquaintance was very great. In the kindest and most amiable manner she communicated to me the results of her long experience, and added advice and rules of conduct, which proved afterwards highly useful.

I arrived in Hamburgh on the 12th of May; and, as early as the 13th, might have embarked on board a fine fast-sailing brig, which, besides, was christened the "Ida," like myself. With a heavy heart I saw this fine vessel set sail. I was obliged to remain behind, as I had promised my travelling companion to await his arrival. Week after week elapsed, with nothing but the fact of my staying with my relatives to lighten the dreariness of suspense; at last, about the middle of June, the Count came, and shortly afterwards we found a vessel—a Danish brig, the "Caroline," Captain Bock, bound for Rio Janeiro.

I had now before me a long voyage, which could not be made under two months at the least, and which, possibly, might last three or four. Luckily I had already lived for a considerable period on board sailing vessels during my former travels, and was therefore acquainted with their arrangements, which are very different from those of steamers. On board a steamer everything is agreeable and luxurious; the vessel pursues her rapid course independent of the wind, and the passengers enjoy good and fresh provisions, spacious cabins, and excellent society.

In sailing vessels all this is very different, as, with the exception of the large East Indiamen, they are not fitted up for passengers. In them the cargo is looked upon as the principal thing, and in the eyes of the crew passengers are a troublesome addition, whose comfort is generally very little studied. The captain is the only person who takes any interest in them, since a third or even the half of the passage-money falls to his share.

The space, too, is so confined, that you can hardly turn yourself round in the sleeping cabins, while it is quite impossible to stand upright in the berths. Besides this, the motion of a sailing vessel is much stronger than that of a steamer; on the latter, however, many affirm that the eternal vibration, and the disagreeable odour of the oil and coals, are totally insupportable. For my own part, I never found this to be the case; it certainly is unpleasant, but much easier to bear than the many inconveniences always existing on board a sailing vessel. The passenger is there a complete slave to every whim or caprice of the captain, who is an absolute sovereign and holds uncontrolled sway over everything. Even the food depends upon his generosity, and although it is generally not absolutely bad, in the best instances, it is not equal to that on board a steamer.

The following form the ordinary diet: tea and coffee without milk, bacon and junk, soup made with pease or cabbage, potatoes, hard dumplings, salted cod, and ship-biscuit. On rare occasions, ham, eggs, fish, pancakes, or even skinny fowls, are served out. It is very seldom, in small ships, that bread can be procured.

To render the living more palatable, especially on a long voyage, passengers would do well to take with them a few additions to the ship's fare. The most suitable are: portable soup and captain's biscuit—both of which should be kept in tin canisters to preserve them from mouldiness and insects—a good quantity of eggs, which, when the vessel is bound for a southern climate, should first be dipped in strong lime-water or packed in coal-dust; rice, potatoes, sugar, butter, and all the ingredients for making sangaree and potato-salad, the former being very

8

strengthening and the latter very cooling. I would strongly recommend those who have children with them to take a goat as well.

As regards wine, passengers should take especial care to ask the captain whether this is included in the passage-money, otherwise it will have to be purchased from him at a very high rate.

There are also other objects which must not be forgotten, and above all a mattress, bolster, and counterpane, as the berths are generally unfurnished. These can be purchased very cheaply in any seaport town.

Besides this, it is likewise advisable to take a stock of coloured linen. The office of washerwoman is filled by a sailor, so that it may easily be imagined that the linen does not return from the wash in the best possible condition.

When the sailors are employed in shifting the sails, great care must be taken to avoid injury by the falling of any of the ropes. But all these inconveniences are comparatively trifling; the greatest amount of annoyance begins towards the end of the voyage. The captain's mistress is his ship. At sea he allows her to wear an easy *negligé*, but in port she must appear in full dress. Not a sign of the long voyage, of the storms, of the glowing heat she has suffered, must be visible. Then begins an incessant hammering, planing, and sawing; every flaw, every crack or injury is made good, and, to wind up, the whole vessel is painted afresh. The worst of all, however, is the hammering when the cracks in the deck are being repaired and filled up with pitch. This is almost unbearable.

But enough of annoyances. I have described them merely to prepare, in some degree, those who have never been to sea. Persons residing in sea-port towns do not, perhaps, stand in need of this, for they hear these matters mentioned every day; but such is not the case with us poor souls, who have lived all our lives in inland cities. Very often we hardly know how a steamer or a sailing vessel looks, much less the mode of life on board them. I speak from experience, and know too well what I myself suffered on my first voyage, simply because, not having been warned beforehand, I took nothing with me save a small stock of linen and clothes.

At present I will proceed with the progress of my voyage. We embarked on the evening of the 28th of June, and weighed anchor before daybreak of the 29th. The voyage did not commence in any very encouraging manner; we had very little, in fact almost no wind at all, and compared to us every pedestrian appeared to be running a race: we made the nine miles to Blankenese in seven hours.

Luckily the slow rate at which we proceeded was not so disagreeable, as, at first, for a considerable period we beheld the magnificent port, and afterwards could admire, on the Holstein side, the beautiful country houses of the rich Hamburghers, situated upon charming eminences and surrounded by lovely gardens. The opposite side, belonging to Hanover, is as flat and monotonous as the other is beautiful. About here the Elbe, in many places, is from three to four

9

miles broad.

Before reaching Blankenese the ships take in their stock of water from the Elbe. This water, although of a dirty and thick appearance, is said to possess the valuable quality of resisting putridity for years.

We did not reach Glückstadt (37 miles from Hamburgh) before the morning of the 30th. As there was not now a breath of wind, we were entirely at the mercy of the stream, and began drifting back. The captain, therefore, ordered the men to cast anchor, and profited by the leisure thus forced upon him to have the chests and boxes made fast on the deck and in the hold. We idlers had permission granted us to land and visit the town, in which, however, we found but little to admire.

There were eight passengers on board. The four cabin places were taken by Count B——, myself, and two young people who hoped to make their fortune sooner in the Brazils than in Europe. The price of a passage in the first cabin was 100 dollars (£20 16s. 8d.), and in the steerage 50 dollars (£10 8s. 4d.).

In the steerage, besides two worthy tradesmen, was a poor old woman who was going, in compliance with the wish of her only son, who had settled in the Brazils, to join him there, and a married woman whose husband had been working as a tailor for the last six years in Rio Janeiro. People soon become acquainted on board ship, and generally endeavour to agree as well as possible, in order to render the monotony of a long voyage at all supportable.

On the 1st of July we again set sail in rather stormy weather. We made a few miles, but were soon obliged to cast anchor once more. The Elbe is here so wide, that we could hardly see its banks, and the swell so strong, that sea-sickness began to manifest itself among our company. On the 2nd of July, we again attempted to weigh anchor, but with no better success than the day before. Towards evening we saw some dolphins, called also *tummler*, or tumblers, as well as several gulls, which announced to us that we were fast nearing the sea.

A great many vessels passed quickly by us. Ah! they could turn to account the storm and wind which swelled out their sails, and drove them rapidly towards the neighbouring port. We grudged them their good fortune; and perhaps we had to thank this specimen of Christian love on our part, that on the 3rd of July, we had not got further than Cuxhaven, seventy-four miles from Hamburgh.

The 4th of July was a beautifully fine day, for those who could remain quietly on shore; but for those on board ship it was bad enough, as there was not the slightest breath of wind stirring. To get rid of our lamentations, the captain launched out in praises of the charming little town, and had us conveyed to land. We visited the town, as well as the bathing establishment and the lighthouse, and afterwards actually proceeded as far as a place called the "Bush," where, as we were told, we should find a great abundance of strawberries. After wandering about, over fields and meadows, for a good hour in the glowing heat, we found

10

the Bush, it is true, but instead of strawberries, discovered only frogs and adders there.

We now proceeded into the scanty wood, where we saw about twenty tents erected. A bustling landlord came up, and offering us some glasses of bad milk, said that every year a fair is held in the Bush for three weeks, or rather, on three successive Sundays, for during the week days the booths are closed. The landlady also came tripping towards us, and invited us, in a very friendly manner, to spend the next Sunday with them. She assured us that we should "amuse ourselves charmingly;" that we elder members of the company should find entertainment in the wonderful performances of the tumblers and jugglers, and the younger gentlemen find spruce young girls for partners in the dance.

We expressed ourselves much pleased at this invitation, promised to be sure to come, and then extended our walk to Ritzebüttel, where we admired a small castle and a miniature park.

5th July. Nothing is so changeable as the weather: yesterday we were revelling in sunshine, and today we were surrounded by a thick, dark fog; and yet this, bad as it was, we found more agreeable than the fine weather of the day before, for a slight breeze sprang up, and at nine o'clock in the morning, we heard the rattling of the capstan, as the anchor was being weighed. In consequence of this, the young people were obliged to give up the idea of an excursion to the Bush, and defer all dancing with pretty girls until their arrival in another hemisphere, for it was fated that they should not set foot in Europe again.

The transition from the Elbe to the North Sea is scarcely perceptible, as the Elbe is not divided into different channels, but is eight or ten miles broad at its mouth. It almost forms a small sea of itself, and has even the green hue of one. We were, consequently, very much surprised, on hearing the captain exclaim, in a joyful tone, "We are out of the river at last." We imagined that we had long since been sailing upon the wide ocean.

In the afternoon, we bore in sight of the island of Heligoland, which belongs to the English, and presented really a magical appearance, as it rose out from the sea. It is a barren, colossal rock; and had I not learned, from one of the newest works on geography, that it was peopled by about 2,500 souls, I should have supposed the whole island to have been uninhabited. On three sides, the cliffs rise so precipitously from the waves, that all access is impossible.

We sailed by the place at a considerable distance, and saw only the towers of the church and lighthouse, in addition to the so-called "Monk," a solitary, perpendicular rock, that is separated from the main body, between which and it there sparkles a small strip of sea.

The inhabitants are very poor. The only sources of their livelihood are fishing and bathing visitors. A great number of the latter come every year, as the bathing, on account of the extraordinary swell, is reckoned extremely efficacious.

11

Unfortunately, great fears are entertained that this watering-place cannot exist much longer, as every year the island decreases in size, from the continual falling away of large masses of rock, so that some day the whole place may disappear into the sea.

From the 5th to the 10th of July, we had continued stormy and cold weather, with a heavy sea, and great rolling of the ship. All we poor "land-lubbers" were suffering from sea sickness. We first entered the British Channel, also called "La Manche" (420 miles from Cuxhaven) in the night of the 10-11th.

We awaited with impatience the rising of the sun, which would display to our gaze two of the mightiest powers in Europe. Luckily, the day was fine and clear, and the two kingdoms lay before us, in such magnificence and proximity, that the beholder was almost inclined to believe that a sister people inhabited both countries.

On the coast of England, we saw the North Foreland, the Castle of Sandown, and the town of Deal, stretching out at the foot of the cliffs, which extend for many miles, and are about 150 feet high. Further on, we came in sight of the South Foreland; and lastly, the ancient castle of Dover, that sits right bravely enthroned upon an eminence, and overlooks the surrounding country, far and wide. The town itself lies upon the sea-shore.

Opposite Dover, at the narrowest part of the channel, we distinguished, on the French coast, Cape Grisnez, where Napoleon erected a small building, in order, it is said, to be at least able to see England; and, further on, the obelisk raised in memory of the camp at Boulogne, by Napoleon, but completed under Louis Philippe.

The wind being unfavourable, we were obliged, during the night, to tack in the neighbourhood of Dover. The great darkness which covered both land and sea rendered this maneuvre a very dangerous one; firstly, on account of the proximity of the coast; and, secondly, on account of the number of vessels passing up and down the channel. To avoid a collision, we hung out a lantern on the foremast, while, from time to time, a torch was lighted, and held over the side, and the bell frequently kept sounding: all very alarming occurrences to a person unused to the sea.

For fourteen days were we prisoners in the 360 miles of the Channel, remaining very often two or three days, as if spell-bound, in the same place, while we were frequently obliged to cruise for whole days to make merely a few miles; and near Start we were overtaken by a tolerably violent storm. During the night I was suddenly called upon deck. I imagined that some misfortune had happened, and hastily throwing a few clothes on, hurried up—to enjoy the astonishing spectacle of a "sea-fire." In the wake of the vessel I behold a streak of fire so strong that it would have been easy to read by its light; the water round the ship looked like a glowing stream of lava, and every wave, as it rose up, threw out sparks of fire.

The track of the fish was surrounded by dazzling inimitable brilliancy, and far and wide everything was one dazzling coruscation.

This extraordinary illumination of the sea is of very unfrequent occurrence, and rarely happens after long-continued, violent storms. The captain told me that he had never yet beheld the sea so lighted up. For my part, I shall never forget the sight.

A second, and hardly less beautiful, spectacle came under our observation at another time, when, after a storm, the clouds, gilt by the rays of the sun, were reflected as in a mirror on the bosom of the sea. They glittered and shone with an intensity of colour which surpassed even those of the rainbow.

We had full leisure to contemplate Eddystone Lighthouse, which is the most celebrated building of the kind in Europe, as we were cruising about for two days in sight of it. Its height, and the boldness and strength with which it is built, are truly wonderful; but still more wonderful is its position upon a dangerous reef, situated ten miles from the coast; at a distance, it seems to be founded in the sea itself.

We often sailed so near the coast of Cornwall, that not only could we plainly perceive every village, but even the people in the streets and in the open country. The land is hilly and luxuriant, and appears carefully cultivated.

During the whole time of our cruising in the Channel, the temperature was cold and raw, the thermometer seldom being higher than 65° to 75° Fah.

At last, on the 24th of July, we came to the end of the Channel, and attained the open sea; the wind was tolerably favourable, and on the 2nd of August we were off Gibraltar, where we were becalmed for twenty-four hours. The captain threw several pieces of white crockeryware, as well as a number of large bones overboard, to show how beautifully green such objects appeared as they slowly sank down beneath the sea; of course this can only be seen in a perfect calm.

In the evening we were greatly delighted by numbers of moluscæ shining through the water; they looked exactly like so many floating stars, about the size of a man's hand; even by day we could perceive them beneath the waves. They are of a brownish red, and in form resemble a toadstool; many had a thick pedicle, somewhat fimbriated on the under part; others, instead of the pedicle, had a number of threads hanging down from them.

4th August. This was the first day that it was announced by the heat that we were in a southern latitude; but, as was also the case the following day, the clear dark blue sky that generally overarches the Mediterranean in such exceeding loveliness, was still wanting. We found, however, some slight compensation for this in the rising and setting of the sun, as these were often accompanied by unusual forms and colours of the clouds.

We were now off Morocco, and were fortunate enough today to perceive a great

13

number of bonitos. Every one on board bestirred himself, and on every side fish hooks were cast overboard; unluckily only one bonito allowed himself to be entrapped by our friendly invitations; he made a dart at the bait, and his good-natured confidence procured us a fresh meal, of which we had long been deprived.

On the 5th of August we saw land for the first time for twelve days. The sun was rising as the little island of Porto Santo greeted our sight. It is formed of peaked mountains, which, by their shape, betray their volcanic origin. A few miles in advance of the island stands the beautiful Falcon Rock, like a sentinel upon the look-out. We sailed past Madeira (23 miles from Porto Santo) the same day, but unluckily at such a distance that we could only perceive the long mountain chains by which the island is intersected. Near Madeira lie the rocky Deserta Islands, which are reckoned as forming part of Africa.

Near these islands we passed a vessel running under reefed sails before the wind, whence the captain concluded that she was a cruiser looking after slavers.

On the 6th of August we beheld, for the first time, flying fish, but at such a distance that we could scarcely distinguish them.

On the 7th of August we neared the Canary Isles, but unfortunately, on account of the thick fog, we could not see them. We now caught the trade wind, that blows from the east, and is anxiously desired by all sailors.

In the night of the 9-10th we entered the tropics. We were now in daily expectation of greater heat and a clearer sky, but met with neither. The atmosphere was dull and hazy, and even in our own raw fatherland the sky could not have been so overcast, except upon some days in November. Every evening the clouds were piled upon one another in such a way that we were continually expecting to see a water-spout; it was generally not before midnight that the heavens would gradually clear up, and allow us to admire the beautiful and dazzling constellations of the South.

The captain told us that this was the fourteenth voyage he had made to the Brazils, during which time he had always found the heat very easily borne, and had never seen the sky otherwise than dull and lowering. He said that this was occasioned by the damp, unhealthy coast of Guinea, the ill effects of which were perceptible much further than where we then were, although the distance between us was 350 miles.

In the tropics the quick transition from day to night is already very perceptible; 35 or 40 minutes after the setting of the sun the deepest darkness reigns around. The difference in the length of day and night decreases more and more the nearer you approach the Equator. At the Equator itself the day and night are of equal duration.

All the 14th and 15th of August we sailed parallel with the Cape de Verde Islands,

14

from which we were not more than 23 miles distant, but which, on account of the hazy state of the weather, we could not see.

During this period we used to be much amused by small flocks of flying-fish, which very often rose from the water so near the ship's side that we were enabled to examine them minutely. They are generally of the size and colour of a herring; their side fins, however, are longer and broader, and they have the power of spreading and closing them like little wings. They raise themselves about twelve or fifteen feet above the water, and then, after flying more than a distance of a hundred feet, dive down again for a moment beneath the waves, to recommence directly afterwards: this occurs most frequently when they are pursued by bonitos or other foes. When they were flying at some distance from the ship they really looked like elegant birds. We very frequently saw the bonitos also, who were pursuing them, endeavour to raise themselves above the water, but they seldom succeeded in raising more than their head.

It is very difficult to catch one of these little denizens of the air, as they are to be secured neither by nets or hooks; but sometimes the wind will drive them, during the night, upon the deck, where they are discovered, in the morning, dead, not having sufficient strength to raise themselves from dry places; in this way I obtained a few specimens.

Today, August 15th, we enjoyed a most interesting sight. We happened, exactly at 12 o'clock, to be in the sun's zenith, and the sunbeams fell so perpendicularly that every object was perfectly shadowless. We put books, chairs, ourselves in the sun, and were highly delighted with this unusual kind of amusement. Luckily we had chanced to be at the right spot at the right time; had we, at the same hour, been only one degree nearer or one degree further, we should have lost the entire sight; when we saw it we were 14° 6' (a minute is equal to a nautical mile).

All observations with the sextant {9} were out of the question until we were once more some degrees from the zenith.

17th August. Shoals of tunny-fish, (fish four and five feet long, and belonging to the dolphin tribe,) were seen tumbling about the ship. A harpoon was quickly procured, and one of the sailors sent out with it on the bowsprit; but whether he had bad luck, or was unskilled in the art of harpooning, he missed his mark. The most wonderful part of the story, though, was that all the fish disappeared as if by magic, and did not appear again for some days; it seemed as if they had whispered and warned each other of the threatened danger.

All the oftener, however, did we see another inhabitant of the sea, namely, that beautiful mollusca, the physolida, called by the sailors *Portugiesisches Segel-schiff,* (Portuguese sailing-ship.) When floating upon the surface of the sea, with its long crest, which it can elevate or depress at pleasure, it really resembles a delicate tiny little sailing vessel. I was very desirous of catching one of these little creatures, but this could only be effected by means of a net, which I had not got, nor had I

15

either needle or twine to make one. Necessity, however, is the mother of invention; so I manufactured a knitting needle of wood, unravelled some thick string, and in a few hours possessed a net. Very soon afterwards a mollusca had been captured, and placed in a tub filled with sea water. The little creature's body is about six inches long and two inches high; the crest extends over the whole of the back, and in the middle, where it is highest, measures about an inch and a half. Both the crest and body are transparent, and appear as if tinged with rose colour; from the belly, which is violet, are suspended a number of threads or arms of the same colour.

I hung the little thing up to dry at the stern, outside the ship; some of the threads reached down into the water (a depth of at least twelve feet), but most of them fell off. After the animal was dead, the crest remained erect, and the body perfectly filled out, but the beautiful rose colour gradually changed to white.

18th August. Today we had a heavy thunder-storm, for which we were very grateful, as it cooled the air considerably. Between 1° and 2°, or 3° North latitude, frequent changes in the weather are very common. For instance, on the morning of the 20th we were overtaken by a strong wind, which lashed up the sea to a great height, and continued until evening, when it gave way to a tropical shower, which we at home should call a perfect water-spout. The deck was instantaneously transformed into a lake, while at the same time the wind had so completely fallen that even the rudder enjoyed a holiday.

This rain cost me a night's rest, for when I went to take possession of my berth, I found the bed-clothes drenched through and through, and was fain to content myself with a wooden bench for a couch.

On the 27th of August we got beyond these hostile latitudes, and were received by the anxiously desired south-east trade wind, which hurried us quickly on our voyage.

We were now very near the Equator, and, like all other travellers, wished very much to see the celebrated constellations of the south. I myself was most interested in the Southern Cross; and, as I could not find it among the stars, I begged the captain to point it out to me. Both he and the first mate, however, said that they had never heard of it, and the second mate was the only one to whom it did not appear entirely unknown. With his help, we really did discover in the spangled firmament four stars, which had something of the form of a somewhat crooked cross, but were certainly not remarkable in themselves, nor did they excite the least enthusiasm amongst us. A most magnificent spectacle was, on the contrary, formed by Orion, Jupiter, and Venus; the latter, indeed, shone so brilliantly that her gleams formed a silver furrow across the waves.

The great frequency of falling stars is another fact that I cannot corroborate. They are, perhaps, more frequent than in cold climates, but are far from being as common as is said: and as for their size, I saw only one which surpassed ours; and

16

this appeared about three times as large as an ordinary star.

For some days also we had now seen the Cape, or Magellan's Clouds, and also the so-called Black Cloud. The first are bright, and, like the Milky Way, are formed of numberless small stars, invisible to the naked eye; the latter presents a black appearance, and is said to be produced by the absence of all stars whatever from this part of the heavens.

All these different signs prepared us for the most interesting moment of our voyage—namely, passing the line.

On the 29th of August, at 10 o'clock P.M., we saluted the southern hemisphere for the first time. A feeling nearly allied to pride excited every one, but more especially those who crossed the line for the first time. We shook each other by the hand, and congratulated one another mutually, as if we had done some great and heroic deed. One of the passengers had brought with him a bottle or two of champagne to celebrate the event: the corks sprang gaily in the air, and with a joyful "huzza," the health of the new hemisphere was drunk.

No festivities took place among the crew. This is at present the case in most vessels, as such amusements seldom end without drunkenness and disorder. The sailors, however, could not let the cabin-boy, who passed the line for the first time, go quite scot-free; so he was well christened in a few buckets of salt water.

Long before passing the line, we passengers had frequently spoken of all the sufferings and tortures we should be subjected to at the Equator. Every one had read or heard something exceedingly horrible, which he duly communicated to all the rest. One expected headache or colic; a second had pictured to himself the sailors falling down from exhaustion; a third dreaded such a fearful degree of heat, that it would not only melt the pitch, {11} but would so dry up the ship, that nothing but continual throwing water over it could prevent its catching fire; while a fourth feared that all the provisions would be spoilt, and ourselves nearly starved to death.

For my own part, I had already congratulated myself on the tragical stories I should be able to present to my readers; I beheld them shedding tears at the narration of the sufferings we had experienced, and I already appeared to myself half a martyr. Alas! I was sadly deceived. We all remained in perfectly good health; not a sailor sank exhausted; the ship did not catch fire; and the provisions were not spoilt—they were just as bad as before.

3rd September. From 2° to 3° South latitude the wind is very irregular, and frequently excessively violent. Today we passed the 8° South latitude, without seeing land, which put the captain in the best of humours. He explained to us, that if we had seen land, we should have been obliged to retrace our course almost to the line, because the current sets in with such violence towards the land, that the voyage could only be made at a proper distance.

17

7th September. Between 10° and 20° South latitude we again met with very peculiar prevalent winds. They are called *vamperos*, and oblige the sailor to be always on his guard, as they spring up very suddenly, and are often extremely violent. We were overtaken by one during the night, but, luckily, it was not of the worst kind. In a few hours it had entirely passed over, but the sea did not become calm again for a considerable time.

On the 9th and 11th of September, we encountered some short gusts of the *vamperos*, the most violent being the last.

12th and 13th of September. The first was termed by the captain merely "a stiffish breeze;" but the second was entered in the log {12} as "a storm." The stiffish breeze cost us one sail; the storm, two. During the time it lasted, the sea ran so high, that it was with the greatest difficulty we could eat. With one hand we were obliged to grasp the plate, and at the same time to hold fast on to the table, while, with the other, we managed, with considerable difficulty, to convey the food to our mouth. At night, I was obliged to "stow" myself firmly in my berth with my cloaks and dresses, to protect my body from being bruised black and blue.

On the morning of the 13th, I was on deck at break of day. The helmsman led me to the side of the vessel, and told me to hold my head overboard, and inhale the air. I breathed a most beautiful perfume of flowers. I looked round in astonishment, and imagined that I must already be able to see the land: it was, however, still far distant, the soft perfume being merely drifted to us by the wind. It was very remarkable that inside the ship this perfume was not at all perceptible.

The sea itself was covered with innumerable dead butterflies and moths, which had been carried out to sea by the storm. Two pretty little birds, quite exhausted by their long flight, were resting upon one of the yards.

For us, who, during two months and a half, had seen nothing but sky and water, all these things were most satisfactory; and we looked out anxiously for Cape Frio, which we were very near. The horizon, however, was lowering and hazy, and the sun had not force enough to tear the murky veil asunder. We looked forward with joy to the next morning, but during the night were overtaken by another storm, which lasted until 2 o'clock. The ship's course was changed, and she was driven as far as possible into the open sea; so that, in the end, we were glad enough to reach, the next day, the same position we had occupied the morning before.

Today we caught no glimpse of land; but a few gulls and albatrosses from Cape Frio warned us that we were near it, and afforded us some little amusement. They swam close up to the ship's side, and eagerly swallowed every morsel of bread or meat that was thrown to them. The sailors tried to catch some with a hook and line, and were fortunate enough to succeed. They were placed upon the deck, and, to my great surprise, I perceived that they were unable to raise themselves from it. If we touched them, they merely dragged themselves, with great difficulty, a few

18

paces further, although they could rise very easily from the surface of the water, and fly extremely high.

One of the gentlemen was exceedingly anxious to kill and stuff one of them, but the superstition of the sailors was opposed to this. They said that if birds were killed on board ship, their death would be followed by long calms. We yielded to their wishes and restored the little creatures to the air and waves, their native elements.

This was another proof that superstition is still deep-rooted in the minds of sailors. Of this we had afterwards many other instances. The captain, for example, was always very averse to the passengers amusing themselves with cards or any other game of chance; in another vessel, as I was informed, no one was allowed to write on Sunday, etc. Empty casks or logs of wood were also very frequently thrown overboard during a calm—probably as sacrifices to the deities of the winds.

On the morning of the 16th of September we at last had the good fortune to perceive the mountains before Rio Janeiro, and soon singled out the *Sugarloaf*. At 2 o'clock, P.M., we entered the bay and port of Rio Janeiro.

Immediately at the entrance of the bay are several conical rocks, some of which, like the Sugarloaf, rise singly from the sea, while others are joined at the base, and are almost inaccessible. {13} Between these "ocean mountains," if I may be allowed the expression, are seen the most remarkably beautiful views; now extraordinary ravines, then some charmingly situated quarter of the town, presently the open sea, and the moment after some delightful bay. From the bay itself, at the end of which the capital is built, rise masses of rock, serving as foundations to different fortifications. On some of these eminences are chapels and fortresses. Ships are obliged to pass as near as possible to one of the largest of the latter, namely, Santa Cruz, in order that their papers may be examined.

From this fortress, to the right, stretches the beautiful mountain range of the Serados-Orgõas, which, in conjunction with other mountains and hills, fringes a lovely bay, on the shores of which lie the little town of Praya-grande, some few villages and detached farmhouses.

At the extremity of the principal bay, stands Rio Janeiro, surrounded by a tolerably high chain of mountains (among which is the Corcovado, 2,100 feet high), behind which, more inland, is the Organ Mountain, which owes its name to its many gigantic peaks placed upright one against the other like the pipes of an organ. The highest peak is 5,000 feet high.

One portion of the town is concealed by the Telegraph Mountain, and several hills, on which, besides the Telegraph, there is a monastery of Capuchin monks and other smaller buildings. Of the town itself are seen several rows of houses and open squares, the Great Hospital, the Monasteries of St. Luzia and Moro do Castello, the Convent of St. Bento, the fine Church of St. Candelaria, and some

19

portions of the really magnificent aqueduct. Close to the sea is the Public Garden (*passeo publico*) of the town, which, from its fine palm trees, and elegant stone gallery, with two summer-houses, forms a striking object. To the left, upon eminences, stand some isolated churches and monasteries, such as St. Gloria, St. Theresa, etc. Near these are the Praya Flamingo and Botafogo, large villages with beautiful villas, pretty buildings, and gardens, which stretch far away until lost in the neighbourhood of the Sugarloaf, and thus close this most wonderful panorama. In addition to all this, the many vessels, partly in the harbour before the town, partly anchored in the different bays, the rich and luxuriant vegetation, and the foreign and novel appearance of the whole, help to form a picture, of whose beauties my pen, unfortunately, can never convey an adequate idea.

It rarely happens that a person is so lucky as to enjoy, immediately on his arrival, so beautiful and extensive a view as fell to my lot; fogs, clouds, or a hazy state of the atmosphere, very often conceal certain portions, and thus disturb the wonderful impression of the whole. Whenever this is the case, I would advise every one, who intends stopping any time in Rio Janeiro, to take a boat, on a perfectly clear day, as far as Santa Cruz, in order to behold this peculiarly beautiful prospect.

It was almost dark before we reached the place of anchorage. We were first obliged to stop at Santa Cruz to have the ship's papers examined, and then appear before an officer, who took from us our passports and sealed letters; then before a surgeon, who inspected us to see that we had not brought the plague or yellow fever; and lastly, before another officer, who took possession of different packets and boxes, and assigned us the spot to anchor in.

It was now too late for us to land, and the captain alone proceeded on shore. We, however, remained for a long time on deck, contemplating the magnificent picture before us, until both land and sea lay shrouded in night.

With a light heart did we all retire to rest; the goal of our long voyage had been attained without any misfortune worthy of being mentioned. A cruel piece of intelligence was in store for the poor tailor's wife alone; but the good captain did not break it to her today, in order to let her enjoy an undisturbed night's rest. As soon as the tailor heard that his wife was really on her passage out, he ran off with a negress, and left nought behind but—debts.

The poor woman had given up a sure means of subsistence in her native land (she supported herself by cleaning lace and ladies' apparel), and had devoted her little savings to pay the expenses of her voyage, and all to find herself deserted and helpless in a strange hemisphere. {14}

From Hamburgh to Rio Janeiro is about 8,750 miles.

20

CHAPTER II. ARRIVAL AND SOJOURN IN RIO JANEIRO.

INTRODUCTION—ARRIVAL—DESCRIPTION OF THE TOWN—THE BLACKS AND THEIR RELATIONS TO THE WHITES—ARTS AND SCIENCES—FESTIVALS OF THE CHURCH—BAPTISM OF THE IMPERIAL PRINCESS—FETE IN THE BARRACKS—CLIMATE AND VEGETATION—MANNERS AND CUSTOMS—A FEW WORDS TO EMIGRANTS.

I remained in Rio Janeiro above two months, exclusive of the time devoted to my different excursions into the interior of the country; it is very far from my intention, however, to tire the reader with a regular catalogue of every trifling and ordinary occurrence. I shall content myself with describing the most striking features in the town, and likewise in the manners and customs of the inhabitants, according to the opportunities I possessed during my stay to form an opinion of them. I shall then give an account of my various excursions in an Appendix, and afterwards resume the thread of my journal.

It was on the morning of the 17th of September that, after the lapse of nearly two months and a half, I first set foot upon dry land. The captain himself accompanied the passengers on shore, after having earnestly advised each one separately to be sure and smuggle nothing, more especially sealed letters. "In no part of the world," he assured us, "were the Custom-house officers so strict, and the penalties so heavy."

On coming in sight of the guard ship, we began to feel quite frightened from this description, and made up our minds that we should be examined from top to toe. The captain begged permission to accompany us on shore; this was immediately granted, and the whole ceremony was completed. During the entire period that we lived on board the ship, and were continually going and coming to and from the town, we never were subjected to any search; it was only when we took chests and boxes with us that we were obliged to proceed to the Custom-house, where all effects are strictly examined, and a heavy duty levied upon merchandise, books, etc., etc.

We landed at the Praya dos Mineiros, a disgusting and dirty sort of square, inhabited by a few dozen blacks, equally disgusting and dirty, who were squatted on the ground, and praising at the top of their voices the fruits and sweetmeats which they were offering for sale. Thence we proceeded directly into the principal street (*Rua Direita*), whose only beauty consists in its breadth. It contains several public buildings, such as the Post-office, the Custom-house, the Exchange, the Guard-house, etc.; all of which, however, are so insignificant in appearance, that any one would pass them by unnoticed, if there were not always a number of people loitering before them.

At the end of this street stands the Imperial Palace, a commonplace, large building, exactly resembling a private house, without the least pretensions to taste or architectural beauty. The square before it (*Largo do Paço*), whose only ornament, a plain fountain, is extremely dirty, and serves at night as a sleeping place for a number of poor free negroes, who, on getting up in the morning, perform the various duties of their toilet in public with the most supreme indifference. A part of the square is walled off and employed as a market for fish, fruit, vegetables, and poultry.

Of the remaining streets the Rua Misericorda and the Rua Ouvidor are the most interesting. The latter contains the finest and largest shops; but we must not expect the magnificent establishments we behold in the cities of Europe—in fact, we meet with little that is beautiful or costly. The flower-shops were the only objects of particular attraction for me. In these shops are exposed for sale the most lovely artificial flowers, made of birds' feathers, fishes' scales, and beetles' wings.

Of the squares, the finest is the Largo do Rocio; the largest, the Largo St. Anna. In the first, which is always kept tolerably clean, stand the Opera-house, the Government-house, the Police-office, etc. This, too, is the starting-place for most of the omnibuses, which traverse the town in all directions.

The last-named square is the dirtiest in the whole town. On crossing it for the first time, I perceived lying about me half putrid cats and dogs—and even a mule in the same state. The only ornament of this square is a fountain, and I almost think I should prefer it if the fountain were, in this case, taken away; for, as soft water is not very abundant in Rio Janeiro, the washerwoman's noble art pitches its tent wherever it finds any, and most willingly of all when, at the same time, it meets with a good drying ground. The consequence is, that in the Largo St. Anna there is always such an amount of washing and drying, of squalling and screaming, that you are glad to get away as quickly as possible.

There is nothing remarkable in the appearance of the churches, either inside or out. The Church and Cloister of St. Bento and the Church of St. Candelaria are the most deceptive; from a distance they have a very imposing look.

The houses are built in the European fashion, but are small and insignificant; most of them have only a ground-floor or single story,—two stories are rarely met with. Neither are there any terraces and verandahs adorned with elegant trellis-work and flowers, as there are in other warm countries. Ugly little balconies hang from the walls, while clumsy wooden shutters close up the windows, and prevent the smallest sunbeam from penetrating into the rooms, where everything is enveloped in almost perfect darkness. This, however, is a matter of the greatest indifference to the Brazilian ladies, who certainly never over-fatigue themselves with reading or working.

The town offers, therefore, very little in the way of squares, streets, and buildings, which, for a stranger, can prove in the least attractive; while the people that he meets are truly shocking—nearly all being negroes and negresses, with flat, ugly noses, thick lips, and short woolly hair. They are, too, generally half naked, with only a few miserable rags on their backs, or else they are thrust into the worn-out European-cut clothes of their masters. To every four or five blacks may be reckoned a mulatto, and it is only here and there that a white man is to be seen.

This horrible picture is rendered still more revolting by the frequent bodily infirmities which everywhere meet the eye: among these elephantiasis, causing horrible club-feet, is especially conspicuous; there is, too, no scarcity of persons afflicted with blindness and other ills. Even the cats and dogs, that run about the gutters in great numbers, partake of the universal ugliness: most of them are covered with the mange, or are full of wounds and sores. I should like to be endowed with the magic power of transporting hither every traveller who starts back with affright from the lanes of Constantinople, and asserts that the sight of the interior of this city destroys the effect produced by it when viewed at a distance.

It is true that the interior of Constantinople is exceedingly dirty, and that the number of small houses, the narrow streets, the unevenness of the pavement, the filthy dogs, etc., do not strike the beholder as excessively picturesque; but then he soon comes upon some magnificent edifice of the time of the Moors or Romans, some wondrous mosque or majestic palace, and can continue his walk through endless cemeteries and forests of dreamy cypresses. He steps aside before a pasha or priest of high rank, who rides by on his noble steed, surrounded by a brilliant retinue; he encounters Turks in splendid costumes, and Turkish women with eyes that flash through their veils like fire; he beholds Persians with their high caps, Arabs with their nobly-formed features, dervises in fools'-caps and plaited petticoats like women, and, now and then, some carriage, beautifully painted and gilt, drawn by superbly caparisoned oxen. All these different objects fully make up for whatever amount of dirtiness may occasionally be met with. In Rio Janeiro, however, there is nothing that can in any way amuse, or atone for the horrible and disgusting sights which everywhere meet the eye.

It was not until I had been here several weeks that I became somewhat accustomed to the appearance of the negroes and mulattoes. I then discovered many very pretty figures among the young negresses, and handsome, expressive countenances among the somewhat dark-complexioned Brazilian and Portuguese women; the men seem, as regards beauty, to be less favoured.

The bustle in the streets is far less than what I had been led to expect from the many descriptions I had heard, and is certainly not to be compared to that at Naples or Messina. The greatest amount of noise is made by those negroes who carry burdens, and especially by such as convey the sacks full of coffee on board the different vessels; they strike up a monotonous sort of song, to the tune of which they keep step, but which sounds very disagreeable. It possesses, however, one advantage; it warns the foot passenger, and affords him time to get out of the way.

In the Brazils, every kind of dirty or hard work, whether in doors or out, is performed by the blacks, who here, in fact, replace the lower classes. Many, however, learn trades, and frequently are to be compared to the most skilful Europeans. I have seen blacks in the most elegant workshops, making wearing apparel, shoes, tapestry, gold or silver articles, and met many a nattily dressed negro maiden working at the finest ladies' dresses, or the most delicate embroidery. I often thought I must be dreaming when I beheld these poor creatures, whom I had pictured to myself as roaming free through their native forests, exercising such occupations in shops and rooms! Yet they do not appear to feel it as much as might be supposed—they were always merry, and joking over their work.

Among the so-called educated class of the place, there are many who, in spite of all the proofs of mechanical skill, as well as general intelligence which the blacks often display, persist in asserting that they are so far inferior to the whites in mental power, that they can only be looked upon as a link between the monkey tribe and the human race. I allow that they are somewhat behind the whites in intellectual culture; but I believe that this is not because they are deficient in understanding, but because their education is totally neglected. No schools are erected for them, no instruction given them—in a word, not the least thing is done to develop the capabilities of their minds. As was the case in old despotic countries, their minds are purposely kept enchained; for, were they once to awake from their present condition, the consequences to the whites might be fearful. They are four times as numerous as the latter, and if they ever become conscious of this superiority, the whites might probably be placed in the position that the unhappy blacks have hitherto occupied.

But I am losing myself in conjectures and reasonings which may, perhaps, become the pen of a learned man, but certainly not mine, since I assuredly do not possess the necessary amount of education to decide upon such questions; my object is merely to give a plain description of what I have seen.

Although the number of slaves in the Brazils is very great, there is nowhere such a thing as a slave-market. The importation of them is publicly prohibited, yet thousands are smuggled in every year, and disposed of in some underhand manner, which every one knows, and every one employs. It is true, that English ships are constantly cruising off the coasts of Brazil and Africa, but even if a slaver happen to fall into their hands, the poor blacks, I was told, were no more free than if they had come to the Brazils. They are all transported to the English colonies, where, at the expiration of ten years, they are supposed to be set at liberty. But during this period, their owners allow the greater number to die—of course, in the returns only—and the poor slaves remain slaves still; but I repeat that I only know this from hearsay.

After all, slaves are far from being as badly off as many Europeans imagine. In the

24

Brazils they are generally pretty well treated; they are not overworked, their food is good and nutritious, and the punishments are neither particularly frequent nor heavy. The crime of running away is the only one which is visited with great rigour. Besides a severe beating, they have fetters placed round their neck and feet; these they have to wear for a considerable period. Another manner of punishment consists in making them wear a tin mask, which is fastened with a lock behind. This is the mode of punishment adopted for those who drink, or are in the habit of eating earth or lime. During my long stay in the Brazils, I only saw one negro who had got on a mask of this description. I very much doubt whether, on the whole, the lot of these slaves is not less wretched than that of the peasants of Russia, Poland, or Egypt, who are *not* called slaves.

I was one day very much amused at being asked to stand godmother to a negro, which I did, although I was not present at either baptism or confirmation. There is a certain custom here, that when a slave has done anything for which he expects to be punished, he endeavours to fly to some friend of his owner, and obtain a note, asking for the remission of his punishment. The writer of such a letter has the title of godfather bestowed on him, and it would be accounted an act of the greatest impoliteness not to grant the godfather's request. In this way, I myself was fortunate enough to save a slave from punishment.

The town is tolerably well lighted, and the lighting is continued to a considerable distance, on all sides, beyond the town itself; this measure was introduced on account of the great number of blacks. No slave dare be seen in the streets later than 9 o'clock in the evening, without having a pass from his master, certifying that he is going on business for him. If a slave is ever caught without a pass, he is immediately conveyed to the House of Correction, where his head is shaved, and he himself obliged to remain until his master buys his freedom for four or five milreis. (8s. 8d., or 10s. 10d.) In consequence of this regulation, the streets may be traversed with safety at any hour of the night.

One of the most disagreeable things in Rio Janeiro is the total absence of sewers. In a heavy shower, every street becomes a regular stream, which it is impossible to pass on foot; in order to traverse them, it is requisite to be carried over by negroes. At such times, all intercourse generally ceases, the streets are deserted, parties are put off, and even the payment of bills of exchange deferred. It is very seldom that people will hire a carriage, for it is an absurd custom here, to pay as much for a short drive, as if the carriage were required for the whole day; in both cases the charge is six milreis (13s.) The carriages are half-covered ones, with seats for two, and are drawn by a pair of mules, on one of which the driver rides. Carriages and horses like the English are very seldom to be met with.

As regards the arts and sciences, I may mention the Academy of Fine Arts, the Museum, Theatre, etc. In the Academy of Fine Arts is something of everything, and not much of anything—a few figures and busts, most in plaster, a few architectural plans and pencil drawings, and a collection of very old oil paintings. It really seemed to me as if some private picture gallery had been carefully weeded of all the rubbish in it, which had then been put here out of the way. Most of the oil paintings are so injured, that it is scarcely possible to make out what they are intended to represent, which, after all, is no great loss. The only thing respectable about them is their venerable antiquity. A startling contrast is produced by the copies of them made by the students. If the colours in the old pictures are faded, in the modern ones they blaze with a superfluity of vividness; red, yellow, green, etc., are there in all their force; such a thing as mixing, softening, or blending them, has evidently never been thought of. Even at the present moment, I really am at a loss to determine whether the worthy students intended to found a new school for colouring, or whether they merely desired to make up in the copies for the damage time had done the originals.

There were as many blacks and mulattoes among the students as whites, but the number of them altogether was inconsiderable.

Music, especially singing and the pianoforte, is almost in a more degraded position than painting. In every family the young ladies play and sing; but of tact, style, arrangement, time, etc., the innocent creatures have not the remotest idea, so that the easiest and most taking melodies are often not recognisable. The sacred music is a shade better, although even the arrangements of the Imperial Chapel itself are susceptible of many improvements. The military bands are certainly the best, and these are generally composed of negroes and mulattoes.

The exterior of the Opera-house does not promise anything very beautiful or astonishing, and the stranger is, consequently, much surprised to find, on entering, a large and magnificent house with a deep stage. I should say it could contain more than 2,000 persons. There are four tiers of spacious boxes rising one above the other, the balustrades of which, formed of delicately-wrought iron trellis-work, give the theatre a very tasty appearance. The pit is only for men. I was present at a tolerably good representation, by an Italian company, of the opera of *Lucrezia Borgia*; the scenery and costumes are not amiss.

If, however, I was agreeably surprised by my visit to the theatre, I experienced quite a contrary feeling on going to the Museum. In a land so richly and luxuriously endowed by Nature, I expected an equally rich and magnificent museum, and found a number of very fine rooms, it is true, which one day or other may be filled, but which at present are empty. The collection of birds, which is the most complete of all, is really fine; that of the minerals is very defective; and those of the quadrupeds and insects poor in the extreme. The objects which most excited my curiosity, were the heads of four savages, in excellent preservation; two of them belonged to the Malay, and two to the New Zealand tribes. The latter especially I could not sufficiently contemplate, completely covered as they were with tattooing of the most beautiful and elegant design, and so well preserved that they seemed only to have just ceased to live.

During the period of my stay in Rio Janeiro, the rooms of the Museum were undergoing repairs, and a new classification of the different objects was also talked of. In consequence of this, the building was not open to the public, and I have to thank the kindness of Herr Riedl, the director, for allowing me to view it. He acted himself as my guide; and, like me, regretted that in a country where the formation of a rich museum would be so easy a task, so little had been done.

I likewise visited the studio of the sculptor Petrich, a native of Dresden, who came over at the unsolicited command of the court, to execute a statue of the emperor in Carrara marble. The emperor is represented the size of life, in a standing position, and arrayed in his imperial robes, with the ermine cloak thrown over his shoulder. The head is strikingly like, and the whole figure worked out of the stone with great artistic skill. I believe this statue was destined for some public building.

I was fortunate enough during my stay in Rio Janeiro to witness several different public festivals.

The first was on the 21st of September, in the Church of St. Cruz, on the occasion of celebrating the anniversary of the patron saint of the country. Early in the morning several hundred soldiers were drawn up before the church, with an excellent band, which played a number of lively airs. Between ten and eleven, the military and civil officers began gradually to arrive, the subordinate ones, as I was told, coming first. On their entrance into the church, a brownish-red silk cloak, which concealed the whole of the uniform, was presented to each. Every time that another of a higher rank appeared, all those already in the church rose from their seats, and advancing towards the new comer as far as the church door, accompanied him respectfully to his place. The emperor and his wife arrived the last of all. The emperor is extremely young—not quite one and twenty—but six feet tall, and very corpulent; his features are those of the Hapsburg-Lothering family. The empress, a Neapolitan princess, is small and slim, and forms a strange contrast when standing beside the athletic figure of her husband.

High mass, which was listened to with great reverence by every one, began immediately after the entrance of the court, and after this was concluded the imperial pair proceeded to their carriage, presenting the crowd, who were waiting in the church, their hands to kiss as they went along. This mark of distinction was bestowed not only on the officers and officials of superior rank, but on every one who pressed forward to obtain it.

A second, and more brilliant festival occurred on the 19th of October; it was the emperor's birth-day, and was celebrated by high mass in the Imperial Chapel. This chapel is situated near the Imperial Palace, to which it is connected by means of a covered gallery. Besides the imperial family, all the general officers, as well as the first officials of the state, were present at the mass, but in full uniform, without the ugly silk cloaks. Surrounding all was a row of Lancers (the body-guard). It is impossible for any but an eye-witness to form an idea of the richness and profusion of the gold embroidery, the splendid epaulets, and beautifully set orders, etc., displayed on the occasion, and I hardly believe that anything approaching it could be seen at any European court.

During high mass, the foreign ambassadors, and the ladies and gentlemen admitted to court, assembled in the palace, where, on the emperor's return, every one was admitted to kiss his hand.

The ambassadors, however, took no part in this proceeding, but merely made a simple bow.

This edifying ceremony could easily be seen from the square, as the windows are very near the ground, and were also open. On such occasions continual salutes are fired from the imperial ships, and sometimes from others in the harbour.

On the 2nd of November I saw a festival of another description—namely, a religious one. During this and the following days, old and young proceed from one church to another, to pray for the souls of the departed.

They have a singular custom here of not burying all their dead in the church-yard, many bodies being placed, at an additional expense, in the church itself. For this purpose, there are, in every church, particular chambers, with catacombs formed in the walls. The corpse is strewed with lime, and laid in a catacomb of this description, where, after a lapse of eight or ten months, the flesh is completely eaten away. The bones are then taken out, cleaned by boiling, and collected in an urn, on which is engraved the name, birth-day, etc., of the deceased. These urns are afterwards set up in the passages of the church, or sometimes even taken home by the relations.

On All-souls' day, the walls of the chambers are hung with black cloth, gold lace, and other ornaments, and the urns are richly decorated with flowers and ribbons, and are lighted up by a great number of tapers in silver candelabra and chandeliers, placed upon high stands. From an early hour in the morning until noon, the women and young girls begin praying very fervently for the souls of their deceased relations, and the young gentlemen, who are quite as curious as those in Europe, go to see the young girls pray.

Females on this day are dressed in mourning, and often wear, to the great disgust of the curious young gentlemen before mentioned, a black veil over their head and face. No one, by the way, is allowed to wear a bonnet at any festival of the church.

But the most brilliant of the public festivals I saw here, was the christening of the imperial princess, which took place on the 15th of November, in the Imperial Chapel, which is connected with the palace.

Towards 3 o'clock in the afternoon a number of troops were drawn up in the

28

court-yard of the palace, the guards were distributed in the corridors and the church, while the bands played a series of pleasing melodies, frequently repeating the National Anthem, which the late emperor, Peter I., is said to have composed. Equipage after equipage began to roll up to the palace, and set down the most brilliantly attired company of both sexes.

At 4 o'clock the procession began to leave the palace. First, came the court band, clothed in red velvet, and followed by three heralds, in old Spanish costume, magnificently decorated hats and feathers, and black velvet suits. Next walked the officers of the law, and the authorities of every rank, chamberlains, court physicians, senators, deputies, generals, and ecclesiastics, privy councillors and secretaries; and, lastly, after this long line of different personages, came the lord steward of the young princess, whom he bore upon a magnificent white velvet cushion, edged with gold lace. Immediately behind him followed the emperor, and the little princess's nurse, surrounded by the principal nobles and ladies of the court. On passing through the triumphal arch of the gallery, and coming before the pallium of the church, the emperor took his little daughter {23a} into his own arms, and presented her to the people; an act which pleased me exceedingly, and which I considered extremely appropriate.

The empress, with her ladies, had likewise already arrived in the church through the inner corridors, and the ceremony commenced forthwith. The instant the princess was baptized, the event was announced to the whole town by salvos of artillery, volleys of musketry, and the discharge of rockets. {23b} At the conclusion of the ceremony, which lasted above an hour, the procession returned in the same order in which it had arrived, and the chapel was then opened to the people. I was curious enough to enter with the rest, and, I must own, I was quite surprised at the magnificence and taste with which the building was decorated. The walls were covered with silk and velvet hangings, ornamented with gold fringe, while rich carpets were spread underfoot. On large tables, in the middle of the nave, were displayed the most valuable specimens of the church plate, gold and silver vases, immense dishes, plates, and goblets, artistically engraved, and ornamented with embossed or open work; while magnificent vessels of crystal, containing the most beautiful flowers, and massive candelabra, with innumerable lights, sparkled in the midst. On a separate table, near the high altar, were all the costly vessels and furniture which had been employed at the christening; and, in one of the side chapels, the princess's cradle, covered with white satin, and ornamented with gold lace. In the evening, the town, or rather, the public buildings, were illuminated. The proprietors of private houses are not required to light up; and they either avail themselves of their privilege, or at most, hang out a few lanterns—a fact which will be readily understood, when it is known that such illuminations last for six or eight days. The public buildings, on the contrary, are covered from top to bottom with countless lamps, which look exactly like a sea of fire.

The most original and really amusing fêtes to celebrate the christening of the

29

princess, were those given on several evenings in some of the barracks: even the emperor himself made his appearance there for a few moments on different occasions. They were also the only fêtes I saw here which were not mixed up with religious solemnities. The sole actors in them were the soldiers themselves, of whom the handsomest and most active had previously been selected, and exercised in the various evolutions and dances. The most brilliant of these fêtes took place in the barracks of the Rua Barbone. A semicircular and very tasty gallery was erected in the spacious court-yard, and in the middle of the gallery were busts of the imperial couple. This gallery was set apart for the ladies invited, who made their appearance as if dressed for the most splendid ball: at the entrance of the court-yard they were received by the officers, and conducted to their places. Before the gallery stood the stage, and at each side of the latter were ranged rows of seats for the less fashionable females; beyond these seats was standing-room for the men.

At eight o'clock the band commenced playing, and shortly afterwards the representation began. The soldiers appeared, dressed in various costumes, as Highlanders, Poles, Spaniards, etc.; nor was there any scarcity of *danseuses*, who, of course, were likewise private soldiers. What pleased me most was, that both the dress and behaviour of the military young ladies were highly becoming. I had expected at least some little exaggeration, or at best no very elegant spectacle; and was therefore greatly astonished, not only with the correctness of the dances and evolutions, but also with the perfect propriety with which the whole affair was conducted.

The last fête that I saw took place on the 2nd of December, in celebration of the emperor's birth-day. After high mass, the different dignitaries again waited on the emperor, to offer their congratulations, and were admitted to the honour of kissing his hand, etc. The imperial couple then placed themselves at a window of the palace, while the troops defiled before them, with their bands playing the most lively airs. It would be difficult to find better dressed soldiers than those here: every private might easily be mistaken for a lieutenant, or at least a non-commissioned officer; but unluckily, their bearing, size, and colour, are greatly out of keeping with the splendour of their uniform—a mere boy of fourteen standing next to a full-grown, well-made man, a white coming after a black, and so on.

The men are pressed into the service; the time of serving is from four to six years.

I had heard and read a great deal in Europe of the natural magnificence and luxury of the Brazils—of the ever clear and smiling sky, and the extraordinary charm of the continual spring; but though it is true that the vegetation is perhaps richer, and the fruitfulness of the soil more luxuriant and vigorous than in any other part of the world, and that every one who desires to see the working of nature in its greatest force and incessant activity, must come to Brazil; still it must not be thought that all is good and beautiful, and that there is nothing which will not weaken the magical effect of the first impression.

Although every one begins by praising the continual verdure and the uninterrupted splendour of spring met with in this country, he is, in the end, but too willing to allow, that even this, in time, loses its charm. A little winter would be preferable, as the reawakening of nature, the resuscitation of the slumbering plants, the return of the sweet perfume of spring, enchants us all the more, simply because during a short period we have been deprived of it.

I found the climate and the air exceedingly oppressive; and the heat, although at that period hardly above 86° in the shade, very weakening. During the warm months, which last from the end of December to May, the heat rises in the shade to 99°, and in the sun to above 122°. In Egypt, I bore a greater amount of heat with far greater ease; a circumstance which may perhaps be accounted for by the fact, that the climate is there drier, while here there is always an immense degree of moisture. Fogs and mists are very common; the hills and eminences, nay, even whole tracts of country, are often enveloped in impenetrable gloom, and the whole atmosphere loaded with damp vapours.

In the month of November I was seriously indisposed for a considerable period. I suffered, especially in the town, from an oppressive feeling of fatigue and weakness; and to the kindness and friendship of Herr Geiger, the Secretary to the Austrian Consulate, and his wife, who took me with them into the country, and showed me the greatest attention, do I alone owe my recovery. I ascribed my illness altogether to the unusual dampness of the atmosphere.

The most agreeable season is said to be the winter (from June to October); that, with a temperature of from 63° to 72°, is mostly dry and clear. This period is generally selected by the inhabitants for travelling. During the summer, violent thunder-storms are of frequent occurrence: I myself only saw three during my stay in the Brazils, all of which were over in an hour and a half. The lightning was almost incessant, and spread like a sheet of fire over the greater portion of the horizon; the thunder, on the other hand, was inconsiderable.

Clear, cloudless days (from 16th September to 9th December) were so rare, that I really could have counted them; and I am at a loss to understand how so many travellers have spoken of the ever beautiful, smiling, and blue sky of the Brazils. This must be true of some other portion of the year.

A fine evening and long twilight is another source of enjoyment which may be said to be unknown: at sunset every one hastens home, as it is immediately followed by darkness and damp.

In the height of summer the sun sets at about a quarter past 6, and all the rest of the year at 6 o'clock; twenty or thirty minutes afterwards, night sets in.

The mosquitoes, ants, baraten, and sand-fleas are another source of annoyance;

31

many a night have I been obliged to sit up, tormented and tortured by the bite of these insects. It is hardly possible to protect provisions from the attacks of the baraten and ants. The latter, in fact, often appear in long trains of immeasureable length, pursuing their course over every obstacle which stands in the way. During my stay in the country at Herr Geiger's, I beheld a swarm of this description traverse a portion of the house. It was really most interesting to see what a regular line they formed; nothing could make them deviate from the direction they had first determined on. Madame Geiger told me that she was one night awoke by a horrible itching; she sprang immediately out of bed, and beheld a swarm of ants of the above description pass over her bed. There is no remedy for this; the end of the procession, which often lasts four or six hours, must be waited for with patience. Provisions are to some extent protected from them, by placing the legs of the tables and presses in plates filled with water. Clothes and linen are laid in tightly-fitting tin canisters, to protect them, not only from the ants, but also from the baraten and the damp.

The worst plague of all, however, are the sand-fleas, which attach themselves to one's toes, underneath the nails, or sometimes to the soles of the feet. The moment a person feels an itching in these parts he must immediately look at the place; if he sees a small black point surrounded by a small white ring, the former is the flea, and the latter the eggs which it has laid in the flesh. The first thing done is to loosen the skin all round as far as the white ring is visible; the whole deposit is then extracted, and a little snuff strewed in the empty space. The best plan is to call in the first black you may happen to see, as they all perform this operation very skilfully.

As regards the natural products of the Brazils, a great many of the most necessary articles are wanting in the list. It is true that there are sugar and coffee, but no corn, no potatoes, and none of our delicious varieties of fruit. The flour of manioc, which is mixed up with the other materials of which the dishes are composed, supplies the place of bread, but is far from being so nutritious and strengthening, while the different kinds of sweet-tasting roots are certainly not to be compared to our potatoes. The only fruit, which are really excellent, are the oranges, bananas and mangoes. Their celebrated pine-apples are neither very fragrant nor remarkably sweet; I certainly have eaten much finer flavoured ones that had been grown in a European hot-house. The other kinds of fruit are not worth mentioning. Lastly, with the two very necessary articles of consumption, milk and meat, the former is very watery, and the latter very dry.

On instituting a comparison between the Brazils and Europe, both with respect to the impression produced by the whole, as also to the separate advantages and disadvantages of each, we shall, perhaps, at first find the scale incline towards the former country, but only to turn ultimately with greater certainty in favour of the latter.

The Brazils is, perhaps, the most interesting country in the world for travellers;

but for a place of permanent residence I should most decidedly prefer Europe.

I saw too little of the manners and customs of the country to be qualified to pronounce judgment upon them, and I shall therefore, on this head, confine myself to a few remarks. The manners seem, on the whole, to differ but little from those of Europe. The present possessors of the country, as is well known, derive their descent from Portugal, and the Brazilians might very aptly be termed "Europeans translated into Americans;" and it is very natural, that in this "translation" many peculiarities have been lost, while others have stood forth in greater relief. The strongest feature in the character of the European-American is the greed for gold; this often becomes a passion, and transforms the most faint-hearted white into a hero, for it certainly requires the courage of one to live alone, as planter, on a plantation with perhaps some hundred slaves, far removed from all assistance, and with the prospect of being irrevocably lost in the event of any revolt.

This grasping feeling is not confined to the men alone; it is found among the women as well, and is greatly encouraged by a common custom here, agreeably to which, a husband never assigns his wife so much for pin-money, but, according to his means, makes her a present of one or more male or female slaves, whom she can dispose of as she chooses. She generally has them taught how to cook, sew, embroider, or even instructed in some trade, and then lets them out, by the day, week, or month, [27] to people who possess no slaves of their own; or she lets them take in washing at home, or employs them in the manufacture of various ornamental objects, fine pastry, etc, which she sends them out to sell. The money for these things belongs to her, and is generally spent in dress and amusement.

In the case of tradesmen, and professional men, the wife is always paid for whatever assistance she may lend her husband in his business.

Morality, unfortunately, is not very general in the Brazils; one cause of this may be traced to the manner in which the children are first brought up. They are confided entirely to the care of blacks. Negresses suckle them when they are infants, their nurses are negresses, their attendants are negresses—and I have often seen girls of eight or ten years of age taken to school, or any other place, by young negroes. The sensuality of the blacks is too well known for us to be surprised, with such a state of things, at the general and early demoralization. In no other place did I ever behold so many children with such pale and worn faces as in the streets of Rio Janeiro. The second cause of immorality here is, without doubt, the want of religion. The Brazils are thoroughly Catholic—perhaps there are no countries save Spain and Italy, that can be compared to them. Almost every day there is some procession, service, or church-festival; but these are attended merely for the sake of amusement, while the true religious feeling is entirely wanting.

We may also ascribe to this deep demoralization and want of religion the frequent occurrence of murders, committed not for the sake of robbery or theft, but from motives of revenge and hatred. The murderer either commits the deed himself, or has it perpetrated by one of his slaves, who is ready to lend himself for the purpose, in consideration of a mere trifle. The discovery of the crime need cause the assassin no anxiety, provided he is rich; for in this country everything, I was assured, can be arranged or achieved with money. I saw several men in Rio Janeiro who had, according to report, committed either themselves, or by the means of others, not one, but several murders, and yet they not only enjoyed perfect liberty, but were received in every society.

In conclusion, I beg leave to address a few words to those of my countrymen who think of leaving their native land, to seek their fortune on the distant coast of Brazil—a few words which I could desire to see as far spread and as well known as possible.

There are people in Europe not a whit better than the African slave-dealers, and such people are those who delude poor wretches with exaggerated accounts of the richness of America and her beautiful territories, of the over-abundance of the products of the soil, and the lack of hands to take advantage of them. These people, however, care little about the poor dupes; their object is to freight the vessels belonging to them, and to effect this they take from their deluded victim the last penny he possesses.

During my stay here, several vessels arrived with unfortunate emigrants of this description; the government had not sent for them, and therefore would afford them no relief; money they had none, and, consequently, could not purchase land, neither could they find employment in working on the plantations, as no one will engage Europeans for this purpose, because, being unused to the warm climate, they would soon succumb beneath the work. The unhappy wretches had thus no resource left; they were obliged to beg about the town, and, in the end, were fain to content themselves with the most miserable occupations. A different fate awaits those who are sent for by the Brazilian government to cultivate the land or colonize the country: these persons receive a piece of uncleared ground, with provisions and other help; but if they come over without any money at all, even their lot is no enviable one. Want, hunger, and sickness destroy most of them, and but a very small number succeed, by unceasing activity and an iron constitution, in gaining a better means of livelihood than what they left behind them in their native land. Those only who exercise some trade find speedy employment and an easy competency; but even this will, in all probability, soon be otherwise, for great numbers are pouring in ever year, and latterly the negroes themselves have been, and are still being, more frequently taught every kind of trade.

Let every one, therefore, obtain trustworthy information before leaving his native land; let him weigh calmly and deliberately the step he is about to take, and not allow himself to be carried away by deceptive hopes. The poor creature's misery on being undeceived is so much the more dreadful, because he does not learn the truth until it is too late—until he has already fallen a victim to poverty and want.

CHAPTER III. EXCURSIONS IN THE NEIGHBOURHOOD OF RIO JANEIRO.

THE WATERFALLS NEAR TESCHUKA—BOA VISTA—THE BOTANICAL GARDENS AND THEIR ENVIRONS—THE CORCOVADO MOUNTAINS, 2,253 FEET ABOVE THE LEVEL OF THE SEA— PALACES OF THE IMPERIAL FAMILY—THE NEWLY-FOUNDED GERMAN COLONY OF PETROPOLIS—ATTEMPT AT MURDER, BY A MARROON NEGRO.

An excursion to the waterfalls near Teschuka, to Boa Vista, and the Botanical Gardens, is one of the most interesting near the city; but it requires two days, as it takes a long time to see the Botanical Gardens alone.

Count Berchthold and myself proceeded as far as Andaracky (four miles) in an omnibus, and then continued our journey on foot, between patches of wood and low hills. Elegant country houses are situated upon the eminences and along the high road, at short distances from each other.

When we had walked four miles, a path to the right conducted us to a small waterfall, neither very high nor well supplied, but still the most considerable one in the vicinity of Rio Janeiro. We then returned to the high road, and in half an hour reached a little elevated plain, whence the eye ranged over a valley of the most remarkable description, one portion of it being in a state of wild chaotic confusion, and the other resembling a blooming garden. In the former were strewed masses of broken granite, from which, in some places, larger blocks reared their heads, like so many Collossi; while in others large fragments of rocks lay towering one above the other; in the second portion stood the finest fruit trees in the midst of luxuriant pastures. This romantic valley is enclosed on three sides by noble mountains, the fourth being open, and disclosing a full view of the sea.

In this valley we found a small *venda*, where we recruited ourselves with bread and wine, and then continued our excursion to the so-called "Great Waterfall," with which we were less astonished than we had been with the smaller one. A very shallow sheet of water flowed down over a broad but nowise precipitous ledge of rock into the valley beneath.

After making our way through the valley, we came to the Porto Massalu, where a number of trunks of trees, hollowed out and lying before the few huts situated in the bay, apprized us that the inhabitants were fishermen. We hired one of these beautiful conveyances to carry us across the little bay. The passage did not take more than a quarter of an hour at the most, and for this, as strangers, we were compelled to pay two thousand reis (4s.).

We had now at one moment to wade through plains of sand, and the next to clamber over the rocks by wretched paths. In this laborious fashion we proceeded for at least twelve miles, until we reached the summit of a mountain, which rises like the party-wall of two mighty valleys. This peak is justly called the Boa Vista. The view extends over both valleys, with the mountain ranges and rows of hills which intersect them, and embraces, among other high mountains, the Corcovado and the "Two Brothers;" and, in the distance, the capital, with the surrounding country-houses and villages, the various bays and the open sea.

Unwillingly did we leave this beautiful position; but being unacquainted with the distance we should have to go before reaching some hospitable roof, we were obliged to hasten on; besides which negroes are the only persons met with on these lonely roads, and a *rencontre* with any of them by night is a thing not at all to be desired. We descended, therefore, into the valley, and resolved to sleep at the first inn we came to.

More fortunate than most people in such cases, we not only found an excellent hotel with clean rooms and good furniture, but fell in with company which amused us in the highest degree. It consisted of a mulatto family, and attracted all my attention. The wife, a tolerably stout beauty of about thirty, was dressed out in a fashion which, in my own country, no one, save a lady of an exceedingly vulgar taste would ever think of adopting—all the valuables she possessed in the world, she had got about her. Wherever it was possible to stick anything of gold or silver, there it was sure to be. A gown of heavy silk and a real cashmere enveloped her dark brown body, and a charming little white silk bonnet looked very comical placed upon her great heavy head. The husband and five children were worthy of their respective wife and mother; and, in fact, this excess of dress extended even to the nurse, a real unadulterated negress, who was also overloaded with ornaments. On one arm she had five and on the other six bracelets of stones, pearls, and coral, but which, as far as I could judge, did not strike me as being particularly genuine.

When the family rose to depart, two landaus, each with four horses, drove up to the door, and man and wife, children and nurse, all stepped in with the same majestic gravity.

As I was still looking after the carriages, which were rolling rapidly towards the town, I saw some one on horseback nodding to me: it was my friend, Herr Geiger. On hearing that we intended to remain for the night where we were, he persuaded us to accompany him to the estate of his father-in-law, which was situated close at hand. In the latter gentleman, we made the acquaintance of a most worthy and cheerful old man of seventy years of age, who, at that period, was Directing Architect and Superintendant of the Fine Arts under Government. We admired his beautiful garden and charming residence, built, with great good taste, in the Italian style.

36

Early on the following morning, I accompanied Count Berchthold to the botanical gardens. Our curiosity to visit these gardens was very great: we hoped to see there magnificent specimens of trees and flowers from all parts of the world —but we were rather disappointed. The gardens have been founded too recently, and none of the large trees have yet attained their full growth; there is no very great selection of flowers or plants; and to the few that are there, not even tickets are affixed, to acquaint the visitor with their names. The most interesting objects for us, were the monkey's bread-tree, with its gourds weighing ten or twenty-five pounds, and containing a number of kernels, which are eaten, not only by monkeys, but also by men—the clove, camphor, and cocoa-tree, the cinnamon and tea bush, etc. We also saw a very peculiar kind of palm-tree: the lower portion of the trunk, to the height of two or three feet, was brown and smooth, and shaped like a large tub or vat; the stems that sprang from this were light green, and like the lower part, very smooth, and at the same time shining, as if varnished; they were not very high, and the crest of leaves, as is the case with other palms, only unfolded itself at the top of the tree. Unfortunately, we were unable to learn the names of this kind of palm; and in the whole course of my voyage, I never met with another specimen.

We did not leave the gardens before noon: we then proceeded on foot four miles as far as Batafogo, and thence reached the city by omnibus.

Herr Geiger had invited Count Berchtholdt, Herr Rister, (a native of Vienna), and myself to an excursion to the Corcovado mountains; and accordingly, on the 1st November, at a time when we are often visited by storms and snow, but when the sun is here in his full force, and the sky without a cloud, at an early hour in the morning did we commence our pilgrimage.

The splendid aqueduct was our guide as far as the springs from which it derives the water, which point we reached in an hour and a half, having been so effectually protected by the deep shade of lovely woods, that even the intense heat of the sun, which reached during the day more than 117°, (in the sun), scarcely annoyed us.

We stopped at the springs; and, on a sign from Herr Geiger, an athletic negro made his appearance, loaded with a large hamper of provisions—everything was soon prepared—a white cloth was spread out, and the eatables and drinkables placed upon it. Our meal was seasoned with jokes and good humour; and when we started afresh on our journey, we felt revived both in body and mind.

The last cone of the mountain gave us some trouble: the route was very precipitous, and lay over bare, hot masses of rock. But when we did reach the top, we were more than repaid by seeing spread before us such a panorama, as most assuredly is very seldom to be met with in the world. All that I had remarked on my entrance into the port, lay there before me, only more clearly defined and more extended, with innumerable additional objects. We could see the whole town, all the lower hills, which half hid it from my view on my arrival, the large bay, reaching as far as the Organ mountain; and, on the other side, the romantic valley, containing the botanical gardens, and a number of beautiful country-houses.

I recommend every one who comes to Rio Janeiro, although it be only for a few days, to make this excursion, since from this spot he can, with one glance, perceive all the treasures which nature, with so truly liberal a hand, has lavished upon the environs of this city. He will here see virgin forests, which, if not quite as thick and beautiful as those farther inland, are still remarkable for their luxuriant vegetation. Mimosæ and Aarren bäume of a gigantic size, palms, wild coffee-trees, orchidæn, parasites and creepers, blossoms and flowers, without end; birds of the most brilliant plumage, immense butterflies, and sparkling insects, flying in swarms from blossom to blossom, from branch to branch. A most wonderful effect also is produced by the millions of fire-flies, which find their way into the very tops of the trees, and sparkle between the foliage like so many brightly twinkling stars.

I had been informed that the ascent of this mountain was attended with great difficulty. I did not, however, find this to be the case, since the summit may be reached with the greatest ease in three hours and three quarters, while three parts of the way can also be performed on horseback.

The regular residence of the imperial family may be said to be the Palace of Christovao, about half an hour's walk from the town. It is there that the emperor spends most of the year, and where also all political councils are held, and state business transacted.

The palace is small, and is distinguished neither for taste nor architectural beauty: its sole charm is its situation. It is placed upon a hill, and commands a view of the Organ mountain, and one of the bays. The palace garden itself is small, and is laid out in terraces right down into the valley below: a larger garden, that serves as a nursery for plants and trees, joins it. Both these gardens are highly interesting for Europeans, since they contain a great number of plants, which either do not exist at all in Europe, or are only known from dwarf specimens in hot-houses. Herr Riedl, who has the management of both gardens, was kind enough to conduct us over them himself, and to draw my attention more especially to the tea and bamboo plantations.

Ponte de Cascher(four miles from the town) is another imperial garden. There are three mango trees here, which are very remarkable, from their age and size. Their branches describe a circle of more than eighty feet in circumference, but they no longer bear fruit. Among the most agreeable walks in the immediate vicinity of the town, I may mention the Telegraph mountain, the public garden (Jardin publico), the Praya do Flamingo, and the Cloisters of St. Gloria and St. Theresia, etc.

I had heard so much in Rio Janeiro of the rapid rise of Petropolis, a colony founded by Germans in the neighbourhood of Rio Janeiro, of the beauty of the country where it was situated, and of the virgin forests through which a part of the road ran—that I could not resist the temptation of making an excursion thither. My travelling companion, Count Berchthold, accompanied me; and, on the 26th September, we took two places on board one of the numerous barks which sail regularly every day for the Porto d'Estrella, (a distance of twenty or twenty-two nautical miles), from which place the journey is continued by land. We sailed through a bay remarkable for its extremely picturesque views, and which often reminded me vividly of the peculiar character of the lakes in Sweden. It is surrounded by ranges of lovely hills, and is dotted over with small islands, both separate and in groups, some of which are so completely overgrown with palms, as well as other trees and shrubs, that it seems impossible to land upon them, while others either rear their solitary heads like huge rocks from the waves, or are loosely piled one upon the other. The round form of many of the latter is especially remarkable: they almost seem to have been cut out with a chisel.

Our bark was manned by four negroes and a white skipper. At first we ran before the wind with full sails, and the crew took advantage of this favourable opportunity to make a meal, consisting of a considerable quantity of flour of manioc, boiled fish, roasted mil, (Turkish corn), oranges, cocoa-nuts, and other nuts of a smaller description; indeed, there was even white bread, which for blacks is a luxury; and I was greatly delighted to see them so well taken care of. In two hours the wind left us, and the crew were obliged to take to the oars, the manner of using which struck me as very fatiguing. At each dip of the oar into the water, the rower mounts upon a bench before him, and then, during the stroke, throws himself off again with his full force. In two hours more, we left the sea, and taking a left-hand direction, entered the river Geromerim, at the mouth of which is an inn, where we stopped half an hour, and where I saw a remarkable kind of lighthouse, consisting of a lantern affixed to a rock. The beauty of the country is now at an end—that is, in the eyes of the vulgar: a botanist would, at this point, find it more than usually wonderful and magnificent; for the most beautiful aquatic plants, especially the Nymphia, the Pontedera, and the Cyprian grass are spread out, both in the water and all round it. The two former twine themselves to the very top of the nearest sapling, and the Cyprian grass attains a height of from six to eight feet. The banks of the river are flat, and fringed with underwood and young trees; the background is formed by ranges of hills. The little houses, which are visible now and then, are built of stone, and covered with tiles, yet, nevertheless, they present a tolerably poverty-stricken appearance.

After sailing up the river for seven hours, we reached, without accident, Porto d'Estrella, a place of some importance, since it is the emporium for all the merchandise which is sent from the interior, and then conveyed by water to the capital. There are two good inns; and, besides these, a large building (similar to a Turkish Khan) and an immense tiled roof, supported on strong stone pillars. The first was appropriated to the merchandise, and the second to the donkey drivers, who had arranged themselves very comfortably underneath it, and were preparing their evening meal over various fires that were blazing away very cheerfully. Although fully admitting the charms of such quarters for the night, we preferred retiring to the Star Inn, where clean rooms and beds, and skilfully spiced dishes, possessed more attraction for us.

27th September. From Porto d'Estrella to Petropolis, the distance is seven leagues. This portion of the journey is generally performed upon mules, the charge for which is four milreis (8s. 8d.) each, but as we had been told in Rio Janeiro that the road afforded a beautiful walk, parts of it traversing splendid woods, and that it was besides much frequented, and perfectly safe, being the great means of communication with Minas Gueras, we determined to go on foot, and that the more willingly, as the Count wished to botanize, and I to collect insects. The first eight miles lay through a broad valley, covered with thick brambles and young trees, and surrounded with lofty mountains. The wild pine-apples at the side of the road presented a most beautiful appearance; they were not quite ripe, and were tinged with the most delicate red. Unfortunately, they are far from being as agreeable to the taste as they are to the sight, and consequently are very seldom gathered. I was greatly amused with the humming-birds, of which I saw a considerable number of the smallest species. Nothing can be more graceful and delicate than these little creatures. They obtain their food from the calyx of the flowers, round which they flutter like butterflies, and indeed are very often mistaken for them in their rapid flight. It is very seldom that they are seen on a branch or twig in a state of repose. After passing through the valley, we reached the Serra, as the Brazilians term the summit of each mountain that they cross; the present one was 3,000 feet high. A broad paved road, traversing virgin forests, runs up the side of the mountain.

I had always imagined that in virgin forests the trees had uncommonly thick and lofty trunks; I found that this was not here the case. The vegetation is probably too luxuriant, and the larger trunks are suffocated and rot beneath the masses of smaller trees, bushes, creepers, and parasites. The two latter description of plants are so abundant, and cover so completely the trees, that it is often impossible to see even the leaves, much less the stems and branches. Herr Schleierer, a botanist, assured us that he once found upon one tree six and thirty different kinds of creepers and parasites.

We gathered a rich harvest of flowers, plants, and insects, and loitered along, enchanted with the magnificent woods and not less beautiful views, which stretched over hill and dale, towards the sea and its bays, and even as far as the capital itself.

Frequent truppas, {34a} driven by negroes, as well as the number of pedestrians we met, eased our minds of every fear, and prevented us from regarding it as at all remarkable that we were being continually followed by a negro. As, however, we arrived at a somewhat lonely spot, he sprang suddenly forward, holding in one hand a long knife and in the other a lasso, {34b} rushed upon us, and gave us to understand, more by gestures than words, that he intended to murder, and then drag us into the forest.

We had no arms, as we had been told that the road was perfectly safe, and the only weapons of defence we possessed were our parasols, if I except a clasp knife, which I instantly drew out of my pocket and opened, fully determined to sell my life as dearly as possible. We parried our adversary's blows as long as we could with our parasols, but these lasted but a short time; besides, he caught hold of mine, which, as we were struggling for it, broke short off, leaving only a piece of the handle in my hand. In the struggle, however, he dropped his knife, which rolled a few steps from him; I instantly made a dash, and thought I had got it, when he, more quick than I, thrust me away with his feet and hands, and once more obtained possession of it. He waved it furiously over my head, and dealt me two wounds, a thrust and a deep gash, both in the upper part of the left arm; I thought I was lost, and despair alone gave me the courage to use my own knife. I made a thrust at his breast; this he warded off, and I only succeeded in wounding him severely in the hand. The Count sprang forward, and seized the fellow from behind, and thus afforded me an opportunity of raising myself from the ground. The whole affair had not taken more than a few seconds. The negro's fury was now roused to its highest pitch by the wounds he had received: he gnashed his teeth at us like a wild beast, and flourished his knife with frightful rapidity. The Count, in his turn, had received a cut right across the hand, and we had been irrevocably lost, had not Providence sent us assistance. We heard the tramp of horses' hoofs upon the road, upon which the negro instantly left us and sprang into the wood. Immediately afterwards two horsemen turned a corner of the road, and we hurried towards them; our wounds, which were bleeding freely, and the way in which our parasols were hacked, soon made them understand the state of affairs. They asked us which direction the fugitive had taken, and, springing from their horses, hurried after him; their efforts, however, would have been fruitless, if two negroes, who were coming from the opposite side, had not helped them. As it was, the fellow was soon captured. He was pinioned, and, as he would not walk, severely beaten, most of the blows being dealt upon the head, so that I feared the poor wretch's skull would be broken. In spite of this he never moved a muscle, and lay, as if insensible to feeling, upon the ground. The two other negroes were obliged to seize hold of him, when he endeavoured to bite every one within his reach, like a wild beast, and carry him to the nearest house. Our preservers, as well as the Count and myself, accompanied them. We then had our wounds dressed, and afterwards continued our journey; not, it is true, entirely devoid of fear, especially when we met one or more negroes but without any further mishap, and with a continually increasing admiration of the beautiful scenery.

The colony of Petropolis is situated in the midst of a virgin forest, at an elevation of 2,500 feet above the level of the sea, and, at the time of our visit, it had been

41

founded about fourteen months, with the especial purpose of furnishing the capital with certain kinds of fruit and vegetables, which, in tropical climates, will thrive only in very high situations. A small row of houses already formed a street, and on a large space that had been cleared away stood the wooden carcase of a larger building—the Imperial Villa, which, however, would have some difficulty in presenting anything like an imperial appearance, on account of the low doors that contrasted strangely with the broad, lofty windows. The town is to be built around the villa, though several detached houses are situated at some distance away in the woods. One portion of the colonists, such as mechanics, shop-keepers, etc., had been presented with small plots of ground for building upon, near the villa; the cultivators of the soil had received larger patches, although not more than two or three yokes. What misery must not these poor people have suffered in their native country to have sought another hemisphere for the sake of a few yokes of land!

We here found the good old woman who had been our fellow passenger from Germany to Rio Janeiro, in company with her son. Her joy at being once more able to share in the toils and labours of her favourite had, in this short space of time, made her several years younger. Her son acted as our guide, and conducted us over the infant colony, which is situated in broad ravines; the surrounding hills are so steep, that when they are cleared of timber and converted into gardens, the soft earth is easily washed away by heavy showers.

At a distance of four miles from the colony, a waterfall foams down a chasm which it has worn away for itself. It is more remarkable for its valley-like enclosure of noble mountains, and the solemn gloom of the surrounding woods, than for its height or body of water.

29th September. In spite of the danger we had incurred in coming, we returned to Porto d'Estrella on foot, went on board a bark, sailed all night, and arrived safely in Rio Janeiro the next morning. Every one, both in Petropolis and the capital, was so astonished at the manner in which our lives had been attempted, that if we had not been able to show our wounds we should never have been believed. The fellow was at first thought to have been drunk or insane, and it was not till later that we learned the real motives of his conduct. He had some time previously been punished by his master for an offence, and on meeting us in the wood, he no doubt thought that it was a good opportunity of satisfying, with impunity, his hatred against the whites.

CHAPTER IV. JOURNEY INTO THE INTERIOR OF THE BRAZILS.

THE TOWNS OF MORROQUEIMADO (NOVO FRIBURGO) AND ALDEA DO PEDRO—PLANTATIONS OF THE EUROPEANS—BURNING FORESTS—VIRGIN FORESTS—LAST SETTLEMENT OF THE WHITES —VISIT TO THE INDIANS, ALSO CALLED PURIS OR RABOCLES— RETURN TO RIO JANEIRO.

This second journey I also made in company of Count Berchthold, after having resolved on penetrating into the interior of the country, and paying a visit to the primitive inhabitants of the Brazils.

2nd October. We left Rio Janeiro in the morning, and proceeded in a steamer as far as the port of Sampajo, a distance of twenty-eight miles. This port lies at the mouth of the river Maccacu, but consists of only one inn and two or three small houses. We here hired mules to take us to the town of Morroqueimado, eighty miles off.

I may take this opportunity of remarking that it is the custom in the Brazils to hire the mules without muleteers—a great mark of confidence on the part of the owners towards travellers. Arrived at their destination the animals are delivered up at a certain place fixed on by the proprietor. We preferred, however, to take a muleteer with us, as we were not acquainted with the road, a piece of precaution we regretted the less, on finding the way frequently obstructed with wooden gates, which had always to be opened and shut again.

The price for hiring a mule was twelve milreis (£1 6s.).

As we arrived at Porto Sampajo by 2 o'clock, we resolved on going on as far as Ponte do Pinheiro, a distance of sixteen miles. The road lay mostly through valleys covered with large bushes and surrounded by low rocks. The country wore a general aspect of wildness, and only here and there were a few scanty pasture-grounds and poverty-stricken huts to be seen.

The little town of Ponte de Cairas, which we passed, consists of a few shops and vendas, a number of smaller houses, an inconsiderable church, and an apothecary's; the principal square looked like a meadow. Ponte do Pinheiro is rather larger. We experienced here a very good reception, and had an excellent supper, consisting of fowls stewed in rice, flour of manioc, and Portuguese wine; we had also good beds and breakfasts; the whole cost us, however, four milreis (8s. 8d.).

43

3rd October. We did not set off till 7 o'clock: here, as everywhere else in the country, there is no getting away early in the morning.

The scenery was of the same character as that passed the day before, except that we were approaching the more lofty mountains. The road was tolerably good, but the bridges across the streams and sloughs execrable; we esteemed ourselves fortunate whenever we passed one without being compelled to stop. After a ride of three hours (nine miles), we reached the great Sugar-Fazenda {38} de Collegio, which in its arrangements is exactly like a large country seat. To the spacious residence is attached a chapel, with the offices lying all around; the whole is enclosed by a high wall.

Far and wide stretched the fields and low eminences, covered with sugar canes: unfortunately, we could not see the mode of preparing the sugar, as the canes were not yet ripe.

A planter's fortune in the Brazils is calculated by the number of his slaves. There were eight hundred of them on the plantation we were viewing—a large property, since each male slave costs from six to seven hundred milreis (£60 to £70).

Not far from this fazenda, to the right of the high road, lies another very considerable one, called Papagais; besides these we saw several smaller plantations, which lent a little animation to the uniformity of the scene.

St. Anna (sixteen miles distance) is a small place, consisting of only a few poor houses, a little church, and an apothecary's; the last is a necessary appendage to every Brazilian village, even though it only contains twelve or fifteen huts. We here made a repast of eggs with a bottle of wine, and gave our mules a feed of mil, for which a cheating landlord, Herr Gebhart, charged us three milreis (6s. 6d.)

Today we did not proceed further than Mendoza (twelve miles), a still more insignificant place than St. Anna. A small shop and a venda were the only houses at the road-side, though in the background we perceived a manioc-fazenda, to which we paid a visit. The proprietor was kind enough first to offer us some strong coffee, without milk (a customary mark of attention in the Brazils), and then to conduct us over his plantation.

The manioc plant shoots out stalks from four to six feet in height, with a number of large leaves at their upper extremities. The valuable portion of the plant is its bulbous root, which often weighs two or three pounds, and supplies the place of corn all through the Brazils. It is washed, peeled, and held against the rough edge of a millstone, turned by a negro, until it is completely ground away. The whole mass is then gathered into a basket, plentifully steeped in water, and is afterwards pressed quite dry by means of a press. Lastly it is scattered upon large iron plates, and slowly dried by a gentle fire kept up beneath. It now resembles a very coarse kind of flour; and is eaten in two ways—wet and dry. In the first case, it is mixed with hot water until it forms a kind of porridge; in the second, it is handed round, under the form of coarse flour, in little baskets, and every one at table takes as

44

much as he chooses, and sprinkles it over his plate.

4th October. The mountain ranges continue drawing nearer and nearer to each other, and the woods become thicker and more luxuriant. The various creeping plants are indescribably beautiful: not only do they entirely cover the ground, but they are so intertwined with the trees that their lovely flowers hang on the highest branches, and look like the blossoms of the trees themselves. But there are likewise trees whose own yellow and red blossoms resemble the most beautiful flowers; while there are others whose great white leaves stand out like silver from the surrounding mass of flowery green. Woods like these might well be called "the giant gardens of the world." The palm-trees have here almost disappeared.

We soon reached the mountain range we had to cross, and on our way often ascended such elevated spots that we had a free view extending as far back as the capital. On the top of the mountain (Alta da Serra, sixteen miles from Mendoza) we found a venda. From this spot the distance to Morroqueimado is sixteen miles, which took us a long time, as the road is either up or down hill the whole way. We were continually surrounded by the most magnificent woodlands, and were only rarely reminded by a small plantation of *kabi*, [39] or mil, that we were in the neighbourhood of men. We did not perceive the little town until we had surmounted the last eminence and were in its immediate vicinity. It lies in a large and picturesque hollow, surrounded by mountains at an elevation of 3,200 feet above the level of the sea. As night was near at hand, we were glad enough to reach our lodgings, which were situated on one side of the town, in the house of a German named Linderoth; they were very comfortable, and, as we afterwards found, exceedingly reasonable, seeing that for our rooms and three good meals a-day we only paid one milreis (2s. 2d.).

5th October. The small town of Novo Friburgo, or Morroqueimado, was founded about fifteen years since by French, Swiss, and Germans. It contains not quite a hundred substantial houses, the greater part of which form an extremely broad street, while the others lie scattered about, here and there.

We had already heard, in Rio Janeiro, a great deal of the Messrs. Beske and Freese, and been particularly recommended not to forget to pay a visit to each. Herr Beske is a naturalist, and resides here with his wife, who is almost as scientific as himself. We enjoyed many an hour in their entertaining society, and were shown many interesting collections of quadrupeds, birds, serpents, insects, etc.; the collection of these last, indeed, was more rich and remarkable than that in the Museum of Rio Janeiro. Herr Beske has always a great many orders from Europe to send over various objects of natural history. Herr Freese is the director and proprietor of an establishment for boys, and preferred establishing his school in this cool climate than in the hot town beneath. He was kind enough to show us all his arrangements. As it was near evening when we paid our visit, school was already over; but he presented all his scholars to us, made them perform a few gymnastic exercises, and proposed several questions on geography, history,

45

arithmetic, etc., which, without exception, they answered very carefully and correctly. His establishment receives sixty boys, and was quite full, although the annual charge for each boy is one thousand milreis (£108 6s. 8d.).

6th October. We had at first intended to stop only one day in Novo Friburgo, and then continue our journey. Unfortunately, however, the wound which the Count had received on our excursion to Petropolis became, through the frequent use of the hand and the excessive heat, much worse; inflammation set in, and he was consequently obliged to give up all ideas of going any further. With my wounds I was more fortunate, for, as they were on the upper part of the arm, I had been enabled to pay them a proper degree of care and attention; they were now proceeding very favourably, and neither dangerous nor troublesome. I had, therefore, no resource left but either to pursue my journey alone, or to give up the most interesting portion of it, namely, my visit to the Indians. To this last idea I could by no means reconcile myself; I inquired, therefore, whether the journey could be made with any degree of safety, and as I received a sort of half-satisfactory answer, and Herr Lindenroth found me also a trusty guide, I procured a good double-barrelled pistol and set out undaunted upon my trip.

We at first remained for some time in the midst of mountain ranges, and then again descended into the warmer region beneath. The valleys were generally narrow, and the uniform appearance of the woods was often broken by plantations. The latter, however, did not always look very promising, most of them being so choked up with weeds that it was frequently impossible to perceive the plant itself, especially when it was young and small. It is only upon the sugar and coffee plantations that any great care is bestowed.

The coffee-trees stand in rows upon tolerably steep hillocks. They attain a height of from six to twelve feet, and begin to bear sometimes as soon as the second, but in no case later than the third year, and are productive for ten years. The leaf is long and slightly serrated, the blossom white, while the fruit hangs down in the same manner as a bunch of grapes, and resembles a longish cherry, which is first green, then red, brown, and nearly black. During the time it is red, the outer shell is soft, but ultimately becomes perfectly hard, and resembles a wooden capsule. Blossoms and fruit in full maturity are found upon the trees at the same time, and hence the harvest lasts nearly the whole year. The latter is conducted in two ways. The berries are either gathered by hand, or large straw mats are spread underneath, and the trees well shaken. The first method is the more troublesome, but, without comparison, the better one.

Another novelty, which I saw here for the first time, were the frequent burning forests, which had been set on fire to clear the ground for cultivation. In most cases I merely saw immense clouds of smoke curling upwards in the distance, and desired nothing more earnestly than to enjoy a nearer view of such a conflagration. My wish was destined to be fulfilled today, as my road lay between a burning forest and a burning *rost*. {40} The intervening space was not, at the

46

most, more than fifty paces broad, and was completely enveloped in smoke. I could hear the cracking of the fire, and through the dense vapour perceive thick, forked columns of flame shoot upwards towards the sky, while now and then loud reports, like those of a cannon, announced the fall of the large trees. On seeing my guide enter this fiery gulf, I was, I must confess, rather frightened; but I felt assured, on reflecting, that he would certainly not foolishly risk his own life, and that he must know from experience that such places were passable.

At the entrance sat two negroes, to point out the direction that wayfarers had to follow, and to recommend them to make as much haste as possible. My guide translated for me what they said, and spurred on his mule; I followed his example, and we both galloped at full speed into the smoking pass. The burning ashes now flew around us in all directions, while the suffocating smoke was even more oppressive than the heat; our beasts, too, seemed to have great difficulty in drawing breath, and it was as much as we could do to keep them in a gallop. Fortunately we had not above 500 or 600 paces to ride, and consequently succeeded in making our way safely through.

In the Brazils a conflagration of this kind never extends very far, as the vegetation is too green and offers too much opposition. The wood has to be ignited in several places, and even then the fire frequently goes out, and when most of the wood is burnt, many patches are found unconsumed. Soon after passing this dangerous spot, we came to a magnificent rock, the sides of which must have risen almost perpendicularly to a height of 600 or 800 feet. A number of detached fragments lay scattered about the road, forming picturesque groups.

To my great astonishment, I learned from my guide that our lodging for the night was near at hand; we had scarcely ridden twenty miles, but he affirmed that the next venda where we could stop, was too far distant. I afterwards discovered that his sole object was to spin out the journey, which was a very profitable one for him, since, besides good living for himself, and fodder for his two mules, he received four milreis (8s. 8d.) a-day. We put up, therefore, at a solitary venda, erected in the middle of the forest, and kept by Herr Molasz.

During the day we had suffered greatly from the heat; the thermometer standing, in the sun, at 119° 75' Fah.

The circumstance which must strike a traveller most forcibly in the habits of the colonists and inhabitants of the Brazils, is the contrast between fear and courage. On the one hand, every one you meet upon the road is armed with pistols and long knives, as if the whole country was overrun with robbers and murderers; while, on the other, the proprietors live quite alone on their plantations, and without the least apprehension, in the midst of their numerous slaves. The traveller, too, fearlessly passes the night in some venda, situated in impenetrable woods, with neither shutters to the windows nor good locks to the doors, besides which the owner's room is a considerable distance from the chambers of the guests, and it would be utterly impossible to obtain any assistance from the

47

servants, who are all slaves, as they live either in some corner of the stable, or in the loft. At first I felt very frightened at thus passing the night alone, surrounded by the wild gloom of the forest, and in a room that was only very insecurely fastened; but, as I was everywhere assured that such a thing as a forcible entry into a house had never been heard of, I soon dismissed my superfluous anxiety, and enjoyed the most tranquil repose.

I know very few countries in Europe where I should like to traverse vast forests, and pass the night in such awfully lonely houses, accompanied by only a hired guide.

On the 7th of October, also, we made only a short day's journey of twenty miles, to the small town of Canto Gallo. The scenery was of the usual description, consisting of narrow, circumscribed valleys and mountains covered with endless forests. If little fazendas, and the remains of woods which had been set on fire, had not, every now and then, reminded us of the hand of man, I should have thought that I was wandering through some yet undiscovered part of Brazil.

The monotony of our journey was rather romantically interrupted by our straying for a short distance from the right road. In order to reach it again, we were obliged to penetrate, by untrodden paths, through the woods; a task presenting difficulties of which a European can scarcely form an idea. We dismounted from our mules, and my guide threw back, on either side, the low-hanging branches, and cut through the thick web of creepers; while, one moment, we were obliged to climb over broken trunks, or squeeze ourselves between others, at the next we sank knee-deep among endless parasitical plants. I began almost to despair of ever effecting a passage, and, even up to the present day, am at a loss to understand how we succeeded in escaping from this inextricable mass.

The little town of Canto Gallo is situated in a narrow valley, and contains about eighty houses. The venda stands apart, the town not being visible from it. The temperature here is warm as in Rio Janeiro.

On my return to the venda, after a short walk to the town, I applied to my landlady, in order to obtain a near and really correct idea of a Brazilian household. The good woman, however, gave herself very little trouble, either in looking after the house or the kitchen; as is the case in Italy, this was her husband's business. A negress and two young negroes cooked, the arrangements of the kitchen being of the most primitive simplicity. The salt was pressed fine with a bottle; the potatoes, when boiled, underwent the same process—the latter were also subsequently squeezed in the frying-pan with a plate, to give them the form of a pancake; a pointed piece of wood served for a fork, etc. There was a large fire burning for every dish.

Every one whose complexion was white, sat down with us at table. All the dishes, consisting of cold roast beef, black beans with boiled *carna secca*, {42} potatoes, rice, manioc flour, and boiled manioc roots, were placed upon the table at the same time, and every one helped himself as he pleased. At the conclusion of our meal, we had strong coffee without milk. The slaves had beans, *carna secca*, and manioc flour.

8th October. Our goal today was the Fazenda Boa Esperanza, twenty-four miles off. Four miles beyond Canto Gallo, we crossed a small waterfall, and then entered one of the most magnificent virgin forests I had yet beheld. A small path, on the bank of a little brook conducted us through it. Palms, with their majestic tops, raised themselves proudly above the other trees, which, lovingly interlaced together, formed the most beautiful bowers; orchids grew in wanton luxuriance upon the branches and twigs; creepers and ferns climbed up the trees, mingling with the boughs, and forming thick walls of blossoms and flowers, which displayed the most brilliant colours, and exhaled the sweetest perfume; delicate humming-birds twittered around our heads; the pepper-pecker, with his brilliant plumage, soared shyly upwards; parrots and parroquets were swinging themselves in the branches, and numberless beautifully marked birds, which I only knew from having seen specimens in the Museum, inhabited this fairy grove. It seemed as if I was riding in some fairy park, and I expected, every moment, to see sylphs and nymphs appear before me.

I was so happy, that I felt richly recompensed for all the fatigue of my journey. One thought only obscured this beautiful picture; and that was, that weak man should dare to enter the lists with the giant nature of the place, and make it bend before his will. How soon, perhaps, may this profound and holy tranquillity be disturbed by the blows of some daring settler's axe, to make room for the wants of men!

I saw no dangerous animals save a few dark green snakes, from five to seven feet long; a dead ounce, that had been stripped of its skin; and a lizard, three feet in length, which ran timidly across our path. I met with no apes; they appear to conceal themselves deeper in the woods, where no human footstep is likely to disturb them in their sports and gambols.

During the whole distance from Canto Gallo to the small village of St. Ritta (sixteen miles), if it had not again been for a few coffee plantations, I should have thought the place completely forgotten by man.

Near St. Ritta are some gold-washings in the river of the same name, and not far from them, diamonds also are found. Since seeking or digging for diamonds is no longer an imperial monopoly, every one is at liberty to employ himself in this occupation, and yet it is exercised as much as possible in secret. No one will acknowledge looking for them, in order to avoid paying the State its share as fixed by law. The precious stones are sought for and dug out at certain spots, from heaps of sand, stones, and soil, which have been washed down by the heavy rains.

I had found lodgings in a venda for the last time, the preceding evening, at Canto Gallo. I had now to rely upon the hospitality of the proprietors of the fazendas.

49

Custom requires that, on reaching a fazenda, any person who desires to stop the middle of the day or the night there, should wait outside and ask, through the servant, permission to do so. It is not until his application is granted, which is almost always the case, that the traveller dismounts from his mule, and enters the building.

They received me at the Fazenda of Boa Esperanza in the most friendly manner, and, as I happened to arrive exactly at dinner-time (it was between 3 and 4 o'clock), covers were immediately laid for me and my attendant. The dishes were numerous, and prepared very nearly in the European fashion.

Great astonishment was manifested in every venda and fazenda at seeing a lady arrive accompanied only by a single servant. The first question was, whether I was not afraid thus to traverse the woods alone; and my guide was invariably taken on one side, and questioned as to way I travelled. As he was in the habit of seeing me collect flowers and insects, he supposed me to be a naturalist, and replied that my journey had a scientific object.

After dinner, the amiable lady of the house proposed that I should go and see the coffee-plantations, warehouses, etc.; and I willingly accepted her offer, as affording me an opportunity of viewing the manner in which the coffee was prepared, from beginning to end.

The mode of gathering it I have already described. When this is done, the coffee is spread out upon large plots of ground, trodden down in a peculiar manner, and enclosed by low stone walls, scarcely a foot high, with little drain-holes in them, to allow of the water running off in case of rain. On these places the coffee is dried by the glowing heat of the sun, and then shaken in large stone mortars, ten or twenty of which are placed beneath a wooden scaffolding, from which wooden hammers, set in motion by water power, descend into the mortars, and easily crush the husks. The mass, thus crushed, is then placed in wooden boxes, fastened in the middle of a long table, and having small openings at each side, through which both the berry itself and the husk fall slowly out. At the table are seated negroes, who separate the berry from the husk, and then cast it into shallow copper cauldrons, which are easily heated. In these it is carefully turned, and remains until it is quite dried. This last process requires some degree of care, as the colour of the coffee depends upon the degree of heat to which it is exposed; if dried too quickly, instead of the usual greenish colour, it contracts a yellowish tinge.

On the whole, the preparation of coffee is not fatiguing, and even the gathering of it is far from being as laborious as reaping is with us. The negro stands in an upright posture when gathering the berry, and is protected by the tree itself against the great heat of the sun. The only danger he incurs is of being bitten by some venomous snake or other—an accident, however, which, fortunately, rarely happens.

The work on a sugar-plantation, on the contrary, is said to be exceedingly laborious, particularly that portion of it which relates to weeding the ground and cutting the cane. I have never yet witnessed a sugar-harvest, but, perhaps, may do so in the course of my travels.

All work ceases at sunset, when the negroes are drawn up in front of their master's house for the purpose of being counted, and then, after a short prayer, have their supper, consisting of boiled beans, bacon, *carna secca*, and manioc flour, handed out to them.

At sunrise, they again assemble, are once more counted, and, after prayers and breakfast, go to work.

I had an opportunity of convincing myself in this, as well as in many other fazendas, vendas, and private houses, that the slaves are by far not so harshly treated as we Europeans imagine. They are not overworked, perform all their duties very leisurely, and are well kept. Their children are frequently the playmates of their master's children, and knock each other about as if they were all equal. There may be cases in which certain slaves are cruelly and undeservedly punished; but do not the like instances of injustice occur in Europe also?

I am certainly very much opposed to slavery, and should greet its abolition with the greatest delight, but, despite this, I again affirm that the negro slave enjoys, under the protection of the law, a better lot than the free fellah of Egypt, or many peasants in Europe, who still groan under the right of soccage. The principal reason of the better lot of the slave, compared to that of the miserable peasant, in the case in point, may perhaps partly be, that the purchase and keep of the one is expensive, while the other costs nothing.

The arrangements in the houses belonging to the proprietors of the fazendas are extremely simple. The windows are unglazed, and are closed at night with wooden shutters. In many instances, the outer roof is the common covering of all the rooms, which are merely separated from one another by low partitions, so that you can hear every word your neighbour says, and almost the breathing of the person sleeping next to you. The furniture is equally simple: a large table, a few straw sofas, and a few chairs. The wearing apparel is generally hung up against the walls; the linen alone being kept in tin cases, to protect it from the attacks of the ants.

In the country, the children of even the most opulent persons run about frequently without shoes or stockings. Before they go to bed they have their feet examined to see whether any sand-fleas have nestled in them; and if such be the case, they are extracted by the elder negro children.

9th October. Early in the morning I took leave of my kind hostess, who, like a truly careful housewife, had wrapped up a roasted fowl, manioc flour, and a cheese for me, so that I was well provisioned on setting off.

51

The next station, Aldea do Pedro, on the banks of the Parahyby, was situated at a distance of sixteen miles. Our way lay through magnificent woods, and before we had traversed half of it, we arrived at the river Parahyby, one of the largest in the Brazils, and celebrated, moreover, for the peculiar character of its bed, which is strewed with innumerable cliffs and rocks; these, owing to the low state of the stream, were more than usually conspicuous. On every side rose little islands, covered with small trees or underwood, lending a most magic appearance to the river. During the rainy season, most of these cliffs and rocks are covered with water, and the river then appears more majestic. On account of the rocks it can only be navigated by small boats and rafts.

As you proceed along the banks, the scenery gradually changes. The fore-part of the mountain ranges subside into low hills, the mountains themselves retreat, and the nearer you approach Aldea do Pedro, the wider and more open becomes the valley. In the background alone are still visible splendid mountain ranges, from which rises a mountain higher than the rest, somewhat more naked, and almost isolated. To this my guide pointed, and gave me to understand that our way lay over it, in order to reach the Puris, who lived beyond.

About noon I arrived at Aldea do Pedro, which I found to be a small village with a stone church; the latter might, perhaps, contain 200 persons. I had intended continuing my journey to the Puris the same day, but my guide was attacked with pains in his knee, and could not ride further. I had, therefore, no resource but to alight at the priest's, who gave me a hearty welcome; he had a pretty good house, immediately adjoining the church.

10th October. As my guide was worse, the priest offered me his negro to replace him. I thankfully accepted his offer, but could not set off before 1 o'clock, for which I was, in some respects, not sorry, as it was Sunday, and I hoped to see a great number of the country people flock to mass. This, however, was not the case; although it was a very fine day there were hardly thirty people at church. The men were dressed exactly in the European fashion; the women wore long cloaks with collars, and had white handkerchiefs upon their heads, partly falling over their faces as well; the latter they uncovered in church. Both men and women were barefooted.

As chance would have it, I witnessed a burial and a christening. Before mass commenced, a boat crossed over from the opposite bank of the Parahyby, and on reaching the side, a hammock, in which was the deceased, was lifted out. He was then laid in a coffin which had been prepared for the purpose in a house near the churchyard. The corpse was enveloped in a white cloth, with the feet and half the head protruding beyond it; the latter was covered with a peaked cap of shining black cloth.

The christening took place before the burial. The person who was to be christened was a young negro of fifteen, who stood with his mother at the church door. As the priest entered the church to perform mass, he christened him, in

52

passing by, without much ceremony or solemnity, and even without sponsors; the boy, too, seemed to be as little touched by the whole affair as a new born infant. I do not believe that either he or his mother had the least idea of the importance of the rite.

The priest then hurriedly performed mass, and read the burial service over the deceased, who had belonged to rather a wealthy family, and therefore was respectably interred. Unfortunately, when they wanted to lower the corpse into its cold resting-place, the latter was found to be too short and too narrow, and the poor wretch was so tossed about, coffin and all, that I expected every moment to see him roll out. But all was of no avail, and after a great deal of useless exertion no other course was left but to place the coffin on one side and enlarge the grave, which was done with much unwillingness and amid an unceasing volley of oaths.

This fatiguing work being at last finished, I returned to the house, where I took a good *déjeuner à la fourchette* in company with the priest, and then set out with my black guide.

We rode for some time through a broad valley between splendid woods, and had to cross two rivers, the Parahyby and the Pomba, in trunks of trees hollowed out. For each of these wretched conveyances I was obliged to pay one milreis (2s. 2d.), and to incur great danger into the bargain; not so much on account of the stream and the small size of the craft, as of our mules, which, fastened by their halter, swam alongside, and frequently came so near that I was afraid that we should be every moment capsized.

After riding twelve miles further, we reached the last settlement of the whites. {47} On an open space, which had with difficulty been conquered from the virgin forest, stood a largish wooden house, surrounded by a few miserable huts, the house serving as the residence of the whites, and the huts as that of the slaves. A letter which I had brought from the priest procured me a welcome.

The manner of living in this settlement was of such a description that I was almost tempted to believe that I was already among savages.

The large house contained an entrance hall leading into four rooms, each of which was inhabited by a white family. The whole furniture of these rooms consisted of a few hammocks and straw mats. The inhabitants were cowering upon the floor, playing with the children, or assisting one another to get rid of their vermin. The kitchen was immediately adjoining the house, and resembled a very large barn with openings in it; upon a hearth that took up nearly the entire length of the barn, several fires were burning, over which hung small kettles, and at each side were fastened wooden spits. On these were fixed several pieces of meat, some of which were being roasted by the fire and some cured by the smoke. The kitchen was full of people: whites, Puris, and negroes, children whose parents were whites and Puris, or Puris and negroes—in a word, the place was like a book of specimens containing the most varied ramifications of the three

53

principal races of the country.

In the court-yard was an immense number of fowls, beautifully marked ducks and geese; I also saw some extraordinarily fat pigs, and some horribly ugly dogs. Under some cocoa-palms and tamarind-trees, were seated white and coloured people, separate and in groups, mostly occupied in satisfying their hunger. Some had got broken basins or pumpkin-gourds before them, in which they kneaded up with their hands boiled beans and manioc flour; this thick and disgusting-looking mess they devoured with avidity. Others were eating pieces of meat, which they likewise tore with their hands, and threw into their mouths alternately with handfuls of manioc flour. The children, who also had their gourds before them, were obliged to defend the contents valiantly; for at one moment a hen would peck something out, and, at the next, a dog would run off with a bit, or sometimes even a little pig would waggle up, and invariably give a most contented grunt when it had not performed the journey for nothing.

While I was making these observations, I suddenly heard a merry cry outside the court-yard; I proceeded to the place from which it issued, and saw two boys dragging towards me a large dark brown serpent; certainly more than seven feet long, at the end of a bast-rope. It was already dead, and, as far as I could learn from the explanations of those about me, it was of so venomous a kind, that if a person is bitten by it, he immediately swells up and dies.

I was rather startled at what I heard, and determined at least not to set out through the wood just as evening was closing in, as I might have to take up my quarters for the night under some tree; I therefore deferred my visit to the savages until the next morning. The good people imagined that I was afraid of the savages, and earnestly assured me that they were a most harmless race, from whom I had not the least to fear. As my knowledge of Portuguese was limited to a few words, I found it rather difficult to make myself understood, and it was only by the help of gesticulations, with now and then a small sketch, that I succeeded in enlightening them as to the real cause of my fear.

I passed the night, therefore, with these half savages, who constantly showed me the greatest respect, and overwhelmed me with attention. A straw mat, which, at my request, was spread out under shelter in the court-yard, was my bed. They brought me for supper a roast fowl, rice, and hard eggs, and for dessert, oranges and tamarind-pods; the latter contain a brown, half sweet, half sour pulp, very agreeable to the taste. The women lay all round me, and by degrees we managed to get on wonderfully together.

I showed them the different flowers and insects I had gathered during the day. This, doubtless, induced them to look upon me as a learned person, and, as such, to impute to me a knowledge of medicine. They begged me to prescribe for different cases of illness: bad ears, eruptions of the skin, and in the children, a considerable tendency to scrofula, etc. I ordered lukewarm baths, frequent fomentations, and the use of oil and soap, applied externally and rubbed into the body. May Heaven grant that these remedies have really worked some good!

On the 11th of October, I proceeded into the forest, in company with a negress and a Puri, to find out the Indians. At times, we had to work our way laboriously through the thicket, and then again we would find narrow paths, by which we pursued our journey with greater ease. After eight hours' walking, we came upon a number of Puris, who led us into their huts, situated in the immediate vicinity, where I beheld a picture of the greatest misery and want: I had often met with a great deal of wretchedness in my travels, but never so much as I saw here!

On a small space, under lofty trees, five huts, or rather sheds, formed of leaves, were erected, eighteen feet long, by twelve feet broad. The frames were formed of four poles stuck in the ground, with another reaching across; and the roof, of palm-leaves, through which the rain could penetrate with the utmost facility. On three sides, these bowers were entirely open. In the interior hung a hammock or two; and on the ground glimmered a little fire, under a heap of ashes, in which a few roots, Indian corn, and bananas, were roasting. In one corner, under the roof, a small supply of provisions was hoarded up, and a few gourds were scattered around: these are used by the savages instead of plates, pots, water-jugs, etc. The long bows and arrows, which constitute their only weapons, were leaning in the background against the wall.

I found the Indians still more ugly than the negroes. Their complexion is a light bronze, stunted in stature, well-knit, and about the middle size. They have broad and somewhat compressed features, and thick, coal-black hair, hanging straight down, which the women sometimes wear in plaits fastened to the back of the head, and sometimes falling down loose about them. Their forehead is broad and low, the nose somewhat flattened, the eyes long and narrow, almost like those of the Chinese, and the mouth large, with rather thick lips. To give a still greater effect to all these various charms, a peculiar look of stupidity is spread over the whole face, and is more especially to be attributed to the way in which their mouths are always kept opened.

Most of them, both men and women, were tattooed with a reddish or blue colour, though only round the mouth, in the form of a moustache. Both sexes are passionately fond of smoking, and prefer brandy to everything. Their dress was composed of a few rags, which they had fastened round their loins.

I had already heard, in Novo Friburgo, a few interesting particulars concerning the Puris, which I will here relate.

The number of the Brazilian Indians at the present time is calculated at about 500,000, who live scattered about the forests in the heart of the country. Not more than six or seven families ever settle on the same spot, which they leave as soon as the game in the neighbourhood has been killed, and all the fruit and roots consumed. A large number of these Indians have been christened. They are always ready, for a little brandy or tobacco, to undergo the ceremony at the

55

shortest notice, and only regret that it cannot be repeated more frequently, as it is soon over. The priest believes that he has only to perform the rite in order to gain another soul for heaven, and afterwards gives himself very little concern, either about the instruction or the manners and morals of his converts. These, it is true, are called Christians, or *tamed savages*, but live in the same heathen manner that they previously did. Thus, for instance, they contract marriages for indefinite periods; elect their Caciques (chiefs) from the strongest and finest men; follow all their old customs on the occasion of marriages and deaths, just the same as before baptism.

Their language is very poor: they are said, for example, only to be able to count one and two, and are therefore obliged, when they desire to express a larger number, to repeat these two figures continually. Furthermore, for *today, to-morrow*, and *yesterday*, they possess only the word *day*, and express their more particular meaning by signs; for *today*, they say *day*, and feel their head, or point upwards; for *to-morrow*, they again use the word *day*, and point their fingers in a straightforward direction; and for *yesterday*, they use the same word, and point behind them.

The Puris are said to be peculiarly adapted for tracking runaway negroes, as their organs of smell are very highly developed. They smell the trace of the fugitive on the leaves of the trees; and if the negro does not succeed in reaching some stream, in which he can either walk or swim for a considerable distance, it is asserted that he can very seldom escape the Indian engaged in pursuit of him. These savages are also readily employed in felling timber, and cultivating Indian corn, manioc, etc., as they are very industrious, and think themselves well paid with a little tobacco, brandy, or coloured cloth. But on no account must they be compelled to do anything by force: they are free men. They seldom, however, come to offer their assistance unless they are half-starved.

I visited the huts of all these savages; and as my guides had trumpeted forth my praises as being a woman of great knowledge, I was here asked my advice for the benefit of every one who was ill.

In one of the huts, I found an old woman groaning in her hammock. On my drawing nearer, they uncovered the poor creature, and I perceived that all her breast was eaten up by cancer. She seemed to have no idea of a bandage, or any means of soothing the pain. I advised her to wash the wound frequently with a decoction of mallows, {50} and, in addition to this, to cover it over with the leaves of the same plant. I only trust that my advice procured her some trifling relief.

This horrible disease unfortunately does not appear to be at all rare among the Puris, for I saw many of their women, some of whom had large hard swellings, and others even small tumours on the breast.

After having sufficiently examined everything in the huts, I went with some of the savages to shoot parrots and monkeys. We had not far to go in order to meet with

56

both; and I had now an opportunity of admiring the skill with which these people use their bows. They brought down the birds even when they were on the wing, and very seldom missed their mark. After shooting three parrots and an ape, we returned to the huts.

The good creatures offered me the best hut they possessed, and invited me to pass the night there. Being rather fatigued by the toilsome nature of my journey on foot, the heat, and the hunting excursion, I very joyfully accepted their proposition: the day, too, was drawing to a close, and I should not have been able to reach the settlement of the whites before night. I therefore spread out my cloak upon the ground, arranged a log of wood so as to serve instead of a pillow, and for the present seated myself upon my splendid couch. In the meanwhile, my hosts were preparing the monkey and the parrots, by sticking them on wooden spits, and roasting them before the fire. In order to render the meal a peculiarly dainty one, they also buried some Indian corn and roots in the cinders. They then gathered a few large fresh leaves off the trees, tore the roasted ape into several pieces with their hands, and placing a large portion of it, as well as a parrot, Indian corn, and some roots upon the leaves, put it before me. My appetite was tremendous, seeing that I had tasted nothing since the morning. I therefore immediately fell to on the roasted monkey, which I found superlatively delicious: the flesh of the parrot was far from being so tender and palatable.

After our meal, I begged the Indians to perform one of their dances for me—a request with which they readily complied. As it was already dark, they brought a quantity of wood, which they formed into a sort of funeral pile, and set on fire: the men then formed a circle all round, and began the dance. They threw their bodies from side to side in a most remarkably awkward fashion, but always moving the head forwards in a straight line. The women then joined in, remaining, however, at some little distance in the rear of the men, and making the same awkward movements. They now began a most horrible noise, which was intended for a song, at the same time distorting their features in a frightful manner. One of them stood near, playing upon a kind of stringed instrument, made out of the stem of a cabbage-palm, and about two feet, or two feet and a half, in length. A hole was cut in it in a slanting direction, and six fibres of the stem had been raised up, and kept in an elevated position at each end, by means of a small bridge. The fingers were then used for playing upon these as upon a guitar: the tone was very low, disagreeable, and hoarse.

This first dance they named the Dance of Peace or Joy. The men then performed a much wilder one alone. After providing themselves for the purpose with bows, arrows, and stout clubs, they again formed a circle, but their movements were much quicker and wilder than in the first instance, and they likewise hit about them with their clubs in a horrible fashion. They then suddenly broke their rank, strung their bows, placed their arrows ready, and went through the pantomime of shooting after a flying foe, uttering at the same time the most piercing cries, which echoed through the whole forest. I started up in affright, for I really believed that

I was surrounded by enemies, and that I was delivered up into their power, without any chance of help or assistance. I was heartily glad when this horrible war-dance came to a conclusion.

After retiring to rest, and when all around had gradually become hushed into silence, I was assailed by apprehensions of another description: I thought of the number of wild beasts, and the horrible serpents that might perhaps be concealed quite close to me, and then of the exposed situation I was in. This kept me awake a long time, and I often fancied I heard a rustling among the leaves, as if one of the dreaded animals were breaking through. At length, however, my weary body asserted its rights. I laid my head upon my wooden pillow, and consoled myself with the idea that the danger was, after all, not so great as many of we travellers wish to have believed, otherwise how would it be possible for the savages to live as they do, without any precautions, in their open huts!

On the 12th of October, early in the morning, I took leave of the savages, and made them a present of various bronze ornaments, with which they were so delighted that they offered me everything they possessed. I took a bow with a couple of arrows, as mementos of my visit; returned to the wooden house, and having also distributed similar presents there, mounted my mule, and arrived late in the evening at Aldea do Pedro.

On the morning of the 13th of October, I bade the obliging priest farewell, and with my attendant, who, by this time was quite recovered, began my journey back to Novo Friburgo, and, in this instance, although I pursued the same road, was only three days instead of four on the way.

On arriving I found Count Berchthold, who was now quite well. We determined, therefore, before returning to Rio Janeiro, to make a little excursion to a fine waterfall, about twelve miles from Novo Friburgo. By mere chance we learned that the christening of the Princess Isabella would take place on the 19th, and, as we did not wish to miss this interesting ceremony, we preferred returning directly. We followed the same road we had taken in coming, till about four miles before reaching Ponte de Pinheiro, and then struck off towards Porto de Praja. This road was thirty-two miles longer by land, but so much shorter by sea, that the passage is made by steamer from Porto de Praja to Rio Janeiro in half an hour. The scenery around Pinheiro was mostly dull and tedious, almost like a desert, the monotony of which was only broken here and there by a few scanty woods or low hills. We were not lucky enough to see the mountains again until we were near the capital.

I must here mention a comical mistake of Herr Beske, of Novo Friburgo, which we at first could not understand, but which afterwards afforded a good deal of amusement. Herr Beske had recommended us a guide, whom he described as a walking encyclopædia of knowledge, and able to answer all our questions about trees, plants, scenery, etc., in the most complete manner. We esteemed ourselves exceedingly fortunate to obtain such a phœnix of a guide, and immediately took advantage of every opportunity to put his powers to the test. He could, however, tell us nothing at all; if we asked him the name of a river, he replied that it was too small, and had no name. The trees, likewise, were too insignificant, the plants too common. This ignorance was rather too much; we made inquiry, and found that Herr Beske had not intended to send us the guide we had, but his brother, who, however, had died six months previously—a circumstance which Herr Beske must have forgotten.

On the evening of the 18th of October, we arrived safely in Rio Janeiro. We immediately inquired about the christening, and heard it had been put off till the 15th of November, and that on the 19th of October only the Emperor's anniversary would be kept. We had thus hurried back to no purpose, without visiting the waterfall near Novo Friburgo, which we might have admired very much at our leisure.

On our return we only came eight miles out of our way.

CHAPTER V. THE VOYAGE ROUND CAPE HORN.

DEPARTURE FROM RIO JANEIRO—SANTOS AND ST. PAULO—CIRCUMNAVIGATION OF CAPE HORN—THE STRAITS OF MAGELLAN—ARRIVAL IN VALPARAISO—8TH DECEMBER, 1846, TO 2ND MARCH, 1847.

When I paid £25 for my place in the fine English barque, "John Renwick," Captain Bell, the latter promised me that he would be ready to sail on the 25th of November at the latest, and would stop at no intermediate port, but shape his course direct to Valparaiso. The first part of this promise I believed, because he assured me that every day he stopped cost him £7; and the second, because, as a general rule, I willingly believe every one, even ship captains. In both particulars, however, was I deceived; for it was not until the 8th of December that I received a notice to go on board that evening and then for the first time the captain informed me that he must run into Santos, to lay in a stock of provisions, which were there much cheaper than in Rio Janeiro; that he also intended clearing out a cargo of coal and taking in another of sugar. He did not tell me till we arrived in Santos itself, where he also assured me that all these different matters would not take him more than three or four days.

I took leave of my friends and went on board in the evening; Count Berchthold and Messrs. Geiger and Rister accompanying me to the ship.

Early in the morning of the 9th of December we weighed anchor, but the wind was so unfavourable that we were obliged to tack the whole day in order to gain the open sea, and it was not until about 10 A.M. that we lost sight of land.

There were eight passengers besides myself; five Frenchmen, one Belgian, and two citizens of Milan. I looked upon the latter as half countrymen of mine, and we were soon very good friends.

It was the second time this year that the two Italians were making the voyage round Cape Horn. Their first had not been fortunate; they reached Cape Horn in winter, which in those cold southern latitudes lasts from April till about November. {53} They were unable to circumnavigate the Cape, being driven back by violent contrary winds and storms, against which they strove for fourteen weary days without making the least progress. The crew now lost courage, and affirmed that it would be advisable to turn back and wait for more favourable winds. The captain, however, was not of this opinion, and succeeded so well in working upon the pride of the crew that they once more engaged in their conflict with the elements. It was, however, for the last time, for the very same night a tremendous sea broke over the ship, tearing away all her upper works, and sweeping the captain and six of the sailors overboard. The water poured in torrents into the cabins, and drove every one from the berths. The bulwarks, boats, and binnacle were carried clean off, and the mainmast had to be cut away. The sailors then turned the ship about, and after a long and dangerous voyage, succeeded in bringing her, dismasted as she was, into Rio Janeiro.

This story was not very encouraging, but the fine weather and our good ship relieved us of all anxiety. With regard to the vessel, we could not have chosen a better. It had large, comfortable cabins, an exceedingly good-natured and obliging captain, and a bill of fare which must have contented the most dainty palate. Every day we had roast or stewed fowls, ducks, or geese, fresh mutton or pork, eggs variously prepared, plum-pudding and tarts; to all this were added side dishes of ham, rice, potatoes, and other vegetables; and for dessert, dried fruit, nuts, almonds, cheese, etc. There was also plenty of bread, fresh baked every day, and good wine. We all unanimously acknowledged that we had never been so well treated, or had so good a table in any sailing vessel before; and we could, therefore, in this respect, look forward to our voyage without any apprehension.

On the 12th of December we hove in sight of the mountain ranges of Santos, and at 9 o'clock the same evening we reached a bay which the captain took for that of the same name. Lighted torches were repeatedly held over the vessel's side to summon a pilot; no pilot, however, made his appearance, and we were therefore obliged to trust to chance, and anchor at the mouth of the bay.

On the morning of the 13th a pilot came on board, and astonished us with the intelligence that we had anchored before the wrong bay. We had some trouble in working our way out, and anchoring about noon in the right one. A pretty little chateau-like building immediately attracted our attention. We took it for some advanced building of the town, and congratulated one another on having reached our temporary destination so quickly. On approaching nearer, however, we could perceive no signs of the town, and learned that the building was a small fort, and that Santos was situated in a second bay, communicating with the first by a small arm of the sea. Unluckily, the wind had by this time fallen, and we were obliged to be at anchor all day, and it was not until the 14th that a slight breeze sprang up and wafted us into port.

Santos is most charmingly situated at the entrance of a large valley. Picturesque hills, adorned with chapels and detached houses, rise on each side, and immediately beyond are considerable mountain ranges, spreading in a semi-circle round the valley, while a lovely island forms a most beautiful foreground to the whole.

We had scarcely landed before the captain informed us that we must stop for at least five days. The Italians, one of the Frenchmen, and myself determined that we would take advantage of this delay to make an excursion to St. Paulo, the largest inland town of the Brazils, and about forty miles from Santos. The same evening we hired mules, for which we paid five milreis (10s. 10d.) each, and set out upon our trip.

15th December. Early in the morning, we armed ourselves with well-charged double-barrelled pistols, having been alarmed by accounts of the Maroon negroes, {55} about a hundred of whom were said to be at that time lurking in the mountains, and to be so daring that they extended their inroads as far as the vicinity of Santos itself.

The first eight miles led through the valley to the lofty range of mountains which we had to cross. The road was good, and more frequented than any I had yet seen in the Brazils. Handsome wooden bridges traverse the rivers Vicente and Cubatao; one of these bridges is actually covered, but then every one is charged a pretty high toll.

In one of the vendas at the foot of the mountain we fortified ourselves with some excellent pan-cakes, laid in a stock of sugar-canes, the juice of which is excessively refreshing in the great heat, and then proceeded to scale the Serra, 3,400 feet high. The road was execrable; full of holes, pits, and puddles, in which our poor beasts often sank above their knees. We had to skirt chasms and ravines, with torrents rolling loudly beneath, yet not visible to us, on account of the thick underwood which grew over them. Some part of the way, too, lay through virgin forests, which, however, were not nearly so beautiful or thick as some I had traversed on my excursion to the Puris. There were hardly any palm-trees, and the few there were, reminded us, from their thin stems and scanty foliage, of those of a colder climate.

The prospect from the Serra struck us all with astonishment. The entire valley with its woods and prairies was spread far and wide before our sight as far as the bays, the little detached huts being quite indistinguishable, while only a part of the town and a few masts of ships were perceptible in the distance.

A turning in the road soon shut out this charming picture from our gaze; we then

61

left the Serra and entered upon a woody, uneven tract, alternating with large level grass-plots, covered with low brushwood, and innumerable mole-hills, two feet high.

Half way from Santos to St. Paulo is a place called Rio Grande, the houses of which lie, after the Brazilian fashion, so far apart, that no one would suppose they had any connection with each other. The owner of the mules used on this journey resides here, and here, likewise, the money for their hire is paid. If the traveller desires to proceed immediately he has fresh mules given him, but, should he prefer stopping the afternoon or night, he finds very good victual and clean rooms, for which he has nothing to pay, as they are included in the five milreis (10s. 10d.), charged for the mules.

We snatched a hasty morsel or two, and then hurried on, in order to complete the second half of the road before sunset. The plain became broader and broader the nearer we approached the town; the beauty of the scenery falls off very much, and for the first time since I left Europe, did I see fields and hills of sand. The town itself, situated upon a hill, presents a tolerable appearance; it contains about 22,000 inhabitants, and is a place of considerable importance for the internal commerce of the country. In spite of this, however, it has neither an inn nor any other place where strangers can alight.

After inquiring for a long time in vain for lodgings, we were directed to a German and a Frenchman, with the remark that both received lodgers out of pure politeness. We first went to the German, who very bluntly cut us short by saying that he had no room. From him we proceeded to the Frenchman, who sent us to a Portuguese, and on visiting the latter we received the same answer we had obtained from the German.

We were now greatly embarrassed; the more so, because the wearisome nature of our journey had so fatigued the Frenchman that he was hardly able any longer to sit upright in his saddle.

In this critical position I thought of the letter of recommendation that Herr Geiger had given me in Rio Janeiro, for a German gentleman of the name of Loskiel, who had settled here. I had intended not to deliver this letter until the next day, but "necessity knows no law," and so I paid my visit the same evening.

He was kind enough to interest himself for us in the warmest manner imaginable. He gave one of the gentlemen and myself lodgings in his own house, and our two companions in that of a neighbour of his, inviting all of us to dine at his table. We now learned that in St. Paulo no one, not even an hotel-keeper, will receive a stranger if he be not provided with a letter of recommendation. It is certainly a lucky thing for travellers that this strange custom is not prevalent everywhere.

16th December. After having completely recovered ourselves from the fatigues of our yesterday's ride, our first thought was to view the curiosities of the town. We asked our hospitable host for information on this point, but he merely shrugged his shoulders, and said, that he knew of no curiosities, unless, indeed, we chose to look upon the Botanical Garden in the light of one.

We went out, therefore, after breakfast, and first of all viewed the town: where we found that the number of large and well-built houses was, in comparison to the size of the two places, greater than in Rio Janeiro, although even here, there was nothing like taste or peculiar architectural style. The streets are tolerably wide, but present an extraordinarily deserted appearance, the universal silence being broken only by the insupportable creaking of the country people's carts. These carts rest upon two wheels, or rather two wooden disks, which are often not even hooped with iron to keep them together. The axle, which is likewise of wood, is never greased, and thus causes the demoniacal kind of music to which I alluded.

A peculiarity of dress, very remarkable in this hot climate, is here prevalent: all the men, with the exception of the slaves, wear large cloth cloaks, one half of which they throw over their shoulder; I even saw a great many women enveloped in long, broad cloth capes.

In St. Paulo there is a High School. Those who study there, and come from the country or the smaller towns, are exposed to the inconvenience of being refused lodgings under any one's roof. They are obliged to hire and furnish houses for themselves, and be their own housekeepers.

We visited several churches which possess very little worth looking at, either inside or out, and then concluded by proceeding to the Botanical Garden, which also contains no object of any interest, with the exception of a plantation of Chinese teas.

All our sight-seeing did not occupy us more than a few hours, and we could very conveniently have begun our journey back to Santos the next morning; but the Frenchman, who, on account of the great fatigue he had suffered, had not accompanied us in our walk, begged us to put off our return for half a day longer, and to arrange it in such a manner, that we should pass the night in Rio Grande. We willingly acceded to his wish, and set out upon the afternoon of the 17th, after thanking our kind host most cordially for his hospitable entertainment. In Rio Grande we found an excellent supper, convenient sleeping apartments, and a good breakfast the next morning. About 12 o'clock on the 18th of December, we arrived safely in Santos, and the Frenchman then confessed to us he had felt so fatigued on arriving at St. Paulo, from his long ride, that he was afraid of being seriously ill. However, he recovered himself completely in a few days, but assured us, that it would be some time before he again accompanied us on one of our trips.

The first question we put to the captain was: "When do you weigh anchor?" to which he very politely replied, that as soon as he had cleared out 200 tons of coal, and shipped 6,000 sacks of sugar, he should be ready to set sail, and in consequence of this we had to remain three whole weary weeks in Santos.

We were still in Santos when we celebrated New-Year's Day, 1847, and at last, on the 2nd of January, were lucky enough to bid the town adieu; but did not proceed far, for in the first bay the wind fell, and did not spring up again till after midnight. It was now Sunday, and no true Englishman will set sail on a Sunday; we remained, therefore, lying at anchor the whole of the 3rd of January, looking with very melancholy feelings after two ships, whose captains, in spite of the holiness of the day, had profited by the fresh breeze, and sailed gaily past us.

On the same evening we saw a vessel, which our captain affirmed was a slaver, run into the bay. It kept as far as possible from the fort, and cast anchor at the most outward extremity of the bay. As the night was clear and moonlight we walked late upon deck, when, true enough, we saw little boats laden with negroes pulling in shore. An officer, indeed, came from the fort to inquire into the doings of this suspicious craft; but the owner seemed to afford him a satisfactory account, for he left the ship, and the slaves continued during the whole night to be quietly and undisturbedly smuggled in as before.

On the morning of the 4th of January, as we sailed past the vessel, we beheld a great number of the poor creatures still standing upon the deck. Our captain inquired of the slave-dealer how many slaves he had had on board, and we learned with astonishment that the number amounted to 670. Much has already been said and written upon this horrible trade; it is everywhere execrated, and looked upon as a blot on the human race, and yet it still continues to flourish.

This day promised to turn out a very melancholy one in many respects. We had hardly lost sight of the slaver before one of our own crew had nearly committed suicide. The steward, a young mulatto, had contracted the bad habit of indulging too much in liquor. The captain had often threatened to punish him severely, but all to no purpose; and this morning he was so intoxicated that the sailors were obliged to lay him in a corner of the forecastle, where he might sleep himself sober. Suddenly, however, he leapt up, clambered on to the forepart of the ship, and threw himself into the sea. Luckily, it was almost a calm, the water was quite still, and we had hopes of saving him. He soon reappeared at the side of the vessel, and ropes were thrown him from every side. The love of life was awakened in his breast, and caused him to grasp involuntarily at the ropes, but he had not strength enough to hold on. He again sank, and it was only after great exertion that the brave sailors succeeded in rescuing him from a watery grave. Hardly had he recovered his senses ere he endeavoured to throw himself in again, exclaiming that he had no wish to live. The man was raving mad, and the captain was obliged to have him bound hand and foot, and chained to the mast. On the following day he was deprived of his office, and degraded to the rank of subordinate to a new steward.

5th January. Mostly calms. Our cook caught, today, a fish three feet long, and remarkable for the manner in which it changed colour. When it came out of the water it was a bright yellow, to which colour it owes its name of Dorado. At the expiration of one or two minutes the brilliant yellow changed into a light sky-blue, and after its death its belly again turned to a beautiful light yellow, but the back was a brownish green. It is reckoned a great delicacy, but, for my own part, I found its flesh rather dry.

On the 9th of January we were off the Rio Grande. In the evening everything seemed to promise a violent storm; the captain consulted his barometer every second almost, and issued his orders according to its indications. Black clouds now began to drive towards us, and the wind increased to such a pitch that the captain had all the hatchways carefully fastened down, and the crew ready to reef the sails at a moment's notice. At a little past 8, the hurricane broke forth. Flash after flash of lightning darted across the horizon from every side, and lighted the sailors in their work; the agitated waves being illuminated with the most dazzling brilliancy. The majestic rolling of the thunder drowned the captain's voice, and the white foaming billows broke with such terrific force over the deck, that it appeared as if they would carry everything with them into the depths of the ocean. Unless there had been ropes stretched on each side of the ship for the sailors to catch hold of, the latter would most certainly have been washed away. Such a storm as this affords much food for reflection. You are alone upon the boundless ocean, far from all human help, and feel more than ever that your life depends upon the Almighty alone. The man who, in such a dreadful and solemn moment, can still believe there is no God, must indeed be irretrievably struck with mental blindness. A feeling of tranquil joy always comes over me during such great convulsions of Nature. I very often had myself bound near the binnacle, and let the tremendous waves break over me, in order to absorb, as it were, as much of the spectacle before me as possible; on no occasion did I ever feel alarmed, but always confident and resigned.

At the expiration of four hours the storm had worn itself out, and was succeeded by a perfect calm.

On the 10th of January we caught sight of several sea-turtles and a whale. The latter was only a young one, about forty feet long.

11th January. We were now off the Rio Plata, {59} and found the temperature very perceptibly cooler.

Up to the present time we had seen no signs of sea-tangle or molluscæ, but during the night we beheld some molluscæ for the first time, shining like stars at a great depth below the surface of the water.

In these latitudes the constellation of the southern cross keeps increasing in brilliancy and beauty, though it is far from being as wonderful as it is said to be. The stars in it, four in number, and disposed somewhat in the following manner, **** are, it is true, large and splendid; but they did not excite, either in myself or any other person of our company, much more admiration than the other constellations.

65

As a general rule, many travellers exaggerate a great deal. On the one hand, they often describe things which they have never seen themselves, and only know from hearsay; and, on the other, they adorn what they really have seen with a little too much imagination.

16th January. In 37° South lat. we fell in with a strong current, running from south to north, and having a yellow streak down the middle of it. The captain said that this streak was caused by a shoal of small fishes. I had some water drawn up in a bucket, and really found a few dozen living creatures, which, in my opinion, however, belonged rather to some species of molluscæ than to any kind of fish. They were about three-quarters of an inch long, and as transparent as the most delicate water-bubbles; they were marked with white and light yellow spots on the forepart of their bodies, and had a few feelers underneath.

In the night of the 20th to 21st of January we were overtaken by a very violent storm, which so damaged our mainmast that the captain determined on running into some haven on the first opportunity, and putting in a new one. For the present the old one was made fast with cables, iron chains, and braces.

In 43° North lat. we saw the first sea-tangle. The temperature had by this time very perceptibly decreased in warmth, the glass often standing no higher than 59° or 63° Fah.

23rd January. We were so near Patagonia that we could distinctly make out the outline of the coast.

26th January. We still kept near the land. In 50° South lat. we saw the chalky mountains of Patagonia. Today we passed the Falkland Islands, which stretched from 51° to 52° South lat. We did not see them, however, as we kept as near the land as possible, in order not to miss the Straits of Magellan. For some days the captain had been studying an English book, which, in his opinion, clearly proved that the passage through the Straits of Magellan was far less dangerous and far shorter than that round Cape Horn. I asked him how it happened that other sailors knew nothing of this valuable book, and why all vessels bound for the western coast of America went round Cape Horn? He could give me no other answer than that the book was very dear, and that that was the reason no one bought it. {60}

To me this bold idea of the captain's was extremely welcome. I already pictured in my mind the six-feet tall Patagonians putting off to us in their boats; I saw myself taking their mussels, plants, ornaments, and weapons in exchange for coloured ribbons and handkerchiefs; while, to render my satisfaction complete, the captain said that he should land at Port Famine (a Patagonian haven) to supply the injured portion of our mainmast. How thankful was I, in secret, to the storm for having reduced our ship to her present condition.

Too soon, however, were all my flattering hopes and dreams dispelled. On the 27th of January the latitude and longitude were taken, and it was then found that

66

the Straits of Magellan were twenty-seven minutes (or nautical miles) behind us, but as we were becalmed, the captain promised, in case a favourable wind should spring up, to endeavour to return as far as the Straits.

I placed no more confidence in this promise, and I was right. About noon a scarcely perceptible breeze sprang up, which the captain, in high spirits, pronounced a favourable one—for rounding Cape Horn. If he had ever really intended to pass through the Straits, he would only have had to cruise about for a few hours, for the wind soon changed and blew directly in the desired direction.

28th January. We were constantly so near Terra del Fuego that we could make out every bush with the naked eye. We could have reached the land in an hour, without retarding our voyage in the least, for we were frequently becalmed; but the captain would not consent, as the wind might spring up every instant.

The coast appeared rather steep, but not high; the foreground was composed of meagre pasture alternating with tracts of sand, and in the background were ranges of woody hills, beyond which rose snow-covered mountains. On the whole, the country struck me as being much more inhabitable than the Island of Iceland, which I had visited a year and a half previously. The temperature, too, must here be higher, as even at sea we had 54° 5' and 59° Fah.

I saw three kinds of sea-tangle, but could only obtain a specimen of one, resembling that which I had seen in 44° South lat. The second kind was not very different, and it was only the third that had pointed leaves, several of which together formed a sort of fan several feet long and broad.

On the 30th of January we passed very near the Staten Islands, lying between 56° and 57° South lat. They are composed of bare high mountains, and separated from Terra del Fuego by an arm of the sea, called Le Maire, only seven miles long and about the same distance across.

The captain told us, seaman-like, that on one occasion of his sailing through these Straits, his ship had got into a strong current, and regularly danced, turning round during the passage at least a thousand times! I had already lost a great deal of confidence in the captain's tales, but I kept my eye steadily fixed upon a Hamburgh brig, that happened to be sailing ahead, to see whether she would dance; but neither she nor our own bark was so obliging. Neither vessels turned even once, and the only circumstance worthy of remark was the heaving and foaming of the waves in the Strait, while at both ends the sea lay majestically calm before our eyes. We had passed the Strait in an hour, and I took the liberty of asking the captain why our ship had not danced, to which he replied that it was because we had had both wind and current with us. It is, perhaps, possible that under other circumstances the vessel might have turned round once or twice, but I strongly doubt its doing so a thousand times. This was, however, a favourite number with our worthy captain. One of the gentlemen once asked him some question about the first London hotels, and was told that it was impossible to remember their names, as there were above a thousand of the first class.

Near the Strait Le Maire begins, in the opinion of seamen, the dangerous part of the passage round Cape Horn, and ends off the Straits of Magellan. Immediately we entered it we were greeted with two most violent bursts of wind, each of which lasted about half an hour; they came from the neighbouring icy chasms in the mountains of Terra del Fuego, and split two sails, and broke the great studding sail-yard, although the sailors were numerous and quick. The distance from the end of the Strait Le Maire to the extreme point of the Cape is calculated to be not more than seventy miles, and yet this trifling passage cost us three days.

At last, on the 3rd of February, we were fortunate enough to reach the southernmost point of America, so dreaded by all mariners. Bare, pointed mountains, one of which looks like a crater that has fallen in, form the extremity of the mighty mountain-chain, and a magnificent group of colossal black rocks (basalt?), of all shapes and sizes, are scattered at some distance in advance, and are separated only by a small arm of the sea. The extreme point of Cape Horn is 600 feet high. At this spot, according to our works on geography, the Atlantic Ocean changes its name and assumes that of the Pacific. Sailors, however, do not give it the latter designation before reaching the Straits of Magellan, as up to this point the sea is continually stormy and agitated, as we learned to our cost, being driven by violent storms as far back as 60° South lat. Besides this, we lost our top-mast, which was broken off, and which, in spite of the heavy sea, had to be replaced; the vessel, meanwhile, being so tossed about, that we were often unable to take our meals at the table, but were obliged to squat down upon the ground, and hold our plates in our hands. On one of these fine days the steward stumbled with the coffee-pot, and deluged me with its burning contents. Luckily, only a small portion fell upon my hands, so that the accident was not a very serious one.

After battling for fourteen days with winds and waves, with rain and cold, {62} we at last arrived off the western entrance to the Straits of Magellan, having accomplished the most dangerous portion of our voyage. During these fourteen days we saw very few whales or albatrosses, and not one iceberg.

We thought that we should now quietly pursue our way upon the placid sea, trusting confidently in its peaceful name. For three whole days we had nothing to complain of; but in the night of the 19th to the 20th of February, we were overtaken by a storm worthy of the Atlantic itself, which lasted for nearly twenty-four hours, and cost us four sails. We suffered most damage from the tremendous waves, which broke with such fury over the ship, that they tore up one of the planks of the deck, and let the water into the cargo of sugar. The deck itself was like a lake, and the portholes had to be opened in order to get rid of the water more quickly. The water leaked in the hold at the rate of two inches an hour. We could not light any fire, and were obliged to content ourselves with bread and cheese and raw ham, which we with great difficulty conveyed to our mouth as we sat upon the ground.

The last cask of lamp oil, too, fell a sacrifice to this storm, having been torn from its fastenings, and broken into pieces. The captain was very apprehensive of not having enough oil to light the compass till we arrived at Valparaiso; and all the lamps on the ship were, in consequence, replaced by candles, and the small quantity of oil remaining kept for the compass. In spite of all these annoyances, we kept up our spirits, and even, during the storm, we could scarcely refrain from laughing at the comical positions we all fell into whenever we attempted to stand up.

The remainder of the voyage to Valparaiso was calm, but excessively disagreeable. The captain wished to present a magnificent appearance on arriving, so that the good people might believe that wind and waves could not injure his fine vessel. He had the whole ship painted from top to bottom with oil colours; even the little doors in the cabins were not spared this infliction. Not content with creating a most horrible disturbance over our heads, the carpenter invaded even our cabins, filling all our things with sawdust and dirt, so that we poor passengers had not a dry or quiet place of refuge in the whole ship. Just as much as we had been pleased with Captain Bell's politeness during all the previous part of the voyage, were we indignant at his behaviour during the last five or six days. But we could offer no resistance, for the captain is an autocrat on board his own ship, knowing neither a constitution nor any other limit to his despotic power.

At 6 o'clock in the morning of the 2nd of March, we ran into the port of Valparaiso.

CHAPTER VI. ARRIVAL AND RESIDENCE IN VALPARAISO.

APPEARANCE OF THE TOWN—PUBLIC BUILDINGS—A FEW OBSERVATIONS ON THE MANNERS AND CUSTOMS OF THE LOWER CLASSES—THE EATING-HOUSES OF POLANEA—THE CHERUB (ANGELITO)—THE RAILROAD—GOLD AND SILVER MINES.

The appearance of Valparaiso is dull and monotonous. The town is laid out in two long streets at the foot of dreary hills, which look like gigantic masses of sand, but which really consist of large rocks covered with thin layers of earth and sand. On some of these hills are houses, and on one of them is the churchyard, which, combined with the wooden church towers, built in the Spanish style, relieves, in a slight degree, the wearisome uniformity of the prospect. Not less astounding than the deserted look of the port, was the miserably wretched landing-place, which is composed of a high wooden quay, about 100 feet long, stretching out into the sea, with narrow steps, like ladders, against the side. It was a most pitiable sight to see a lady attempting to go up or down: all persons who were in the least weak or awkward, had to be let down with ropes.

The two principal streets are tolerably broad, and very much frequented, especially by horsemen. Every Chilian is born a horseman; and some of their horses are such fine animals, that you involuntarily stop to admire their proud action, their noble bearing, and the nice symmetry of their limbs.

The stirrups are curiously formed, consisting of long, heavy pieces of wood, hollowed out, and into which the rider places the tips of his feet. The spurs are remarkably large, and are often about four inches in diameter.

The houses are constructed completely in the European style, with flat Italian roofs. The more ancient buildings have only a ground floor, and are small and ugly, while most of the modern ones have a spacious and handsome first floor. The interior, too, of the latter is generally very tasty. Large steps conduct into a lofty well-ventilated entrance-hall on the first floor, from which the visitor passes, through large glass doors, into the drawing-room and other apartments. The drawing-room is the pride, not only of every European who has settled in the country, but also of the Chilians, who often spend very large sums in the decorations. Heavy carpets cover all the floor; rich tapestry hangs against the walls; furniture and mirrors of the most costly description are procured from Europe; and on the tables are strewed magnificent albums, adorned with the most artistic engravings. The elegant fire-places, however, convinced me that the winters here are not as mild as the inhabitants would fain have had me believe.

Of all the public buildings, the Theatre and the Exchange are the finest. The interior of the former is very neat, and contains a roomy pit and two galleries, portioned off as boxes. The inhabitants of the town patronise the theatre a great deal, but not so much on account of the Italian operas played there, as for the sake of possessing a common place of meeting. The ladies always come in full dress, and mutual visits are made in the boxes, all of which are very spacious, and beautifully furnished with mirrors, carpets, sofas, and chairs.

The second fine building, the Exchange, comprises a good-sized, cheerful hall, with convenient rooms adjoining. From the hall there is a pleasant view over the town and sea. The building belonging to the "German Club" contains some fine apartments, with reading and card rooms.

The only thing that pleased me about the churches were the towers, which consist of two or three octagons, placed one above the other, and each one supported by eight columns. They are composed of wood, the altars and pillars of the nave being of the same material. The nave itself presents rather a poor and naked appearance, occasioned in a great degree by the absence of sittings. The men stand, and the women bring with them little carpets, which they spread before them, and on which they either kneel or sit. Ladies in easy circumstances have their carpets brought by their maids. The cathedral is called La Matriza.

The public promenades of Valparaiso are not very pleasant, as most of the side-walks and roads are covered almost a foot deep with sand and dust, which the slightest breath of wind is sufficient to raise in thick clouds. After 10 o'clock in the morning, when the sea-breeze begins blowing, the whole town is very often enveloped by it. A great many persons are said to die here from diseases of the chest and lungs. The most frequented places of resort are Polanka and the lighthouse. Near the latter, especially, the prospect is very beautiful, extending, as it does, on a clear day, as far as some of the majestic snow-covered spurs of the Andes.

The streets, as I have already mentioned, are tolerably lively: peculiar omnibuses and cabriolets traverse them frequently. The fare from one end of the town to the other is one real (2½d.) There are also a great number of asses, mostly employed in carrying water and provisions.

The lower classes are remarkably ugly. The Chilians have a yellowish brown complexion, thick black hair, most unpleasant features, and such a peculiarly repulsive cast of countenance, that any physiognomist would straightway pronounce them to be robbers or pickpockets at the least. Captain Bell had told me a great deal of the extraordinary honesty of these people; and, in his usual exaggerated manner, assured us that a person might leave a purse of gold lying in the street, with the certainty of finding it the next day on the same spot; but, in spite of this, I must frankly confess, that for my own part, I should be rather fearful of meeting these honest creatures, even by day, in a lonely spot, with the money in my pocket.

I had subsequently opportunities of convincing myself of the fallaciousness of the captain's opinion, for I often met with convicts, chained together, and employed in the public buildings and cleaning the roads. The windows and doors, too, are secured with bolts and bars in a manner almost unknown in any town of Europe. At night, in all the streets, and on all the hills which are inhabited, are parties of police, who call out to one another in exactly the same manner that the advanced posts do during a campaign. Mounted patrols also traverse the town in every direction, and persons returning alone from the theatre or from a party, often engage their services to conduct them home. Burglariously entering a house is punished with death. All these precautions do not, most decidedly, argue much for the honesty of the people.

I will take this opportunity of mentioning a scene, of which I was myself an eye-witness, as it happened before my window. A little boy was carrying a number of plates and dishes on a board, when the latter unluckily slipped from his grasp, and all the crockery lay in fragments at his feet. At first, the poor fellow was so frightened that he stood like a column, gazing with a fixed look at the pieces, and then began to cry most bitterly. The passers-by stopped, it is true, to look at the unfortunate child, but did not evince the least compassion; they laughed, and went on. In any other place, they would have raised a little subscription, or at least pitied and consoled him, but certainly would not have seen anything to laugh at. The circumstance is of itself a mere trifle, but it is exactly by such trifles that we

71

are often enabled to form a true estimate of people's real characters.

Another adventure, also, but of quite a different and most horrible kind, happened during my stay in Valparaiso.

As I have already remarked, it is the custom here, as well as in many countries of Europe, to sentence criminals to hard labour on public works. One of the convicts endeavoured to bribe his gaoler to let him escape, and so far succeeded that the latter promised on his paying an ounce (17 Spanish dollars—£3 8s.) to give him an opportunity for flight. The prisoners are allowed every morning and afternoon to receive the visits of their friends and relations, and likewise to accept provisions from them. The wife of the convict in question profited by this regulation to bring her husband the necessary money; and on receiving this, the gaoler arranged matters so that on the next morning the convict was not fastened to the same chain with a fellow-criminal, as is usually the case, but could walk alone, and thus easily get clear off, more especially as the spot in which they worked was a very lonely one.

The whole affair was very cunningly arranged, but either the gaoler changed his mind, or, perhaps, from the beginning had intended to act as he did—he fired at the fugitive, and shot him dead.

It is very seldom that any pure descendants of the original inhabitants are to be seen; we met with only two. They struck me as very similar to the Puris of Brazil, except that they have not such small ugly-shaped eyes. In this country there are no slaves.

The dress of the Chilians is quite in the European taste, especially as regards the women. The only difference with the men is that, instead of a coat, they frequently wear the Poncho, which is composed of two pieces of cloth or merino, each about one ell broad and two ells long. The two pieces are sewn together, with the exception of an opening in the middle for the head to pass through; the whole garment reaches down to the hips, and resembles a square cape. The Poncho is worn of all colours, green, blue, bright red, etc., and looks very handsome, especially when embroidered all round with coloured silk, which is the case when the wearer is opulent. In the streets, the women invariably wear large scarfs, which they draw over their heads in church.

My intention, on coming to Chili, was to stop for a few weeks in order to have time for an excursion to the capital, Santiago, and after that to proceed to China, as I had been told in Rio Janeiro that there was a ship from Valparaiso to China every month. Unfortunately this was not the case. I found that vessels bound to that country were very seldom to be met with, but that there happened to be one at that moment, which would sail in five or six days. I was generally advised not to lose the opportunity, but rather to abandon my design of visiting Santiago. I reflected for a little, and agreed to do so, although with a heavy heart; and in order to avoid all disappointment, immediately went to the captain, who offered to take me for 200 Spanish dollars (£40). I agreed, and had five days left, which I determined to spend in carefully examining Valparaiso and its environs. I should have had plenty of time to pay Santiago a flying visit, since it is only 130 miles from Valparaiso, but the expenses would have been very heavy, as there is no public conveyance, and consequently I should have been obliged to hire a carriage for myself. Besides this, I should have derived but little satisfaction from the mere superficial impressions which would have been all I could have obtained of either town.

I contented myself, therefore, with Valparaiso alone. I toiled industriously up the surrounding hills and mountains, visited the huts of the lower classes, witnessed their national dances, etc., determined that here at least I would become acquainted with everything.

On some of the hills, especially on the Serra Allegri, there are the most lovely country-houses, with elegant gardens, and a most beautiful view over the sea. The prospect inland is not so fine, as chains of tall, naked, ugly mountains rise up behind the hills, and completely shut in the scene.

The huts of the poor people are miserably bad, being mostly built of clay and wood, and threatening to fall down every moment. I hardly ventured to enter them, thinking that the interior was of a piece with the exterior, and was consequently astonished at seeing not only good beds, chairs, and tables, but very often elegant little altars adorned with flowers. The inmates, too, were far from being badly dressed, and the linen hung out before many of these hovels struck me as superior to much that I had seen at the windows of some of the most elegant houses situated in the principal streets of the towns of Sicily.

A very good idea of the manners and customs of the people may be easily obtained by strolling, on Sundays and *fête* days, near Polanka, and visiting the eating-houses.

I will introduce my reader to one of these places. In one corner, on the ground, burns a fierce fire, surrounded by innumerable pots and pans, between which are wooden spits with beef and pork, simmering and roasting in the most enticing manner. An ungainly wooden framework, with a long broad plank on it, occupies the middle of the room, and is covered with a cloth whose original colour it would be an impossibility to determine. This is the table at which the guests sit. During the dinner itself the old patriarchal customs are observed, with this difference, that not only do all the guests eat out of one dish, but that all the eatables are served up in one, and one only. Beans and rice, potatoes and roast beef, Paradise apples and onions, etc., etc., lie quietly side by side, and are devoured in the deepest silence. At the end of the repast, a goblet, filled with wine, or sometimes merely water, is passed from hand to hand, and after this had gone round, the company begin to talk. In the evening dancing is vigorously pursued to the music of a guitar; unfortunately, it was Lent during my visit, when all public amusements are prohibited. The people themselves, however, were not so particular, and were only too ready, for a few reaux, to go through the Sammaquecca and Refolosa—the national dances of the country. I had soon seen sufficient; the gestures and movements of the dancers were beyond all description unbecoming, and I could but pity the children, whose natural modesty cannot fail to be nipped in the bud by witnessing the performance of these dances.

I was equally displeased with a remarkable custom prevalent here, in accordance with which the death of a little child is celebrated by its parents as a grand festival. They name the deceased child an *angelito*, (little angel), and adorn it in every possible way. Its eyes are not closed, but, on the contrary, opened as wide as possible, and its cheeks are painted red; it is then dressed out in the finest clothes, crowned with flowers, and placed in a little chair in a kind of niche, which also is ornamented with flowers. The relations and neighbours then come and wish the parents joy at possessing such an angel; and, during the first night, the parents, relations, and friends execute the wildest dances, and feast in the most joyous fashion before the angelito. I heard that in the country it was not unusual for the parents to carry the little coffin to the churchyard themselves, followed by the relations with the brandy bottle in their hands, and giving vent to their joy in the most outrageous manner.

A merchant told me that one of his friends, who holds a judicial appointment, had, a short time previous, been called to decide a curious case. A grave-digger was carrying one of these deceased angels to the churchyard, when he stept into a tavern to take a dram. The landlord inquired what he had got under his poncho, and on learning that it was an angelito, offered him two reaux for it. The gravedigger consented; the landlord quickly arranged a niche with flowers in the drinking-room, and then hastened to inform the whole neighbourhood what a treasure he had got. They all came, admired the little angel, and drank and feasted in its honour. But the parents also soon heard of it, hurried down to the tavern, took away their child, and had the landlord brought before the magistrate. On hearing the case, the latter could scarcely restrain from laughing, but arranged the matter amicably, as such a crime was not mentioned in the statute book.

The manner in which patients are conveyed to the hospital here is very remarkable. They are placed upon a simple wooden armchair, with one band fastened in front of them to prevent their falling off, and another beneath for them to place their feet on—a most horrible sight when the sick person is so weak that he can no longer hold himself in an upright posture.

I was not a little astonished on hearing that, in this country, where there is yet no post, or, indeed, any regular means of conveyance from one place to another, that a railroad was about being constructed from here to Santiago. The work has been undertaken by an English company, and the necessary measurements already begun. As the localities are very mountainous, the railroad will have to make considerable windings, in order to profit by the level tracts, and this will occasion an enormous outlay, quite out of proportion to the present state of trade or the amount of passenger traffic. At present, there are not more than two or three vehicles a day from one place to the other, and if by chance ten or fifteen passengers come from Santiago to Valparaiso, the thing is talked of over the whole town. This has given rise to the belief that the construction of a railroad has merely been seized on as an excuse, in order to enable those concerned to search about the country undisturbed for gold and silver.

Persons discovering mines are highly favoured, and have full right of property to their discovery, being obliged merely to notify the same to the government. This licence is pushed to such an extent, that if, for instance, a person can advance any plausible grounds for asserting that he has found a mine in a particular spot, such as under a church or house, etc., he is at liberty to have either pulled down, provided he is rich enough to pay for the damage done.

About fifteen years ago, a donkey driver accidentally hit upon a productive silver mine. He was driving several asses over the mountain, when one of them ran away. He seized a stone, and was about to throw it after the animal, but stumbled and fell to the ground, while the stone escaped from his grasp, and rolled away. Rising in a great passion, he snatched a second from the earth, and had drawn his arm to throw the stone, when he was struck by its uncommon weight. He looked at it more closely, and perceived that it was streaked with rich veins of pure silver. He preserved the stone as a treasure, marked the spot, drove his asses home, and then communicated his important discovery to one of his friends, who was a miner. Both of them then returned to the place, which the miner examined, and pronounced the soil full of precious ore. Nothing was now wanting save capital to carry on their operations. This they procured by taking the miner's employer into partnership, and in a few years all three were rich men.

The six days had now elapsed, and the captain sent me a message to be on board with my bag and baggage the next day, as he intended putting out to sea in the evening; but on the morning of his intended departure, my evil genius conducted a French man-of-war into the harbour. Little imagining that this was destined to overturn all my plans, I proceeded very tranquilly to the landing-place, where I met the captain hastening to meet me, with a long story about his half-cargo, and the necessity he was under of completing his freight with provisions for the use of the French garrison at Tahiti, and so forth: in a word, the end of the matter was, that I was informed we should have to stop another five days.

In the first burst of my disappointment, I paid a visit to the Sardinian Consul, Herr Bayerbach, and told him of the position in which I was placed. He consoled me, in a most kind and gentlemanly manner, as well as he could; and on learning that I had already taken up my quarters on board, insisted on my occupying a chamber in his country-house in the Serra Allegri. Besides this, he introduced me to several families, where I passed many very pleasant hours, and had the opportunity of inspecting some excellent collections of mussel-shells and insects.

Our departure was again deferred from day to day; so that, although, in this manner, I spent fifteen days in Chili, I saw nothing more of it than Valparaiso and its immediate neighbourhood.

As Valparaiso is situated to the south of the Equator, and, as is well known, the seasons of the southern hemisphere are exactly the contrary of those of the northern, it was now autumn. I saw (34° South latitude) almost the same kinds of fruits and vegetables as those we have in Germany, especially grapes and melons. The apples and pears were not so good nor so abundant as with us.

In conclusion, I will here give a list of the prices which travellers have to pay for certain things:—

A room that is at all decent in a private house costs four or five reaux (2s.) a day; the table d'hôte a piaster (4s.); but washing is more expensive than anything else, on account of the great scarcity of water, for every article, large or small, costs a real (6d.). A passport, too, is excessively dear, being charged eight Spanish dollars (£1 12s.).

CHAPTER VII. THE VOYAGE FROM VALPARAISO TO CANTON VIA TAHITI.

DEPARTURE FROM VALPARAISO—TAHITI—MANNERS AND CUSTOMS OF THE PEOPLE—FÊTE AND BALL IN HONOUR OF LOUIS PHILIPPE—EXCURSIONS—A TAHITIAN DINNER—THE LAKE VAIHIRIA—THE DEFILE OF FANTAUA AND THE DIADEM— DEPARTURE—ARRIVAL IN CHINA.

On the 17th of March, Captain Van Wyk Jurianse sent me word that his ship was ready for sea, and that he should set sail the next morning. The news was very unwelcome to me, as, for the last two days, I had been suffering from English cholera, which on board ship, where the patient cannot procure meat broth or any other light nourishment, and where he is always more exposed to the sudden changes of the weather than he is on shore, is very apt to be attended with grave results. I did not, however, wish to miss the opportunity of visiting China, knowing how rarely it occurred, nor was I desirous of losing the two hundred dollars (£40) already paid for my passage, and I therefore went on board, trusting in my good luck, which had never forsaken me on my travels.

During the first few days, I endeavoured to master my illness by observing a strict diet, and abstaining from almost everything, but to no purpose. I still continued to suffer, until I luckily thought of using salt-water baths. I took them in a large tub, in which I remained a quarter of an hour. After the second bath, I felt much better, and after the sixth, I was completely recovered. I merely mention this malady, to which I was very subject in warm climates, that I may have the opportunity of remarking, that sea-baths or cooling drinks, such as buttermilk, sour milk, sherbet, orangeade, etc., are very efficacious remedies.

The ship in which I made my present voyage, was the Dutch barque Lootpuit, a fine, strong vessel, quite remarkable for its cleanliness. The table was pretty good, too, with the exception of a few Dutch dishes, and a superfluity of onions. To these, which played a prominent part in everything that was served up, I really could not accustom myself, and felt greatly delighted that a large quantity of this noble production of the vegetable kingdom became spoilt during the voyage.

The captain was a polite and kind man, and the mates and sailors were also civil and obliging. In fact, as a general rule, in every ship that I embarked in, I was far from finding seamen so rough and uncivil as travellers often represent them to be. Their manners are certainly not the most polished in the world, neither are they extraordinarily attentive or delicate, but their hearts and dispositions are mostly good.

After three days' sailing, we saw, on the 21st March, the island of St. Felix, and on the morning following, St. Ambrosio. They both consist of naked, inhospitable masses of rock, and serve at most as resting places for a few gulls.

We were now within the tropics, but found the heat greatly moderated by the trade wind, and only unbearable in the cabin.

For nearly a month did we now sail on, without the slightest interruption, free from storms, with the same monotonous prospect of sky and water before us, until, on the 19th of April, we reached the Archipelago of the Society Islands. This Archipelago, stretching from 130° to 140° longitude, is very dangerous, as most of the islands composing it scarcely rise above the surface of the water; in fact, to make out David Clark's Island, which was only twelve miles distant, the captain was obliged to mount to the shrouds.

During the night of the 21st to the 22nd of April we were overtaken by a sudden and violent storm, accompanied by heavy thunder; this storm our captain termed a thunder-gust. While it lasted flashes of lightning frequently played around the mast-top, occasioned by electricity. They generally flutter for two or three minutes about the most elevated point of any object, and then disappear.

The night of the 22nd to the 23rd of April was a very dangerous one; even the captain said so. We had to pass several of the low islands in dark rainy weather, which completely concealed the moon from us. About midnight our position was rendered worse by the springing up of a strong wind, which, together with incessant flashes of lightning, caused us to expect another squall; luckily, however, morning broke, and we escaped both the storm and the islands.

In the course of the day we passed the Bice Islands, and two days later, on the 25th of April, we beheld one of the Society Islands, Maithia.

On the following morning, being the thirty-ninth of our voyage, we came in sight of Tahiti, and the island opposite to it, Emao, also called Moreo. The entrance into Papeiti, the port of Tahiti, is exceedingly dangerous; it is surrounded by reefs of coral as by a fortress, while wild and foaming breakers, rolling on every side, leave but a small place open through which a vessel can steer.

A pilot came out to meet us, and, although the wind was so unfavourable that the sails had to be trimmed every instant, steered us safely into port. Afterwards, when we had landed, we were congratulated heartily on our good fortune; every one had watched our course with the greatest anxiety, and, at the last turn the ship took, expected to see her strike upon a coral reef. This misfortune had happened to a French man-of-war, that at the period of our arrival had been lying at anchor for some months, engaged in repairing the damage done.

Before we could come to an anchor we were surrounded by half-a-dozen pirogues, or boats, manned by Indians, who climbed up from all sides upon the deck to offer us fruit and shell-fish, but not as formerly for red rags or glass beads —such golden times for travellers are over. They demanded money, and were as grasping and cunning in their dealings as the most civilized Europeans. I offered one of them a small bronze ring; he took it, smelt it, shook his head, and gave me to understand that it was not gold. He remarked another ring on my finger, and seizing hold of my hand, smelt this second ring as well, then twisted his face into a friendly smile, and made signs for me to give him the ornament in question. I afterwards had frequent opportunities of remarking that the natives of these islands have the power of distinguishing between pure and counterfeit gold by the smell.

Some years ago the island of Tahiti was under the protection of the English, but at present it is under that of the French. It had long been a subject of dispute between the two nations, until a friendly understanding was at last come to in November, 1846. Queen Pomaré, who had fled to another island, had returned to Papeiti five weeks before my arrival. She resides in a four-roomed house, and dines daily, with her family, at the governor's table. The French government is having a handsome house built for her use, and allows her a pension of 25,000 francs per annum (£1,041 13s. 4d.). No stranger is allowed to visit her without the governor's permission, but this is easily obtained.

Papeiti was full of French troops, and several men-of-war were lying at anchor.

The place contains three or four thousand inhabitants, and consists of a row of small wooden houses, skirting the harbour, and separated by small gardens. In the immediate background is a fine wood, with a number of huts scattered about in different parts of it.

The principal buildings are—the governor's house, the French magazines, the military bakehouse, the barracks, and the queen's house, which however is not quite completed. Besides these, a number of small wooden houses were in the course of erection, the want of them being greatly felt; at the time of my visit even officers of high rank were obliged to be contented with the most wretched huts.

I went from hut to hut in the hopes of being able to obtain some small room or other; but in vain, all were already occupied. I was at last obliged to be satisfied with a small piece of ground, which I found at a carpenter's, whose room was already inhabited by four different individuals. I was shown a place behind the door, exactly six feet long and four broad. There was no flooring but the earth itself; the walls were composed of wicker work; a bed was quite out of the question, and yet for this accommodation I was obliged to pay one florin and thirty kreutzers a-week (about 7s.)

The residence or hut of an Indian consists simply of a roof of palm-trees, supported on a number of poles, with sometimes the addition of walls formed of wicker-work. Each hut contains only one room, from twenty to fifty feet long, and from ten to thirty feet broad, and is frequently occupied by several families at the same time. The furniture is composed of finely woven straw mats, a few coverlids, and two or three wooden chests and stools; the last, however, are reckoned articles of luxury. Cooking utensils are not wanted, as the cookery of the Indians does not include soups or sauces, their provisions being simply roasted between hot stones. All they require is a knife, and a cocoa shell for water.

Before their huts, or on the shore, lie their piroques, formed of the trunks of trees hollowed out, and so narrow, small, and shallow, that they would constantly be overturning, if there were not on one side five or six sticks, each about a foot long, fastened by a cross-bar to preserve the equilibrium. In spite of this, however, one of these boats is very easily upset, unless a person steps in very cautiously. When, on one occasion, I proceeded in a piroque to the ship, the good-hearted captain was horror-struck, and, in his concern for my safety, even reprimanded me severely, and besought me not to repeat the experiment a second time.

The costume of the Indians has been, since the first settlement of the missionaries (about fifty years ago), tolerably becoming, especially in the neighbourhood of Papeiti. Both men and women wear round their loins a kind of apron, made of coloured stuff, and called a *pareo*; the women let it fall as low down as their ancles; the men not farther than the calf of the leg. The latter have a short coloured shirt underneath it, and again beneath that, large flowing trousers. The women wear a long full blouse. Both sexes wear flowers in their ears, which have such large holes bored in them that the stalk can very easily be drawn through. The women, both old and young, adorn themselves with garlands of leaves and flowers, which they make in the most artistic and elegant manner. I have often seen men, too, weaving the same kind of ornament.

On grand occasions, they cast over their ordinary dress an upper garment, called a *tiputa*, the cloth of which they manufacture themselves from the bark of the bread and cocoa trees. The bark, while still tender, is beaten between two stones, until it is as thin as paper; it is then coloured yellow and brown.

One Sunday I went into the meeting-house to see the people assembled there. {73} Before entering they all laid aside their flowers, with which they again ornamented themselves at their departure. Some of the women had black satin blouses on, and European bonnets of an exceedingly ancient date. It would not be easy to find a more ugly sight than that of their plump, heavy heads and faces in these old-fashioned bonnets.

During the singing of the psalms there was some degree of attention, and many of the congregation joined in very becomingly; but while the clergyman was performing the service, I could not remark the slightest degree of devotion in any of them; the children played, joked, and ate, while the adults gossiped or slept; and although I was assured that many could read and even write, I saw only two old men who made any use of their Bibles.

The men are a remarkably strong and vigorous race, six feet being by no means an uncommon height amongst them. The women, likewise, are very tall, but too muscular—they might even be termed unwieldy. The features of the men are handsomer than those of the women. They have beautiful teeth and fine dark eyes, but generally a large mouth, thick lips, and an ugly nose, the cartilage being slightly crushed when the child is born, so that the nose becomes flat and broad. This fashion appears to be most popular with the females, for their noses are the ugliest. Their hair is jet black and thick, but coarse; the women and girls generally wear it plaited in two knots. The colour of their skin is a copper-brown. All the natives are tattooed, generally from the hips half down the legs, and frequently this mode of ornamenting themselves is extended to the hands, feet, or other parts of the body. The designs resemble arabesques; they are regular and artistic in their composition, and executed with much taste.

That the population of this place should be so vigorous and well-formed is the more surprising, if we reflect on their depraved and immoral kind of life. Little girls of seven or eight years old have their lovers of twelve or fourteen, and their parents are quite proud of the fact. The more lovers a girl has the more she is respected. As long as she is not married she leads a most dissolute life, and it is said that not all the married women make the most faithful wives possible.

I had frequent opportunities of seeing the national dances, which are the most unbecoming I ever beheld, although every painter would envy me my good fortune. Let the reader picture to himself a grove of splendid palms, and other gigantic trees of the torrid zone, with a number of open huts, and a crowd of good-humoured islanders assembled beneath, to greet, in their fashion, the lovely evening, which is fast approaching. Before one of the huts a circle is formed, and in the centre sit two herculean and half-naked natives, beating time most vigorously on small drums. Five similar colossi are seated before them, moving the upper parts of their bodies in the most horrible and violent manner, and more especially the arms, hands, and fingers; the latter they have the power of moving

80

in every separate joint. I imagine, that by these gestures they desired to represent how they pursue their enemy, ridicule his cowardice, rejoice at their victory, and so forth. During all this time they howl continually in a most discordant manner, and make the most hideous faces. At the commencement, the men appear alone upon the scene of action, but after a short time two female forms dart forward from among the spectators, and dance and rave like two maniacs; the more unbecoming, bold, and indecent their gestures, the greater the applause. The whole affair does not, at most, last longer than two minutes, and the pause before another dance is commenced not much longer. An evening's amusement of this description often lasts for hours. The younger members of society very seldom take any part in the dances.

It is a great question whether the immorality of these islanders has been lessened by French civilization. From my own observations, as well as from what I was told by persons well informed on the subject, I should say that this has not yet been the case, and that, for the present, there is but little hope of its being so: while, on the other side, the natives have acquired a number of useless wants, in consequence of which, the greed for gold has been fearfully awakened in their breasts. As they are naturally very lazy, and above all things disinclined to work, they have made the female portion of the community the means of gaining money. Parents, brothers, and even husbands, offer to their foreign masters those belonging to them, while the women themselves offer no opposition, as in this manner they can obtain the means for their own display, and money for their relations without trouble. Every officer's house is the rendezvous of several native beauties, who go out and in at every hour of the day. Even abroad they are not particular; they will accompany any man without the least hesitation, and no gentleman ever refuses a conductress of this description.

As a female of an advanced age, I may be allowed to make a few observations upon such a state of things, and I frankly own that, although I have travelled much and seen a great deal, I never witnessed such shameful scenes of public depravity.

As a proof of what I assert, I will mention a little affair which happened one day before my hut.

Four fat graces were squatted on the ground smoking tobacco, when an officer, who happened to be passing, caught a glimpse of the charming picture, rushed up at double quick pace and caught hold of one of the beauties by the shoulder. He began by speaking softly to her, but as his anger increased, he changed his tone to one of loud abuse. But neither entreaties nor threats produced the slightest effect upon the delicate creature to whom they were addressed; she remained coolly in the same position, continuing to smoke with the greatest indifference, and without deigning even to cast upon her excited swain a look, far less answer him a word. He became enraged to such a pitch, that he so far forgot himself as to loosen the golden ear-rings from her ears, and threatened to take away all the

81

finery he had given her. Even this was not sufficient to rouse the girl from her stolid calmness, and the valiant officer was, at last, obliged to retreat from the field of battle.

From his conversation, which was half in French and half in the native dialect, I learned that in three months the girl had cost him about four hundred francs in dress and jewellery. Her wishes were satisfied, and she quietly refused to have anything more to say to him.

I very often heard the feeling, attachment, and kindness of this people spoken of in terms of high praise, with which, however, I cannot unreservedly agree. Their kindness I will not precisely dispute; they readily invite a stranger to share their hospitality, and even kill a pig in his honour, give him a part of their couch, etc.; but all this costs them no trouble, and if they are offered money in return, they take it eagerly enough, without so much as thanking the donor. As for feeling and attachment, I should almost be inclined to deny that they possessed them in the slightest degree; I saw only sensuality, and none of the nobler sentiments. I shall return to this subject when describing my journey through the island.

On the 1st of May I witnessed a highly interesting scene. It was the fête of Louis Philippe, the King of the French; and the governor, Monsieur Bruat, exerted himself to the utmost to amuse the population of Tahiti. In the forenoon, there was a tournament on the water, in which the French sailors were the performers. Several boats with lusty oarsmen put out to sea. In the bows of each boat was a kind of ladder or steps, on which stood one of the combatants with a pole. The boats were then pulled close to one another, and each combatant endeavoured to push his antagonist into the water. Besides this, there was a *Mât de Cocagne*, with coloured shirts, ribbons, and other trifles fluttering at the top, for whoever chose to climb up and get them. At 12 o'clock the chiefs and principal personages were entertained at dinner. On the grass plot before the governor's house were heaped up various sorts of provisions, such as salt meat, bacon, bread, baked pork, fruits, etc.; but instead of the guests taking their places all around, as we had supposed they would have done, the chiefs divided everything into different portions, and each carried his share home. In the evening there were fireworks, and a ball.

No part of the entertainment amused me more than the ball, where I witnessed the most startling contrasts of art and nature. Elegant Frenchwomen side by side with their brown, awkward sisters, and the staff officers in full uniform, in juxtaposition with the half-naked islanders. Many of the natives wore, on this occasion, broad white trousers, with a shirt over them; but there were others who had no other garments than the ordinary short shirt and the pareo. One of the chiefs who appeared in this costume, and was afflicted with Elephantiasis, {76} offered a most repulsive spectacle.

This evening I saw Queen Pomaré for the first time. She is a woman of 36 years of age, tall and stout, but tolerably well preserved—as a general rule, I found that the women here fade much less quickly than in other warm climates—her face is

82

far from ugly, and there is a most good-natured expression round her mouth, and the lower portion of her face. She was enveloped in a sky-blue satin gown, or rather, sort of blouse, ornamented all round with two rows of rich black blond. She wore large jessamine blossoms in her ears, and a wreath of flowers in her hair, while in her hand she carried a fine pocket handkerchief beautifully embroidered, and ornamented with broad lace. In honour of the evening, she had forced her feet into shoes and stockings, though on other occasions she went barefoot. The entire costume was a present from the King of the French.

The queen's husband, who is younger than herself, is the handsomest man in Tahiti. The French jokingly call him the Prince Albert of Tahiti, not only on account of his good looks, but because, like Prince Albert in England, he is not named "the king," but simply, "the queen's consort." He had on the uniform of a French general, which became him very well; the more so, that he was not in the least embarrassed in it. The only drawback were his feet, which were very ugly and awkward.

Besides these two high personages, there was in the company another crowned head, namely, King Otoume, the owner of one of the neighbouring islands. He presented a most comical appearance, having put on, over a pair of full but short white trousers, a bright yellow calico coat, that most certainly had not been made by a Parisian artiste, for it was a perfect model of what a coat ought not to be. This monarch was barefoot.

The queen's ladies of honour, four in number, as well as most of the wives and daughters of the chiefs, were dressed in white muslin. They had also flowers in their ears, and garlands in their hair. Their behaviour and deportment were surprising, and three of the young ladies actually danced French quadrilles with the officers, without making a fault in the figures. I was only anxious for their feet, as no one, save the royal couple, wore either shoes or stockings. Some of the old women had arrayed themselves in European bonnets, while the young ones brought their children, even the youngest, with them, and, to quiet the latter, suckled them without ceremony before the company.

Before supper was announced, the queen disappeared in an adjoining room to smoke a cigar or two, while her husband passed the time in playing billiards.

At table I was seated between Prince Albert of Tahiti and the canary-coloured King Otoume. They were both sufficiently advanced in the rules of good breeding to show me the usual civilities; that is, to fill my glass with water or wine, to hand me the various dishes, and so on; but it was evident that they were at great trouble to catch the tone of European society. Some of the guests, however, forgot their parts now and then: the queen, for instance, asked, during the dessert, for a second plate, which she filled with sweetmeats, and ordered to be put on one side for her to take home with her. Others had to be prevented from indulging too much in the generous champagne; but, on the whole, the entertainment passed off in a becoming and good-humoured manner.

83

I subsequently dined with the royal family several times at the governor's. The queen then appeared in the national costume, with the coloured pareo and chemise, as did also her husband. Both were barefoot. The heir apparent, a boy of nine years old, is affianced to the daughter of a neighbouring king. The bride, who is a few years older than the prince, is being educated at the court of Queen Pomaré, and instructed in the Christian religion, and the English and Tahitian languages.

The arrangements of the queen's residence are exceedingly simple. For the present, until the stone house which is being built for her by the French government is completed, she lives in a wooden one containing four rooms, and partly furnished with European furniture.

As peace was now declared in Tahiti, there was no obstacle to my making a journey through the whole island. I had obtained a fortnight's leave of absence from the captain, and was desirous of devoting this time to a trip. I imagined that I should have been able to join one or other of the officers, who are often obliged to journey through the island on affairs connected with the government. To my great surprise I found, however, that they had all some extraordinary reason why it was impossible for me to accompany them at that particular time. I was at a loss to account for this incivility, until one of the officers themselves told me the answer to the riddle, which was this: every gentleman always travelled with his mistress.

Monsieur ---, {78} who let me into the secret, offered to take me with him to Papara, where he resided; but even he did not travel alone, as, besides his mistress, Tati, the principal chief of the island, and his family, accompanied him. This chief had come to Papeiti to be present at the fete of the 1st of May.

On the 4th of May we put off to sea in a boat, for the purpose of coasting round to Papara, forty-two miles distant. I found the chief Tati to be a lively old man nearly ninety years of age, who remembered perfectly the second landing of the celebrated circumnavigator of the globe, Captain Cook. His father was, at that period, the principal chief, and had concluded a friendly alliance with Cook, and, according to the custom then prevalent at Tahiti, had changed names with him.

Tati enjoys from the French government a yearly pension of 6,000 francs (£240), which, after his death, will fall to his eldest son.

He had with him his young wife and five of his sons; the former was twenty-three years old, and the ages of the latter varied from twelve to eighteen. The children were all the offspring of other marriages, this being his fifth wife.

As we had not left Papeiti till nearly noon, and as the sun sets soon after six o'clock, and the passage between the numberless rocks is highly dangerous, we landed at Paya (22 miles), where a sixth son of Tati's ruled as chief.

The island is intersected in all directions by noble mountains, the loftiest of which, the Oroena, is 6,200 feet high. In the middle of the island the mountains separate, and a most remarkable mass of rock raises itself from the midst of them. It has the form of a diadem with a number of points, and it is to this circumstance that it owes its name. Around the mountain range winds a forest girdle, from four to six hundred paces broad; it is inhabited, and contains the most delicious fruit. Nowhere did I ever eat such bread-fruit, mangoes, oranges, and guavas, as I did here. As for cocoa-nuts, the natives are so extravagant with them, that they generally merely drink the water they contain, and then throw away the shell and the fruit. In the mountains and ravines there are a great quantity of plantains, a kind of banana, which are not commonly eaten, however, without being roasted. The huts of the natives lie scattered here and there along the shore; it is very seldom that a dozen of these huts are seen together.

The bread-fruit is somewhat similar in shape to a water-melon, and weighs from four to six pounds. The outside is green, and rather rough and thin. The natives scrape it with mussel-shells, and then split the fruit up long ways into two portions, which they roast between two heated stones. The taste is delicious; it is finer than that of potatoes, and so like bread that the latter may be dispensed with without any inconvenience. The South Sea Islands are the real home of the fruit. It is true that it grows in other parts of the tropics, but it is very different from that produced here. In Brazil, for instance, where the people call it monkeys' bread, it weighs from five to thirty pounds, and is full inside of kernels, which are taken out and eaten when the fruit is roasted. These kernels taste like chestnuts.

The mango is a fruit resembling an apple, and of the size of a man's fist; both the rind and the fruit itself are yellow. It tastes a little like turpentine, but loses this taste more and more the riper it gets. This fruit is of the best description; it is full and juicy, and has a long, broad kernel in the middle. The bread and mango trees grow to a great height and circumference. The leaves of the former are about three feet long, a foot and a-half broad, and deeply serrated; while those of the latter are not much larger than the leaves of our own apple-trees.

Before reaching Paya, we passed several interesting places, among which may be mentioned Foar, a small French fort, situated upon a hill. Near Taipari it is necessary to pass between two rows of dangerous breakers, called the "Devil's Entrance." The foaming waves rose in such volume and to so great a height, that they might almost be mistaken for walls. In the plain near Punavia is a large fort supported by several towers, built upon the neighbouring hills. At this point the scenery is beautiful. The mountain range breaks here, so that the eye can follow for a long distance the windings of a picturesque valley, with the black and lofty mountain Olofena in the background.

Delighted as I was, however, with the beauty of the objects around me, I was no less pleased with those beneath. Our boat glided along over countless shallows, where the water was as clear as crystal, so that the smallest pebble at the bottom was distinctly visible. I could observe groups and clusters of coloured coral and madrepore-stone, whose magnificence challenges all description. It might be said that there was a quantity of fairy flower and kitchen gardens in the sea, full of gigantic flowers, blossoms, and leaves, varied by fungi and pulse of every description, like open arabesque work, the whole interspersed with pretty groups of rocks of every hue. The most lovely shell-fish were clinging to these rocks, or lying scattered on the ground, while endless shoals of variegated fish darted in and out between them, like so many butterflies and humming-birds. These delicate creatures were scarcely four inches long, and surpassed in richness of colour anything I had ever seen. Many of them were of the purest sky-blue, others a light yellow, while some, again, that were almost transparent, were brown, green, etc.

On our arrival at Paya, about 6 in the evening, the young Tati had a pig, weighing eighteen or twenty pounds, killed and cooked, after the fashion of Tahiti, in honour of his father. A large fire was kindled in a shallow pit, in which were a number of stones. A quantity of bread-fruit (majoré), that had been first peeled and split into two portions with a very sharp wooden axe, was then brought. When the fire had gone out, and the stones heated to the requisite degree, the pig and the fruit were laid upon them, a few other heated stones placed on the top, and the whole covered up with green branches, dry leaves, and earth.

During the time that the victuals were cooking, the table was laid. A straw mat was placed upon the ground, and covered with large leaves. For each guest there was a cocoa-nut shell, half-filled with *miti*, a sourish beverage extracted from the cocoa-palm.

In an hour and a half the victuals were dug up. The pig was neither very artistically cooked nor very enticing, but cut up as quick as lightning, being divided by the hand and knife into as many portions as there were guests, and each person had his share, together with half a bread-fruit, handed to him upon a large leaf. There was no one at our rustic table besides the officer, his mistress, the old Tati, his wife, and myself, as it is contrary to the custom of the country for the host to eat with his guests, or the children with their parents. With the exception of this ceremony, I did not observe any other proof of love or affection between the father and son. The old man, for instance, although ninety years of age, and suffering besides from a violent cough, was obliged to pass the night under nothing but a light roof, open to the weather, while his son slept in his well-closed huts.

On the 5th of May, we left Taipari with empty stomachs, as old Tati was desirous of entertaining us at one of his estates about two hours' journey distant.

On our arrival, and as soon as the stones were heated for our meal, several of the natives out of the neighbouring huts hastened to profit by the opportunity to cook their provisions as well, bringing with them fish, pieces of pork, bread-fruit, plantains, and so on. The fish and meat were enveloped in large leaves. For our use, besides bread-fruit and fish, there was a turtle weighing perhaps more than twenty pounds. The repast was held in a hut, to which the whole neighbourhood also came, and forming themselves into groups a little on one side of us principal guests, eat the provisions they had brought with them. Each person had a cocoa-nut shell full of *miti* before him; into this he first threw every morsel and took it out again with his hand, and then what remained of the miti was drunk at the end of the meal. We had each of us a fresh cocoa-nut with a hole bored in it, containing at least a pint of clear, sweet-tasting water. This is erroneously termed by us "Milk," but it only becomes thick and milky when the cocoa-nut is very stale, in which condition it is never eaten in these islands.

Tati, with his family, remained here, while we proceeded to Papara, an hour's walk. The road was delightful, leading mostly through thick groves of fruit-trees; but it would not suit a person with a tendency to hydrophobia, for we were obliged to wade through more than half a dozen streams and brooks.

At Papara, Monsieur --- possessed some landed property, with a little wooden four-roomed house, in which he was kind enough to give me a lodging.

We here heard of the death of one of Tati's sons, of which he numbered twenty-one. He had been dead three days, and his friends were awaiting Tati to pay the last honours to the deceased. I had intended to make an excursion to the Lake Vaihiria, but deferred doing so, in order to be present at the burial. On the following morning, 6th May, I paid a visit to the hut of the deceased. Monsieur --- gave me a new handkerchief to take with me as a present—a relic of the old superstition which the people of this island have introduced into Christianity. These presents are supposed to calm the soul of the deceased. The corpse was lying in a narrow coffin, upon a low bier, both of which were covered with a white pall. Before the bier were hung two straw mats, on which were spread the deceased's clothes, drinking vessels, knives, and so forth, while on the other, lay the presents, making quite a heap, of shirts, pareos, pieces of cloth, etc., all so new and good that they might have served to furnish a small shop.

Old Tati soon entered the hut, but quickly returned into the open air, stopping only a few instants, as the corpse was already most offensive. He sat down under a tree, and began talking very quietly and unconcernedly with the neighbours, as if nothing had happened. The female relatives and neighbours remained in the hut; they, too, chatted and gossiped very contentedly, and moreover ate and smoked. I was obliged to have the wife, children, and relations of the deceased pointed out to me, for I was unable to recognise them by their demeanour. In a little time, the stepmother and wife rose, and throwing themselves on the coffin, howled for half an hour; but it was easy to see that their grief did not come from the heart. Their moaning was always pitched in the same monotonous key. Both then returned with smiling faces and dry eyes to their seats, and appeared to resume the conversation at the point at which they had broken it off. The deceased's canoe was burnt upon the shore.

I had seen enough, and returned to my quarters to make some preparations for my trip to the lake the next day. The distance is reckoned to be eighteen miles, so that the journey there and back may be performed in two days with ease, and yet a guide had the conscience to ask ten dollars (£2) for his services. With the assistance of old Tati, however, I procured one for three dollars (12s.).

Pedestrian trips are very fatiguing in Tahiti, since it is so richly watered that the excursionist is constantly obliged to wade through plains of sand and rivers. I was very suitably clothed for the purpose, having got strong men's shoes, without any stockings, trousers, and a blouse, which I had fastened up as high as my hips. Thus equipped I began, on the 7th of May, my short journey, in company with my guide. In the first third of my road, which lay along the coast, I counted about thirty-two brooks which we were obliged to walk through. We then struck off, through ravines, into the interior of the island, first calling, however, at a hut to obtain some refreshment. The inmates were very friendly, and gave us some bread-fruit and fish, but very willingly accepted a small present in exchange.

In the interior, the fine fruit-trees disappear, and their place is supplied by plantains, tarros, and a kind of bush, growing to the height of twelve feet, and called Oputu (Maranta); the last, in fact, grew so luxuriantly, that we frequently experienced the greatest difficulty in making our way through. The tarro, which is planted, is from two to three feet high, and has fine large leaves and tubercles, similar to the potato, but which do not taste very good when roasted. The plantain, or banana, is a pretty little tree, from fifteen to twenty feet high, with leaves like those of the palm, and a stem which is often eight inches in diameter, but is not of wood, but cane, and very easily broken. It belongs properly to the herbiferous species, and grows with uncommon rapidity. It reaches its full growth the first year: in the second it bears fruit, and then dies. It is produced from shoots, which generally spring up near the parent tree.

Through one mountain stream, which chafed along the ravine over a stony bed, and in some places was exceedingly rapid, and, in consequence of the rain that had lately fallen, was frequently more than three feet deep, we had to wade sixty-two times. My guide caught hold of me by the hand whenever we passed a dangerous spot, and dragged me, often half swimming, after him. The water constantly reached above my hips, and all idea of getting dry again was totally out of the question. The path also became at every step more fatiguing and dangerous. I had to clamber over rocks and stones covered to such an extent with the foliage of the oputu that I never knew with any degree of certainty where I was placing my foot. I received several severe wounds on my hands and feet, and frequently fell down on the ground, when I trusted for support to the treacherous stem of a banana, which would break beneath my grasp. It was really a breakneck sort of excursion, which is very rarely made even by the officers, and certainly never by ladies.

In two places the ravine became so narrow, that the bed of the stream occupied its whole extent. It was here that the islanders, during the war with the French, built stone walls five feet in height to protect them against the enemy, in case they should have attacked them from this side.

In eight hours' time we had completed the eighteen miles, and attained an elevation of 1,800 feet. The lake itself was not visible until we stood upon its shores, as it lies in a slight hollow; it is about 800 feet across. The surrounding scenery is the most remarkable. The lake is so closely hemmed in by a ring of lofty and precipitous green mountains, that there is no room even for a footing between the water and the rocks, and its bed might be taken for an extinguished volcano filled with water—a supposition which gains additional force from the masses of basalt which occupy the foreground. It is plentifully supplied with fish, one kind of which is said to be peculiar to the locality; it is supposed that the lake has a subterranean outlet, which as yet remains undiscovered.

To cross the lake, it is either necessary to swim over or trust oneself to a dangerous kind of boat, which is prepared by the natives in a few minutes. Being desirous of making the attempt, I intimated this by signs to my guide. In an instant he tore off some plantain-branches, fastened them together with long, tough grass, laid a few leaves upon them, launched them in the water, and then told me to take possession of this apology for a boat. I must own that I felt rather frightened, although I did not like to say so. I stept on board, and my guide swam behind and pushed me forward. I made the passage to the opposite side and back without any accident, but I was in truth rather alarmed the whole time. The boat was small, and floated under rather than upon the water—there was nothing I could support myself with, and every minute I expected to fall into the lake. I would not advise any one who cannot swim ever to follow my example.

After I had sufficiently admired the lake and the surrounding scenery, we retraced our way for some hundred yards, until we reached a little spot roofed over with leaves. Here my guide quickly made a good fire, after the Indian fashion. He took a small piece of wood, which he cut to a fine point, and then selecting a second piece, he made in it a narrow furrow not very deep. In this he rubbed the pointed stick until the little particles which were detached during the operation began to smoke. These he threw into a quantity of dry leaves and grass which he had got together for the purpose, and swung the whole several times round in the air, until it burst out into flames. The entire process did not take more than two minutes.

For our supper, he gathered a few plantains and laid them on the fire. I profited by the opportunity to dry my clothes, by sitting down near the fire, and turning first one side towards it, and then the other. Half wet through, and tolerably fatigued, I retired to my couch of dry leaves immediately after partaking of our scanty meal.

It is a fortunate circumstance that in these wild and remote districts neither men nor beasts afford the slightest grounds for apprehension; the former are very quiet and peaceably inclined, and, with the exception of a few wild boars, the latter are not dangerous. The island is especially favoured; it contains no poisonous or hurtful insects or reptiles. It is true there are a few scorpions, but so small and harmless, that they may be handled with impunity. The mosquitoes alone were the source of very considerable annoyance, as they are in all southern countries.

8th May. It began to rain very violently during the night, and in the morning I was sorry to see that there was not much hope of its clearing up; on the contrary, the clouds became blacker and blacker, and collecting from all sides, like so many evil spirits, poured down in torrents upon the innocent earth. Nevertheless, in spite of this, there was no other course open to us but to bid defiance to the angry water deity, and proceed upon our journey. In half an hour I was literally drenched; this being the case, I went on uncomplainingly, as it was impossible for me to become wetter than I was.

On my return to Papara, I found that Tati's son was not buried, but the ceremony took place the next day. The clergyman pronounced a short discourse at the side of the grave; and, as the coffin was being lowered, the mats, straw hat, and clothes of the deceased, as well as a few of the presents, were thrown in with it. The relations were present, but as unconcerned as I was myself.

The graveyard was in the immediate vicinity of several *murais*. The latter are small four-cornered plots of ground surrounded by stone walls three or four feet high, where the natives used to deposit their dead, which were left exposed upon wooden frames until the flesh fell from the bones. These were then collected and buried in some lonely spot.

The same evening I witnessed a remarkable mode of catching fish. Two boys waded out into the sea, one with a stick, and the other with a quantity of burning chips. The one with the stick drove the fish between the rocks, and then hit them, the other lighting him in the meanwhile. They were not very fortunate, however. The more common and successful manner of fishing is with nets.

Almost every day Monsieur --- had visits from officers who were passing, accompanied by their mistresses. The reader may easily imagine that the laws of propriety were not, however, always strictly observed, and as I had no desire to disturb the gentlemen in their intellectual conversation and amusement, I retired with my book into the servants' room. They, too, would laugh and joke, but, at least, in such a manner that there was no occasion to blush for them.

It was highly amusing to hear Monsieur --- launch out in praise of the attachment and gratitude of his Indian beauty; he would have altered his tone had he seen her behaviour in his absence. On one occasion I could not help telling one of the gentlemen my opinion of the matter, and expressing my astonishment that they could treat these grasping and avaricious creatures with such attention and kindness, to load them with presents, anticipate their every wish, and forgive and put up with their most glaring faults. The answer I received was: that these ladies, if not so treated and loaded with presents, would quickly run off, and that, in fact, even by the kindest attentions they never allowed themselves to be influenced very long.

From all I saw, I must repeat my former assertion, that the Tahitian people are endowed with none of the more noble sentiments of humanity, but that their only pleasures are merely animal. Nature herself encourages them to this in an extraordinary manner. They have no need to gain their bread by the sweat of their brow; the island is most plentifully supplied with beautiful fruit, tubercles of all descriptions, and tame pigs, so that the people have really only to gather the fruit and kill the pigs. To this circumstance is to be attributed the difficulty that exists of obtaining any one as servant or in any other capacity. The most wretched journeyman will not work for less than a dollar a-day; the price for washing a dozen handkerchiefs, or any other articles, is also a dollar (4s.), not including soap. A native, whom I desired to engage as guide, demanded a dollar and a half a day.

I returned from Papara to Papeiti in the company of an officer and his native beauty; we walked the thirty-six miles in a day. On our way, we passed the hut of the girl's mother, where we partook of a most splendid dish. It was composed of bread-fruit, mangoes, and bananas, kneaded together into a paste, and cooked upon hot stones. It was eaten, while warm, with a sauce of orange juice.

On taking leave, the officer gave the girl a present of a dollar to give her mother; the girl took it as indifferently as if it were not of the slightest value, and her mother did exactly the same, neither of them pronouncing one word of thanks, or manifesting the least sign of satisfaction.

We now and then came upon some portions of the road, the work of public offenders, that were most excellently constructed. Whenever an Indian is convicted of a crime, he is not chained in a gang, like convicts in Europe, but condemned to make or mend a certain extent of road, and the natives fulfil the tasks thus imposed with such punctuality, that no overseer is ever necessary. This kind of punishment was introduced under King Pomaré, and originated with the natives themselves—the Europeans have merely continued the practice.

At Punavia we entered the fort, where we refreshed ourselves, in military fashion, with bread, wine, and bacon, and reached our journey's end at 7 o'clock in the morning.

Besides Papara, I visited also Venus Point, a small tongue of land where Cook observed the transit of Venus. The stone on which he placed his instruments still remains. On my way, I passed the grave, or *murai*, of King Pomaré I. It consists of a small piece of ground, surrounded by a stone wall, and covered with a roof of palm-leaves. Some half-decayed pieces of cloth and portions of wearing apparel were still lying in it.

One of my most interesting excursions, however, was that to Fantaua and the Diadem. The former is a spot which the Indians considered impregnable; but where, nevertheless, they were well beaten by the French during the last war.

Monsieur Bruat, the governor, was kind enough to lend me his horses, and to allow me the escort of a non-commissioned officer, who could point out to me each position of the Indians and French, as he had himself been in the engagement.

For more than two hours, we proceeded through horrible ravines, thick woods, and rapid mountain torrents. The ravines often became so narrow as to form so many defiles, with such precipitous and inaccessible sides, that here, as at Thermopylæ, a handful of valiant warriors might defy whole armies. As a natural consequence, the entrance of Fantaua is regarded as the real key to the whole island. There was no other means of taking it than by scaling one of its most precipitous sides, and pressing forward upon the narrow ledge of rock above, so as to take the enemy in the rear. The governor, Monsieur Bruat, announced that he would confide this dangerous enterprise to volunteers, and he soon had more than he could employ. From those chosen, a second selection of only sixty-two men was made: these divested themselves of every article of clothing save their shoes and drawers, and took no other arms save their muskets.

After clambering up for twelve hours, and incurring great danger, they succeeded, by the aid of ropes, and by sticking pointed iron-rods and bayonets into the rock, in reaching the crest of the mountain, where their appearance so astonished the Indians, that they lost all courage, threw down their arms, and surrendered. They said that those who were capable of deeds like this, could not be men but spirits, against whom all hopes of resistance were out of the question altogether.

At present, there is a small fort built at Fantaua, and on one of its highest points stands a guard-house. The path leading to it is over a small ledge of rock, skirted on each side by a yawning abyss. Persons affected with giddiness can only reach it with great difficulty, if indeed they can do so at all. In this last case, they are great losers, for the prospect is magnificent in the extreme, extending over valleys, ravines, and mountains without number (among the latter may be mentioned the colossal rock called the "Diadem"), thick forests of palms and other trees; and beyond all these, the mighty ocean, broken into a thousand waves against the rocks and reefs, and in the distance mingling with the azure sky.

Near the fort, a waterfall precipitates itself perpendicularly down a narrow ravine. Unfortunately, the bottom of it is concealed by jutting rocks and promontories, and the volume of water is rather small; otherwise, this fall would, on account of its height, which is certainly more than 400 feet, deserve to be classed among the most celebrated ones with which I am acquainted.

The road from the fort to the Diadem is extremely fatiguing, and fully three hours are required to accomplish the journey. The prospect here is even more magnificent than from the fort, as the eye beholds the sea over two sides of the island at the same time.

This excursion was my last in this beautiful isle, as I was obliged to embark on the next day, the 17th of May. The cargo was cleared, and the ballast taken on board. All articles to which the French troops are accustomed, such as flour, salted meat, potatoes, pulse, wine, and a variety of others, have to be imported. {86}

I felt extremely reluctant to leave; and the only thing that tended at all to cheer my spirits, was the thought of my speedy arrival in China, that most wonderful of all known countries.

We left the port of Papeiti on the morning of the 17th of May, with a most favourable wind, soon passed in safety all the dangerous coral-reefs which surround the island, and in seven hours' time had lost sight of it altogether. Towards evening, we beheld the mountain ranges of the island of Huaheme, which we passed during the night.

The commencement of our voyage was remarkably pleasant. Besides the favourable breeze, which still continued, we enjoyed the company of a fine Belgian brig, the Rubens, which had put to sea at the same time as ourselves. It was seldom that we approached near enough for the persons on board to converse with each other; but whoever is at all acquainted with the endless uniformity of long voyages, will easily understand our satisfaction at knowing we were even in the neighbourhood of human beings.

We pursued the same track as far as the Philippine Islands, but on the morning of the third day our companion had disappeared, leaving us in ignorance whether she had out-sailed us or we her. We were once more alone on the endless waste of waters.

On the 23rd of May, we approached very near to the low island of Penchyn. A dozen or two of the natives were desirous of honouring us with a visit, and pulled stoutly in six canoes towards our ship, but we sailed so fast that they were soon left a long way behind. Several of the sailors affirmed, that these were specimens of real savages, and that we might reckon ourselves fortunate in having escaped their visit. The captain, too, appeared to share this opinion, and I was the only person who regretted not having formed a more intimate acquaintance with them.

28th May. For some days we had been fortunate enough to be visited, from time to time, with violent showers; a most remarkable thing for the time of year in this climate, where the rainy season commences in January and lasts for three months, the sky for the remaining nine being generally cloudless. This present exception was the more welcome from our being just on the Line, where we should otherwise have suffered much from the heat. The thermometer stood at only 81° in the shade, and 97° in the sun.

Today at noon we crossed the Line, and were once more in the northern hemisphere. A Tahitian sucking-pig was killed and consumed in honour of our successful passage, and our native hemisphere toasted in real hock.

On the 4th of June, under 8° North latitude, we beheld again, for the first time,

93

the lovely polar star.

On the 17th of June, we passed so near to Saypan, one of the largest of the Ladrone Islands, that we could make out the mountains very distinctly. The Ladrone and Marianne Islands are situated between the 13° and 21° North latitude, and the 145° and 146° East longitude.

On the 1st of July we again saw land: this time it was the coast of Lucovia, or Luzon, the largest of the Philippines, and lying between the 18° and 19° North latitude, and the 125° and 119° East longitude. The port of Manilla is situated on the southern coast of the island.

In the course of the day we passed the island of Babuan, and several detached rocks, rising, colossus like, from the sea. Four of them were pretty close together, and formed a picturesque group. Some time afterwards we saw two more.

In the night of the 1st-2nd of July, we reached the western point of Luzon, and entered on the dangerous Chinese Sea. I was heartily glad at last to bid adieu to the Pacific Ocean, for a voyage on it is one of the most monotonous things that can be imagined. The appearance of another ship is a rare occurrence; and the water is so calm that it resembles a stream. Very frequently I used to start up from my desk, thinking that I was in some diminutive room ashore; and my mistake was the more natural, as we had three horses, a dog, several pigs, hens, geese, and a canary bird on board, all respectively neighing, barking, grunting, cackling, and singing, as if they were in a farm-yard.

6th July. For the first few days after entering the Chinese sea, we sailed pretty well in the same fashion we had done in the Pacific—proceeding slowly and quietly on our way. Today we beheld the coast of China for the first time, and towards evening we were not more than thirty-three miles from Macao. I was rather impatient for the following morning. I longed to find my darling hope realized, of putting my foot upon Chinese ground. I pictured the mandarins with their high caps, and the ladies with their tiny feet, when in the middle of the night the wind shifted, and on the 7th of July we had been carried back 115 miles. In addition to this, the glass fell so low, that we dreaded a *Tai-foon*, which is a very dangerous kind of storm, or rather hurricane, that is very frequent in the Chinese sea during the months of July, August, and September. It is generally first announced by a black cloud on the horizon, with one edge dark red, and the other half-white; and this is accompanied by the most awful torrents of rain, by thunder, lightning, and the violent winds, which arise simultaneously on all sides, and lash the waters up mountains high. We took every precaution in anticipation of our dangerous enemy, but for once they were not needed: either the hurricane did not break out at all, or else it broke out at a great distance from us; for we were only visited by a trifling storm of no long duration.

On the 8th of July we again reached the vicinity of Macao, and entered the Straits of Lema. Our course now lay between bays and reefs, diversified by groups of the

94

most beautiful islands, offering a series of most magnificent and varied views.

On the 9th of July we anchored in Macao Roads. The town, which belongs to the Portuguese, and has a population of 20,000 inhabitants, is beautifully situated on the sea-side, and surrounded by pleasing hills and mountains. The most remarkable objects are the palace of the Portuguese governor, the Catholic monastery of Guia, the fortifications, and a few fine houses which lie scattered about the hills in picturesque disorder.

Besides a few European ships, there were anchored in the roads several large Chinese junks, while a great number of small boats, manned by Chinese, were rocking to and fro around us.

CHAPTER VIII. CHINA.

MACAO—HONG-KONG—VICTORIA—VOYAGE ON BOARD A CHINESE JUNK—THE SI-KIANG, CALLED ALSO THE TIGRIS— WHAMPOA—CANTON, OR KUANGTSCHEU-FU—MODE OF LIFE PURSUED BY EUROPEANS—THE CHINESE MANNERS AND CUSTOMS—CRIMINALS AND PIRATES—MURDER OF VAUCHÉE— PROMENADES AND EXCURSIONS.

A year before my arrival in China, it would have seemed hardly credible to me that I should ever succeed in taking my place among the small number of Europeans who are acquainted with that remarkable country, not from books alone, but from actual observation; I never believed that I should really behold the Chinese, with their shaven heads, long tails, and small, ugly, narrow eyes, the exact counterparts of the representations of them which we have in Europe.

We had hardly anchored, before a number of Chinese clambered up on deck, while others remained in their boats, offering for sale a variety of beautifully made articles, with fruit and cakes, laid out in great order, so as to form in a few seconds a regular market round the vessel. Some of them began praising their wares in broken English; but on the whole, they did not drive a very flourishing business, as the crew merely bought a few cigars, and a little fruit.

Captain Jurianse hired a boat, and we immediately went on shore, where each person on landing had to pay half a Spanish dollar (2s.) to the mandarin: I subsequently heard that this imposition was shortly afterwards abolished. We proceeded to the house of one of the Portuguese merchants established there, passing through a large portion of the town on our way thither. Europeans, both men and women, can circulate freely, without being exposed to a shower of stones, as is frequently the case in other Chinese towns. The streets, which are exclusively inhabited by Chinese, presented a very bustling aspect. The men were in many cases seated out of doors in groups, playing at dominoes, while locksmiths, carpenters, shoemakers, and many others were either working, talking, playing, or dining in the numerous booths. I observed but few women, and these were of the lower classes. Nothing surprised and amused me more than the manner in which the Chinese eat; they have two little sticks, with which they very skilfully convey their victuals into their mouths. This process, however, cannot be so successfully practised with rice, because it does not hold together; they therefore hold the plate containing it close to their mouths, and push it in by the aid of the sticks, generally letting a portion of it fall back again, in no very cleanly fashion, into the plate. For liquids they use round spoons of porcelain.

The style in which the houses are built, did not strike me as very remarkable; the front generally looks out upon the courtyard or garden.

Among other objects which I visited was the grotto, in which the celebrated Portuguese poet, Camoens, is said to have composed the Lusiade. He had been banished, A.D. 1556, to Macao, on account of a satirical poem he had written, *Disperates no India*, and remained in banishment several years before receiving a pardon. The grotto is charmingly situated upon an eminence not far from the town.

As there was no business to be done, the captain resolved to put to sea again the next morning, and offered in the most friendly manner to take me as his guest to Hong-Kong, as I had only agreed for a passage as far as Macao. I accepted his invitation with the greater pleasure, as I had not a single letter to any one in Macao; besides which, it is very seldom that there is an opportunity of proceeding to Hong-Kong.

On account of the shallowness of the water, our ship was hove to at rather a long distance from the shore, where it was exposed to an attack from the pirates, who are here very daring and numerous. In consequence of this, every precaution was taken, and the watch doubled for the night.

As late as the year 1842 these pirates attacked a brig that was lying at anchor in the Macao Roads, murdering the crew and plundering the vessel. The captain had remained on shore, and the sailors had carelessly given themselves up to sleep, leaving only one man to keep watch. In the middle of the night a schampan— which is the name given to a vessel smaller than a junk—came alongside the brig. One of the rowers then came on board, pretending he had a letter from the captain; and as the sailor went near the lantern to read the letter, he received from the pirate a blow upon his head which laid him senseless on the deck; the rest of those in the boat, who had hitherto remained concealed, now scaled the side of the brig, and quickly overpowered the slumbering crew.

In our case, however, the night passed without any incident worth noting; and on the morning of the 10th of July, having first taken on board a pilot, we proceeded to Hong-Kong, a distance of sixty nautical miles. The voyage proved highly interesting, on account of the varied succession of bays, creeks, and groups of islands which we had to pass.

The English obtained Hong-Kong from the Chinese at the conclusion of the war in 1842, and founded the port of Victoria, which contains at present a large number of palace-like houses built of stone.

The Europeans who have settled here, and who are not more than two or three hundred in number, are far from being contented, however, as trade is not half as good as they at first expected it would be. Every merchant is presented by the English government with a plot of ground, on condition of his building on it. Many of them erected, as I before mentioned, splendid edifices, which they would now be glad to sell for half the cost price, or even very frequently to give the ground and foundations, without asking the smallest sum in return.

I resolved to stop only a few days in Victoria, as it was my wish to arrive at Canton as soon as possible.

In addition to the great politeness he had previously shown me, Captain Jurianse conferred another favour, by allowing me, during my stay here, to live and lodge on board his ship, thereby saving me an expense of 16s. or 24s. {91a} a day; and, besides this, the boat which he had hired for his own use was always at my disposal. I must also take this opportunity of mentioning that I never drank, on board any other vessel, such clear and excellent water—a proof that it is not so easily spoilt by the heat of the tropics, or a protracted period, as is generally imagined. It all depends upon care and cleanliness, for which the Dutch are especially celebrated; and I only wish that every captain would, in this respect at least, imitate their example. It is rather too bad for passengers to be obliged to quench their thirst with thick and most offensive water—a disagreeable necessity I was subjected to on board every other sailing vessel in which I made a voyage of any length.

Victoria is not very pleasantly situated, being surrounded by barren rocks. The town itself has a European stamp upon it, so that were it not for the Chinese porters, labourers, and pedlars, a person would hardly believe he was in China. I was much struck at seeing no native women in the streets, from which it might be concluded that it was dangerous for a European female to walk about as freely as I did; but I never experienced the least insult, or heard the slightest word of abuse from the Chinese; even their curiosity was here by no means annoying.

In Victoria I had the pleasure of becoming acquainted with the well-known Herr Gützlaff, {91b} and four other German missionaries. They were studying the Chinese language; and wore the Chinese costume, with their heads shaved like the natives, and with large cues hanging down behind. No language is so difficult to read and write as the Chinese; it contains more than four thousand characters, and is wholly composed of monosyllables. Little brushes dipped in Indian ink are used for writing, the writing itself extending down the paper from right to left.

97

I had not been above a few days in Victoria before I had an opportunity of proceeding to Canton on board a small Chinese junk. A gentleman of the name of Pustan, who is settled as a merchant here, and whom I found excessively kind, endeavoured very earnestly to dissuade me from trusting myself among the Chinese without any protector, and advised me either to take a boat for myself or a place in the steamer; but both these means were too dear for my small finances, since either would have cost twelve dollars, whereas a passage in the junk was only three. I must also add, that the appearance and behaviour of the Chinese did not inspire me with the slightest apprehension. I looked to the priming of my pistols, and embarked very tranquilly on the evening of the 12th of July.

A heavy fall of rain, and the approach of night, soon obliged me to seek the interior of the vessel, where I passed my time in observing my Chinese fellow-travellers.

The company were, it is true, not very select, but behaved with great propriety, so that there was nothing which could prevent my remaining among them. Some were playing at dominoes, while others were extracting most horrible sounds from a sort of mandolin with three strings; all, however, were smoking, chatting, and drinking tea, without sugar, from little saucers. I, too, had this celestial drink offered to me on all sides. Every Chinese, rich or poor, drinks neither pure water nor spirituous liquors, but invariably indulges in weak tea with no sugar.

At a late hour in the evening I retired to my cabin, the roof of which, not being completely waterproof, let in certain very unwelcome proofs that it was raining outside. The captain no sooner remarked this than he assigned me another place, where I found myself in the company of two Chinese women, busily engaged in smoking out of pipes with bowls no bigger than thimbles, and in consequence they could not take more than four or five puffs without being obliged to fill their pipes afresh.

They soon remarked that I had no stool for my head. They offered me one of theirs, and would not be satisfied until I accepted it. It is a Chinese custom to use, instead of pillows, little stools of bamboo or strong pasteboard. They are not stuffed, but are rounded at the top, and are about eight inches high, and from one to three feet long. They are far more comfortable than would at first be imagined.

13th July. On hurrying upon deck early in the morning to view the mouth of the Si-Kiang, or Tigris, I found that we had already passed it, and were a long way up the river. I saw it, however, subsequently, on my return from Canton to Hong-Kong. The Si-Kiang, which is one of the principal rivers of China, and which, at a short distance before entering the sea, is eight nautical miles broad, is so contracted by hills and rocks at its mouth, that it loses one half of its breadth. The surrounding country is fine, and a few fortifications on the summits of some of the hills, give it rather a romantic appearance.

Near Hoo-man, or Whampoa, the stream divides into several branches; that which flows to Canton being called the Pearl stream. Although Whampoa of itself is an insignificant place, it is worthy of note, as being the spot where, from the shallowness of the water, all deeply laden ships are obliged to anchor.

Immense plantations of rice, skirted by bananas and other fruit-trees, extend along the banks of the Pearl stream. The trees are sometimes prettily arranged in alleys, but are planted far less for ornament than for use. Rice always requires a great deal of moisture, and the trees are planted in order to impart a greater degree of solidity to the soil, and also to prevent the possibility of its being washed away by the force of the stream. Pretty little country houses of the genuine Chinese pattern, with their sloping, pointed, indented roofs, and their coloured tiles inlaid with different hues, were scattered here and there, under groups of shady trees, while pagodas (called Tas) of various styles, and from three to nine stories high, raised their heads on little eminences in the neighbourhood of the villages, and attracted attention at a great distance. A number of fortifications, which, however, look more like roofless houses than anything else, protect the stream.

For miles below Canton, the villages follow one another in quick succession. They are mostly composed of miserable huts, built for the most part on piles driven into the river, and before them lie innumerable boats, which also serve as dwellings.

The nearer we approached Canton, the busier became the scene on the river, and the greater the number of ships and inhabited boats. I saw some junks of most extraordinary shape, having poops that hung far over the water, and provided with large windows and galleries, and covered in with a roof, like a house. These vessels are often of immense size, and of a thousand tons' burden. I also saw some Chinese men-of-war, flat, broad, and long, and mounting twenty or thirty cannons. {93} Another object of interest was the mandarins' boats, with their painted sides, doors, and windows, their carved galleries, and pretty little silk flags, giving them the appearance of the most charming houses; but what delighted me most was the flower-boats, with their upper galleries ornamented with flowers, garlands, and arabesques. A large apartment and a few cabinets, into which the interior is divided, are reached through doors and windows which have almost a Gothic appearance. Mirrors and silk hangings adorn the walls, while glass chandeliers and coloured paper lanterns, between which swing lovely little baskets with fresh flowers, complete the magic scene.

These flower-boats are always stationary, and are frequented by the Chinese as places of amusement, both by day and night. Plays are acted here, and ballets and conjuring performed. Women, with the exception of a certain class, do not frequent these places; Europeans are not exactly prevented from entering them, but are exposed, especially in the present unfavourable state of public opinion, to insult and even injury.

In addition to these extraordinary vessels, let the reader picture to himself thousands of small boats (schampans), some at anchor, some crossing and passing in all directions, with fishermen casting their nets, and men and children amusing themselves by swimming, and he will have some idea of the scene I witnessed. I often could not avoid turning away with terror at seeing the little children playing and rolling about upon the narrow boats, I expected every instant that one or other of them would certainly fall overboard. Some parents are cautious enough to fasten hollow gourds, or bladders filled with air, on their children's backs, until they are six years old, so as to prevent them sinking so quickly, if they should happen to tumble into the water.

All these multifarious occupations—this ceaseless activity, this never-ending bustle, form so peculiar a feature, that it is hardly possible for a person who has not been an eye-witness to obtain a correct idea of it.

It is only during the last few years that we European women have been allowed to visit or remain in the factories at Canton. I left the vessel without any apprehension; but first, I had to consider how I should find my way to the house of a gentleman named Agassiz, for whom I had brought letters of recommendation. I explained to the captain, by signs, that I had no money with me, and that he must act as my guide to the factory, where I would pay him. He soon understood me, and conducted me to the place, and the Europeans there showed me the particular house I wanted.

On seeing me arrive, and hearing the manner in which I had travelled, and the way that I had walked from the vessel to his house, Mr. Agassiz was extremely surprised, and would hardly credit that I had met with no difficulties or injury. From him I learned what risks I, as a woman, had run in traversing the streets of Canton with no escort but a Chinese guide. Such a thing had never occurred before, and Mr. Agassiz assured me that I might esteem myself as exceedingly fortunate in not having been insulted by the people in the grossest manner, or even stoned. Had this been the case, he told me that my guide would have immediately taken to flight, and abandoned me to my fate.

I had certainly remarked, on my way from the vessel to the factory, that both old and young turned back to look after me, and that they hooted and pointed at me with their fingers; the people ran out of the booths, and gradually formed a crowd at my heels. I had, however, no alternative but to preserve my countenance; I walked, therefore, calmly on, and perhaps it is to the very fact of my manifesting no fear that I escaped unmolested.

I had not intended to stop long in Canton, as, since the last war between the English and Chinese, Europeans are obliged to be more careful than ever how they show themselves in public. This hatred is more especially directed against women, as it is declared in one of the Chinese prophecies that a woman will some day or other conquer the Celestial Empire. On account of this, I entertained but slight hopes of seeing anything here, and thought of proceeding directly to the port of Shanghai, in the north of China, where, as I was informed, it was far easier to obtain access both among the nobility and lower classes. Fortunately, however, I made the acquaintance of a German gentleman, Herr von Carlowitz, who had been settled for some time in Canton. He offered, in the kindest manner, to act as my Mentor, on condition that I should arm myself with patience until the mail from Europe, which was expected in a few days, had come in. {95} At such times the merchants are so busy and excited, that they have no leisure to think of anything but their correspondence. I was, therefore, obliged to wait, not only until the steamer had arrived, but until it had left again, which it did not do until a week had elapsed. I have to thank Mr. Agassiz that the time did not hang heavily upon my hands; I was most kindly and hospitably entertained, and enjoyed the opportunity of noting the mode of life of those Europeans who have settled in the country.

Very few take their families with them to China, and least of all to Canton, where both women and children are closely imprisoned in their houses, which they can only leave in a well-closed litter. Besides this, everything is so dear, that living in London is cheap in comparison. Lodgings of six rooms, with a kitchen, cost about 700 or 800 dollars a-year (£140 or £160). A man-servant receives from four to eight dollars a-month, and female servants nine or ten dollars, as Chinese women will not wait upon a European unless greatly overpaid. In addition to all this, there is a custom prevalent here, of having a separate person for each branch of household duty, which renders a large number of servants indispensable.

A family of only four persons requires at least eleven or twelve domestics, if not more. In the first place, every member of the family must have an attendant especially for his or her use; then there is a man-cook, a number of nursery-maids, and several coolies for the more menial duties, such as cleaning the rooms, carrying the wood and water, and so forth. In spite of this number of servants, the attendance is frequently very bad; for, if one or other of them happens to be out, and his services are required, his master must wait until he returns, as no servant could ever be prevailed upon to do another's duty.

At the head of the whole household is the comprador, who is a kind of major-domo. To his care are confided all the plate, furniture, linen, and other effects; he engages all the servants, provides for their board, and anything else they may require, and answers for their good conduct, deducting, however, two dollars a-month from the wages of each, in return for his services. He makes all the purchases, and settles all the bills, giving in the sum total at the end of the month, without descending into the items.

Besides these domestic duties, the comprador is also entrusted with the money belonging to his master's firm; hundreds of thousands of dollars pass through his hands, and he is responsible for the genuineness of every one. He has persons in his own employment who pay and receive all monies, and who examine and test every separate coin with the most marvellous rapidity. They take a whole handful of dollars at a time, and toss them up separately with the finger and thumb: this

101

enables them to determine whether each "rings" properly, and on the coin falling into their hand again, reversed, they examine the second side with a glance. A few hours are sufficient to pass several thousand dollars in review; and this minute inspection is very necessary, on account of the number of false dollars made by the Chinese. Each piece of money is then stamped with the peculiar mark of the firm, as a guarantee of its genuineness, so that it at last becomes exceedingly thin and broad, and frequently falls to bits; no loss is, however, occasioned by this, as the amount is always reckoned by weight. Besides dollars, little bars of pure unstamped silver are used as a circulating medium; small portions, varying in size, being cut off them, according to the sum required. The counting-house is situated on the ground floor, in the comprador's room. The Europeans have nothing to do with the money, and, in fact, never even carry any for their private use.

The comprador has no fixed salary, but receives a stated per-centage upon all business transactions: his per-centage upon the household expenses is not fixed, but is not on that account less certain. On the whole, these compradors are very trustworthy. They pay down a certain sum, as caution-money, to some mandarin, and the latter answers for them.

The following is a tolerably correct account of the mode of life pursued by the Europeans settled here. As soon as they are up, and have drunk a cup of tea in their bed-room, they take a cold bath. A little after 9 o'clock, they breakfast upon fried fish or cutlets, cold roast meat, boiled eggs, tea, and bread and butter. Every one then proceeds to his business until dinner-time, which is generally 4 o'clock. The dinner is composed of turtle-soup, curry, roast meat, hashes, and pastry. All the dishes, with the exception of the curry, are prepared after the English fashion, although the cooks are Chinese. For dessert there is cheese, with fruit; such as pine-apples, long-yen, mangoes, and lytchi. The Chinese affirm that the latter is the finest fruit in the whole world. It is about the size of a nut, with a brown verrucous outside; the edible part is white and tender, and the kernel black. Long-yen is somewhat smaller, but is also white and tender, though the taste is rather watery. Neither of these fruits struck me as very good. I do not think the pine-apples are so sweet, or possessed of that aromatic fragrance which distinguishes those raised in our European greenhouses, although they are much larger.

Portuguese wines and English beer are the usual drinks—ice, broken into small pieces, and covered up with a cloth, is offered with each. The ice is rather a costly article, as it has to be brought from North America. In the evening, tea is served up.

During meal-times, a large punkah is employed to diffuse an agreeable degree of coolness through the apartment. The punkah is a large frame, from eight to ten feet long, and three feet high, covered with white Indian cloth, and fastened to the ceiling. A rope communicates, through the wall, like a bell-pull, with the next room, or the ground floor, where a servant is stationed to keep it constantly in motion, and thus maintain a pleasing draught.

102

As may be seen from what I have said, the living here is very dear for Europeans. The expense of keeping a house may be reckoned at 30,000 francs (6,000 dollars —£1,200) at the lowest; a very considerable sum, when we reflect how little it procures, neither including a carriage nor horses. There is nothing in the way of amusement, or places of public recreation; the only pleasure many gentlemen indulge in, is keeping a boat, for which they pay 28s. a-month, or they walk in the evenings in a small garden, which the European inhabitants have laid out at their own cost. This garden faces the factory, surrounded on three sides by a wall, and, on the fourth, washed by the Pearl stream.

The living of the Chinese population, on the contrary, costs very little; 60 cash, 1,200 of which make a dollar (4s.), may be reckoned a very liberal daily allowance for each man. As a natural consequence, wages are extremely low; a boat, for instance, may be hired for half a dollar (2s.) a-day, and on this income, a whole family of from six to eight persons will often exist. It is true, the Chinese are not too particular in their food; they eat dogs, cats, mice, and rats, the intestines of birds, and the blood of every animal, and I was even assured that caterpillars and worms formed part of their diet. Their principal dish, however, is rice, which is not only employed by them in the composition of their various dishes, but supplies the place of bread. It is exceedingly cheap; the pekul, which is equal to 124 lbs. English avoirdupois, costing from one dollar and three-quarters to two dollars and a half.

The costume of both sexes, among the lower orders, consists of broad trousers and long upper garments, and is remarkable for its excessive filth. The Chinaman is an enemy of baths and washing; he wears no shirt, and does not discard his trousers until they actually fall off his body. The men's upper garments reach a little below the knee, and the women's somewhat lower. They are made of nankeen, or dark blue, brown, or black silk. During the cold season, both men and women wear one summer-garment over the other, and keep the whole together with a girdle; during the great heat, however, they allow their garments to flutter unconstrained about their body.

All the men have their heads shaved, with the exception of a small patch at the back, the hair on which is carefully cultivated and plaited into a cue. The thicker and longer this cue is, the prouder is its owner; false hair and black ribbon are consequently worked up in it, so that it often reaches down to the ankles. During work, it is twisted round the neck, but, on the owner's entering a room, it is let down again, as it would be against all the laws of etiquette and politeness for a person to make his appearance with his cue twisted up. The women wear all their hair, which they comb entirely back off their forehead, and fasten it in most artistic plaits to the head; they spend a great deal of time in the process, but when their hair is once dressed, it does not require to be touched for a whole week. Both men and women sometimes go about with no covering at all on their head; sometimes they wear hats made of thin bamboo, and very frequently three feet in diameter; these keep off both sun and rain, and are exceedingly durable.

103

On their feet they wear sewed stockings and shoes, formed of black silk, or some material like worsted; the soles, which are more than an inch thick, are made up of layers of strong pasteboard or felt pasted together. The poor people go barefooted.

The houses of the lower classes are miserable hovels, built of wood or brick. The internal arrangements are very wretched: the whole furniture consists of a worthless table, a few chairs, and two or three bamboo-mats, stools for the head, and old counterpanes; yet, with this poverty, there are always sure to be some pots of flowers.

The cheapest mode of living is on board a boat. The husband goes on shore to his work, and leaves his wife to make a trifle by ferrying persons over, or letting out the boat to pleasure parties. One half the boat belongs to the family themselves, and the other half to the persons to whom they let it; and although there is not much room, the whole boat measuring scarcely twenty-five feet in length, the greatest order and cleanliness is everywhere apparent, as each single plank on board is thoroughly scrubbed and washed every morning. Great ingenuity is displayed in turning every inch of space on board these small craft to advantage, and the dexterity is actually pushed so far as to find room for a tiny domestic altar. During the day all the cookery and washing is done, and though at the latter process there is no want of little children, the temporary tenant of the boat does not suffer the least annoyance; nothing offensive meets his eye; and, at the most, he merely hears at rare intervals the whining voice of some poor little wretch. The youngest child is generally tied on its mother's back while she steers; the elder children, too, have sometimes similar burdens, but jump and climb about without the least consideration for them. It has often grieved me to the heart to see the head of an infant scarcely born, thrown from one side to the other with each movement of the child that was carrying it, or the sun darting so fiercely on the poor little creature, who was completely exposed to its rays, that it could hardly open its eyes. For those who have not been themselves witnesses of the fact, it is almost impossible to form an idea of the indigence and poverty of a Chinese boat-family.

The Chinese are accused of killing numbers of their new-born or weakly children. They are said to suffocate them immediately after their birth, and then throw them into the river, or expose them in the streets—by far the most horrible proceeding of the two, on account of the number of swine and houseless dogs, who fall upon, and voraciously devour, their prey. The most frequent victims are the female infants, as parents esteem themselves fortunate in possessing a large number of male children, the latter being bound to support them in their old age; the eldest son, in fact, should the father die, is obliged to take his place, and provide for his brothers and sisters, who, on their part, are bound to yield implicit obedience, and show him the greatest respect. These laws are very strictly observed, and any one infringing them is punished with death.

104

The Chinese consider it a great honour to be a grandfather, and every man who is fortunate enough to be one wears a moustache, as the distinctive sign of his good luck. These thin grey moustaches are the more conspicuous, as the young men not only wear none, but, as a general rule, grow no beard at all.

With regard to the social manners and customs of the Chinese, I am only able to mention a few, as it is exceedingly difficult, and, in fact, almost impossible, for a foreigner to become acquainted with them. I endeavoured to see as much as I could, and mixed on every possible opportunity among the people, afterwards writing down a true account of what I had seen.

On going out one morning, I met more than fifteen prisoners, all with a wooden yoke (*can-gue*) about their necks, being led through the streets. This yoke is composed of two large pieces of wood, fitting into one another, and having from one to three holes in them; through these holes the head, and one or both hands, are stuck, in proportion to the importance of the offence. A yoke of this description varies in weight from fifty to a hundred pounds, and presses so heavily upon the neck and shoulders of the poor wretch who bears it, that he is unable to convey his victuals to his mouth himself, and is compelled to wait till some compassionate soul feeds him. This punishment lasts from a few days to several months; in the latter case the prisoner generally dies.

Another description of punishment is the bastinado with the bamboo, which, when applied to the more tender parts of the body, very often, as early as the fifteenth blow, frees its victim for ever from all his earthly sufferings. Other more severe punishments, which in no way yield the palm to those of the Holy Inquisition, consist in flaying the prisoner alive, crushing his limbs, cutting the sinews out of his feet, and so on. Their modes of carrying out the sentence of death appear to be mild in comparison, and are generally confined to strangling and decapitation, although, as I was informed, in certain extraordinary cases, the prisoner is executed by being sawed in two, or left to die of starvation. In the first case, the unhappy victim is made fast between two planks, and sawed in two longitudinally, beginning with the head; and, in the second, he is either buried up to his head in the ground, and thus left to perish of want, or else is fastened in one of the wooden yokes I have described, while his food is gradually reduced in quantity every day, until at last it consists of only a few grains of rice. In spite of the horrible and cruel nature of these punishments, it is said that individuals are found ready, for a sum of money, to undergo them all, death even included, instead of the person condemned.

In the year 1846, 4,000 people were beheaded at Canton. It is true that they were the criminals of two provinces, which together numbered a population of 9,000,000 souls, but the number is still horrible to contemplate. Is it possible that there could really be so many who should be looked upon as criminals—or are persons sentenced to death for a mere nothing—or are both these suppositions true?

105

I once happened to go near the place of execution, and to my horror beheld a long row of still bleeding heads exposed upon high poles. The relations enjoy the privilege of carrying away and interring the bodies.

There are several different religions in China, the most prevalent being Buddhism. It is marked by great superstition and idolatry, and is mostly confined to the lower classes. The most natural is that of the wise Confucius, which is said to be the religion of the court, the public functionaries, the scholars, and educated classes.

The population of China is composed of a great many very different races: unfortunately, I am unable to describe their several characteristics, as my stay in China was far too short. The people I saw in Canton, Hong-Kong, and Macao, are of middling stature. Their complexion varies with their occupation: the peasants and labourers are rather sun-burnt; rich people and ladies white. Their faces are flat, broad, and ugly; their eyes are narrow, rather obliquely placed, and far apart; their noses broad, and their mouth large. Their fingers I observed were in many cases extremely long and thin; only the rich (of both sexes) allow their nails to grow to an extraordinary length, as a proof that they are not obliged, like their poorer brethren, to gain their livelihood by manual labour. These aristocratic nails are generally half an inch long, though I saw one man whose nails were quite an inch in length, but only on his left hand. With this hand it was impossible for him to raise any flat object, except by laying his hand flat upon it, and catching hold of it between his fingers.

The women of the higher classes are generally inclined to corpulency, a quality which is highly esteemed not in women alone, but in men as well.

Although I had heard a great deal about the small feet of Chinese women, I was greatly astonished at their appearance. Through the kind assistance of a missionary's lady (Mrs. Balt) I was enabled to behold one of these small feet *in naturâ*. Four of the toes were bent under the sole of the foot, to which they were firmly pressed, and with which they appeared to be grown together; the great toe was alone left in its normal state. The fore-part of the foot had been so compressed with strong broad bandages, that instead of expanding in length and breadth, it had shot upwards and formed a large lump at the instep, where it made part and parcel of the leg; the lower portion of the foot was scarcely four inches long, and an inch and a half broad. The feet are always swathed in white linen or silk, bound round with silk bandages and stuffed into pretty little shoes, with very high heels.

To my astonishment these deformed beings tripped about, as if in defiance of us broad-footed creatures, with tolerable ease, the only difference in their gait being that they waddled like geese; they even ran up and down stairs without the aid of a stick.

The only persons exempted from this Chinese method of improving their beauty are girls of the lowest class—that is, those who live in boats; in families of rank they are all subject to the same fate; while in those of the middle classes, as a general rule, it is limited to the eldest daughter.

The worth of a bride is reckoned by the smallness of her feet.

This process of mutilation is not commenced immediately the child is born, but is deferred until the end of the first, or sometimes even third year, nor is the foot after the operation forced into an iron shoe, as many have affirmed, but merely firmly compressed with bandages.

The religion of the Chinese allows them to have a number of wives, but in this respect they are far behind the Mahomedans. The richest have rarely more than from six to twelve, while poor persons content themselves with one.

I visited during my stay in Canton as many workshops of the different artists as I could. My first visit was to the most celebrated painters, and I must frankly own, that the vividness and splendour of their colouring struck me exceedingly. These qualities are generally ascribed to the rice paper on which they paint, and which is of the greatest possible fineness, and as white as milk.

The paintings upon linen and ivory differ very little, as far as the colouring is concerned, from those of our European artists, and the difference is therefore the more visible in their composition, and perspective, which, with the Chinese, are yet in a state of infancy. This is more especially true of perspective. The figures and objects in the back-ground rival in size and brilliancy those in front, while rivers or seas float in the place which should be occupied by clouds. On the other hand, the native artists can copy admirably, {101} and even take likenesses. I saw some portraits so strikingly well drawn, and admirably coloured, that first-rate European artists need not have been ashamed to own them.

The Chinese possess marvellous skill in carving ivory, tortoiseshell, and wood. Among the superior black lacquered articles, especially with flat or raised gold ornaments, I observed some, which were worthy of a place in the most valuable collections of objects of *vertu*. I saw some small work-tables worth at least 600 dollars (£120). The baskets and carpets, made from the bamboo, are also remarkably beautiful.

They are, however, far behind-hand in gold or silver work, which is generally heavy and tasteless; but then again, they have attained great celebrity by their porcelain, which is remarkable not only for its size, but for its transparency. It is true that vases and other vessels four feet high are neither light nor transparent; but cups and other small objects can only be compared to glass for fineness and transparency. The colours on them are very vivid, but the drawings very stiff and bad.

In the manufacture of silks and crape shawls, the Chinese are unsurpassable; the latter especially, in beauty, tastefulness, and thickness, are far preferable to those made in England or France.

107

The knowledge of music, on the other hand, is so little developed, that our good friends of the Celestial Empire might almost, in this respect, be compared to savages—not that they have no instruments, but they do not know how to use them. They possess violins, guitars, lutes (all with strings or wires), dulcimers, wind instruments, ordinary and kettle-drums, and cymbals, but are neither skilled in composition, melody, nor execution. They scratch, scrape, and thump upon their instruments in such a manner, as to produce the finest marrowbone-and-cleaver kind of music imaginable. During my excursions up and down the Pearl stream, I had frequent opportunities of hearing artistic performances of this description on board the mandarin and flower-boats.

In all kinds of deception the Chinese are great adepts, and decidedly more than a match for any Europeans. They have not the slightest sense of honour, and if you detect them, content themselves with saying: "You are more clever or cunning than I." I was told that when they have any live stock, such as calves or pigs, for sale, they compel them, as they are disposed of by weight, to swallow stones or large quantities of water. They also know how to blow out and dress stale poultry, so as to make it look quite fresh and plump.

But it is not the lower classes alone that indulge in cheating and fraud; these agreeable qualities are shared by the highest functionaries. It is a well-known fact, for instance, that there are nowhere so many pirates as in the Chinese sea, especially in the vicinity of Canton; yet no measures are taken to punish or extirpate them, simply because the mandarins do not think it beneath their dignity to secretly share in the profits.

For example, though the opium trade is forbidden, so much of this drug is smuggled in every year, that it is said to exceed in value that of all the tea exported in the same period. {102a} The merchants enter into a private understanding with the officers and mandarins, agreeing to give them a certain sum for every *pikul*, and it is no rare occurrence for a mandarin to land whole cargoes under the protection of his own flag.

In like manner there is said to be on one of the islands near Hong-Kong a very extensive manufactory of false money, which is allowed to be carried on without any interruption, as it pays a tribute to the public functionaries and mandarins. A short time ago, a number of pirate vessels that had ventured too near Canton, were shot into and sunk, the crews lost, and their leader taken. The owners of the vessels petitioned the government to set the prisoners free, and threatened, in case of a refusal, to make extensive disclosures. Every one was convinced that a sum of money accompanied this threatening letter, for shortly after it was reported that the prisoner had escaped.

I myself was witness of a circumstance in Canton, which caused me great uneasiness, and was a pretty good proof of the helplessness or apathy of the Chinese government.

On the 8th of August, Mr. Agassiz set out with a friend, intending to return the same evening. I was left at home alone with the Chinese servants. Mr. Agassiz did not return at the appointed time. At last, about 1 o'clock the next morning, I suddenly heard voices in loud conversation, and a violent knocking at the street door. I at first supposed it to be Mr. Agassiz, and felt much surprise at the late hour of his arrival, but I soon perceived that the disturbance was not in our house, but in that on the opposite side of the way. It is easy to fall into an error of this description, as the houses are situated quite close to each other, and windows are left open day and night. I heard voices exclaim, "Get up,—dress!" and then, "It is horrible—shocking—good heavens?—where did it happen?"—I sprang quickly out of bed and huddled on my gown, thinking either that a fire had broken out in some house or other, or that the people had risen in insurrection. {102b}

Seeing a gentleman at one of the windows, I called and inquired of him what was the matter. He told me hurriedly that intelligence had just arrived that two of his friends who were proceeding to Hong-Kong (Whampoa lay on the road) had been attacked by pirates, and that one was killed and the other wounded. He then immediately retired, so that I was unable to learn the name of the unfortunate victim, and was left all night a prey to the greatest anxiety lest it should be Mr. Agassiz.

Fortunately, this at least was not the case, as Mr. Agassiz returned at 5 o'clock in the morning. I then learned that this misfortune had happened to Monsieur Vauchée, a Swiss gentleman, who had passed many an evening in our house. On the very day of his departure, I met him at a neighbour's, where we had all been in the highest spirits, singing songs and quartettes. At 9 o'clock he went on board the boat, set off at 10, and a quarter of an hour afterwards, in the midst of thousands of schampans and other craft, met his tragical end.

Monsieur Vauchée had intended to proceed to Hong-Kong, and there embark on board a larger vessel for Shanghai; {103} he took with him Swiss watches to the value of 40,000 francs (£1,600), and, in speaking to a friend, congratulated himself on the cautious manner he had packed them up, without letting his servants know anything about it. This, however, could not have been the case: and, as the pirates have spies among the servants in every house, they were unfortunately but too well acquainted with the circumstance.

During my stay in Canton, the house of a European was pulled down by the populace, because it stood upon a piece of ground which, though Europeans were allowed to occupy, they had not hitherto built upon.

In this manner there was hardly a day that we did not hear of acts of violence and mischief, so that we were in a continual state of apprehension, more especially as the report of the near approach of a revolution, in which all the Europeans were to perish, was everywhere bruited about. Many of the merchants had made every preparation for instant flight, and muskets, pistols, and swords were neatly arranged ready for use in most of the counting-houses. Luckily, the time fixed for the revolution passed over, without the populace fulfilling its threats.

The Chinese are cowardly in the highest degree; they talk very large when they are certain they have nothing to fear. For instance, they are always ready to stone, or even kill, a few defenceless individuals, but if they have to fear any opposition, they are sure not to commence the attack. I believe that a dozen good European soldiers would put to flight more than a hundred Chinese. I myself never met with a more dastardly, false, and, at the same time, cruel race, in my life; one proof of this is, that their greatest pleasure consists in torturing animals.

In spite of the unfavourable disposition of the populace, I ventured out a good deal. Herr von Carlowitz was untiring in his kindness to me, and accompanied me everywhere, exposing himself to many dangers on my account, and bearing patiently the insults of the populace, who followed at our heels, and loudly expressed their indignation at the boldness of the European woman in thus appearing in public. Through his assistance, I saw more than any woman ever yet saw in China.

Our first excursion was to the celebrated Temple of Honan, which is said to be one of the finest in China.

This temple is surrounded by numerous out-buildings, and a large garden enclosed with a high wall. You first enter a large fore-court, at the extremity of which a colossal gateway leads into the inner courts. Under the archway of this portico are two War Gods, each eighteen feet high, in menacing attitudes, and with horribly distorted features. They are placed there to prevent evil spirits from entering. A second similar portico, under which are the four Celestial Kings, leads into the inmost court, where the principal temple is situated. The interior of the temple is 100 feet in length, and 100 feet in breadth. The flat roof, from which hang a number of glass chandeliers, lamps, artificial flowers, and silk ribbons, is supported upon several rows of wooden pillars, while the multitude of statues, altars, flower-pots, censers, candelabra, candlesticks, and other ornaments, involuntarily suggest to the mind of the spectator the decoration of a Roman Catholic church.

In the foreground are three altars, and behind these three statues, representing the God Buddha in three different aspects: the past, the present, and the future. These figures, which are in a sitting posture, are of colossal dimensions.

We happened to visit the temple just as service was being performed. It was a kind of mass for the dead, which a mandarin had ordered for his deceased wife. At the right and left altars were the priests, whose garments and gesticulations also resembled those of the Roman Catholics. At the middle altar was the mandarin, piously engaged in prayer, while two stood beside him, fanning him with large fans. {104} He frequently kissed the ground, and every time he did so, three wax tapers were presented to him, which he first elevated in the air, and then gave to one of the priests, who placed them before a statue of Buddha, but without lighting them. The music was performed by three men, one of whom twanged a stringed instrument, while the second struck a metal globe, and the third played the flute.

Besides the principal temple there are various smaller ones, and halls, all adorned with statues of gods. Especial honour is paid to the twenty-four Gods of Pity, and to Kwanfootse, a demi-god of War. Many of the former have four, six, and even eight arms. All these divinities, Buddha himself not excepted, are made of wood, gilt over, and painted with glazing colours.

In the Temple of Mercy we met with an adventure which was nearly attended with unpleasant consequences. A priest, or *bonze*, handed us some little tapers for us to light and offer to his divinity. Herr von Carlowitz and myself had already got the tapers in our hands, and were quite willing to afford him this gratification, when an American missionary, who was with us, tore the tapers from our grasp, and indignantly returned them to the priest, saying, that what we were about to do was an act of idolatry. The priest took the matter very seriously, and, instantly closing the doors, called his companions, who hurried in from all sides, and abused us in the most violent and vociferous fashion, pressing closer every instant. It was with the greatest difficulty that we succeeded in fighting our way to the door, and thus making our escape.

After this little fray, our guide conducted us to the dwelling of the Holy—Pigs! {105} A beautiful stone hall is set apart for their use, which hall these remarkable divinities fill, in spite of all the care bestowed on them, with so horrible a stench, that it is impossible to approach them without holding one's nose. They are taken care of and fed until death summons them away. When we visited the place there were only a pair of these fortunate beings, and their number rarely exceeds three couples.

I was better pleased with the residence of a bonze, which adjoined this holy spot. It consisted of a sitting-room and bed-room merely, but was very comfortably and elegantly fitted up. The walls of the sitting-room were ornamented with carved wood-work, and the furniture was old-fashioned and pleasing: at the back of the apartment, which was flagged, stood a small altar.

We here saw an opium-eater, lying stretched out upon a mat on the floor. At his side was a cup of tea, with some fruit and a little lamp, besides several pipes, with bowls that were smaller than a thimble. On our entrance, he was just inhaling the intoxicating smoke from one of them. It is said that some of the Chinese opium smokers consume from twenty to thirty grains a-day. As he was not altogether unconscious of our presence, he managed to raise himself, laid by his pipe, and dragged himself to a chair. His eyes were fixed and staring, and his face deadly pale, presenting altogether a most pitiable and wretched spectacle.

Last of all, we were conducted to the garden, where the bonzes, at their death, are burnt—a particular mark of distinction, as all other people are interred. A simple mausoleum, about thirty feet square, and a few small private monuments, were all that was to be seen. None of them had any pretensions to elegance, being built of the simplest masonry. In the former of these edifices are preserved the bones of the persons who have been burnt, and among them are also buried the rich Chinese, whose heirs pay pretty handsomely to obtain such an honour for them. At a little distance stands a small tower, eight feet in diameter and eighteen in height, with a small pit, where a fire can be kindled, in the floor. Over this pit is an armchair, to which the deceased bonze is fastened in full costume. Logs and dry brushwood are disposed all round, and the whole is set fire to, and the doors closed. In an hour they are again opened, the ashes strewed around the tower, and the bones preserved until the period for opening the mausoleum, which is only once every year.

A striking feature in the garden is this beautiful water-rose, or lotus-flower (*nymphæa nelumbo*), which was originally a native of China. The Chinese admire this flower so much, that they have ponds dug in their gardens expressly for it. It is about six inches in diameter, and generally white—very rarely pale red. The seeds resemble in size and taste those of the hazel; and the roots, when cooked, are said to taste like artichokes.

There are more than a hundred bonzes who reside in the temple of Honan. In their ordinary dress, they differ nothing from the common Chinamen, the only means of recognising them being by their heads, which are *entirely* shaved. Neither these nor any other priests can boast, as I was told, of being in the least respected by the people.

Our second excursion was to the Half-way Pagoda, so called by the English from its lying half way between Canton and Whampoa. We went up the Pearl stream to it. It stands upon a small eminence near a village, in the midst of immense fields of rice, and is composed of nine stories, 170 feet high. Its circumference is not very considerable, but nearly the same all the way up, which gives it the look of a tower. I was informed that this pagoda was formerly one of the most celebrated in China, but it has long ceased to be used. The interior was completely empty; there were neither statues nor any other ornaments; nor were there any floors to prevent the eye from seeing to the very top. On the outside, small balconies without railings surround each story, to which access is gained by steep and narrow flights of stairs. These projecting balconies produce a very fine effect, being built of coloured bricks, very artistically laid, and faced with variegated tiles. The bricks are placed in rows, with their points jutting obliquely outwards, so that the points project about four inches over one another. At a distance, the work seems as if it were half pierced through, and from the beautiful colours and fineness of the tiles, a person might easily mistake the entire mass for porcelain.

While we were viewing the pagoda, the whole population of the village had assembled round about us, and as they behaved with tolerable quietness, we determined on paying a visit to the village itself. The houses, or rather huts, were small and built of brick, and with the exception of their flat roofs, presented nothing peculiar. The rooms did not possess a ceiling of their own, but were simply covered by the roof; the floor was formed of earth closely pressed together, and the internal walls consisted partly of bamboo-mats. What little furniture there was, was exceedingly dirty. About the middle of the village was a small temple, with a few lamps burning dimly before the principal divinity.

What struck me most was the quantity of poultry, both in and out of the huts, and we had to take the greatest care to avoid treading on some of the young brood. The chickens are hatched, as they are in Egypt, by artificial heat.

On our return from the village to the pagoda, we saw two schampans run in shore, and a number of swarthy, half-naked, and mostly armed men jump out, and hasten through the fields of rice directly to where we were. We set them down as pirates, and awaited the upshot with a considerable degree of uneasiness. We knew that, if we were right in our supposition, we were lost without hope; for, at the distance we were from Canton, and entirely surrounded by Chinese, who would have been but too ready to lend them assistance, it would have been doubly easy for pirates to dispatch us. All idea of escape or rescue was out of the question.

While these thoughts were flashing across our minds, the men kept approaching us, and at length their leader introduced himself as the captain of a Siamese man-of-war. He informed us, in broken English, that he had not long arrived with the Governor of Bangkok, who was proceeding for the rest of the way to Pekin by land. Our fears were gradually dispelled, and we even accepted the friendly invitation of the captain to run alongside his ship and view it, on our return. He came in the boat with us, and took us on board, where he showed us everything himself: the sight, however, was not a particularly attractive one. The crew looked very rough and wild; they were all dressed in a most slovenly and dirty manner, so that it was utterly impossible to distinguish the officers from the common men. The vessel mounted twelve guns and sixty-eight hands.

The captain set before us Portuguese wine and English beer, and the evening was far advanced before we reached home.

The longest trip that can be made from Canton is one twenty miles up the Pearl stream, and Mr. Agassiz was kind enough to procure me this pleasure. He hired a good boat, which he furnished abundantly with eatables and drinkables, and invited a missionary, who had made the trip several times, Herr von Carlowitz, and myself. The company of a missionary is as yet by far the safest escort in China. These gentlemen speak the language; they become gradually acquainted with the people, and travel about, with hardly any obstacle to speak of, all round the vicinity of Canton.

About a week before we had decided on going, a few young gentlemen had

113

endeavoured to make the same excursion, but had been fired upon from one of the fortresses that lie on the banks of the river, and compelled to turn back half-way. When we approached the fortress in question, the crew of our boat refused to proceed any further, until we had almost employed violence to make them do so. We also were fired into, but fortunately not until we were more than half past the fortress. Having escaped the danger, we pursued our course without further interruption, landed at several hamlets, visited the so-called Herren Pagoda, and took a good view of everything that was to be seen. The scenery all round was charming, and displayed to our view large plains with rice, sugar, and tea-plantations, picturesque clumps of trees, lovely hills, and more elevated mountain ranges rising in the distance. On the declivities of the hills, we beheld a number of graves, which were marked by single, upright stones.

The Herren Pagoda has three stories, with a pointed roof, and is distinguished for its external sculpture. It has no balconies outside, but, instead of this, a triple wreath of leaves round each story. In the first and second story, to which access is gained by more than usually narrow stairs, are some small altars with carved idols. We were not allowed to go into the third story, under the excuse that there was nothing to be seen there.

The villages we visited, resembled more or less, that we had seen near the Half-way Pagoda.

During this journey I was an eye-witness of the manner in which the missionaries dispose of their religious tracts. The missionary who had been kind enough to accompany us, took this opportunity of distributing among the natives some seeds that should bring forth good fruit. He had 500 tracts on board our boat, and every time that another boat approached us, a circumstance that was of frequent occurrence, he stretched himself as far as possible over the side with half a dozen tracts in his hand, and made signs to the people to approach and take them. If people did not obey his summons, we rowed up to them, and the missionary gratified them with his tracts in dozens, and went his way rejoicing, in anticipation of the good which he did not doubt they would effect.

Whenever we arrived at a village, however, matters reached even a higher pitch. The servant was obliged to carry whole packs of tracts, which in a moment were distributed among the crowd of curious who had quickly gathered round us.

Every one took what was offered to him, as it cost nothing, and if he could not read it—the tracts were in Chinese—he had at least got so much paper. The missionary returned home delighted; he had disposed of his 500 copies. What glorious news for the Missionary Society, and what a brilliant article for his religious paper, he no doubt transmitted to Europe!

Six young Englishmen made this same excursion up the Pearl stream six months later, stopping at one of the villages and mixing with the people. Unhappily, however, they all fell victims to the fanaticism of the Chinese: they were most barbarously murdered.

There was now no trip of any distance left but one round the walls of the town of Canton, {108} properly so called. This, too, I was shortly enabled to undertake through the kindness of our good friend the missionary, who offered to come as guide to Herr von Carlowitz and myself, under the condition, however, that I should put on male attire. No woman had ever yet ventured to make this trip, and he thought that I ought not to venture in my own dress; I complied with his wish, therefore, and one fine morning early we set out.

For some distance our road lay through narrow streets or alleys paved with large flags. In a small niche somewhere in the front of every house, we saw little altars from one to three feet high, before which, as it was yet early, the night lamps were still burning. An immense quantity of oil is unnecessarily consumed in keeping up this religious custom. The shops now began to be opened. They resemble neat entrance halls, having no front wall. The goods were exposed for sale either in large open boxes or on tables, behind which the shopkeepers sit and work. In one corner of the shop, a narrow staircase leads up into the dwelling-house above.

Here, as in Turkish towns, the same regulation is observed of each trade or calling having its especial street, so that in one nothing but crockery and glass, in another silks, and so on, is to be seen. In the physician's street are situated all the apothecaries' shops as well, as the two professions are united in one and the same person. The provisions, which are very tastily arranged, have also their separate streets. Between the houses are frequently small temples, not differing the least, however, in style from the surrounding buildings: the gods, too, merely occupy the ground floor, the upper stories being inhabited by simple mortals.

The bustle in the streets was astonishing, especially in those set apart for the sale of provisions. Women and girls of the lower classes went about making their purchases, just as in Europe. They were all unveiled, and some of them waddled like geese, in consequence of their crippled feet, which, as I before observed, extends to all ranks. The crowd was considerably increased by the number of porters, with large baskets of provisions on their shoulders, running along, and praising in a loud voice their stock in trade, or warning the people to make way for them. At other times, the whole breadth of the street would be taken up, and the busy stream of human beings completely stopped by the litter of some rich or noble personage proceeding to his place of business. But worse than all were the numerous porters we met at every step we took, carrying large baskets of unsavoury matter.

It is a well known fact, that there is perhaps no nation on the face of the earth equal to the Chinese in diligence and industry, or that profits by, and cultivates, as they do, every available inch of ground. As, however, they have not much cattle, and consequently but little manure, they endeavour to supply the want of it by other means, and hence their great care of anything that can serve as a substitute.

115

All their small streets are built against the city walls, so that we had been going round them for some time before we were aware of the fact. Mean-looking gates or wickets, which all foreigners are strictly prohibited from passing, and which are shut in the evening, lead into the interior of the town.

I was told that it has often happened for sailors, or other strangers, during their walks, to penetrate through one of these entrances into the interior of the town, and not discover their mistake until the stones began flying about their ears.

After threading our way for at least two miles through a succession of narrow streets, we at length emerged into the open space, where we obtained a full view of the city walls, and from the summit of a small hill which was situated near them, a tolerably extensive one over the town itself. The city walls are about sixty feet high, and, for the most part, so overgrown with grass, creeping plants, and underwood, that they resemble a magnificent mass of living vegetation. The town resembles a chaos of small houses, with now and then a solitary tree, but we saw neither fine streets nor squares, nor any remarkable buildings, temples, or pagodas. A single pagoda, five stories high, reminded us of the peculiar character of Chinese architecture.

Our road now lay over fertile eminences, varied with fields and meadows in a high state of cultivation. Many of the hills are used as cemeteries, and are dotted over with small mounds of earth, walled in with stone flags, or rough hewn stones two feet high, frequently covered with inscriptions. Family tombs were also to be seen, dug in the hill, and enclosed with stone walls of the shape of a horse-shoe. All the entrances were built up with stone.

The Chinese do not, however, bury all their dead: they have a remarkable way of preserving them in small stone chambers, consisting of two stone walls and a roof, while the two other sides are left open. In these places, there are never more than from two to four coffins, which are placed upon wooden benches two feet high: the coffins themselves consist of massive trunks of trees hollowed out.

The villages through which we passed presented an animated appearance, but appeared poor and dirty. We were often obliged to hold our noses in passing through the lanes and squares, and very frequently would fain have closed our eyes as well, to avoid the disgusting sight of people covered with eruptions of the skin, tumours, and boils.

In all the villages I saw poultry and swine in great numbers, but not more than three horses and a buffalo-cow; both the horses and the cow were of an extremely small breed.

When we had nearly reached the end of our excursion, we met a funeral. A horrible kind of music gave us warning that something extraordinary was approaching, and we had hardly time to look up and step on one side, before the procession came flying past us at full speed. First came the worthy musicians, followed by a few Chinese, next two empty litters carried by porters, and then the

116

hollow trunk of a tree, representing the coffin, hanging to a long pole, and carried in a similar manner: last of all, were some priests and a crowd of people.

The chief priest wore a kind of white {110} fool's cap, with three points; the other persons, who consisted of men alone, had a kind of white cloth bound round their head or arm.

I was lucky enough to be enabled to visit some of the summer palaces and gardens of the nobility.

The finest of all was certainly that belonging to the Mandarin Howqua. The house itself was tolerably spacious, one story high, with very wide, splendid terraces. The windows looked into the inner courts, and the roof was like those in European buildings, only much flatter. The sloping roofs, with their multitude of points and pinnacles, with their little bells and variegated tiles, are only to be found in the temples and country-houses, but never in the usual residences. At the entrance there were two painted gods: these, according to the belief of the Chinese, keep off evil spirits.

The front part of the house consisted of several reception rooms, without front walls, and immediately adjoining them, on the ground floor, elegant parterres; and on the first floor magnificent terraces, which were also decorated with flowers, and afforded a most splendid view over the animated scene on the river, the enchanting scenery around, and the mass of houses in the villages situated about the walls of Canton.

Neat little cabinets surrounded these rooms, from which they were only separated by walls that in many cases were adorned with the most artistic paintings, and through which the eye could easily penetrate. The most remarkable of these walls were those composed of bamboos, which were as delicate as a veil, and plentifully ornamented with painted flowers, or beautifully written proverbs.

A numberless quantity of chairs and a great many sofas were ranged along the walls, from which I inferred that the Chinese are as much accustomed to large assemblages as ourselves. I observed some arm-chairs most skilfully cut out of a single piece of wood; others with seats of beautiful marble-slabs; and others again of fine coloured tiles or porcelain. Among various objects of European furniture, we saw some handsome mirrors, clocks, vases, and tables of Florentine mosaic, or variegated marble. There was also a most extraordinary collection of lamps and lanterns hanging from the ceilings, and consisting of glass, transparent horn, and coloured gauze or paper, ornamented with glass beads, fringe, and tassels. Nor was there any scarcity of lamps on the walls, so that when the apartments are entirely lighted up, they must present a fairy-like appearance.

As we had been fortunate enough to reach this house without being stoned, we were emboldened to visit the Mandarin Howqua's large pleasure-garden, situated on a branch of the Pearl stream, about three-quarters of a mile from the house. We had, however, hardly entered the branch of the river, before the crew wanted to turn back, having observed a mandarin's junk, with all its flags hoisted, a signal that the owner himself was on board. They were unwilling to venture on conveying us Europeans past the vessel, for fear they should be punished, or stoned to death, along with ourselves, by the people. We obliged them to proceed, passed close by the junk, and then landed, and continued our excursion on foot. A large crowd of people soon collected in our rear, and began pushing the children up against us, in order to excite our rage; but arming ourselves with patience, we moved quietly on, and reached, without any accident, the garden gates, which we instantly closed behind us.

The garden was in a perfect state of cultivation, but without the least pretension to taste in its arrangement. On every side were summer-houses, kiosks, and bridges, and all the paths and open spots were lined with large and small flower-pots, in which were flowers and dwarfed fruit-trees of every description.

The Chinese are certainly adepts in the art of diminishing the size of, or rather crippling their trees, many of which very often scarcely attain a height of three feet. These dwarf trees are very prevalent in their gardens, and preferred to the most magnificent and shady trees of a natural size. These lilliputian alleys can hardly be considered in good taste, but it is most remarkable with what a large quantity of beautiful fruit the tiny branches are laden.

Besides these toys we also observed figures of all descriptions, representing ships, birds, fish, pagodas, etc., cut out of foliage. In the heads of the animals were stuck eggs, with a black star painted on them to represent the eyes.

There was also no scarcity of rocks, both single and in groups, ornamented with flower-pots, as well as little figures of men and animals, which can be removed at pleasure, so as to form new combinations, a kind of amusement of which the Chinese ladies are said to be very fond. Another source of entertainment, no less popular, as well among the ladies as the gentlemen, consists in kite-flying, and they will sit for hours looking at their paper monsters in the air. There is a large open spot set apart for this purpose in the garden of every Chinese nobleman. We noticed an abundance of running water and ponds, but we did not observe any fountains.

As everything had passed off so well, Herr von Carlowitz proposed that we should go and see the garden of the Mandarin Puntiqua, which I was very anxious to do, as the mandarin had ordered a steam-boat to be built there by a Chinese, who had resided thirteen years in North America, where he had studied.

The vessel was so far advanced that it was to be launched in a few weeks. The artist showed us his work with great satisfaction, and was evidently very much pleased at the praise we bestowed upon him for it. He attached great importance to his knowledge of the English language, for when Herr von Carlowitz addressed him in Chinese, he answered in English, and requested us to continue the conversation in that idiom. The machinery struck us as not being constructed with the usual degree of neatness for which the Chinese are famous, and also appeared far too large for the small vessel for which it was intended. Neither I nor my companion would have had the courage to have gone in her on her experimental trip.

The mandarin who had the vessel built, had gone to Pekin to obtain a "button" as his reward for being the first person to launch a steamer in the Chinese empire. The builder himself will, in all probability, be obliged to rest contented with the consciousness of his talent.

From the ship-yard we proceeded to the garden, which was very large but greatly neglected. There were neither alleys nor fruit trees, rocks nor figures; but, to make up for these, an insufferable quantity of summer-houses, bridges, galleries, little temples, and pagodas.

The dwelling-house consisted of a large hall and a number of small chambers. The walls were ornamented, both inside and out, with carved wood-work, and the roof abundantly decorated with points and pinnacles.

In the large halls plays and other entertainments are sometimes enacted for the amusement of the ladies, who are universally confined to their houses and gardens, which can only be visited by strangers in their absence. {112}

A number of peacocks, silver-pheasants, mandarin-ducks, and deer are preserved in their gardens. In one corner was a small, gloomy bamboo plantation, in which were some family graves; and not far off a small earthen mound had been raised, with a wooden tablet, on which was a long poetical inscription in honour of the favourite snake of the mandarin, which was buried there.

After duly inspecting everything, we set off on our road home, and reached there in safety.

I was not so fortunate a few days later on visiting a tea-factory. The proprietor conducted me himself over the workshops, which consisted of large halls, in which six hundred people, including a great many old women and children, were at work. My entrance occasioned a perfect revolt. Old and young rose from work, the elder portion lifting up the younger members of the community in their arms and pointing at me with their fingers. The whole mass then pressed close upon me and raised so horrible a cry that I began to be alarmed. The proprietor and his overseer had a difficult task to keep off the crowd, and begged me to content myself with a hasty glance at the different objects, and then to quit the building as soon as possible.

In consequence of this I could only manage to observe that the leaves of the plant are thrown for a few seconds into boiling water, and then placed in flat iron pans, fixed slantingly in stone-work, where they are slightly roasted by a gentle

119

heat, during which process they are continually stirred by hand. As soon as they begin to curl a little, they are thrown upon large planks, and each single leaf is rolled together. This is effected with such rapidity, that it requires a person's undivided attention to perceive that no more than one leaf is rolled up at a time. After this, all the leaves are placed once more in the pan. Black tea takes some time to roast, and the green is frequently coloured with Prussian blue, an exceedingly small quantity of which is added during the second roasting. Last of all the tea is once more shaken out upon the large boards, in order that it may be carefully inspected, and the leaves that are not entirely closed are rolled over again.

Before I left, the proprietor conducted me into his house, and treated me to a cup of tea prepared after the fashion in which it is usually drunk by rich and noble Chinese. A small quantity was placed in a China cup, boiling water poured upon it, and the cup then closed with a tightly-fitting cover. In a few seconds the tea is then drank and the leaves left at the bottom. The Chinese take neither sugar, rum, nor milk with their tea; they say that anything added to it, and even the stirring of it, causes it to lose its aroma; in my cup, however, a little sugar was put.

The tea-plant, which I saw in the plantations round about Canton, was at most six feet high; it is not allowed to grow any higher, and is consequently cut at intervals. Its leaves are used from the third to the eighth year; and the plant is then cut down, in order that it may send forth new shoots, or else it is rooted out. There are three gatherings in the year; the first in March, the second in April, and the third, which lasts for three months, in May. The leaves of the first gathering are so delicate and fine that they might easily be taken for the blossom, which has no doubt given rise to the error that the so-called "bloom or imperial tea" is supposed not to consist of the leaves but of the blossom itself. {114} This gathering is so hurtful to the plant that it often perishes.

I was informed that the tea which comes from the neighbourhood of Canton is the worst, and that from the provinces somewhat more to the north the best. The tea manufacturers of Canton are said to possess the art of giving tea that has been frequently used, or spoiled by rain, the appearance of good tea. They dry and roast the leaves, colour them yellow with powdered kurkumni, or light green with Prussian blue, and then roll them tightly up. The price of the tea sent to Europe varies from fifteen to sixty dollars (£3 to £12) a pikul, of 134 lb. English weight. The kind at sixty dollars does not find a very ready market; the greater part of it is exported to England. The "bloom" is not met with in trade.

I must mention a sight which I accidentally saw, one evening, upon the Pearl stream. It was, as I afterwards heard, a thanksgiving festival in honour of the gods, by the owners of two junks that had made a somewhat long sea voyage without being pillaged by pirates, or overtaken by the dangerous typhoon.

Two of the largest flower boats, splendidly illuminated, were floating gently down the stream. Three rows of lamps were hung round the upper part of the vessels, forming perfect galleries of fire; all the cabins were full of chandeliers and lamps, and on the forecastle large fires were burning out of which rockets darted at intervals with a loud report, although they only attained the elevation of a few feet. On the foremost vessel there was a large mast erected, and hung with myriads of coloured paper lamps up to its very top, forming a beautiful pyramid. Two boats, abundantly furnished with torches and provided with boisterous music, preceded these two fiery masses. Slowly did they float through the darkness of the night, appearing like the work of fairy hands. Sometimes they stopped, when high flames, fed with holy perfumed paper, flickered upwards to the sky.

Perfumed paper, which must be bought from the priests, is burnt at every opportunity, and very frequently beforehand, after every prayer. From the trade in this paper the greater portion of the priests' income is derived.

On several occasions, accompanied by Herr von Carlowitz, I took short walks in the streets near the factory. I found the greater pleasure in examining the beautiful articles of Chinese manufacture, which I could here do at my leisure, as the shops were not so open as those I saw during my excursion round the walls of Canton, but had doors and windows like our own, so that I could walk in and be protected from the pressure of the crowd. The streets, also, in this quarter were somewhat broader, well paved, and protected with mats or planks to keep off the burning heat of the sun.

In the neighbourhood of the factory, namely in Fousch-an, where most of the manufactories are situated, a great many places may be reached by water, as the streets, like those in Venice, are intersected by canals. This quarter of Canton, however, is not the handsomest, because all the warehouses are erected on the sides of the canals, where the different workmen have also taken up their residence in miserable huts that, built half upon the ground and half upon worm-eaten piles, stretch far out over the water.

I had now been altogether, from July 13th to August 20th, five weeks in Canton. The season was the hottest in the whole year, and the heat was really insupportable. In the house, the glass rose as high as $94\frac{1}{2}°$, and out of doors, in the shade, as high as $99°$. To render this state of things bearable, the inhabitants use, besides the punkas in the rooms, wicker-work made of bamboo. This wicker-work is placed before the windows and doors, or over those portions of the roofs under which the workshops are situated. Even whole walls are formed of it, standing about eight or ten feet from the real ones, and provided with entrances, window-openings, and roofs. The houses are most effectually disguised by it.

On my return to Hong-Kong, I again set out on board a junk, but not so fearlessly as the first time; the unhappy end of Monsieur Vauchée was still fresh in my memory. I took the precaution of packing up the few clothes and linen I had in the presence of the servants, that they might be convinced that any trouble the pirates might give themselves on my account would be thrown away.

121

On the evening of the 20th of August I bade Canton, and all my friends there, farewell; and at 9 o'clock I was once again floating down the Si-Kiang, or Pearl stream, famous for the deeds of horror perpetrated on it.

CHAPTER IX. THE EAST INDIES—SINGAPORE.

ARRIVAL IN HONG-KONG—THE ENGLISH STEAMER—SINGAPORE PLANTATIONS—A HUNTING PARTY IN THE JUNGLE—A CHINESE FUNERAL—THE FEAST OF LANTERNS—TEMPERATURE AND CLIMATE.

The passage from Canton to Hong-Kong was accomplished without any circumstance worthy of notice, save the time it took, in consequence of the prevalence of contrary winds the whole way. We were, it is true, woke up the first night by the report of guns; but I expect they were not fired at us, as we were not molested. My travelling companions, the Chinese, also behaved themselves on this occasion with the greatest politeness and decorum; and, had I been enabled to look into the future, I would willingly have given up the English steamer and pursued my journey as far as Singapore on board a junk. But as this was impossible, I availed myself of the English steamer, "Pekin," of 450 horse-power, Captain Fronson commander, which leaves for Calcutta every month.

As the fares are most exorbitant, {116} I was advised to take a third-class ticket, and hire a cabin from one of the engineers or petty officers; I was greatly pleased with the notion, and hastened to carry it out. My astonishment, however, may be imagined when, on paying my fare, I was told that the third-class passengers were not respectable, that they were obliged to sleep upon deck, and that the moon was exceedingly dangerous, etc. It was in vain that I replied I was the best judge of my own actions; I was obliged, unless I chose to remain behind, to pay for one of the second places. This certainly gave me a very curious idea of English liberty.

On the 25th of August, at 1 o'clock, P.M., I went on board. On reaching the vessel I found no servant in the second places, and was obliged to ask a sailor to take my luggage into the cabin. This latter was certainly anything but comfortable. The furniture was of the most common description, the table was covered with stains and dirt, and the whole place was one scene of confusion. I inquired for the sleeping cabin, and found there was but one for both sexes. I was told to apply to one of the officials, who would no doubt allow me to sleep somewhere else. I did so, and obtained a neat little cabin in consequence, and the steward was kind enough to propose that I should take my meals with his wife. I did not, however, choose to accept the offer; I paid dearly enough, Heaven knows, and did not choose to accept everything as a favour. Besides, this was the first English steamer I had ever been on board, and I was curious to learn how second-class passengers were treated.

The company at our table consisted not only of the passengers, of whom there were three besides myself, but of the cooks and waiters of the first-class places, as well as of the butcher; or, in a word, of every one of the attendants who chose to take "pot-luck" with us. As for any etiquette in the article of costume, that was entirely out of the question. Sometimes one of the company would appear without either coat or jacket; the butcher was generally oblivious of his shoes and stockings; and it was really necessary to be endowed with a ravenous appetite to be enabled to eat anything with such a set.

The bill of fare was certainly adapted to the crew and their costume, but decidedly not to the passengers, who had to pay thirteen dollars (£2 12s.) a day each for provisions.

The table-cloth was full of stains, and, in lieu of a napkin, each guest was at liberty to use his handkerchief. The knives and forks had white and black horn handles, with notched blades, and broken prongs. On the first day we had no spoons at all; on the second we had one between us, and this one was placed on the table in solitary grandeur during the entire voyage. There were only two glasses, and those of the most ordinary description, which circulated from mouth to mouth; as I was a female, instead of my turn of the glasses, I had, as a peculiar mark of distinction, an old tea-cup with the handle knocked off.

The head cook, who did the honours, pleaded in excuse for all this discomfort, that they happened this voyage to be short of servants. This struck me as really a little too *naïve*, for when I paid my money I paid for what I ought to have then, and not for what I might have another time.

As I said before, the provisions were execrable; the remnants of the first cabin were sent to us poor wretches. Two or three different things would very often be side by side in the most friendly and brotherly manner upon one dish, even although their character was widely different; that was looked upon as a matter of no import, which was also the case as to whether the things came to table hot or cold.

On one occasion, during tea, the head cook was in unusually good humour, and remarked, "I spare no possible pains to provide for you. I hope you want for nothing." Two of the passengers, Englishmen, replied, "No, that's true!" The third, who was a Portuguese, did not understand the importance of the assertion. As a native of Germany, not possessing the patriotic feeling of an English subject in the matter, I should have replied very differently had I not been a women, and if, by so replying, I could have effected a change for the better.

The only light we had was from a piece of tallow candle, that often went out by eight o'clock. We were then under the necessity of sitting in the dark or going to bed.

123

In the morning the cabin served as a barber's shop, and in the afternoon as a dormitory, where the cooks and servants, who were half dead with sleep, used to come and slumber on the benches.

In order to render us still more comfortable, one of the officers pitched upon our cabin as quarters for two young puppies, who did nothing but keep up one continued howl; he would not have dared to put them in the sailors' cabin, because the latter would have kicked them out without farther ceremony.

My description will, in all probability, be considered exaggerated, especially as there is an old opinion that the English are, above all other people, justly celebrated for their comfort and cleanliness. I can, however, assure my readers that I have spoken nothing but the truth; and I will even add that, although I have made many voyages on board steam-ships, and always paid second fare, never did I pay so high a price for such wretched and detestable treatment. In all my life I was never so cheated. The only circumstance on board the ship to which I can refer with pleasure was the conduct of the officers, who were, without exception, obliging and polite.

I was very much struck with the remarkable degree of patience exhibited by my fellow-passengers. I should like to know what an Englishman, who has always got the words "comfort" and "comfortable" at the top of his tongue, would say, if he were treated in this manner on board a steamer belonging to any other nation?

For the first few days of our voyage we saw no land, and it was not until the 28th of August that we caught sight of the rocky coast of Cochin China. During the whole of the 29th we steered close along the coast, but could see no signs of either human beings or habitations, the only objects visible being richly wooded mountain-ranges; in the evening, however, we beheld several fires, which might have been mistaken for the signals from lighthouses, and proved that the country was not quite uninhabited.

During the following day we only saw a large solitary rock called "The Shoe." It struck me as being exactly like the head of a shepherd's dog.

On the 2nd of September we neared Malacca. Skirting the coast are tolerably high, well-wooded mountain-ranges, infested, according to all accounts, by numerous tigers, that render all travelling very dangerous.

On the 3rd of September we ran into the port of Singapore; but it was so late in the evening, that we could not disembark.

On the following morning I paid a visit to the firm of Behu and Meyer, to whom I had letters of introduction. Madame Behu was the first German lady I had met since my departure from Hamburgh. I cannot say how delighted I was at forming her acquaintance. I was once more able to give free vent to my feelings in my own native tongue. Madame Behu would not hear of my lodging in an hotel; I was immediately installed as a member of her own amiable family. My original plan was to have remained but a short period in Singapore, and then proceed in a sailing vessel to Calcutta, as I had a perfect horror of English steamers, and as I had been told that opportunities continually presented themselves. I waited, however, week after week in vain, until, in spite of my unwillingness, I was obliged to embark in a comfortable English steamer at last. {118}

The Europeans lead pretty much the same kind of life at Singapore that they do at Canton, with this difference, however, that the merchants reside with their families in the country, and come to town every morning for business. Each family is obliged to keep a large staff of servants, and the lady of the house meddles very little in domestic matters, as these are generally altogether entrusted to the major-domo.

The servants are Chinese, with the exception of the *seis* (coachmen or grooms), who are Bengalese. Every spring, whole shiploads of Chinese boys, from ten to fifteen years old, come over here. They are generally so poor that they cannot pay their passage. When this is the case, the captain brings them over on his own account, and is paid beforehand, by the person engaging them, their wages for the first year. These young people live very economically, and when they have a little money, return generally to their native country, though many hire themselves as journeymen, and stop altogether.

The Island of Singapore has a population of 55,000 souls, 40,000 of whom are Chinese, 10,000 Malays, or natives, and 150 Europeans. The number of women is said to be very small, in consequence of the immigrants from China and India consisting only of men and boys.

The town of Singapore and its environs contain upwards of 20,000 inhabitants. The streets struck me as being broad and airy, but the houses are not handsome. They are only one story high; and, from the fact of the roof's being placed directly above the windows, appear as if they were crushed. On account of the continual heat, there is no glass in any of the windows, but its place is supplied by sun-blinds.

Every article of merchandise has here, as at Canton, if not its own peculiar street, at least its own side of the street. The building in which meat and vegetables are sold, is a fine handsome edifice resembling a temple.

As a natural result of the number of persons of different nations congregated upon this island, there are various temples, none of which are worthy of notice, however, with the exception of that belonging to the Chinese. It is formed like an ordinary house, but the roof is ornamented in the usual Chinese fashion to rather too great an extent. It is loaded with points and pinnacles, with circles and curves without end, all of which are formed of coloured tiles or porcelain, and decorated with an infinity of arabesques, flowers, dragons, and other monsters. Over the principal entrance are small stone bas-reliefs, and both the exterior and interior of the building can boast of a profusion of carved wood-work richly gilt.

125

Some fruit and biscuits of various descriptions, with a very small quantity of boiled rice, were placed upon the altar of the Goddess of Mercy. These are renewed every evening, and whatever the goddess may leave is the perquisite of the bonzes. On the same altar lay pretty little wooden counters cut in an oval shape, which the Chinese toss up in the air; it is held to be a sign of ill-luck if they fall upon the reverse side, but if they fall upon the other, this is believed to betoken good fortune. The worthy people are in the habit of tossing them up until they fall as desired.

Another manner of learning the decrees of fate consists in placing a number of thin wooden sticks in a basin, and then shaking them until one falls out. Each of these sticks is inscribed with a certain number, corresponding with a sentence in a book of proverbs. This temple was more frequented by the people than those in Canton. The counters and sticks seemed to exercise great influence over the congregation, for it was only round them that they gathered.

There is nothing further to be seen in the town, but the environs, or rather the whole island, offers the most enchanting sight. The view cannot certainly be called magnificent or grand, since one great feature necessary to give it this character, namely, mountains, is entirely wanting. The highest hill, on which the governor's house and the telegraph are situated, is scarcely more than 200 feet high, but the luxuriant verdancy, the neat houses of the Europeans in the midst of beautiful gardens, the plantations of the most precious spices, the elegant areca and feathered palms, with their slim stems shooting up to a height of a hundred feet, and spreading out into the thick feather-like tuft of fresh green, by which they are distinguished from every other kind of palms, and, lastly, the jungle in the back-ground, compose a most beautiful landscape, and which appears doubly lovely to a person like myself, just escaped from that prison ycleped Canton, or from the dreary scenery about the town of Victoria.

The whole island is intersected with excellent roads, of which those skirting the sea-shore are the most frequented, and where handsome carriages, and horses from New Holland, and even from England, {120a} are to be seen. Besides the European carriages, there are also certain vehicles of home manufacture called palanquins, which are altogether closed and surrounded on all sides with jalousies. Generally, there is but one horse, at the side of which both the coachman and footman run on foot. I could not help expressing my indignation at the barbarity of this custom, when I was informed that the residents had wanted to abolish it, but that the servants had protested against it, and begged to be allowed to run beside the carriage rather than sit or stand upon it. They cling to the horse or vehicle, and are thus dragged along with it.

Hardly a day passed that we did not drive out. Twice a week a very fine military band used to play on the esplanade close to the sea, and the whole world of fashionables would either walk or drive to the place to hear the music. The carriages were ranged several rows deep, and surrounded by young beaux on foot and horseback; any one might have been excused for imagining himself in an European city. As for myself, it gave me more pleasure to visit a plantation, or some other place of the kind, than to stop and look on what I had so often witnessed in Europe. {120b}

I frequently used to visit the plantations of nutmegs and cloves, and refresh myself with their balsamic fragrance. The nutmeg-tree is about the size of a fine apricot-bush, and is covered from top to bottom with thick foliage; the branches grow very low down the stem, and the leaves shine as if they were varnished. The fruit is exactly similar to an apricot covered with yellowish-brown spots. When ripe it bursts, exposing to view a round kernel about the size of a nut, enclosed in a kind of net-work of a fine deep red: this network is known as mace. It is carefully separated from the nutmeg itself, and dried in the shade. While undergoing this process, it is frequently sprinkled with sea-water, to prevent its original tint turning black instead of yellow. In addition to this net-work, the nutmeg is covered with a thin, soft rind. The nutmeg itself is also dried, then smoke-dried a little, and afterwards, to prevent its turning mouldy, dipped several times in sea-water, containing a weak solution of lime.

The clove-tree is somewhat smaller, and cannot boast of such luxuriant foliage, or such fine large leaves as the nutmeg-tree. The cloves are the buds of the tree gathered before they have had time to blossom. They are first smoked, and then laid for a short time in the sun.

Another kind of spice is the areca-nut, which hangs under the crown of the palm of the same name, in groups containing from ten to twenty nuts each. It is somewhat larger than a nutmeg, and its outer shell is of so bright a colour, that it resembles the gilt nuts which are hung upon the Christmas-trees in Germany. The kernel is almost the same colour as the nutmeg, but it has no net-work: it is dried in the shade.

The Chinese and natives of the place chew this nut with betel-leaf and calcined mussel-shells. They strew the leaf with a small quantity of the mussel-powder, to which they add a very small piece of the nut, and make the whole into a little packet, which they put into their mouth. When they chew tobacco at the same time, the saliva becomes as red as blood, and their mouths, when open, look like little furnaces, especially if, as is frequently the case with the Chinese, the person has his teeth dyed and filed. The first time I saw a case of the kind I was very frightened: I thought the poor fellow had sustained some serious injury, and that his mouth was full of blood.

I also visited a sago manufactory. The unprepared sago is imported from the neighbouring island of Borromeo, and consists of the pith of a short, thick kind of palm. The tree is cut down when it is seven years old, split up from top to bottom, and the pith, of which there is always a large quantity, extracted; it is then freed from the fibres, pressed in large frames, and dried at the fire or in the sun. At this period it has still a yellowish tinge. The following is the manner in which it

127

is grained: The meal or pith is steeped in water for several days, until it is completely blanched; it is then once more dried by the fire or in the sun, and passed under a large wooden roller, and through a hair sieve. When it has become white and fine, it is placed in a kind of linen winnowing-fan, which is kept damp in a peculiar manner. The workman takes a mouthful of water, and spurts it out like fine rain over the fan, in which the meal is alternately shaken and moistened in the manner just mentioned, until it assumes the shape of small globules, which are constantly stirred round in large, flat pans until they are dried, when they are passed through a second sieve, not quite so fine as the first, and the larger globules separated from the rest.

The building in which the process takes place is a large shed without walls, its roof being supported upon the trunks of trees.

I was indebted to the kindness of the Messrs. Behu and Meyer for a very interesting excursion into the jungle. The gentlemen, four in number, all well provided with fowling-pieces, having determined to start a tiger, besides which they were obliged to be prepared for bears, wild boars, and large serpents. We drove as far as the river Gallon, where we found two boats in readiness for us, but, before entering them, paid a visit to a sugar-refining establishment situated upon the banks of the river.

The sugar-cane was piled up in stacks before the building, but there had only been sufficient for a day's consumption, as all that remained would have turned sour from the excessive heat. The cane is first passed under metal cylinders, which press out all the juice; this runs into large cauldrons, in which it is boiled and then allowed to cool. It is afterwards placed in earthen jars, where it becomes completely dry.

The buildings resembled those I have described when speaking of the preparation of sago.

After we had witnessed the process of sugar-baking, we entered the boats, and proceeded up the stream. We were soon in the midst of the virgin forests, and experienced, at every stroke of the oars, greater difficulty in forcing our passage, on account of the numerous trunks of trees both in and over the stream. We were frequently obliged to land and lift the boats over these trees, or else lie flat down, and thus pass under them as so many bridges. All kinds of brushwood, full of thorns and brambles, hung down over our heads, and even some gigantic leaves proved a serious obstacle to us. These leaves belonged to a sort of palm called the Mungkuang. Near the stem they are five inches broad, but their length is about twelve feet, and as the stream is scarcely more than nine feet wide, they reached right across it.

The natural beauty of the scene was so great, however, that these occasional obstructions, so far from diminishing, actually heightened the charm of the whole. The forest was full of the most luxuriant underwood, creepers, palms, and

128

fern plants; the latter, in many instances sixteen feet high, proved a no less effectual screen against the burning rays of the sun than did the palms and other trees.

My previous satisfaction was greatly augmented on seeing several apes skipping about on the highest branches of the trees, while others were heard chattering in our immediate vicinity. This was the first time I had seen these animals in a state of perfect freedom, and I secretly felt very much delighted that the gentlemen with me did not succeed in shooting any of the mischievous little creatures: they brought down, however, a few splendid lories (a sort of small parrot of the most beautiful plumage) and some squirrels. But our attention was soon attracted by a much more serious object. We remarked in the branches of one of the trees a dark body, which, on nearer inspection, we found to be that of a large serpent, lying coiled up, and waiting, probably, to dart upon its prey. We ventured pretty near, but it remained quite motionless without turning its eyes from us, and little thinking how near its death was. One of the gentlemen fired, and hit it in the side. As quick as lightning, and with the greatest fury, it darted from the tree, but remained fast, with its tail entangled in a bough. It kept making springs at us, with its forked tongue exposed to view, but all in vain, as we kept at a respectable distance. A few more shots put an end to its existence, and we then pulled up under the bough on which it was hanging. One of the boatmen, a Malay, made a small noose of strong, tough grass, which he threw round the head of the serpent, and thus dragged it into the boat. He also told us that we should be sure to find a second not far off, as serpents of this kind always go in pairs, and, true enough, the gentlemen in the other boat had already shot the second, which was also coiled up on the branch of a large tree.

These serpents were of a dark green colour, with beautiful yellow streaks, and about twelve feet in length. I was told that they belonged to the boa species.

After having proceeded eight English miles in four hours, we left the boats, and following a narrow footpath, soon reached a number of plots of ground, cleared from trees, and planted with pepper and gambir.

The pepper-tree is a tall bush-like plant, that, when trained and supported with props, will attain a height varying from fifteen to eighteen feet. The pepper grows in small, grape-like bunches, which are first red, then green, and lastly, nearly black. The plant begins to bear in the second year.

White pepper is not a natural production, but is obtained by dipping the black pepper several times in sea-water: this causes it to lose its colour, and become a dirty white. The price of a pikul of white pepper is six dollars (24s.), whereas that of a pikul of black is only three dollars (12s.).

The greatest height attained by the gambir plant is eight feet. The leaves alone are used in trade: they are first stripped off the stalk, and then boiled down in large coppers. The thick juice is placed in wide wooden vessels, and dried in the sun; it

129

is then cut into slips three inches long and packed up. Gambir is an article that is very useful in dyeing, and hence is frequently exported to Europe. Pepper plantations are always to be found near a plantation of the gambir plant, as the former are always manured with the boiled leaves of the latter.

Although all the work on the plantations, as well as every other description of labour at Singapore, is performed by free labourers, I was told that it cost less than if it were done by slaves. The wages here are very trifling indeed; a common labourer receives three dollars a month, without either board or lodging; and yet with this, he is enabled not only to subsist himself, but to maintain a family. Their huts, which are composed of foliage, they build themselves; their food consists of small fish, roots, and a few vegetables. Nor is their apparel more expensive; for, beyond the immediate vicinity of the town, and where all the plantations are situated, the children go about entirely naked, while the men wear nothing more than a small apron about a hand's-breadth wide, and fastened between the legs: the women are the only persons dressed with anything like propriety.

The plantations that we now saw, and which we reached about 10 o'clock, were cultivated by Chinese. In addition to their huts of leaves, they had erected a small temple, where they invited us to alight. We immediately spread out upon the altar some refreshments, which Madame Behu, like a good housewife, had given us; but, instead of imitating the Chinese, and sacrificing them to the gods, we were wicked enough to devour them ravenously ourselves.

When we had satisfied our hunger, we skinned the serpent and then made a present of it to the Chinese; but they gave us to understand that they would not touch it, at which I was greatly surprised, since they will generally eat anything. I was afterwards convinced that this was all pretence, for on returning some hours later from our hunting excursion and going into one of their huts, we found them all seated round a large dish in which were pieces of roast meat of the peculiar round shape of the serpent. They wanted to hide the dish in a great hurry, but I entered very quickly and gave them some money to be allowed to taste it. I found the flesh particularly tender and delicate, even more tender than that of a chicken.

But I have quite forgotten to describe our hunting excursion. We asked the labourers if they could not put us on the track of a tiger; they described to us a part of the wood where one was reported to have taken up his abode a few days previously, and we immediately set off. We had great difficulty in forcing our way through the forest, having, at every instant, to clamber over prostrate trees, creep through brambles or cross over swamps, but we had, at all events, the satisfaction of progressing, which we certainly should not have had in the forests of Brazil, where such an undertaking would have been impracticable. It is true that there were creepers and orchids, but not in such numbers as in Brazil, and the trees, too, stand far wider apart. We saw some splendid specimens, towering to a height of above a hundred feet. The objects which interested us most were the ebony and kolim trees. The timber of the first is of two kinds, a layer of brownish-yellow

130

surrounding the inner stem, which composes that portion especially known as ebony.

The kolim-tree diffuses an excessively strong odour, similar to that of onions, indicating its site at some distance off. The fruit tastes extremely like onions, and is very often used by the common people, but its odour and taste are too strong for Europeans. I merely just touched a piece of fresh rind, and my hands smelt of it the next morning.

We beat about the forest for some hours without meeting the game of which we were in search. We once thought that we had found the lair, but we soon found that we were mistaken. One of the gentlemen, too, affirmed that he heard the growl of a bear; it must, however, have been a very gentle growl, as no one else heard it, although we were all close together.

We returned home without any further addition to our stock of game, but highly delighted with our agreeable trip.

Although Singapore is a small island, and all means have been used and rewards offered for the extirpation of the tigers, they have failed. Government gives a premium of a hundred dollars, and the Society of Singapore Merchants a similar sum for every tiger killed. Besides this, the valuable skin belongs to the fortunate hunter, and even the flesh is worth something, as it is eagerly bought by the Chinese for eating. The tigers, however, swim over from the neighbouring peninsula of Malacca, which is only separated from Singapore by a very narrow channel, and hence it will be impossible to eradicate them entirely.

The varieties of fruit found at Singapore are very numerous and beautiful. Among the best may be reckoned the mangostan, which is said to grow only here and in Java. It is as big as a middling-sized apple. The rind is a deep brown on the outside and scarlet inside, and the fruit itself is white, and divided naturally into four or five sections: it almost melts in the mouth, and has an exquisite flavour. The pine-apples are much more juicy, sweeter, and considerably larger than those at Canton; I saw some which must have weighed about four pounds. Whole fields are planted with them, and when they arrive at full maturity, three or four hundred may be bought for a dollar. They are often eaten with salt. There is also another kind of fruit, "sauersop," which also often weighs several pounds, and is green outside and white or pale yellow inside. It very much resembles strawberries in taste, and, like them, is eaten with wine and sugar. The gumaloh is divided into several distinct slices, and resembles a pale yellow orange, but is not so sweet and juicy; many people, however, prefer it; it is at least five times as large as an orange. In my opinion, however, the palm of excellence is borne away by the "custard apple," which is covered with small green scales. {125} The inside, which is full of black pips, is very white, as soft as butter, and of the most exquisite flavour. It is eaten with the help of small spoons.

A few days before my departure from Singapore, I had an opportunity of

131

witnessing the burial of a Chinese in easy circumstances. The procession passed our house, and in spite of a temperature of 113° Fah., I went with it to the grave, which was three or four miles distant, and was too much interested in the ceremony to leave until it was concluded, although it lasted nearly two hours.

At the head of the procession was a priest, and at his side a Chinese with a lantern two feet high, covered with white cambric. Then came two musicians, one of whom beat a small drum at intervals, and the other played the cymbals. These persons were followed by the coffin, with a servant holding a large open parasol over that part of it on which the head of the deceased lay. Alongside walked the eldest son or the nearest male relative, carrying a small white flag, and with his hair hanging in disorder over his shoulders. The relations were all dressed in the deepest mourning—that is to say, entirely in white; the men had even got white caps on, and the women were so enveloped in white cloths that it was impossible to see so much as their faces. The friends and attendants, who followed the coffin in small groups without order or regularity, had all got a white strip of cambric bound round their head, their waist, or their arm. As soon as it was remarked that I had joined the procession, a man who had a quantity of these strips, came up and offered me one, which I took and bound round my arm.

The coffin, which consisted of the trunk of a large tree, was covered with a dark-coloured cloth; a few garlands of flowers were suspended from it, and some rice, tied up in a cloth, was placed upon it. Four-and-twenty men bore this heavy burden on immense poles: their behaviour was excessively lively, and every time they changed, they began quarrelling or laughing among themselves. Nor did the other personages in the ceremony display either grief or respect; they ate, drank, smoked, and talked, while some carried cold tea in small pails for the benefit of such as might be thirsty. The son alone held himself aloof; he walked, according to custom, plunged in deep sorrow by the side of the coffin.

On reaching the road that led to the last resting place, the son threw himself upon the ground, and, covering up his face, sobbed very audibly. After a little, he got up again and tottered behind the coffin, so that two men were obliged to support him; he appeared very ill and deeply moved. It is true, I was afterwards informed that this grief is mostly merely assumed, since custom requires that the chief mourner shall be, or pretend to be, weak and ill with sorrow.

On arriving at the grave, which was seven feet deep, and dug on the declivity of a hill, they laid the pall, flowers, and rice on one side, and then, after throwing in a vast quantity of gold and silver paper, lowered the coffin, which I then for the first time perceived was of the finest workmanship, lacquered and hermetically closed. At least half an hour was taken up by this part of the proceedings. The relations at first threw themselves on the ground, and, covering their faces, howled horribly, but finding the burial lasted rather long, sat down in a circle all round, and taking their little baskets of betel, burnt mussel-shells, and areca-nuts, began chewing away with the greatest composure.

132

After the coffin was lowered into the grave, one of the attendants advanced to the upper part of it, and opened the small packet of rice, on which he placed a sort of compass. A cord was then handed to him. He placed it over the middle of the compass, and altered its position until it lay exactly in the same direction as the needle. A second cord, with a plummet attached, was then held to the first and let down into the grave, and the coffin moved backwards and forwards according to this line, until the middle was in the same direction as the needle: this arrangement consumed at least another quarter of an hour.

After this, the coffin was covered over with numberless sheets of white paper, and the person who had conducted the previous operation made a short speech, during which the children of the deceased threw themselves upon the ground. When it was finished, the speaker threw a few handfuls of rice over the coffin and to the children, who held up the corner of their outer garments so as to catch as many of the grains as possible; but as they only succeeded in obtaining a few, the speaker gave about a handful more, which they tied up carefully in the corner of their dress, and took away with them.

The grave was at last filled in, when the relations set up a most dismal howl, but, as far as I could remark, every eye was dry.

After this, boiled fowls, ducks, pork, fruit, all kinds of pastry, and a dozen cups full of tea, together with the tea-pot, were placed in two rows upon the grave, and six painted wax tapers lighted and stuck in the ground near the refreshments. During all this time, immense heaps of gold and silver paper were set fire to and consumed.

The eldest son now approached the grave again, and threw himself down several times, touching the ground on each occasion with his forehead. Six perfumed paper tapers were handed to him a-light; when he had swung them round in the air a few times he gave them back, when they also, in their turn, were fixed in the earth. The other relations performed the same ceremony.

During all this time, the priest had been sitting at a considerable distance from the grave under the shade of a large parasol, and without taking the slightest share in the proceedings. He now, however, came forward, made a short speech, during which he rang a small bell several times, and his duty was at an end. The refreshments were cleared away, the tea poured over the grave, and the whole company returned home in excellent spirits accompanied by the music, which had also played at intervals over the grave. The provisions, as I was informed, were distributed among the poor.

On the following day I witnessed the celebrated Chinese Feast of Lanterns. From all the houses, at the corners of the roofs, from high posts, etc., were hung innumerable lanterns, made of paper or gauze, and most artistically ornamented with gods, warriors, and animals. In the courts and gardens of the different houses, or, where there were no courts or gardens, in the streets, all kinds of

133

refreshments and fruit were laid out with lights and flowers, in the form of half pyramids on large tables. The people wandered about the streets, gardens, and courts, until nearly midnight, when the edible portions of the pyramids were eaten by the proprietors of them. I was very much pleased with this feast, but with no part of it more than the quiet and orderly behaviour of the people: they looked at all the eatables with a scrutinizing glance, but without touching the smallest fragment.

Singapore is situated 58' (nautical miles) north of the line, in 104° East longitude, and the climate, when compared to that of other southern countries, is very agreeable. During the period of my stay, extending from September 3rd to October 8th, the heat seldom exceeded 83° 75' indoors, and 117° in the sun. There is never any great variation in the temperature, which is the natural consequence of the place being near the equator. The sun always rises and sets at 6 A.M. and 6 P.M. respectively, and is immediately followed by full daylight or perfect night; the twilight hardly lasting ten minutes.

In conclusion, I must remark that Singapore will shortly become the central point of all the Indian steamers. Those from Hong-Kong, Ceylon, Madras, Calcutta, and Europe arrive regularly once a month; there is likewise a Dutch war-steamer from Batavia, and in a little time there will also be steamers running to and fro between this place, and Manilla and Sidney.

CHAPTER X. THE EAST INDIES—CEYLON.

*DEPARTURE FROM SINGAPORE—THE ISLAND OF PINANG—
CEYLON—POINTE DE GALLE—EXCURSION INTO THE INTERIOR—
COLOMBO—CANDY—THE TEMPLE OF DAGOHA—ELEPHANT
HUNT—RETURN TO COLOMBO AND POINTE DE GALLE.*

I once more embarked in an English steamer, the "Braganza," of 350 horse power, that left Singapore for Ceylon on the 7th of October. The distance between the two places is 1,900 miles.

The treatment I experienced on board this vessel was, it is true, a little different from that on board the other, although it was nearly as bad. There were four of us in the second cabin; {128} we dined alone, and had a mulatto servant to attend upon us. Unfortunately, he was afflicted with elephantiasis, and his appearance did not at all tend to whet the edge of our appetites.

During the 7th and 8th of October, we held our course through the Strait of Malacca, which separates Sumatra from the peninsula, and during all this time we never lost sight of land. Malacca is, near the coast, merely hilly; but further in the interior the hills swell into a fine mountain range. To our left lay a number of

134

mountainous islands, which completely intercepted our view of Sumatra.

But if the scenery around us was not remarkable, the spectacle on board the vessel itself was highly interesting. The crew was composed of seventy-nine persons, comprising Chinese, Malays, Cingalese, Bengalese, Hindostanese, and Europeans. As a general rule, those of each country generally took their meals separately with their own countrymen. They all had immense plates of rice, and little bowls full of curry; a few pieces of dried fish supplied the place of bread. They poured the curry over the rice, and mixing the whole together with their hands, made it into small balls which they put into their mouths with a small piece of fish; about half their food used generally to fall back again into their plates.

The costume of these people was very simple. Many of them had nothing more than a pair of short trousers on, with a dirty old turban, and even the place of this was sometimes supplied by a coloured rag, or a cast-off sailor's cap. The Malays wore long cloths wound round their bodies, with one end hanging over their shoulder. The Chinese preserved intact their usual costume and mode of life; and the coloured servants of the ship's officers were the only ones who were occasionally well and even elegantly dressed. Their costume consisted of white trousers, wide upper garments, also white, with white sashes, silk jackets, and small embroidered white caps, or handsome turbans.

The manner in which all these poor coloured people were treated was certainly not in accordance with Christian principles. No one ever addressed them but in the roughest manner, and they were kicked and cuffed about on every occasion; even the dirtiest little European cabin-boy on board was allowed to act in the most cruel manner, and play off the most ignoble practical jokes upon them. Unhappy creatures! how is it possible that they should feel any love for Christians?

On the 9th of October we landed on the small island of Pinang. The town of the same name lies in the midst of a small plain, which forms the half of an isthmus. Not far from the town rises a picturesque mountain range.

I received five hours' leave, which I devoted to riding about in all directions through the town in a palanquin, and even going a little distance into the country. All that I could see resembled what I had already seen at Singapore. The town itself is not handsome, but the contrary is the case with the country houses, which are all situated in beautiful gardens. The island is intersected by a great number of excellent roads.

From one of the neighbouring mountains there is said to be a very fine prospect of Pinang, a part of Malacca, and the sea, and, on the road to the mountain, a waterfall. Unfortunately, the few hours at my disposal did not allow me to see everything.

The greatest portion of the population of this island consists of Chinese, who perform all the manual labour, and engross all the retail trade.

135

On the 11th of October we saw the small island of Pulo-Rondo, which appertains to Sumatra. We now took the shortest line across the Bay of Bengal, and beheld land no more until we came in sight of Ceylon.

On the afternoon of the 17th of October, we neared Ceylon. I strained my anxious eyes to catch a glimpse of it as soon as possible, for it is always described as being a second Eden; some go so far as to affirm that our common father, Adam, settled there on his expulsion from Paradise, and, as a proof of this, adduce the fact of many places in the island, such as Adam's Peak, Adam's Bridge, etc., still bearing his name. I breathed the very air more eagerly, hoping, like other travellers, to inhale the fragrant odours wafted to me from the plantations of costly spices.

It was one of the most magnificent sights I ever beheld, to observe the island rising gradually from the sea, and to mark the numerous mountain ranges, which intersect Ceylon in every direction, becoming every instant more defined, their summits still magically lighted by the setting sun, while the thick cocoa-groves, the hills, and plains lay enveloped in dusky night. The fragrant odours, however, were wanting, and the vessel smelt, as usual, of nothing more than tar, coals, steam, and oil.

About 9 in the evening, we arrived before the harbour at Pointe de Galle, but, as the entrance is very dangerous, we quietly hove-to for the night. On the following morning two pilots came on board and took us safely through the narrow passage of deep water leading into the port.

Hardly were we landed before we were surrounded by a crowd of people with precious stones, pearls, tortoiseshell, and ivory articles for sale. It is possible that a connoisseur may sometimes make a very advantageous purchase; but I would advise those who have not much experience in these things, not to be dazzled by the size and splendour of the said precious stones and pearls, as the natives, according to all accounts, have learnt from Europeans the art of profiting as much as they can by a favourable opportunity.

Pointe de Galle is charmingly situated: in the fore-ground are some fine groups of rock, and in the back-ground, immediately adjoining the little town, which is protected by fortifications, rise magnificent forests of palms. The houses present a neat appearance; they are low, and shaded by trees, which, in the better streets, are planted so as to form alleys.

Pointe de Galle is the place of rendezvous for the steamers from China, Bombay, Calcutta, and Suez. Passengers from Calcutta, Bombay, and Suez, do not stop more than twelve, or, at most, twenty-four hours; but those proceeding from China to Calcutta have to wait ten or fourteen days for the steamer that carries them to their destination. This delay was to me very agreeable, as I profited by it to make an excursion to Candy.

There are two conveyances from Pointe de Galle to Colombo—the mail which leaves every day, and a coach which starts three times a week. The distance is seventy-three English miles, and the journey is performed in ten hours. A place in the mail costs £1 10s., and in the coach 13s. As I was pressed for time, I was obliged to go by the first. The roads are excellent; not a hill, not a stone is there to impede the rapid rate at which the horses, that are changed every eight miles, scamper along.

The greater portion of the road traversed thick forests of cocoa-trees, at a little distance from the sea-shore, and the whole way was more frequented and more thickly studded with houses than anything I ever saw even in Europe. Village followed village in quick succession, and so many separate houses were built between them, that there was not a minute that we did not pass one. I remarked also some small towns, but the only one worthy of notice was Calturi, where I was particularly struck by several handsome houses inhabited by Europeans.

Along the road-side, under little roofs of palm-leaves, were placed large earthen vessels filled with water, and near them cocoa-nut shells to drink out of. Another measure for the accommodation of travellers, which is no less worthy of praise, consists in the establishment of little stone buildings, roofed in, but open at the sides, and furnished with benches. In these buildings many wayfarers often pass the night.

The number of people and vehicles that we met made the journey appear to me very short. There were specimens of all the various races which compose the population of Ceylon. The Cingalese, properly so called, are the most numerous, but, besides these, there are Indians, Mahomedans, Malays, natives of Malabar, Jews, Moors, and even Hottentots. I saw numerous instances of handsome and agreeable physiognomies among those of the first three races; the Cingalese youths and boys, in particular, are remarkably handsome. They possess mild, well-formed features, and are so slim and finely built, that they might easily be mistaken for girls; an error into which it is the more easy to fall from their manner of dressing their hair. They wear no covering on their head, and comb back all their hair, which is then fastened behind by means of a comb, with a flat, broad plate, four inches high. This kind of head-dress looks anything but becoming in the men. The Mahomedans and Jews have more marked features; the latter resemble the Arabs, and, like them, have noble physiognomies. The Mahomedans and Jews, too, are easily recognised by their shaven heads, long beards, and small white caps or turbans. Many of the Indians, likewise, wear turbans; but the most have only a simple piece of cloth tied round their head, which is also the case with the natives of Malacca and Malabar. The Hottentots allow their coal-black hair to fall in rude disorder over their foreheads and half-way down their necks. With the exception of the Mahomedans and Jews, none of these different people bestow much care upon their dress. Save a small piece of cloth of about a hand's-breadth, and fastened between their legs, they go about naked. Those who are at all dressed, wear short trousers and an upper garment.

137

I saw very few women, and these only near their huts, which they appear to leave less than any females with whom I am acquainted. Their dress, also, was exceedingly simple, consisting merely of an apron bound round their loins, a short jacket that exposed rather than covered the upper part of their body, and a sort of rag hanging over their head. Many were enveloped in large pieces of cloth worn loosely about them. The borders and lobes of their ears were pierced and ornamented with ear-rings, while on their feet and arms, and round their necks, they wore chains and bracelets of silver, or some other metal, and round one of their toes an extremely massive ring.

Any one would suppose that, in a country where the females are allowed to show themselves so little, they would be closely wrapped up; but this is not the case. Many had forgotten their jackets and head coverings, especially the old women, who seemed particularly oblivious in this respect, and presented a most repulsive appearance when thus exposed. Among the younger ones I remarked many a handsome and expressive face; only they, too, ought not to be seen without their jackets, as their breasts hang down almost to their knees.

The complexion of the population varies from a dark to a light or reddish brown or copper colour. The Hottentots are black, but without that glossy appearance which distinguishes the negro.

It is extraordinary what a dread all these half-naked people have of the wet. It happened to commence raining a little, when they sprang like so many rope-dancers over every little puddle, and hastened to their huts and houses for shelter. Those who were travelling and obliged to continue their journey, held, instead of umbrellas, the leaves of the great fan-palm (*Corypha umbraculifera*) over their heads. These leaves are about four feet broad, and can be easily held, like fans. One of them is large enough for two persons.

But if the natives dread the rain, they have no fear of the heat. It is said that they run no risk from the rays of the sun, being protected by the thickness of their skulls and the fat beneath.

I was much struck by the peculiarity of some of the waggons, which consisted of wooden two-wheeled cars, roofed with palm leaves stretching out about four feet, before and behind, beyond the body of the car. These projections serve to protect the driver from the rain and the rays of the sun, whichever way they may chance to fall. The oxen, of which there was always only a pair, were yoked at such a distance from the waggon, that the driver could walk very conveniently in the intervening space.

I profited by the half-hour allowed for breakfast to proceed to the sea-shore, whence I observed a number of men busily employed on the dangerous rock in the middle of the most violent breakers. Some of them loosened, by the aid of long poles, oysters, mussels, etc., from the rocks, while others dived down to the bottom to fetch them up. I concluded that there must be pearls contained inside, for I could not suppose that human beings would encounter such risks for the sake of the fish alone; and yet this was the case, for I found, later, that though the same means are employed in fishing for pearls, it is on the eastern coast and only during the months of February and March.

The boats employed by these individuals were of two kinds. The larger ones, which contained about forty persons, were very broad, and composed of boards joined together and fastened with the fibres of the cocoa-tree; the smaller ones were exactly like those I saw in Tahiti, save that they appeared still more dangerous. The bottom was formed of the trunk of an extremely narrow tree, slightly hollowed out, and the sides of the planks are kept in their places by side and cross supports. These craft rose hardly a foot and a half out of the water, and their greatest breadth did not average quite a foot. There was a small piece of plank laid across as a seat, but the rower was obliged to cross his knees from want of room to sit with them apart.

The road, as I before mentioned, lay for the most part through forests of cocoa-trees, where the soil was very sandy and completely free from creepers and underwood; but near trees that did not bear fruit, the soil was rich, and both that and the trees covered with creepers in wild luxuriance. There were very few orchids.

We crossed four rivers, the Tindurch, Bentock, Cattura, and Pandura, two by means of boats, two by handsome wooden bridges.

The cinnamon plantations commenced about ten miles from Colombo; and on this side of the town are all the country-houses of the Europeans. They are very simple, shaded with cocoa-trees and surrounded with stone walls. At 3 o'clock in the afternoon, we drove over two draw-bridges and through two fortified gateways into the town, which is far more pleasantly situated than Pointe de Galle, on account of its nearer proximity to the beautiful mountain ranges.

I only stopped a night here, and on the following morning again resumed my journey in the mail to the town of Candy, which is distant seventy-two miles.

We left on the 20th of October, at 5 o'clock in the morning. Colombo is a very extensive town. We drove through a succession of long, broad streets of handsome houses, all of which latter were surrounded by verandahs and colonnades. I was very much startled at the number of persons lying stretched out at full length under these verandahs, and covered with white clothes. I at first mistook them for corpses, but I soon perceived that their number was too great to warrant that supposition, and I then discovered that they were only asleep. Many, too, began to move and throw off their winding-sheets. I was informed that the natives prefer sleeping in this manner before the houses to sleeping inside of them.

The Calanyganga, an important river, is traversed by a long floating bridge; the road then branches off more and more from the sea-coast, and the character of the scenery changes. The traveller now meets with large plains covered with fine plantations of rice, the green and juicy appearance of which reminded me of our own young wheat when it first shoots up in spring. The forests were composed of mere leaved wood, the palms becoming at every step more rare; one or two might sometimes be seen, here and there, towering aloft like giants, and shading everything around. I can imagine nothing more lovely than the sight of the delicate creepers attached to the tall stems of these palms and twining up to their very crests.

After we had gone about sixteen miles, the country began to assume a more hilly aspect, and we were soon surrounded by mountains on every side. At the foot of each ascent we found extra horses in waiting for us; these were yoked to the ordinary team, and whirled us rapidly over all obstacles. Although there is a rise of about 2,000 feet on the road to Candy, we performed the distance, seventy-two miles, in eleven hours.

The nearer we approached our destination, the more varied and changing became the scenery. At one time we might be closely hemmed in by the mountains, and then the next moment they would stretch away, one above the other, while their summits seemed to contend which should outrival the rest in altitude and beauty of outline. They were covered, to the height of several thousand feet, with luxuriant vegetation, which, for the most part, then generally ceased, and gave way to the bare rock. I was not less interested, however, with the curious teams we sometimes met, than I was with the scenery. It is well known that Ceylon abounds in elephants, many of which are captured and employed for various purposes. Those that I now saw were yoked in twos or threes to large waggons, full of stones for mending the roads.

Four miles before reaching Candy, we came to the river Mahavilaganga, which is spanned by a masterly bridge of one arch. The materials of the bridge are most costly, consisting of satin-wood. In connection with this structure, I learned the following legend.

After the conquest of the island by the English, the natives did not give up the hope of once more attaining their independence, because one of their oracles had declared that it was as impossible for the enemy to obtain a lasting dominion over them, as it was for the opposite banks of the Mahavilaganga to be united by a road. When the bridge was begun, they smiled, and said that it could never be successfully completed. At present, I was told, they think of independence no more.

Near the bridge is a botanical garden which I visited the following day, and was astonished at its excellent arrangement, and the richness of its collection of flowers, plants, and trees.

Opposite the garden is one of the largest sugar-plantations, and, in the neighbourhood, a number of coffee-plantations.

140

In my opinion, the situation of Candy is most beautiful, but many affirm that it is too near the mountains, and lies in a pit. At any rate, this pit is a very lovely one, abounding in the most luxuriant vegetation. The town itself is small and ugly, consisting of nothing but a mass of small shops, with natives passing to and fro. The few houses that belong to Europeans, the places of business, and the barracks, are all outside the town, upon small hills. Large sheets of artificial water, surrounded by splendid stone balustrades, and shaded by alleys of the mighty tulip-tree, occupy a portion of the valley. On the side of one of these basins, stands the famous Buddhist temple of Dagoha, which is built in the Moorish-Hindostanee style, and richly ornamented.

On my leaving the coach, one of the passengers was kind enough to recommend me a good hotel, and to call a native and direct him where to conduct me. When I reached the hotel, the people there said that they were very sorry, but that all their rooms were occupied. I asked them to direct my guide to another establishment, which they did. The rascal led me away from the town, and, pointing to a hill which was near us, gave me to understand that the hotel was situated behind it. I believed him, as all the houses are built far apart; but on ascending the hill, I found nothing but a lonely spot and a wood. I wished to turn back, but the fellow paid no attention to my desire, and continued walking towards the wood. I then snatched my portmanteau from him, and refused to proceed any further. He endeavoured to wrest it from me, when, luckily, I saw in the distance two English soldiers, who hastened up in answer to my cries, and, on seeing this, the fellow ran off. I related my adventure to the soldiers, who congratulated me on the recovery of my luggage, and conducted me to the barracks, where one of the officers was kind enough to give orders that I should be conducted to another hotel.

My first visit was to the temple of Dagoha, which contains a valuable relic of the god Buddha, namely, one of his teeth, and, together with the out-buildings, is surrounded by a wall. The circumference of the principal temple is not very considerable, and the sanctuary, which contains the tooth, is a small chamber hardly twenty feet broad. Within this place all is darkness, as there are no windows, and inside the door, there is a curtain, to prevent the entry of any light. The walls and ceiling are covered with silk tapestry, which, however, has nothing but its antiquity to recommend it. It is true that it was interwoven with gold thread, but it appeared never to have been especially costly, and I cannot believe that it ever produced that dazzling effect which some travellers have described. Half of the chamber was engrossed by a large table, or kind of altar, inlaid with plates of silver, and ornamented round the edges with precious stones. On it stands a bell-shaped case, measuring at the bottom at least three feet in diameter, and the same in height. It is made of silver thickly gilt, and decorated with a number of costly jewels; there is a peacock in the middle entirely formed of precious stones; but all these treasures fail to produce any very great effect, from the clumsy and inartistic fashion in which they are set.

Under the large case there are six smaller ones, said to be of pure gold; under the last is the tooth of the all-powerful divinity. The outer case is secured by means of three locks, two of the keys belonging to which used to be kept by the English governor, while the third remained in the custody of the chief priest of the temple. A short time previous to my visit, however, the government had restored the two keys to the natives with great solemnities, and they are now confided to one of the native *Radschas*, or princes.

The relic itself is only shown to a prince or some other great personage; all other people must be content to believe the priest, who, for a small gratuity, has the politeness to describe the size and beauty of the tooth. The dazzling whiteness of its hue is said to eclipse that of ivory, while its form is described as being more beautiful than anything of the kind ever beheld, and its size to equal that of the tooth of an immense bullock.

An immense number of pilgrims come here every year to pay their adoration to this divine tooth.

"Where ignorance is bliss, 't is folly to be wise." How many people are there among us Christians who believe things which require quite as great an amount of faith? For instance, I remember witnessing, when I was a girl, a festival at Calvaria, in Gallicia, which is still celebrated every year. A great multitude of pilgrims go there to obtain splinters of the true cross. The priests manufacture little crosses of wax, on which, as they assure the faithful, they stick splinters of the real one. These little crosses, wrapped up in paper and packed in baskets, are placed ready for distribution, that is, for sale. Every peasant generally takes three: one to put in his room, one in his stable, and another in his barn. The most wonderful portion of the business is that these crosses must be renewed every year, as in that period they lose their divine power.

But let me return to Candy. In a second temple, adjoining that in which the relic is preserved, are two gigantic hollow statues of the god Buddha in a sitting posture, and both are said to be formed of the finest gold. Before these colossi stand whole rows of smaller Buddhas, of crystal, glass, silver, copper, and other materials. In the entrance hall, likewise, are several stone statues of different gods, with other ornaments, most of them roughly and stiffly executed. In the middle stands a small plain monument of stone, resembling a bell turned upside down; it is said to cover the grave of a Brahmin.

On the outer walls of the principal temple are wretched daubs in fresco, representing the state of eternal punishment. Some of the figures are being roasted, twitched with red-hot pincers, partly baked, or forced to swallow fire. Others again, are jammed between rocks, or having pieces of flesh cut out of their bodies, etc., but fire appears to play the principal part in these punishments.

The doors of the principal temple are made of metal, and the door posts of ivory. On the first are the most beautiful arabesques in basso-relief, and on the second, in inlaid work, representing flowers and other objects. Before the principal entrance, four of the largest elephant's teeth ever found are stuck up by way of ornament.

Ranged round the court-yard are the tents of the priests, who always go about with bare, shaven heads, and whose costume consists of a light yellow upper garment, which nearly covers the whole body. It is said that there were once 500 officiating priests in this temple; at present the divinity is obliged to content himself with a few dozen.

The chief part of the religious ceremonies of the Buddhists consists in presents of flowers and money. Every morning and evening a most horrible instrument, fit to break the drum of one's ear, and called a tam-tam, together with some shrill trumpets and fifes, is played before the door of the temple. To this soon succeeds a crowd of people from all sides, bringing baskets full of the most beautiful flowers, with which the priests adorn the altars, and that in a manner so elegant and tasty, that it cannot be surpassed.

Besides this temple, there are several others in Candy, but only one worth noticing. This is situated at the foot of a rocky hill, out of which has been hewn a statue of Buddha, thirty-six feet high, and over this is built the temple, which is small and elegant. The god is painted with the most glaring colours. The walls of the temple are covered with handsome red cement, and portioned out into small panels, in all of which the god Buddha appears *al fresco*. There are also a few portraits of Vischnu, another god. The colours on the southern wall of the temple are remarkable for their fine state of preservation.

Here, likewise, there is a funeral monument, like that of the Temple of Dagoha, not however, in the building itself, but under the lofty firmament of heaven, and shaded by noble trees.

Attached to the temples are frequently schools, in which the priests fulfil the duties of teachers. Near this particular temple, we saw about a dozen boys—girls are not allowed to attend school—busy writing. The copies for them were written very beautifully, by means of a stylus, on small palm-leaves, and the boys used the same material.

It is well worth any person's while to walk to the great valley through which the Mahavilaganga flows. It is intersected with a countless number of wave-like hills, many of which form regular terraces, and are planted with rice or coffee. Nature is here young and vigorous, and amply rewards the planter's toil. The darker portions of the picture are composed of palms or other trees, and the background consists partly of towering mountains, in a holiday suit of green velvet, partly of stupendous and romantic rocks in all their gloomy nakedness.

I saw many of the principal mountains in Ceylon—giants, 8,000 feet high; but, unfortunately, not the most celebrated one, Adam's Peak, which has an altitude of 6,500 feet, and which, towards the summit is so steep, that it was necessary, in order to enable any one to climb up, to cut small steps in the rock, and let in an iron chain.

But the bold adventurer is amply repaid for his trouble. On the flat summit of the rock is the imprint of a *small* foot, five feet long. The Mahomedans suppose it to be that of our vigorous progenitor, Adam, and the Buddhists that of their large-toothed divinity, Buddha. Thousands of both sects flock to the place every year, to perform their devotions.

There still exists at Candy the palace of the former king, or emperor of Ceylon. It is a handsome stone building, but with no peculiar feature of its own; I should have supposed that it had been built by Europeans. It consists of a ground floor, somewhat raised, with large windows, and handsome porticoes resting upon columns. The only remarkable thing about it is a large hall in the interior, with its walls decorated with some rough and stiffly executed representations of animals in relief. Since the English deposed the native sovereign, the palace has been inhabited by the English resident, or governor.

Had I only arrived a fortnight sooner, I should have witnessed the mode of hunting, or rather snaring, elephants. The scene of operations is a spot on the banks of some stream or other, where these animals go to drink. A large place is enclosed with posts, leading up to which, and also skirted by stout posts, are a series of narrow passages. A tame elephant, properly trained, is then made fast in the middle of the large space, to entice by his cries the thirsty animals, who enter unsuspiciously the labyrinth from which they cannot escape, as the hunters and drivers follow, alarm them by their shouts, and drive them into the middle of the enclosure. The finest are taken alive, by being deprived of food for a short time. This renders them so obedient, that they quietly allow a noose to be thrown over them, and then follow the tame elephant without the least resistance. The others are then either killed or set at liberty, according as they possess fine tusks or not.

The preparations for capturing these animals sometimes last several weeks, as, besides enclosing the spot selected, a great many persons are employed to hunt up the elephants far and wide, and drive them gradually to the watering place.

Persons sometimes go elephant-hunting, armed merely with firearms; but this is attended with danger. The elephant, as is well known, is easily vulnerable in one spot only,—the middle of the skull. If the hunter happens to hit the mark, the monster lies stretched before him at the first shot; but if he misses, then woe to him, for he is speedily trampled to death by the enraged beast. In all other cases the elephant is very peaceable, and is not easily induced to attack human beings.

The Europeans employ elephants to draw and carry burdens—an elephant will carry forty hundred-weight; but the natives keep them more for show and riding.

I left Candy after a stay of three days, and returned to Colombo, where I was obliged to stop another day, as it was Sunday, and there was no mail.

I profited by this period to visit the town, which is protected by a strong fort. It is very extensive; the streets are handsome, broad, and clean; the houses only one story high, and surrounded by verandahs and colonnades. The population is reckoned at about 80,000 souls, of whom about 100 are Europeans, exclusive of the troops, and 200 descendants of Portuguese colonists, who founded a settlement here some centuries ago. The complexion of the latter is quite as dark as that of the natives themselves.

In the morning I attended mass. The church was full of Irish soldiers and Portuguese. The dress of the Portuguese was extremely rich; they wore ample robes with large folds, and short silk jackets; in their ears hung ear-rings of pearls and diamonds, and round their necks, arms, and even ankles, were gold and silver chains.

In the afternoon I took a walk to one of the numerous cinnamon plantations round Colombo. The cinnamon tree or bush is planted in rows; it attains at most a height of nine feet, and bears a white, scentless blossom. From the fruit, which is smaller than an acorn, oil is obtained by crushing and boiling it; the oil then disengages itself and floats on the top of the water. It is mixed with cocoa-oil and used for burning.

There are two cinnamon harvests in the course of the year. The first and principal one takes place from April to July, and the second from November to January. The rind is peeled from the branches by means of knives, and then dried in the sun; this gives it a yellowish or brownish tint. The best cinnamon is a light yellow, and not thicker than pasteboard.

The essential oil of cinnamon, used in medicine, is extracted from the plant itself, which is placed in a vessel full of water, and left to steep for eight to ten days. The whole mass is then transferred to a retort and distilled over a slow fire. In a short time, on the surface of the water thus distilled a quantity of oil collects, and this is then skimmed off with the greatest care.

In the animal kingdom, besides the elephants, I was much struck by the number and tameness of the ravens of Ceylon. In every small town and village may be seen multitudes of these birds, that come up to the very doors and windows and pick up everything. They play the part of scavengers here, just as dogs do in Turkey. The horned cattle are rather small, with humps between the shoulder-blades; these humps consist of flesh and are considered a great dainty.

In Colombo and Pointe de Galle there are likewise a great many large white buffaloes, belonging to the English government, and imported from Bengal. They are employed in drawing heavy loads.

Under the head of fruit, I may mention the pine-apple as being particularly large and good.

I found the temperature supportable, especially in the high country round about Candy, where, after some heavy rain, it might almost be called cold. In the evening

145

and morning the thermometer stood as low as 61° 25' Fah.; and in the middle of the day and in the sun, it did not rise above 79° 25'. In Colombo and Pointe de Galle, the weather was fine, and the heat reached 95° Fah.

On the 26th of October I again reached Pointe de Galle, and on the following day I embarked in another English steamer for India.

CHAPTER XI. MADRAS AND CALCUTTA.

DEPARTURE FROM CEYLON—MADRAS—CALCUTTA—MODE OF LIFE OF THE EUROPEANS—THE HINDOOS—PRINCIPAL OBJECTS OF INTEREST IN THE TOWN—VISIT TO A BABOO—RELIGIOUS FESTIVALS OF THE HINDOOS—HOUSES OF DEATH AND PLACES FOR BURNING THE DEAD—MAHOMEDAN AND EUROPEAN MARRIAGE CEREMONIES.

On the afternoon of the 27th of October I went on board the steamship "Bentinck," of 500 horse-power; but we did not weigh anchor much before evening.

Among the passengers was an Indian prince of the name of Schadathan, who had been made prisoner by the English for breaking a peace he had concluded with them. He was treated with all the respect due to his rank, and he was allowed his two companions, his *mundschi*, or secretary, and six of his servants. They were all dressed in the Oriental fashion, only, instead of turbans, they wore high, round caps, composed of pasteboard covered with gold or silver stuff. They wore also luxuriant long black hair, and beards.

The companions of the prince took their meals with the servants. A carpet was spread out upon the deck, and two large dishes, one containing boiled fowls, and the other pillau, placed upon it; the company used their hands for knives and forks.

28th October. We still were in sight of the fine dark mountain ranges of Ceylon. Now and then, too, some huge detached groups of rocks would be visible towering above the waves.

29th October. Saw no land. A few whales betrayed their presence by the showers of spray they spouted up, and immense swarms of flying fish were startled by the noise of our engines.

On the morning of the 30th of October we came in sight of the Indian continent. We soon approached near enough to the shore to distinguish that it was particularly remarkable for its beauty, being flat and partly covered with yellow sand; in the back-ground were chains of low hills.

146

At 1 o'clock, P.M., we anchored at a considerable distance (six miles) from Madras. The anchoring place here is the most dangerous in the world, the ground-swell being so strong that at no time can large vessels approach near the town, and many weeks often pass without even a boat being able to do so. Ships, consequently, only stop a very short time, and there are rarely more than a dozen to be seen riding at anchor. Large boats, rowed by ten or twelve men, come alongside them to take the passengers, letters, and merchandise ashore.

The steamer stops here eight hours, which may be spent in viewing the town, though any one so doing runs a chance of being left behind, as the wind is constantly changing. I trusted to the good luck which had always attended me during my travels, and made one of the party that disembarked; but we had not got more than half way to land when I was punished for my curiosity. It began to rain most fearfully, and we were very soon wet to the skin. We took refuge in the first coffee-house we saw, situated at the water's edge; the rain had now assumed a tropical character, and we were unable to leave our asylum. As soon as the storm had passed by, a cry was raised for us to return as quickly as possible, as there was no knowing what might follow.

A speculative baker of Madras had come out in the first boat that reached the steamer with ice and biscuits for sale, which he disposed of very much to his profit.

The angry heavens at length took compassion on us and cleared up before sunset. We were then enabled to see the palace-like dwellings of the Europeans, built half in the Grecian and half in the Italian style of architecture, stretching along the shore and beautifully lighted by the sun. Besides these, there were others standing outside the town in the midst of magnificent gardens.

Before we left, a number of natives ventured to us in small boats with fruit, fish, and other trifles. Their boats were constructed of the trunks of four small trees, tightly bound together with thin ropes made of the fibres of the cocoa-tree; a long piece of wood served as an oar. The waves broke so completely over them that I imagined every instant that both boats and men were irretrievably lost.

The good people were almost in a state of nature, and seemed to bestow all their care on their heads, which were covered with pieces of cloth, turbans, cloth or straw caps, or very high and peaked straw hats. The more respectable—among whom may be reckoned the boatmen who brought the passengers and mails— were, however, in many cases, very tastily dressed. They had on neat jackets, and large long pieces of cloth wrapped round their bodies; both the cloths and jackets were white, with a border of blue stripes. On their heads they wore tightly fitting white caps, with a long flap hanging down as far as their shoulders. These caps, too, had a blue border. The complexion of the natives was a dark brown or coffee colour.

Late in the evening, a native woman came on board with her two children. She had paid second-class fare, and was shown a small dark berth not far from the first cabin places. Her younger child had, unfortunately, a bad cough, which prevented some rich English lady, who had likewise a child with her, from sleeping. Perhaps the exaggerated tenderness which this lady manifested for her little son caused her to believe that the cough might be catching; but, be that as it may, the first thing she did on the following morning, was to beg that the captain would transfer mother and children to the deck, which the noble-hearted humane captain immediately did, neither the lady nor himself caring in the least whether the poor mother had or had not, even a warm coverlid to protect her sick child from the night cold and the frequent heavy showers.

Would that this rich English lady's child had only been ill, and exposed with her to the foggy night air, that she might herself have experienced what it is to be thus harshly treated! A person of any heart must almost feel ashamed at belonging to a class of beings who allow themselves to be far surpassed in humanity and kindness by those who are termed savages; no savages would have thus thrust forth a poor woman with a sick child, but would, on the contrary, have taken care of both. It is only Europeans, who have been brought up with Christian principles, who assume the right of treating coloured people according as their whim or fancy may dictate.

On the 1st and 2nd of November we caught occasional glimpses of the mainland, as well as of several little islands; but all was flat and sandy, without the least pretensions to natural beauty. Ten or twelve ships, some of them East Indiamen of the largest size, were pursuing the same route as ourselves.

On the morning of the 3rd of November, the sea had already lost its own beautiful colour, and taken that of the dirty yellow Ganges. Towards evening we had approached pretty close to the mouths of this monster river, for some miles previous to our entering which, the water had a sweet flavour. I filled a glass from the holy stream, and drank it to the health of all those near and dear to me at home.

At 5 o'clock in the afternoon, we cast anchor before Kadscheri, at the entrance of the Ganges, it being too late to proceed to Calcutta, which is sixty nautical miles distant. The stream at this point was several miles broad, so that the dark line of only one of its banks was to be seen.

4th November. In the morning we entered the Hoogly, one of the seven mouths of the Ganges. A succession of apparently boundless plains lay stretched along on both sides of the river. Fields of rice were alternated with sugar plantations, while palm, bamboo, and other trees, sprung up between, and the vegetation extended, in wanton luxuriance, down to the very water's edge; the only objects wanting to complete the picture were villages and human beings, but it was not until we were within about five-and-twenty miles of Calcutta that we saw now and then a wretched village or a few half-naked men. The huts were formed of clay, bamboos, or palm branches, and covered with tiles, rice-straw, or palm leaves. The

148

larger boats of the natives struck me as very remarkable, and differed entirely from those I saw at Madras. The front portion was almost flat, being elevated hardly half a foot above the water while the stern was about seven feet high.

The first grand-looking building, a cotton mill, is situated fifteen miles below Calcutta, and a cheerful dwelling-house is attached. From this point up to Calcutta, both banks of the Hoogly are lined with palaces built in the Greco-Italian style, and richly provided with pillars and terraces. We flew too quickly by, unfortunately, to obtain more than a mere passing glimpse of them.

Numbers of large vessels either passed us or were sailing in the same direction, and steamer after steamer flitted by, tugging vessels after them; the scene became more busy and more strange, every moment, and everything gave signs that we were approaching an Asiatic city of the first magnitude.

We anchored at Gardenrich, four miles below Calcutta. Nothing gave me more trouble during my travels than finding lodgings, as it was sometimes impossible by mere signs and gestures to make the natives understand where I wanted to go. In the present instance, one of the engineers interested himself so far in my behalf as to land with me, and to hire a palanquin, and direct the natives where to take me.

I was overpowered by feelings of the most disagreeable kind the first time I used a palanquin. I could not help feeling how degrading it was to human beings to employ them as beasts of burden.

The palanquins are five feet long and three feet high, with sliding doors and jalousies: in the inside they are provided with mattresses and cushions, so that a person can lie down in them as in a bed. Four porters are enough to carry one of them about the town, but eight are required for a longer excursion. They relieve each other at short intervals, and run so quickly that they go four miles in an hour or even in three-quarters of an hour. These palanquins being painted black, looked like so many stretchers carrying corpses to the churchyard or patients to the hospital.

On the road to the town, I was particularly struck with the magnificent *gauths* (piazzas), situated on the banks of the Hoogly, and from which broad flights of steps lead down to the river. Before these gauths are numerous pleasure and other boats.

The most magnificent palaces lay around in the midst of splendid gardens, into one of which the palanquin-bearers turned, and set me down under a handsome portico before the house of Herr Heilgers, to whom I had brought letters of recommendation. The young and amiable mistress of the house greeted me as a countrywoman (she was from the north and I from the south of Germany), and received me most cordially. I was lodged with Indian luxury, having a drawing-room, a bed-room, and a bath-room especially assigned to me.

149

I happened to arrive in Calcutta at the most unfavourable period possible. Three years of unfruitfulness through almost the whole of Europe had been followed by a commercial crisis, which threatened the town with entire destruction. Every mail from Europe brought intelligence of some failure, in which the richest firms here were involved. No merchant could say, "I am worth so much;"—the next post might inform him that he was a beggar. A feeling of dread and anxiety had seized every family. The sums already lost in England and this place were reckoned at thirty millions of pounds sterling, and yet the crisis was far from being at an end.

Misfortunes of this kind fall particularly hard upon persons who, like the Europeans here, have been accustomed to every kind of comfort and luxury. No one can have any idea of the mode of life in India. Each family has an entire palace, the rent of which amounts to two hundred rupees (£20), or more, a month. The household is composed of from twenty-five to thirty servants; namely—two cooks, a scullion, two water-carriers, four servants to wait at table, four housemaids, a lamp-cleaner, and half-a-dozen seis or grooms. Besides this, there are at least six horses, to every one of which there is a separate groom; two coachmen, two gardeners, a nurse and servant for each child, a lady's maid, a girl to wait on the nurses, two tailors, two men to work the punkahs, and one porter. The wages vary from four to eleven rupees (8s. to £1 2s.) a month. None of the domestics are boarded, and but few of them sleep in the house: they are mostly married, and eat and sleep at home. The only portion of their dress which they have given to them is their turban and belt; they are obliged to find the rest themselves, and also to pay for their own washing. The linen belonging to the family is never, in spite of the number of servants, washed at home, but is all put out, at the cost of three rupees (6s.) for a hundred articles. The amount of linen used is something extraordinary; everything is white, and the whole is generally changed twice a day.

Provisions are not dear, though the contrary is true of horses, carriages, furniture, and wearing apparel. The last three are imported from Europe; the horses come either from Europe, New Holland, or Java.

In some European families I visited there were from sixty to seventy servants, and from fifteen to twenty horses.

In my opinion, the Europeans themselves are to blame for the large sums they have to pay for servants. They saw the native princes and rajahs surrounded by a multitude of idle people, and, as Europeans, they did not wish to appear in anyway inferior. Gradually the custom became a necessity, and it would be difficult to find a case where a more sensible course is pursued.

It is true that I was informed that matters could never be altered as long as the Hindoos were divided into castes. The Hindoo who cleans the room would on no account wait at table, while the nurse thinks herself far too good ever to soil her hands by cleaning the child's washing-basin. There may certainly be some truth in this, but still every family cannot keep twenty, thirty, or even more servants. In China and Singapore, I was struck with the number of servants, but they are not half, nay, not a third so numerous, as they are here.

The Hindoos, as is well known, are divided into four castes—the Brahmins, Khetries, Bices and Sooders. They all sprung from the body of the god Brahma: the first from his mouth, the second from his shoulders, the third from his belly and thighs, and the fourth from his feet. From the first class are chosen the highest officers of state, the priests, and the teachers of the people. Members of this class alone are allowed to peruse the holy books; they enjoy the greatest consideration; and if they happen to commit a crime, are far less severely punished than persons belonging to any of the other castes. The second class furnishes the inferior officials and soldiers; the third the merchants, workmen, and peasants; while the fourth and last provides servants for the other three. Hindoos of all castes, however, enter service when compelled by poverty to do so, but there is still a distinction in the kind of work, as the higher castes are allowed to perform only that of the cleanest kind.

It is impossible for a person of one caste to be received into another, or to intermarry with any one belonging to it. If a Hindoo leaves his native land or takes food from a Paria, he is turned out of his caste, and can only obtain re-admission on the payment of a very large sum.

Besides these castes, there is a fifth class—the Parias. The lot of these poor creatures is the most wretched that can be imagined. They are so despised by the other four castes, that no one will hold the slightest intercourse with them. If a Hindoo happens to touch a Paria as he is passing, he thinks himself defiled, and is obliged to bathe immediately.

The Parias are not allowed to enter any temple, and have particular places set apart for their dwellings. They are miserably poor, and live in the most wretched huts; their food consists of all kinds of offal and even diseased cattle; they go about nearly naked, or with only a few rags at most on them, and perform the hardest and commonest work.

The four castes are subdivided into an immense number of sects, seventy of which are allowed to eat meat, while others are compelled to abstain from it altogether. Strictly speaking, the Hindoo religion forbids the spilling of blood, and consequently the eating of meat; but the seventy sects just mentioned are an exception. There are, too, certain religious festivals, at which animals are sacrificed. A cow, however, is never killed. The food of the Hindoos consists principally of rice, fruit, fish, and vegetables. They are very moderate in their living, and have only two simple meals a day—one in the morning and the other in the evening. Their general drink is water or milk, varied sometimes with cocoa wine.

The Hindoos are of the middle height, slim, and delicately formed; their features

151

are agreeable and mild; the face is oval, the nose sharply chiselled, the lip by no means thick, the eye fine and soft, and the hair smooth and black. Their complexion varies, according to the locality, from dark to light brown; among the upper classes, some of them, especially the women, are almost white.

There are a great number of Mahomedans in India; and as they are extremely skilful and active, most trades and professions are in their hands. They also willingly hire themselves as servants to Europeans.

Men here do that kind of work which we are accustomed to see performed by women. They embroider with white wool, coloured silk, and gold; make ladies' head-dresses, wash and iron, mend the linen, and even take situations as nurses for little children. There are a few Chinese, too, here, most of whom are in the shoemaking trade.

Calcutta, the capital of Bengal, is situated on the Hoogly, which at this point is so deep and broad, that the largest men-of-war and East Indiamen can lie at anchor before the town. The population consists of about 600,000 souls, of whom, not counting the English troops, hardly more than 2,000 are Europeans and Americans. The town is divided into several portions—namely, the Business-town, the Black-town, and the European quarter. The Business-town and Black-town are very ugly, containing narrow, crooked streets, filled with wretched houses and miserable huts, between which there are warehouses, counting-houses, and now and then some palace or other. Narrow paved canals run through all the streets, in order to supply the necessary amount of water for the numerous daily ablutions of the Hindoos. The Business-town and Black-town are always so densely crowded, that when a carriage drives through, the servants are obliged to get down and run on before, in order to warn the people, or push them out of the way.

The European quarter of the town, however, which is often termed the City of Palaces—a name which it richly merits—is, on the contrary, very beautiful. Every good-sized house, by the way, is called, as it is in Venice, a palace. Most of these palaces are situated in gardens surrounded by high walls; they seldom join one another, for which reason there are but few imposing squares or streets.

With the exception of the governor's palace, none of these buildings can be compared for architectural beauty and richness with the large palaces of Rome, Florence, and Venice. Most of them are only distinguished from ordinary dwelling-houses by a handsome portico upon brick pillars covered with cement, and terrace-like roof's. Inside, the rooms are large and lofty, and the stairs of greyish marble or even wood; but neither in doors or out are there any fine statues or sculptures.

The Palace of the governor is as I before said, a magnificent building—one that would be an ornament to the finest city in the world. It is built in the form of a horse-shoe, with a handsome cupola in the centre: the portico, as well as both the wings, is supported upon columns. The internal arrangements are as bad as can possibly be imagined; the supper-room being, for instance, a story higher than the ball-room. In both these rooms there is a row of columns on each side, and the floor of the latter is composed of Agra marble. The pillars and walls are covered with a white cement, which is equal to marble for its polish. The private rooms are not worth looking at; they merely afford the spectator an opportunity of admiring the skill of the architect, who has managed to turn the large space at his command to the smallest imaginable profit.

Among the other buildings worthy of notice are the Town-hall, the Hospital, the Museum, Ochterlony's Monument, the Mint, and the English Cathedral.

The Town-hall is large and handsome. The hall itself extends through one entire story. There are a few monuments in white marble to the memory of several distinguished men of modern times. It is here that all kinds of meetings are held, all speculations and undertakings discussed, and concerts, balls, and other entertainments given.

The Hospital consists of several small houses, each standing in the midst of a grass plot. The male patients are lodged in one house, the females and children in a second, while the lunatics are confined in the third. The wards were spacious, airy, and excessively clean. Only Christians are received as patients.

The hospital for natives is similar, but considerably smaller. The patients are received for nothing, and numbers who cannot be accommodated in the building itself are supplied with drugs and medicines.

The Museum, which was only founded in 1836, possesses, considering the short space of time that has elapsed since its establishment, a very rich collection, particularly of quadrupeds and skeletons, but there are very few specimens of insects, and most of those are injured. In one of the rooms is a beautifully-executed model of the celebrated Tatch in Agra; several sculptures and bas-reliefs were lying around. The figures seemed to me very clumsy; the architecture, however, is decidedly superior. The museum is open daily. I visited it several times, and, on every occasion, to my great astonishment, met a number of natives, who seemed to take the greatest interest in the objects before them.

Ochterlony's Monument is a simple stone column, 165 feet in height, standing, like a large note of admiration, on a solitary grassplot, in memory of General Ochterlony, who was equally celebrated as a statesman and a warrior. Whoever is not afraid of mounting 222 steps will be recompensed by an extensive view of the town, the river, and the surrounding country; the last, however, is very monotonous, consisting of an endless succession of plains bounded only by the horizon.

Not far from the column is a neat little mosque, whose countless towers and cupolas are ornamented with gilt metal balls, which glitter and glisten like so many stars in the heavens. It is surrounded by a pretty court-yard, at the entrance of

153

which those who wish to enter the mosque are obliged to leave their shoes. I complied with this regulation, but did not feel recompensed for so doing, as I saw merely a small empty hall, the roof of which was supported by a few stone pillars. Glass lamps were suspended from the roof and walls, and the floor was paved with Agra marble, which is very common in Calcutta, being brought down the Ganges.

The Mint presents a most handsome appearance; it is built in the pure Grecian style, except that it is not surrounded by pillars on all its four sides. The machinery in it is said to be especially good, surpassing anything of the kind to be seen even in Europe. I am unable to express any opinion on the subject, and can only say that all I saw appeared excessively ingenious and perfect. The metal is softened by heat and then flattened into plates by means of cylinders. These plates are cut into strips and stamped. The rooms in which the operations take place are spacious, lofty, and airy. The motive-power is mostly steam.

Of all the Christian places of worship, the English Cathedral is the most magnificent. It is built in the Gothic style, with a fine large tower rising above half-a-dozen smaller ones. There are other churches with Gothic towers, but these edifices are all extremely simple in the interior, with the exception of the Armenian church, which has the wall near the altar crowded with pictures in gold frames.

The notorious "Black Hole," in which the Rajah Suraja Dowla cast 150 of the principal prisoners when he obtained possession of Calcutta in 1756, is at present changed into a warehouse. At the entrance stands an obelisk fifty feet high, and on it are inscribed the names of his victims.

The Botanical Garden lies five miles distant from the town. It was founded in the year 1743, but is more like a natural park than a garden, as it is by no means so remarkable for its collection of flowers and plants as for the number of trees and shrubs, which are distributed here and there with studied negligence in the midst of large grass-plots. A neat little monument, with a marble bust, is erected to the memory of the founder. The most remarkable objects are two banana-trees. These trees belong to the fig-tree species, and sometimes attain a height of forty feet. The fruit is very small, round, and of a dark-red; it yields oil when burnt. When the trunk has reached an elevation of about fifteen feet, a number of small branches shoot out horizontally in all directions, and from these quantity of threadlike roots descend perpendicularly to the ground, in which they soon firmly fix themselves. When they are sufficiently grown, they send out shoots like the parent trunk; and this process is repeated *ad infinitum*, so that it is easy to understand how a single tree may end by forming a whole forest, in which thousands may find a cool and shady retreat. This tree is held sacred by the Hindoos. They erect altars to the god Rama beneath its shade, and there, too, the Brahmin instructs his scholars.

The oldest of these two trees, together with its family, already describes a

154

circumference of more than 600 feet, and the original trunk measures nearly fifty feet round.

Adjoining the Botanical Garden is the Bishop's College, in which the natives are trained as missionaries. After the Governor's Palace, it is the finest building in Calcutta, and consists of two main buildings and three wings. One of the main buildings is occupied by an extremely neat chapel. The library, which is a noble-looking room, contains a rich collection of the works of the best authors, and is thrown open to the pupils; but their industry does not appear to equal the magnificence of the arrangements, for, on taking a book from the bookcase, I immediately let it fall again and ran to the other end of the room; a swarm of bees had flown upon me from out the bookcase.

The dining and sleeping rooms, as well as all the other apartments, are so richly and conveniently furnished, that a person might easily suppose that the establishment had been founded for the sons of the richest English families, who were so accustomed to comfort from their tenderest infancy that they were desirous of transplanting it to all quarters of the globe; but no one would ever imagine the place had been built for "the labourers in the vineyard of the Lord."

I surveyed this splendid institution with a sadder heart than I might have done, because I knew it was intended for the natives, who had first to put off their own simple mode of life and accustom themselves to convenience and superfluity, only to wander forth into the woods and wildernesses, and exercise their office in the midst of savages and barbarians.

Among the sights of Calcutta may be reckoned the garden of the chief judge, Mr. Lawrence Peel, which is equally interesting to the botanist and the amateur, and which, in rare flowers, plants, and trees, is much richer than the Botanical Garden itself. The noble park, laid out with consummate skill, the luxuriant lawns, interspersed and bordered with flowers and plants, the crystal ponds, the shady alleys, with their bosquets and gigantic trees, all combine to form a perfect paradise, in the midst of which stands the palace of the fortunate owner.

Opposite this park, in the large village of Alifaughur, is situated a modest little house, which is the birthplace of much that is good. It contains a small surgery, and is inhabited by a native who has studied medicine. Here the natives may obtain both advice and medicine for nothing. This kind and benevolent arrangement is due to Lady Julia Cameron, wife of the law member of the Supreme Council of India, Charles Henry Cameron.

I had the pleasure of making this lady's acquaintance, and found her to be, in every respect, an ornament to her sex. Wherever there is any good to be done, she is sure to take the lead. In the years 1846-7, she set on foot subscriptions for the starving Irish, writing to the most distant provinces and calling upon every Englishman to contribute his mite. In this manner she collected the large sum of 80,000 rupees (£8,000.)

155

Lady Peel has distinguished herself also in the field of science, and Bürger's "Leonore" has been beautifully translated by her into English. She is also a kind mother and affectionate wife, and lives only for her family, caring little for the world. Many call her an original; would that we had a few more such originals!

I had brought no letters of recommendation to this amiable woman, but she happened to hear of my travels and paid me a visit. In fact, the hospitality I met with here was really astonishing. I was cordially welcomed in the very first circles, and every one did all in his power to be of use to me. I could not help thinking of Count Rehberg, the Austrian minister at Rio Janeiro, who thought he had conferred a great mark of distinction by inviting me once to his villa; and, to purchase this honour, I had either to walk an hour in the burning heat or to pay six milreis (13s.) for a carriage. In Calcutta, a carriage was always sent for me. I could relate a great many more anecdotes of the worthy count, who made me feel how much I was to blame for not descending from a rich and aristocratic family. I experienced different treatment from the member of the Supreme Council, Charles Henry Cameron, and from the chief judge, Mr. Peel. These gentlemen respected me for myself alone without troubling their heads about my ancestors.

During my stay in Calcutta, I was invited to a large party in honour of Mr. Peel's birthday; but I refused the invitation, as I had no suitable dress. My excuse, however, was not allowed, and I accompanied Lady Cameron, in a simple coloured muslin dress, to a party where all the other ladies were dressed in silk and satin and covered with lace and jewellery; yet no one was ashamed of me, but conversed freely with me, and showed me every possible attention.

A very interesting promenade for a stranger is that to the Strand, or "Maytown," as it is likewise called. It is skirted on one side by the banks of the Hoogly, and on the other by beautiful meadows, beyond which is the noble Chaudrini Road, consisting of rows of noble palaces, and reckoned the finest quarter of Calcutta. Besides this, there is a fine view of the governor's palace, the cathedral, Ochterlony's monument, the magnificent reservoirs, Fort William, a fine prutagon with extensive outworks, and many other remarkable objects.

Every evening, before sunset, all the fashionable world of Calcutta streams hitherward. The purse-proud European, the stuck-up Baboo or Nabob, the deposed Rajah, are to be beheld driving in splendid European carriages, followed by a multitude of servants, in Oriental costume, some standing behind their carriages, and some running before it. The Rajahs and Nabobs are generally dressed in silk robes embroidered with gold, over which are thrown the most costly Indian shawls. Ladies and gentlemen mounted upon English blood horses gallop along the meadows, while crowds of natives are to be seen laughing and joking on their way home, after the conclusion of their day's work. Nor is the scene on the Hoogly less animated; first-class East Indiamen are lying at anchor, unloading or being cleaned out, while numberless small craft pass continually to and fro.

156

I had been told that the population here suffered very much from elephantiasis, and that numbers of poor wretches with horribly swollen feet were to be seen at almost every turn. But this is not true. I did not meet with as many cases of the kind during five weeks here, as I did in one day in Rio Janeiro.

On one occasion I paid a visit to a rich Baboo. The property of the family, consisting of three brothers, was reckoned at £150,000. The master of the house received me at the door, and accompanied me to the reception-room. He was clad in a large dress of white muslin, over which was wound a magnificent Indian shawl, which extended from the hips to the feet, and made up for the transparency of the muslin. One end of the shawl was thrown over his shoulder in the most picturesque manner.

The parlour was furnished in the European fashion. A large hand organ stood in one corner, and in the other a spacious bookcase, with the works of the principal English poets and philosophers; but it struck me that these books were there more for show than use, for the two volumes of Byron's works were turned different ways, while Young's Night Thoughts were stuck between. There were a few engravings and pictures, which the worthy Baboo imagined to be an ornament to the walls, but which were not of so much value as the frames that contained them.

My host sent for his two sons, handsome boys, one seven and the other four years old, and introduced them to me. I inquired, although it was quite contrary to custom to do so, after his wife and daughters. Our poor sex ranks so low in the estimation of the Hindoos, that it is almost an insult to a person to mention any of his female relations. He overlooked this in me, as a European, and immediately sent for his daughters. The youngest, a most lovely baby six months old, was nearly white, with large splendid eyes, the brilliancy of which was greatly increased by the delicate eyelids, which were painted a deep blue round the edges. The elder daughter, nine years old, had a somewhat common coarse face. Her father, who spoke tolerable English, introduced her to me as a bride, and invited me to the marriage which was to take place in six weeks. I was so astonished at this, considering the child's extreme youth, that I remarked he no doubt meant her betrothal, but he assured me that she would then be married and delivered over to her husband.

On my asking whether the girl loved her intended bridegroom, I was told that she would see him for the first time at the celebration of the nuptials. The Baboo informed me further, that every person like himself looked out for a son-in-law as soon as possible, and that the younger a girl married the more honourable was it accounted; an unmarried daughter was a disgrace to her father, who was looked upon as possessed of no paternal love if he did not get her off his hands. As soon as he has found a son-in-law, he describes his bodily and mental qualities as well as his worldly circumstances to his wife, and with this description she is obliged to content herself, for she is never allowed to see her future son-in-law, either as the betrothed, or the husband of her child. The bridegroom is never considered to belong to the family of the bride, but the latter leaves her own relations for those of her husband. No woman, however, is allowed to see or speak with the male relations of her husband, nor dare she ever appear before the men-servants of her household without being veiled. If she wishes to pay a visit to her mother, she is carried to her shut up in a palanquin.

I also saw the Baboo's wife and one of his sisters-in-law. The former was twenty-five years old and very corpulent, the latter was fifteen and was slim and well made. The reason of this, as I was told, is that the females, although married so young, seldom become mothers before their fourteenth year, and until then preserve their original slimness. After their first confinement, they remain for six or eight weeks shut up in their room, without taking the least exercise, and living all the time on the most sumptuous and dainty food. This fattening process generally produces the desired effect. The reader must know that the Hindoos, like the Mahomedans, are partial to corpulent ladies. I never saw any specimens of this kind of beauty, however, among the lower classes.

The two ladies were not very decently attired. Their bodies and heads were enveloped in ample blue and white muslin drapery, embroidered with gold, and bordered with lace of the same material as broad as a man's hand, but the delicate texture {150} was so ethereal, that every outline of the body was visible beneath it. Besides this, whenever they moved their arms the muslin opened and displayed not only their arm, but a portion of their bosom and body. They appeared to pay a great deal of attention to their hair; their chief care seemed to consist in replacing the muslin on their heads, whenever it chanced to fall off. As long as a female is unmarried, she is never allowed to lay aside her head-dress.

These ladies were so overloaded with gold, pearls, and diamonds, that they really resembled beasts of burden. Large pearls, with other precious stones strung together, adorned their head and neck, as likewise did heavy gold chains and mounted gold coins. Their ears, which were pierced all over—I counted twelve holes in one ear—were so thickly laden with similar ornaments, that the latter could not be distinguished from one another; all that was to be seen was a confused mass of gold, pearls, and diamonds. On each arm were eight or ten costly bracelets; the principal one, which was four inches broad, being composed of massive gold, with six rows of small brilliants. I took it in my hand, and found that it weighed at least half a pound. They had gold chains twisted three times round their thighs, and their ankles and feet were also encircled with gold rings and chains; their feet were dyed with henna.

The two ladies then brought me their jewel-cases, and showed me a great many more valuable ornaments. The Hindoos must spend immense sums in jewels and gold and silver embroidered Dacca muslin, as in these articles it is the endeavour of every lady to outrival all her acquaintances. As they had anticipated my arrival, the two ladies were arrayed in their most costly apparel; being determined to exhibit themselves to me in true Indian splendour.

The Baboo also conducted me to the inner apartments looking into the courtyard. Some of these were furnished only with carpets and pillows, the Hindoos not being, in general, partial to chairs or beds; in others, were different pieces of European furniture, such as, tables, chairs, presses, and even bedsteads. A glass case containing dolls, coaches, horses, and other toys, was pointed out to me with peculiar satisfaction; both children and women are very fond of playing with these things, though the women are more passionately fond of cards.

No married woman is allowed to enter the rooms looking out upon the street, as she might be seen by a man from the opposite windows. The young bride, however, profited by her freedom, and tripping before us to the open window, glanced into the busy street.

The wives of the rich Hindoos, or of those belonging to the higher castes, are as much confined to their houses as the Chinese women. The only pleasure that the husband's strictness permits the wife to enjoy, is to pay a visit, now and then, in a carefully closed palanquin, to some friend or relation. It is only during the short time that a woman remains unmarried that she is allowed rather more freedom.

A Hindoo may have several wives; there are, however, but few examples of his availing himself of this privilege.

The husband's relations generally reside in the same house, but each family has its separate household. The elder boys take their meals with their father, but the wife, daughters, and younger boys are not allowed this privilege. Both sexes are extremely fond of tobacco, which they smoke in pipes called hookas.

At the conclusion of my visit, I was offered sweetmeats, fruits, raisins, etc. The sweetmeats were mostly composed of sugar, almonds, and suet, but were not very palatable, owing to the predominance of the suet.

Before leaving the house, I visited the ground-floor to examine the room, in which, once a year, the religious festival called *Natch* is celebrated. This festival, which is the most important one in the Hindoo religion, takes place in the beginning of October, and lasts a fortnight, during which time neither poor nor rich do any business whatever. The master closes his shops and warehouses, and the servant engages a substitute, generally from among the Mahomedans, and then both master and servant spend the fortnight, if not in fasting and prayer, most certainly in doing nothing else.

The Baboo informed me that on these occasions his room is richly ornamented, and a statue of the ten-armed goddess Durga placed in it. This statue is formed of clay or wood, painted with the most glaring colours, and loaded with gold and silver tinsel, flowers, ribbons, and often with even real jewellery. Hundreds of lights and lamps, placed between vases and garlands of flowers, glitter in the room, the court-yard, and outside the house. A number of different animals are offered up as sacrifices; they are not slain, however, in the presence of the goddess, but in some retired part of the house. Priests attend upon the goddess, and female dancers display their talent before her, accompanied by the loud music of the tam-tam. Both priests and *danseuses* are liberally paid. Some of the latter, like our Taglionis and Elslers, earn large sums. During the period of my stay here, there was a Persian *danseuse*, who never appeared for less than 500 rupees (£50.) Crowds of the curious, among whom are numbers of Europeans, flock from one temple to another; the principal guests have sweetmeats and fruit served round to them.

On the last day of the festival the goddess is conveyed with great pomp, and accompanied by music, to the Hoogly, where she is put in a boat, rowed into the middle of the stream, and then thrown overboard in the midst of the shouts and acclamations of the multitude upon the banks. Formerly, the real jewels were thrown in along with the goddess, but carefully fished up again by the priests during the night; at present, the real jewels are replaced on the last day by false ones, or else the founder of the feast takes an opportunity of secretly obtaining possession of them during the goddess's progress to the river. He is obliged to do this very cautiously, however, so as not to be observed by the people. A Natch often costs several thousand rupees, and is one of the most costly items in the expenditure of the rich.

Marriages, too, are said to cost large sums of money. The Brahmins observe the stars, and by their aid calculate the most fortunate day and even hour for the ceremony to take place. It is, however, frequently postponed, at the very last moment, for a few hours longer, as the priest has taken fresh observations, and hit upon a still luckier instant. Of course, such a discovery has to be paid for by an extra fee.

There are several different feasts every year in honour of the four-armed goddess Kally, especially in the village of Kallighat, near Calcutta. There were two during my stay. Before each hut was placed a number of small clay idols, painted with various colours and representing the most horrible creatures. They were exposed there for sale. The goddess Kally, as large as life, had got her tongue thrust out as far as possible between her open jaws; she was placed either before or inside the huts, and was richly decorated with wreaths of flowers.

The temple of Kally is a miserable building, or rather a dark hole, from whose cupola-like roof rise several turrets: the statue here was remarkable for its immense head and horribly long tongue. Its face was painted deep-red, yellow, and sky-blue. I was unable to enter this god-like hole, as I was a woman, and as such was not reckoned worthy of admission into so sacred a place as Kally's temple. I looked in at the door with the Hindoo woman, and was quite satisfied.

The most horrible and distressing scenes occur in the Hindoo dead-houses, and at the places where the corpses are burnt. Those that I saw are situated on the banks of the Hoogly, near the town, and opposite to them is the wood market. The dead-house was small, and contained only one room, in which were four bare bedsteads. The dying person is brought here by his relations, and either placed upon one of the bedsteads, or, if these are all full, on the floor, or, at a push, even before the house in the burning sun. At the period of my arrival, there were five persons in the house and two outside. The latter were completely wrapped up in straw and woollen counterpanes, and I thought they were already dead. On my asking whether or no this was the case, my guide threw off the clothes, and I saw the poor wretches move. I think they must have been half-smothered under the mass of covering. Inside, on the floor, lay a poor old woman, the death-rattle in whose throat proclaimed that her end was fast approaching. The four bedsteads were likewise occupied. I did not observe that the mouths and noses of these poor creatures were stopped up with mud from the Ganges: this may, perhaps, be the case in some other districts. Near the dying persons were seated their relations, quietly and silently waiting to receive their last breath. On my inquiring whether nothing was ever given to them, I was told that if they did not die immediately, a small draught of water from the Ganges was handed to them from time to time, but always decreasing in quantity and at longer intervals, for when once brought to these places, they must die at any price.

As soon as they are dead, and almost before they are cold, they are taken to the place where they are burnt, and which is separated from the high road by a wall. In this place I saw one corpse and one person at the point of death, while on six funeral-piles were six corpses with the flames flaring on high all around them. A number of birds, larger than turkeys, and called here philosophers, {153} small vultures, and ravens were seated upon the neighbouring trees and house-tops, in anxious expectation of the half-burnt corpses. I was horrified. I hurried away, and it was long before I could efface the impression made upon my mind by this hideous spectacle.

In the case of rich people, the burning of the body sometimes costs more than a thousand rupees; the most costly wood, such as rose and sandal wood, being employed for that purpose. Besides this, a Brahmin, music, and female mourners, are necessary parts of the ceremony.

After the body has been burnt, the bones are collected, laid in a vase, and thrown into the Ganges, or some other holy river. The nearest relation is obliged to set fire to the pile.

There are naturally none of these ceremonies among poor people. They simply burn their dead on common wood or cow-dung; and if they cannot even buy these materials, they fasten a stone to the corpse and throw it into the river.

I will here relate a short anecdote that I had from a very trustworthy person. It may serve as an example of the atrocities that are often committed from false ideas of religion.

Mr. N--- was once, during his travels, not far from the Ganges, and was

161

accompanied by several servants and a dog. Suddenly the latter disappeared, and all the calling in the world would not bring him back. He was at last discovered on the banks of the Ganges, standing near a human body, which he kept licking. Mr. N--- went up and found that the man had been left to die, but had still some spark of life left. He summoned his attendants, had the slime and filth washed off the poor wretch's face, and wrapped him well up. In a few days after he was completely recovered. On Mr. N---'s now being about to leave him, the man begged and prayed him not to do so, as he had lost his caste, and would never more be recognised by any of his relations; in a word that he was completely wiped out of the list of the living. Mr. N--- took him into his service, and the man, at the present day, is still in the enjoyment of perfect health. The event narrated occurred years ago.

The Hindoos themselves acknowledge that their customs, with regard to dying persons, occasion many involuntary murders; but their religion ordains that when the physician declares there is no hope left, the person must die.

During my stay in Calcutta, I could learn no more of the manners and customs of the Hindoos than what I have described, but I became acquainted with some of the particulars of a Mahomedan marriage. On the day appointed for the ceremony, the nuptial bed, elegantly ornamented, is carried, with music and festivity, to the house of the bridegroom, and late in the evening, the bride herself is also conveyed there in a close palanquin, with music and torches, and a large crowd of friends, many of whom carry regular pyramids of tapers; that well known kind of firework, the Bengal-fire, with its beautiful light-blue flame, is also in requisition for the evening's proceedings.

On arriving at the bridegroom's house, the newly-married couple alone are admitted; the rest remain outside playing, singing, and hallooing until broad day.

I often heard Europeans remark that they considered the procession of the nuptial couch extremely improper. But as the old saying goes—"A man can see the mote in his neighbour's eye when he cannot perceive the beam in his own;" and it struck me that the manner in which marriages are managed among the Europeans who are settled here, is much more unbecoming. It is a rule with the English, that on the day appointed for the marriage, which takes place towards evening, the bridegroom shall not see his bride before he meets her at the altar. An infringement of this regulation would be shocking. In case the two who are about to marry should have anything to say to each other, they are obliged to do so in writing. Scarcely, however, has the clergyman pronounced the benediction, ere the new married couple are packed off together in a carriage, and sent to spend a week in some hotel in the vicinity of the town. For this purpose, either the hotel at Barrackpore or one of two or three houses at Gardenrich is selected. In case all the lodgings should be occupied, a circumstance of by no means rare occurrence, since almost all marriages are celebrated in the months of November and December, a boat containing one or two cabins is hired, and the young people are condemned to pass the next eight days completely shut up from all their friends, and even the parents themselves are not allowed access to their children.

I am of opinion that a girl's modesty must suffer much from these coarse customs. How the poor creature must blush on entering the place selected for her imprisonment; and how each look, each grin of the landlord, waiters, or boatmen, must wound her feelings!

The worthy Germans, who think everything excellent that does not emanate from themselves, copy this custom most conscientiously.

CHAPTER XII. BENARES.

DEPARTURE FROM CALCUTTA—ENTRANCE INTO THE GANGES— RAJMAHAL—GUR—JUNGHERA—MONGHYR—PATNA— DEINAPOOR—GESIPOOR—BENARES—RELIGION OF THE HINDOOS —DESCRIPTION OF THE TOWN—PALACES AND TEMPLES—THE HOLY PLACES—THE HOLY APES—THE RUINS OF SARANTH—AN INDIGO PLANTATION—A VISIT TO THE RAJAH OF BENARES— MARTYRS AND FAKIRS—THE INDIAN PEASANT—THE MISSIONARY ESTABLISHMENT.

On the 10th of December, after a stay of more than five weeks, I left Calcutta for Benares. The journey may be performed either by land, or else by water, on the Ganges. By land, the distance is 470 miles; by water, 800 miles during the rainy season, and 465 miles more during the dry months, as the boats are compelled to take very circuitous routes to pass from the Hoogly, through the Sonderbunds, into the Ganges.

The land journey is performed in post-palanquins, carried by men, who, like horses, are changed every four or six miles. The traveller proceeds by night as well as day, and at each station finds people ready to receive him, as a circular from the post-office is always sent a day or two before, to prepare them for his arrival. At night the train is increased by the addition of a torch-bearer, to scare off the wild beasts by the glare of his torch. The travelling expenses for one person are about 200 rupees (£20), independent of the luggage, which is reckoned separately.

The journey by water can be accomplished in steamers, one of which leaves almost every week for Allahabad (135 miles beyond Benares). The journey occupies from fourteen to twenty days, as, on account of the numerous sand-banks, it is impossible for the vessel to proceed on her course except in the day-time, and even then it is by no means unusual for her to run aground, especially when the water is low.

The fares to Benares are: first cabin, 257 rupees (£25 14s.); second cabin, 216 rupees (£21 12s.). Provisions, without wine or spirits, three rupees (6s.) a day.

As I had heard so much of the magnificent banks of the Ganges, and of the important towns situated on them, I determined to go by water.

On the 8th of December, according to the advertisement, the steamer "General Macleod," 140 horse-power, commanded by Captain Kellar, was to leave her moorings; but on going on board, I received the gratifying intelligence that we should have to wait twenty-four hours, which twenty-four hours were extended to as much again, so that we did not actually set off before 11 o'clock on the morning of the 10th. We first proceeded down the stream to the sea as far as Katcherie, and on the following day we rounded Mud Point, and entered the Sonderbunds, where we beat about as far as Culna. From there we proceeded up the Gury, a large tributary stream flowing into the Ganges below Rumpurbolea. During the first few days, the scenery was monotonous to the highest degree; there were neither towns nor villages to be seen; the banks were flat, and the prospect everywhere bounded by tall, thick bushes, which the English term *jungles*, that is to say, "virgin forests." For my own part, I could see no "virgin forests," as by this term I understand a forest of mighty trees. During the night, we heard, from time to time, the roaring of tigers. These animals are pretty abundant in these parts, and frequently attack the natives if they happen to remain out late wooding. I was shown the tattered fragment of a man's dress, hung upon a bush, to commemorate the fact of a native having been torn to pieces there by one of these beasts. But they are not the only foes that man has to dread here; the Ganges contains quite as deadly ones, namely—the ravenous crocodiles. These may be seen in groups of six or eight, sunning themselves on the slimy banks of the river or on the numerous sandbanks. They vary in length from six to fifteen feet. On the approach of the steamer, several started up, affrighted by the noise, and glided hastily into the dirty yellow stream.

The different branches of the Sonderbunds and the Gury are often so narrow that there is hardly room for two vessels to pass each other; while, on the other hand, they frequently expand into lakes that are miles across. In spite, too, of the precaution of only proceeding by day, on account of the numerous sandbanks and shallows, accidents are of frequent occurrence. We ourselves did not come off scot free. In one of the narrow branches I have alluded to, while our vessel was stopped to allow another to pass, one of the two ships that we had in tow came with such violence against the steamer, that the sides of a cabin were driven in: luckily, however, no one was injured.

In another arm of the river, two native vessels were lying at anchor. The crews were somewhat slow in perceiving us, and had not time to raise their anchors before we came puffing up to them. The captain did not stop, as he thought there was room to pass, but turned the steamer's head so far in shore, that he ran into the bushes, and left some of the blinds of the cabin-windows suspended as trophies behind him, whereat he was so enraged, that he immediately dispatched two boats to cut the poor creatures' hawsers, thereby causing them to lose their anchors. This was another action worthy of a European!

Near Culna (358 miles from the sea), we entered the Gury, a considerable tributary of the Ganges, which it flows into below Rumpurbolea. The jungles here recede, and their place is occupied by beautiful plantations of rice, and other vegetables. There was, too, no scarcity of villages, only the huts, which were mostly built of straw and palm-leaves, were small and wretched. The appearance of the steamer soon collected all the inhabitants, who left their fields and huts and greeted it with loud huzzas.

15th December. This evening we struck, for the first time, on a sandbank. It cost us some trouble before we could get off again.

16th December. We had entered the Ganges yesterday. At a late hour this evening we hove to near the little village of Commercolly. The inhabitants brought provisions of every description on board, and we had an opportunity of becoming acquainted with the prices of the various articles. A fine wether cost four rupees (8s.); eighteen fowls, a rupee (2s.); a fish, weighing several pounds, an anna (1½d.); eight eggs, an anna; twenty oranges, two annas (3d.); a pound of fine bread, three beis (ld.); and yet, in spite of these ludicrously cheap prices, the captain charged each passenger three rupees (6s.) a-day for his board, which was not even passable! Many of the passengers made purchases here of eggs, new bread, and oranges, and the captain was actually not ashamed to let these articles, which were paid for out of our own pockets, appear at his table that we all paid so dearly for.

18th December. Bealeah, a place of considerable importance, noted for the number of its prisons. It is a depot for criminals, {158a} who are sent here from all parts. The prisoners here cannot be so desirous of escaping as those in Europe, for I saw numbers of them, very slightly ironed, wandering about in groups or alone, in the place itself and its vicinity, without having any gaolers with them. They are properly taken care of, and employed in various kinds of light work. There is a paper manufactory, which is almost entirely carried on by them.

The inhabitants appeared to possess a more than usual degree of fanaticism. I and another passenger, Herr Lau, had gone to take a walk in the place, and were about to enter a small street in which there was a Hindoo temple; but no sooner, however, did the people perceive our intention, than they set up a horrible yelling, and pressed on us so closely, that we held it advisable to restrain our curiosity and turn back.

19th December. Today we perceived the low ranges of the Rajmahal Hills, the first we had seen since we left Madras. In the evening, we were again stuck fast upon a sandbank. We remained tolerably quiet during the night, but, as soon as it was morning, every possible means were adopted to get us off again. The vessels

165

we had in tow were cast off, our steam got up to its highest pitch; the sailors, too, exerted themselves indefatigably, and at noon we were stuck just as fast as we were the evening before. About this time, we perceived a steamer on its way from Allahabad to Calcutta; but our captain hoisted no signals of distress, being very much vexed that he should be seen by a comrade in such a position. The captain of the other vessel, however, offered his assistance of his own accord but his offer was coldly and curtly refused, and it was not until after several hours of the most strenuous exertion that we succeeded in getting off the bank into deep water.

In the course of the day, we touched at Rajmahal, {158b} a large village, which, on account of the thick woods and numerous swamps and morasses around it, is reckoned a most unhealthy place.

It was here that Gur, one of the largest towns of India, once stood. It is said to have been twenty square miles in extent, and to have contained about two millions of inhabitants, and, according to the latest books of travels, the most splendid and considerable ruins are still to be seen there. Those of the so-called "Golden Mosque" are especially remarkable, being very fine and faced with marble; the gateways are celebrated for their great width of span and the solidity of their side walls.

As there was, fortunately, a depot for coals here, we were allowed a few hours to do as we liked. The younger passengers seized the opportunity to go out shooting, being attracted by the splendid forests, the finest I had as yet seen in India. It was certainly reported that they were very much infested with tigers, but this deterred no one.

I also engaged in the chase—although it was one of a different description. I penetrated far and wide, through forest and swamp, in order to discover the ruins. I was successful; but how meagre and wretched they were! The most important were those of two common city-gates, built of sandstone and ornamented with a few handsome sculptures, but without any arches or cupolas. One inconsiderable temple, with four corner towers, was in several places covered with very fine cement. Besides these, there were a few other ruins or single fragments of buildings and pillars scattered around, but all of them together do not cover a space of two square miles.

On the border of the forest, or some hundred paces farther in, were situated a number of huts belonging to the natives, approached by picturesque paths running beneath shady avenues of trees. In Bealeah, the people were very fanatic, while here the men were very jealous. At the conclusion of my excursion, one of the gentlemen passengers had joined me, and we directed our steps towards the habitations of the natives. As soon as the men saw my companion, they called out to their wives, and ordered them to take refuge in the huts. The women ran in from all directions, but remained very quietly at the doors of their dwellings to see us pass, and quite forgot to conceal their faces while they did so.

166

In these parts, there are whole woods of cocoa-palms. This tree is properly a native of India, where it attains a height of eighty feet, and bears fruit in its sixth year. In other countries, it is scarcely fifty feet high, and does not bear fruit before it is twelve or fifteen years old. This tree is, perhaps, the most useful one in the known world. It produces large and nutritious fruit, excellent milk, large leaves that are used for covering in and roofing huts, materials for strong cordage, the clearest oil for burning, mats, woven stuffs, colouring matter, and even a kind of drink called surr, toddy, or palm brandy, and obtained by incisions made in the crown of the tree, to which, during an entire month, the Hindoos climb up every morning and evening, making incisions in the stem and hanging pots underneath to catch the sap which oozes out. The rough condition of the bark facilitates considerably the task of climbing up the tree. The Hindoos tie a strong cord round the trunk and their own body, and another round their feet, which they fix firmly against the tree; they then raise themselves up, drawing the upper rope with their hands and the lower one with the points of their feet, after them. I have seen them climb the highest trees in this manner with the greatest ease in two minutes at the most. Round their bodies they have a belt, to which are suspended a knife and one or two small jars.

The sap is at first quite clear, and agreeably sweet, but begins, in six or eight hours' time, to ferment, and then assumes a whitish tint, while its flavour becomes disagreeably acid. From this, with the addition of some rice, is manufactured strong arrack. A good tree will yield above a gallon of this sap in four-and-twenty hours, but during the year in which the sap is thus extracted, it bears no fruit.

21st December. About 80 miles below Rajmahal, we passed three rather steep rocks rising out of the Ganges. The largest is about sixty feet high; the next in size, which is overgrown with bushes, is the residence of a Fakir, whom the true believers supply with provisions. We could not see the holy man, as it was beginning to grow dark as we passed. This, however, did not cause us so much regret, as that we were unable to visit the Botanical Garden at Bogulpore, which is said to be the finest in all India; but as there was no coal depot at Bogulpore, we did not stop.

On the 22nd of December, we passed the remarkable mountain scenery of Junghera, which rises, like an island of rocks, from the majestic Ganges. This spot was, in former times, looked on as the holiest in the whole course of the river. Thousands of boats and larger vessels were constantly to be seen there, as no Hindoo believed he could die in peace without having visited the place. Numerous Fakirs had established themselves here, strengthening the poor pilgrims with unctuous exhortations, and taking in return their pious gifts. The neighbourhood has, however, at present, lost its reputation for sanctity, and the offerings received are scarcely sufficient to maintain two or three Fakirs.

In the evening we stopped near Monghyr, {160a} a tolerably large town, with

167

some old fortifications. The most conspicuous object is a cemetery, crowded with monuments. The monuments are so peculiar, that had I not seen similar ones in the cemeteries of Calcutta, I should never have imagined that they belonged to any sect of Christians. There were temples, pyramids, immense catafalques, kiosks, etc., all massively built of tiles. The extent of this cemetery is quite disproportioned to the number of Europeans in Monghyr; but the place is said to be the most unhealthy in India, so that when a European is ordered there for any number of years, he generally takes a last farewell of all his friends.

Six miles hence, there are some hot springs, which are looked upon by the natives as sacred.

We had lost sight of the Rajmahal Hills at Bogulpore; on both sides of the river, nothing was now to be seen but an uninterrupted succession of flat plains.

24th December. Patna, {160b} one of the largest and most ancient cities of Bengal, with a population of about 300,000 souls, {161} consists of a long, broad street, eight miles long, with numerous short alleys running into it. The houses, which are mostly constructed of mud, struck me as particularly small and wretched. Under the projecting roofs are exposed for sale goods and provisions of the simplest kind. That part of the street in which the greatest number of these miserable shops are situated, is dignified by the grand name of the "Bazaar." The few houses of a better description might easily be counted without any very great trouble; they are built of tiles, and surrounded by wooden galleries and colonnades prettily carved. In these houses were to be found the best and finest shops.

The temples of the Hindoos, the Ghauts (flights of steps, halls, and gateways) on the Ganges, like the mosques of the Mahomedans, always look a great deal better at a distance than they do on a nearer inspection. The only objects worthy of notice which I saw here, were a few bell-shaped mausoleums, like those in Ceylon, which they greatly surpassed in size, although not in artistic beauty; they were certainly more than 200 feet in circumference, and eighty feet in height. Excessively narrow entrances, with simple doors, conduct into the interior. On the outside, two small flights of steps, forming a semicircle, lead up to the top. The doors were not opened for us, and we were obliged to content ourselves with the assurance that, with the exception of a small, plain sarcophagus there was nothing inside.

Patna is a place of great importance, from the trade in opium, by which many of the natives acquire large fortunes. As a general rule, they make no display of their riches, either as regards their clothes, or in any other public kind of luxury. There are only two sorts of dress—one for those in easy circumstances, which is like that of the Orientals, and one for the poorest classes, which consists of a piece of cloth bound round the loins.

The principal street presents a bustling appearance, being much frequented by carriages, as well as pedestrians. The Hindoos, like the Jews, are such determined foes to walking, that they do not think the worst place in the most wretched cart beneath their acceptance.

The vehicles in most general use are narrow, wooden cars upon two wheels, and composed of four posts with cross-beams. Coloured woollen stuff is hung over these, and a kind of canopy keeps off the sun. There is properly only room for two persons, although I have seen three or four crowded into them. This put me in mind of the Italians, who fill a carriage so that not even the steps are left vacant. These cars are called *baili*. They are closely curtained when women travel in them.

I expected to see the streets here full of camels and elephants, since I had read so much about it in some descriptions: but I saw only bailis drawn by oxen and a few horsemen, but neither camels nor elephants.

Towards evening we drove to Deinapore, {162} which is eight miles from Patna, along an excellent post-road, planted with handsome trees.

Deinapore is one of the largest English military stations, and contains extensive barracks, which almost constitute a town in themselves. The town is but a short distance from the barracks. There are many Mahomedans among the inhabitants, who surpass the Hindoos in industry and perseverance.

I here saw elephants for the first time on the Indian continent. In a serai outside the town there were eight large handsome animals.

When we returned to the ship in the evening, we found it like a camp. All kinds of articles were brought there and laid out for inspection; but the shoemakers were particularly numerous. Their work appeared neat and lasting, and remarkably cheap. A pair of men's boots, for example, cost from one and a half to two rupees (3s. to 4s.); but it is true that twice as much is always asked for them. I saw on this occasion the way in which the European sailors conduct bargains with the natives. One of the engineers wanted to buy a pair of shoes, and offered a quarter of the price asked. The seller, not consenting to this, took his goods back; but the engineer snatched them out of his hand, threw down a few beis more than what he had offered, and hastened to his cabin. The shoemaker pursued him, and demanded the shoes back; instead of which he received several tough blows, and was threatened that if he was not quiet he should be compelled to leave the ship immediately. The poor creature returned half crying to his pack of goods.

A similar occurrence took place on the same evening. A Hindoo boy brought a box for one of the travellers, and asked for a small payment for his trouble; he was not listened to. The boy remained standing by, repeating his request now and then. He was driven away, and as he would not go quietly, blows were had recourse to. The captain happened to pass accidentally, and asked what was the matter. The boy, sobbing, told him; the captain shrugged his shoulders, and the boy was put out of the ship.

169

How many similar and even more provoking incidents have I seen? The so-called "barbarian and heathen people" have good reason to hate us. Wherever the Europeans go they will not give any reward, but only orders and commands; and their rule is generally much more oppressive than that of the natives.

26th December. The custom of exposing dying people on the banks of the Ganges, does not appear to be so general as some travellers state. We sailed on the river for fourteen days, during which time we passed many thickly populated towns and villages, and did not meet with a single case until today. The dying man lay close to the water, and several men, probably his relations, were seated round him, awaiting his decease. One dipped water and mud out of the river with his hands, and put them to the nose and mouth of the dying man. The Hindoos believe that if they die at the river with their mouths full of the holy water, they are quite certain to go to heaven. His relations or friends remain by the dying man till sunset, when they go home, and leave him to his fate. He generally falls a prey to crocodiles. I very seldom saw any floating corpses; only two during the whole journey. Most of the corpses are burnt.

27th December. Ghazipoor is an important place, and is remarkable at a distance for its handsome ghauts. Here stands a pretty monument erected to the memory of Lord Cornwallis, who conquered Tippoo Saib in 1790. Very near is a large establishment for training horses, which is said to turn out remarkably fine ones. But Ghazipoor is most remarkable for its enormous rose-fields, and the rose-water and attar prepared here. The latter is obtained in the following manner:—

Upon forty pounds of roses, with the calixes, sixty pounds of water are poured, and the whole is distilled over a slow fire. From this, about thirty pounds of rose-water are obtained. Another forty pounds of roses are again added to this, and, at the utmost, twenty pounds of water distilled off. This is then exposed during the night to the cold air in pans, and in the morning the oil is found swimming upon the surface and is skimmed off. Not more than an ounce and a half of attar, at the utmost, is obtained from eighty pounds of roses. An ounce of true attar costs, even at Ghazipoor, 40 rupees (£4).

At 10 o'clock on the morning of the 28th, we at length reached the holy town of Benares. We anchored near Radschgaht, where coolies and camels were ready to receive us.

Before taking leave of the Ganges, I must remark that, during the whole journey of about a thousand miles, I did not meet with a single spot remarkable for its especial beauty, or one picturesque view. The banks are either flat or bounded by layers of earth ten or twenty feet in height, and, further inland, sandy plains alternate with plantations or dried-up meadows and miserable jungles. There are, indeed, a great number of towns and villages, but, with the exception of occasional handsome houses and the ghauts, they are composed of a collection of huts. The river itself is frequently divided into several branches, and is sometimes so broad that it resembles a sea rather than a river, for the banks are

170

scarcely visible.

Benares is the most sacred town of India. It is to the Hindoos what Mecca is to the Mahomedans, or Rome to the Catholics. The belief of the Hindoos in its holiness is such that, according to their opinion, every man will be saved who remains twenty-four hours in the town, without reference to his religion. This noble toleration is one of the finest features in the religion and character of this people, and puts to shame the prejudices of many Christian sects.

The number of pilgrims amounts annually to 300,000 or 400,000, and the town is one of the most wealthy in the country, through their trading, sacrifices, and gifts.

This may not be an improper place to make some remarks upon the religion of these interesting people, which I extract from Zimmerman's "Handbook of Travels."

"The foundation of the Hindoo faith is the belief in a superior primitive being, immortality, and a reward of virtue. The chief idea of God is so great and beautiful, its moral so pure and elevated, that its equal has not been found among any other people.

"Their creed is to worship the highest Being, to invoke their guardian gods, to be well-disposed towards their fellow-men, to pity the unfortunate and help them, to bear patiently the inconveniences of life, not to lie or break their word, to read the sacred histories and to give heed to them, not to talk much, to fast, pray, and to bathe at stated periods. These are the general duties which the sacred writings of the Hindoos enforce, without exception, upon all castes or sects.

"Their true and only god is called 'Brahma,' which must not be confounded with Brahma who was created by the former, who is the true, eternal, holy, and unchangeable light of all time and space. The wicked are punished and the good rewarded.

"Out of the Eternal Being proceeded the goddess Bhavani, i.e., Nature, and a host of 1,180 million spirits. Among these there are three demi-gods or superior spirits, Brahma, Vishnu, and Shiva, the Hindoo Trinity, called by them Trimurti.

"For a long time, happiness and content prevailed; but they afterwards revolted, and many gave up their allegiance. The rebels were cast down from on high into the pit of darkness. Hereupon succeeded the transmigration of souls; every animal and every plant was animated by one of the fallen angels, and the remarkable amiability of the Hindoos towards animals is owing to this belief. They look upon them as their fellow-creatures, and will not put any of them to death.

"The Hindoo reverences the great purpose of nature, the production of organized bodies, in the most disinterested and pious manner. Everything tending to this end is to him venerable and holy, and it is in this respect alone that he worships the Lingam.

171

"It may be affirmed, that the superstitions of this creed have only gradually become an almost senseless delusion through corruption and misunderstanding.

"In order to judge of the present state of their religion, it will be sufficient to describe the figures of a few of their chief deities.

"Brahma, as the creator of the world, is represented with four human heads and eight hands; in one hand he holds the scriptures, in the others, various idols. He is not worshipped in any temple, having lost this prerogative on account of his ambitious desire to find out the Supreme Being. However, after repenting of his folly, it was permitted that the Brahmins might celebrate some festivals in his honour, called Poutsché.

"Vishnu, as the maintainer of the world, is represented in twenty-one different forms:—Half fish half man, as tortoise, half lion half man, Buddha, dwarf, etc. The wife of Vishnu is worshipped as the goddess of fruitfulness, plenty, and beauty. The cow is considered sacred to her.

"Shiva is the destroyer, revenger, and the conqueror of Death. He has, therefore, a double character, beneficent or terrible; he rewards or punishes. He is generally hideously represented, entirely surrounded by lightning, with three eyes, the largest of which is in the forehead; he has also eight arms, in each of which he holds something.

"Although these three deities are equal, the religion of the Hindoos is divided into only two sects—the worshippers of Vishnu and those of Shiva. Brahma has no peculiar sect, since he is denied temples and pagodas; however, the whole priestly caste—the Brahmins—may be considered as his worshippers, since they affirm that they proceeded from his head.

"The worshippers of Vishnu have on their foreheads a red or yellowish painted sign of the Jani; the Shiva worshippers, the sign of the Lingam, or an obelisk, triangle, or the sun.

"333,000,000 subordinate deities are recognised. They control the elements, natural phenomena, the passions, acts, diseases, etc. They are represented in different forms and having all kinds of attributes.

"There are also genii, good and evil spirits. The number of the good exceeds that of the bad by about 3,000,000.

"Other objects are also considered sacred by the Hindoos, as rivers, especially the Ganges, which is believed to have been formed from the sweat of Shiva. The water of the Ganges is so highly esteemed, that a trade is carried on in it for many miles inland.

"Among animals, they chiefly look upon the cow, ox, elephant, ape, eagle, swan, peacock, and serpent, as sacred; among plants, the lotus, the banana, and the mango-tree.

172

"The Brahmins have an especial veneration for a stone, which is, according to Sonnerat, a fossil ammonite in slate.

"It is in the highest degree remarkable that there is no representation of the Supreme Being to be found in all Hindostan. The idea appears too great for them; they consider the whole earth as his temple, and worship him under all forms.

"The adherents of Shiva bury their dead; the others either burn them or throw them into the river."

No one can form an accurate idea of India who has not gone beyond Calcutta. This city has become almost European. The palaces, the equipages are European; there are societies, balls, concerts, promenades, almost the same as in Paris or London; and if it was not for the tawny natives in the streets, and the Hindoo servants in the houses, a stranger might easily forget that he was in a foreign country.

It is very different in Benares. The Europeans are isolated there; foreign customs and manners everywhere surround them, and remind them that they are tolerated intruders. Benares contains 300,000 inhabitants, of which scarcely 150 are Europeans.

The town is handsome, especially when seen from the river side, where its defects are not observed. Magnificent rows of steps, built of colossal stones, lead up to the houses and palaces, and artistically built gateways. In the best part of the town, they form a continuous line two miles in length. These steps cost enormous sums of money, and a large town might have been built with the stones employed for them.

The handsome part of the town contains a great number of antique palaces, in the Moorish, Gothic, and Hindoo styles, many of which are six stories high. The gates are most magnificent, and the fronts of the palaces and houses are covered with masterly arabesques and sculptured work; the different stories are richly ornamented with fine colonnades, verandahs, balconies, and friezes. The windows alone did not please me; they were low, small, and seldom regularly arranged. All the houses and palaces have very broad sloping roofs and terraces. The innumerable temples afford a proof of the wealth and piety of the inhabitants of this town. Every Hindoo in good circumstances has a temple in his house, i.e., a small tower, which is frequently only twenty feet high.

The Hindoo temples consist properly of a tower thirty or sixty feet in height, without windows, and having only a small entrance. They appear, especially at a distance, very striking and handsome, as they are either artistically sculptured or richly covered with projecting ornaments, such as pinnacles, small columns, pyramids, leaves, niches, etc.

Unfortunately, many of these beautiful buildings are in ruins. The Ganges here

173

and there undermines the foundations, and palaces and temples sink into the soft earth or fall entirely down. Miserable little huts are in some places built upon these ruins, and disfigure the fine appearance of the town, for even the ruins themselves are still beautiful.

At sunrise, a spectacle is to be seen at the river which has not its counterpart in the world. The pious Hindoos come here to perform their devotions; they step into the river, turn towards the sun, throw three handsful of water upon their heads, and mutter their prayers. Taking into account the large population which Benares contains, besides pilgrims, it will not be exaggeration to say that the daily number of devotees amounts, on the average, to 50,000 persons. Numbers of Brahmins sit in small kiosks, or upon blocks of stone on the steps, close to the water's edge, to receive the charity of the wealthy, and grant them absolution in return.

Every Hindoo must bathe at least once in the day, and particularly in the morning; if he is pious and has time, he repeats the ceremony again in the evening. The women bathe at home.

At the time of the festival called Mala, when the concourse of pilgrims is innumerable, the steps are crowded with masses of human beings, and the river appears as if covered with black spots from the number of the bathers' heads.

The interior of the city is far less handsome than that portion which extends along the Ganges. It contains many palaces; but these have not the same beautiful gateways, colonnades, and verandahs as those already described. Many of these buildings are covered with fine cement, and others are painted with miserable frescoes.

The streets are for the most part both dirty and ugly, and many of them are so narrow, that there is scarcely room for a palanquin to pass. At the corner of almost every house stands the figure of the god Shiva.

Among the temples in the town, the handsomest is the "Bisvishas:" it has two towers connected by colonnades, with their summits covered with golden plates. The temple is surrounded by a wall, but we were allowed to enter the fore-court, and to go as far as the entrance. We saw inside several images of Vishnu and Shiva, wreathed with flowers, and strewn over with grains of rice, wheat, etc. Small bulls of metal or stone stood in the porch, and living white bulls (of which I counted eight) wandered about at liberty. The latter are considered sacred, and are allowed to roam where they please, and are not prevented from satisfying their hunger with even the sacrificial flowers and corn.

These sacred animals do not remain in the temples only—they wander about the streets; and the people turn reverently out of their way, and frequently give them fodder. They do not, however, allow them to eat the corn exposed for sale, as was formerly the case. If one of the sacred animals happen to die, it is either thrown into the river or burnt. They receive in this respect the same honour as the

174

Hindoos themselves.

In the temple, there were men and women who had brought flowers, with which they decorated the images. Some of them also laid a piece of money under the flowers. They then sprinkled them over with Ganges' water, and strewed rice and other corn about.

Near the temple are the most holy places in the town, namely—the so-called "holy well" and the Mankarnika, a large basin of water. The following anecdote is told of the former:—

When the English had conquered Benares, they planted a cannon before the entrance of the temple to destroy the image of the god Mahadeo. The Brahmins, greatly indignant at this, instigated the people to revolt, and they hastened in numerous crowds to the temple. The English, to prevent a disturbance, said to the people: "If your god is stronger than the Christian God, the balls will not hurt him; but if not, he will be broken to pieces." Of course; the latter was the result. The Brahmins, however, did not give up their cause, but declared that they had seen the spirit of their god leave the idol before the cannon was fired, and plunge into the spring near at hand. From this time the spring was considered sacred.

The Mankarnika is a deep basin, paved with stone, about sixty feet long, and of equal breadth; broad steps lead from the four sides into the water. A similar tradition, but connected with the god Shiva, is attached to this place. Both deities are said to have continued to reside in these waters down to the present day. Every pilgrim who visits Benares must, on his arrival, bathe in this holy pool, and, at the same time, make a small offering. Several Brahmins are always present to receive these gifts. They are in no way distinguished by their dress from the bulk of the better classes, but the colour of their skin is clearer, and many of them have very noble features.

Fifty paces from this pool, on the banks of the Ganges, stands a remarkably handsome Hindoo temple, with three towers. Unfortunately, the ground sunk in a few years since, and the towers were thrown out of their proper position: one inclines to the right and the other to the left; the third is almost sunk into the Ganges.

Among the thousand of other temples, there is here and there one which is worth the trouble of a cursory inspection, but I would not advise any one to go much out of their way on their account. The place for burning the dead is very near the holy pool. When we went there, they were just roasting a corpse—the mode of burning cannot be described by any other name, the fire was so small, and the corpse projected over on all sides.

Among the other buildings, the Mosque Aurang Zeb is most worthy of the notice of travellers. It is famous on account of its two minarets, which are 150 feet high, and are said to be the slenderest in the world. They look like two needles, and certainly are more deserving of the name than that of Cleopatra at Alexandria.

175

Narrow winding staircases in the interior lead to the top, upon which a small platform, with a balustrade a foot high, is erected. It is fortunate for those who are not subject to dizziness. They can venture out, and take a bird's-eye view of the endless sea of houses, and the innumerable Hindoo temples; the Ganges also, with its step quays, miles long, lies exposed below. I was told that on very clear, fine days, a distant chain of mountains was perceivable—the day was fine and clear, but I could not see the mountains.

The observatory is a very remarkable and artistic building. It was built by Dscheising, under the intelligent Emperor Akbar, more than two centuries since. There are no ordinary telescopes to be found there: all the instruments are constructed of massive blocks of stone. Upon a raised terrace, to which stone steps lead, stand circular tables, semicircular and quadratic curves, etc. which are covered with signs, writing, and lines. With these instruments, the Brahmins made, and still make, their observations and calculations. We met with several Brahmins busily engaged with calculations and written treatises.

Benares is on the whole the chief seat of Indian learning. Among the Brahmins, 6,000 in number, I was told there were many who give instruction in astronomy, Sanscrit, and other scientific subjects.

The sacred apes are another of the curiosities of Benares. Their principal location is upon some of the immense mango-trees in the suburbs of Durgakund. The animals seemed as if they knew we had come to see them, for they approached quite close to us; but when the servant, whom I had sent for some food for them, returned, and called them to him, it was amusing to see the merry creatures come running from the trees, the roofs of the houses, and the streets. We were in a moment closely surrounded by several hundreds, who fought together in the most comical manner for the fruits and grain. The largest or oldest acted as commander. Wherever there was quarrelling, he rushed in, and commenced thrashing the combatants, threatening them with his teeth, and making a muttering sound, upon which they immediately separated. It was the largest and most comical party of monkeys I ever saw. They were generally more than two feet high, and their skins were a dirty yellow colour.

My kind host took me one day to Sarnath (five miles from Benares), where there are some interesting ruins of three remarkably massive towers. They are not particularly high, and stand upon three artificially raised mounds, a mile distant from each other. Both the mounds and towers are constructed of large bricks. The largest of these towers is still covered in many places with stone slabs, on which traces of arabesques are here and there visible. Numbers of slabs lie scattered about the ground. There are no signs of any such covering on the remaining towers. In each there is a small door and a single apartment.

Excavations were commenced beneath these towers by the English government in the hope of making some discoveries which would throw light upon the origin of these buildings; but nothing was found beyond an empty underground vault.

176

There is a lake close by of artificial construction, which is supplied with water from the Ganges by a canal.

There is a very singular tradition connected with these towers and the lake. "In very ancient times three brothers ruled here, who were giants, and had these buildings erected and the lake excavated, and all in one day. It must, however, be known that a day at that time was equal to two years of modern reckoning. The giants were so tall that they could go from one tower to the other with a step, and the reason these were built so close was their fondness for each other, and their desire to be always together."

An indigo plantation in the neighbourhood, the first I ever saw, was not less interesting to me than these towers and their singular tradition. The indigo plant is herbaceous, and from one to three feet high, with delicate bluish-green leaves. The harvest is generally in August; the plants are cut tolerably low on the principal stem, tied together in bundles, and thrown into large wooden vats. Planks are laid on the tops of the bundles weighted with stones, and water poured on them; generally after sixteen hours, though sometimes after several days, according to the character of the water, fermentation commences. This is the principal difficulty, and everything depends upon its continuance for the proper time. When the water has acquired a dark-green colour, it is transferred to other wooden vessels, lime added, and the whole stirred with wooden spades until a blue deposit takes place. After being allowed to settle, the water is poured off, and the substance remaining behind is put into long linen bags through which the moisture filters. As soon as the indigo is dry, it is broken in pieces and packed.

Shortly before my departure I had the pleasure of being presented to the Rajah through the aid of my fellow-traveller, Mr. Law. He resides in the Citadel Rhamnughur, which lies on the left bank of the Ganges, above the town.

A handsomely ornamented boat awaited us at the bank of the river, and on the other side a palanquin. We soon found ourselves at the entrance of the palace, the gateway of which is lofty and majestic. I expected to have been gratified in the interior by the sight of spacious courts and a handsome style of architecture, but found only irregular courts and small unsymmetrical apartments, destitute of all taste and luxury. In one of the courts was a plain-columned hall on the level of the ground, which served as a reception-room. This hall was overcrowded with glass lustres, lamps, and European furniture; on the walls were some miserable pictures, framed and glazed. Outside was a swarm of servants, who gazed at us with great attention. Presently the prince made his appearance, accompanied by his brother, and some courtiers and attendants, who could scarcely be distinguished the one from the other.

The two princes were very richly dressed; they wore wide trousers, long under and short over garments, all made of satin, embroidered with gold. The elder one, aged thirty-five, wore short silk cuffs, embroidered with gold, the edge set with diamonds; he had several large brilliant rings on his finger, and his silk shoes were covered with beautiful gold embroidery. His brother, a youth of nineteen, whom he had adopted, {170} wore a white turban with a costly clasp of diamonds and pearls. He had large pearls hanging from his ears, and rich massive bracelets on his wrists. The elder prince was a handsome man, with exceedingly amiable and intellectual features; the younger one pleased me far less.

We had scarcely seated ourselves, when a large silver basin with elaborately worked nargillys were brought, and we were invited to smoke. We declined this honour, and the prince smoked alone; he took only a few whiffs from the same nargilly, which was then replaced by another handsomer one.

The behaviour of the princes was very decorous and lively. I regretted that we could communicate only through an interpreter. He inquired whether I had ever seen a Natsch (festival dance). On my answering that I had not, he immediately ordered one to be performed.

In half an hour two female dancers and three musicians appeared. The dancers were dressed in gay gold-embroidered muslin, wide silk trousers, embroidered with gold, which reached to the ground, and quite covered their bare feet. One of the musicians played upon two small drums, the other two on four-stringed instruments, similar to our violins. They stood close behind the dancers, and played without melody or harmony; the dancers making at the same time very animated motions with their arms, hands, and fingers, more than with their feet, on which they wore silver bells, which they rung at intervals. They made handsome and graceful drapings and figures with their over garments. This performance lasted about a quarter of an hour, after which they accompanied the dance with singing. The two sylphides shrieked so miserably that I was in fear for my ears and nerves.

During the performance, sweetmeats, fruits, and sherbet (a cooling, sweet, acidulated beverage) were handed round.

After the dance was ended, the prince asked if I would like to see his garden, which is a mile distant from the palace. I was indiscreet enough to accept his offer.

In company with the young prince we proceeded to the front square of the palace, where elegantly ornamented elephants stood ready. The elder prince's favourite elephant, an animal of uncommon size and beauty, was destined for myself and Mr. Law. A scarlet canopy, with tassels, fringes, and gold embroidered lace, nearly covered the whole animal. A convenient seat was placed upon his broad back, which might be compared to a phaeton without wheels. The elephant was made to kneel down, a ladder was placed against his side, and Mr. Law and myself took our places. Behind us sat a servant, who held an enormously large umbrella over our heads. The driver sat upon the neck of the animal, and pricked it now and then between the ears with a sharp-pointed iron rod.

The young prince, with his attendant and servants, took their places upon the other elephants. Several officers on horseback rode at our side, two soldiers with drawn sabres ran in front of the party to clear the way, and upwards of a dozen soldiers, also with drawn sabres, surrounded us, while a few mounted soldiers brought up the rear.

Although the motion of the elephant is quite as jolting and unpleasant as that of the camel, this truly Indian ride afforded me great pleasure.

When we had arrived at the garden, the young prince seemed by his proud look to ask whether we were not charmed with its magnificence. Our delight was unfortunately assumed, for the garden was far too plain to deserve much praise. In the back-ground of the garden stands a somewhat ruinous royal summer palace.

As we were about leaving the garden, the gardener brought us some beautiful nosegays and delicious fruits—a custom universal in India.

Outside the garden was a very large water-basin, covered with handsome blocks of stone; broad steps led up to the water, and at the corner stood beautiful kiosks, ornamented with tolerably well-executed reliefs.

The Rajah of Benares receives from the English government an annual pension of one lac, that is, 100,000 rupees (£10,000). He is said to receive as much more from his property, and nevertheless to be very much in debt. The causes of this are his great extravagance in clothes and jewellery, his numerous wives, servants, horses, camels, and elephants, etc. I was told that the prince has forty wives, about a thousand servants and soldiers, a hundred horses, fifty camels, and twenty elephants.

On the following morning the Rajah sent to inquire how the excursion had pleased us, and presented me with confectionery, sweetmeats, and the rarest fruits; among others, grapes and pomegranates, which at this time of the year are scarce. They came from Cabul, which is about 700 miles distant from this place.

Finally, I must mention that for many years no one has died in the palace which the Rajah occupies. The reason of this is said to be the following:—"One of the rulers of this palace once asked a Brahmin what would become of the soul of any one who died in the palace. The Brahmin answered that it would go to heaven. The Rajah repeated the same question ninety-nine times, and always received the same answer. But on asking the hundredth time, the Brahmin lost patience, and answered that it would go into a donkey." Since that time every one, from the prince to the meanest servant, leaves the palace as soon as they feel themselves unwell. None of them are desirous of continuing after death the part which they have, perhaps, so frequently commenced in this life.

While in Benares I had two opportunities of seeing the so-called martyrs of the Fakirs (a priestly sect of the Hindoos). These martyrs impose upon themselves the most various tortures: for example, they stick an iron hook through their

179

flesh, and have themselves drawn up to a height of twenty or five-and-twenty feet; or they stand several hours in the day upon one foot, and at the same time stretch their arms in the air, or hold heavy weights in various positions, turn round in a circle for hours together, tear the flesh off their bodies, etc. They frequently torment themselves so much as to be in danger of their lives. These martyrs are still tolerably venerated by the people; however, there are at the present time but a few more remaining. One of the two whom I saw, held a heavy axe over his head, and had taken the bent attitude of a workman hewing wood. I watched him for more than a quarter of an hour; he remained in the same position as firmly and quietly as if he had been turned to stone. He had, perhaps, exercised this useless occupation for years. The other held the point of his foot to his nose.

Another sect of the Fakirs condemn themselves to eat only a little food, and that of the most disgusting kind: the flesh of oxen that have died, half-rotten vegetables, and refuse of every kind, even mud and earth; they say that it is quite immaterial what the stomach is filled with.

The Fakirs all go about almost naked, smear their bodies with cow-dung, not even excepting the face; and then strew ashes over themselves. They paint their breasts and foreheads with the symbolical figures of Vishnu and Shiva, and dye their ragged hair dark reddish brown. It is not easy to imagine anything more disgusting and repulsive than these priests. They wander about all the streets, preaching and doing whatever they fancy; they are, however, far less respected than the martyrs.

One of the gentlemen whose acquaintance I made in Benares, was so obliging as to communicate to me some information as to the relation of the peasants to the government. The peasant has no landed property. All the land belongs either to the English government, the East India Company, or the native princes. It is let out altogether; the principal tenants divide it into small lots, and sublet these to the peasants. The fate of the latter depends entirely upon the disposition of the principal tenant. He determines the amount of rent, and frequently demands the money at a time when the crops are not harvested, and the peasant cannot pay; the poor people are then obliged to sell the unripe crops for half their worth, and their landlord generally contrives to buy it himself in the name of another person. The unfortunate peasant frequently has scarcely a sufficiency left to keep life in himself and his family.

Laws and judges there certainly are in the country, and, as everywhere else, the laws are good and the magistrates just; but it is another question whether the poor ever receive justice. The districts are so extensive, that the peasant cannot undertake a journey of seventy or eighty miles; and even when he lives near, he cannot always reach the presence of the magistrate. The business of the latter is so great, that he cannot himself attend to the details, and generally he is the only European in office, the remaining officials consisting of Hindoos and Mahomedans, whose character—a lamentable fact—is always worse the more

180

they come in contact with Europeans. If, therefore, the peasant comes to the court without bringing a present, he is generally turned away, his petition or complaint is not accepted or listened to; and how is he to bring a present after being deprived of everything by the landlord? The peasant knows this, and therefore seldom makes a complaint.

An Englishman (unfortunately I have forgotten his name) who travelled in India for scientific purposes, proves that the peasants have now to suffer more than formerly under their native princes.

In India, under the so-called "free English government," I found a sad proof that the position of the slaves in Brazil is better than that of the free peasants here. The slave there has not to provide for any of his wants, and he is never burdened with too much work, as the interest of his master would then suffer; for a slave costs seven or eight hundred gulders (£70 or £80), and it is to the interest of his owner that he should be well treated, that he may be longer of service. It cannot be denied that there are cases in which the slaves are tyrannically treated, but this is extremely rare.

Several German and English missionaries reside in the neighbourhood of Benares, and go constantly to the town to preach. At one of these missionary establishments is a Christian village, which contains more than twenty Hindoo families. Nevertheless, Christianity makes scarcely any advance. {173} I inquired of each of the missionaries how many Hindoos or Mahomedans they had baptized in the course of their labours: generally they said, "None;" very seldom, "One." The above mentioned families result from the year 1831, when nearly the whole of India was ravaged by cholera, nervous fever, or famine; the people died, and many children remained orphans, wandering about without a home. The missionaries took these, and brought them up in the Christian religion. They were instructed in all kinds of trades, were housed, married, and their whole maintenance provided for. The descendants of these families are continually educated by the missionaries, and strictly watched: as to new converts, however, there are unfortunately none.

I was present at several examinations: the boys and girls seemed to have been taught well to read, write, reckon, and were well acquainted with religion and geography. The girls were clever embroiderers, they did needle-work very well, and sewed all kinds of things; the boys and men made tables, carpets, bound books, printed, etc. The director and professor of this excellent establishment is the missionary, Mr. Luitpold; his wife has the superintendence of the girls. The whole is sensibly and intelligently arranged and conducted; Mr. and Mrs. Luitpold attend to their *protégés* with true Christian love. But what are a few drops in an immeasurable sea?

181

CHAPTER XIII. ALLAHABAD, AGRA, AND DELHI.

ALLAHABAD—CAUNIPOOR—AGRA—THE MAUSOLEUM OF SULTAN AKBAR—TAJ-MEHAL—THE RUINED TOWN OF FATIPOOR—SIKRI—DELHI—THE MAIN STREET—PUBLIC PROCESSIONS—THE EMPEROR'S PALACE—PALACES AND MOSQUES—OLD DELHI—REMARKABLE RUINS—THE ENGLISH MILITARY STATION.

From Benares, Mr. Law and myself travelled in a post-dock to Allahabad. The distance, which amounts to seventy-six miles, occupies about twelve or thirteen hours. We left the sacred town on the 7th of January, 1848, at 6 o'clock in the evening, and early in the morning found ourselves already near Allahabad, at a long bridge of boats which here crosses the Ganges.

We left the post-dock, and were carried in palanquins to the hotel, about a mile further on. When we arrived there, we found it so occupied by some officers of a regiment on the march, that my travelling companion was received only upon condition that he would content himself with a place in the public-room. In these circumstances, nothing remained for me but to make use of my letter of introduction to Dr. Angus.

My arrival placed the good old gentleman in no little embarrassment: his house was also already filled with travellers. His sister, Mrs. Spencer, however, with great kindness, at once offered me half of her own sleeping apartment.

Allahabad has 25,000 inhabitants. It lies partly upon the Jumna (Deschumna), partly on the Ganges. It is not one of the largest and handsomest, although it is one of the sacred towns, and is visited by many pilgrims. The Europeans reside in handsome garden-houses outside the town.

Among the objects of interest, the fortress with the palace is the most remarkable. It was built during the reign of the Sultan Akbar. It is situated at the junction of the Jumna with the Ganges.

The fortress has been much strengthened with new works by the English. It serves now as the principal depot of arms in British India.

The palace is a rather ordinary building; only a few of the saloons are remarkable for their interior division. There are some which are intersected by three rows of columns, forming three adjoining arcades. In others, a few steps lead into small apartments which are situated in the saloon itself, and resemble large private boxes in theatres.

The palace is now employed as an armoury. It contains complete arms for 40,000 men, and there is also a quantity of heavy ordnance.

In one of the courts stands a metal column thirty-six feet high, called Feroze-Schachs-Laht, which is very well preserved, is covered with inscriptions, and is surmounted by a lion.

A second curiosity in the fort is a small unimportant temple, now much dilapidated, which is considered as very sacred by the Hindoos. To their great sorrow they are not allowed to visit it, as the fort is not open to them. One of the officers told me that, a short time since, a very rich Hindoo made a pilgrimage here, and offered the commandant of the fortress 20,000 rupees (£2,000) to allow him to make his devotions in this temple. The commandant could not permit it.

This fortress also has its tradition:—"When the Sultan Akbar commenced building it, every wall immediately fell in. An oracle said that he would not succeed in its erection before a man voluntarily offered himself as a sacrifice. Such an one presented himself, and made only one condition, that the fortress and town should bear his name. The man was called Brog, and the town is, even at this time, more frequently called Brog by the Hindoos than Allahabad."

In memory of the heroic man, a temple was erected near the fortress, under ground, where he is interred. Many pilgrims come here annually. The temple is quite dark; lights or torches must be used on entering it. It resembles, on the whole, a large handsome cellar, the roof of which rests upon a number of plain columns. The walls are full of niches, which are occupied by idols and figures of deities. A leafless tree is shown as a great curiosity, which grew in the temple and made its way through the stone roof.

I also visited a fine large garden, in which stood four Mahomedan mausoleums. The largest contains a sarcophagus of white marble, which is surrounded by wooden galleries extremely richly and handsomely decorated with mother-of-pearl. Here rests the Sultan Koshru, son of Jehanpuira. Two smaller sarcophagi contain children of the sultan. The walls are painted with stiff flowers and miserable trees, between which are some inscriptions.

One part of the wall is covered with a small curtain. The guide pushed it with great devotion on one side, and showed me the impression of a colossal open hand. He told me that a great-great-uncle of Mohamet once came here to pray. He was powerful, large, and clumsy; when raising himself up, he stumbled against the wall and left the impression of his sacred hand.

These four monuments are said to be upwards of 250 years old. They are constructed of large blocks of stone, and richly decorated with arabesques, friezes, reliefs, etc. The sepulchre of Koshru and the impression of the hand are much venerated by the Mahomedans.

The garden afforded me more pleasure than the monuments—especially on account of the enormous tamarind-trees. I thought that I had seen the largest in Brazil, but the ground, or perhaps the climate, here appears more favourable to this species of trees. Not only is the garden full of such magnificent specimens, but there are beautiful avenues of them round the town. The tamarinds of Allahabad are even mentioned in geographical works.

183

On one side of the lofty wall which surrounds the garden, two caravansaries are built, which are remarkable for their beautiful high portals, their size, and convenient arrangement. They presented an uncommonly lively appearance, containing people in all costumes, horses, oxen, camels, and elephants, and a large quantity of wares in chests, bales, and sacks.

10th January. About 3 in the afternoon, we left Allahabad and continued our journey in a post-dock as far as Agra, with some short stoppages. The distance is nearly 300 miles.

In twenty-two hours we reached Caunipoor (150 miles), on the Ganges, a town which is remarkable for its English settlement.

The journey so far offered little change, an uninterrupted richly-cultivated plain and an unfrequented road. With the exception of a few companies of military, we did not meet a single traveller.

A party of military on the march in India resembles a small emigration company; and, after seeing one, it is easy to form an idea of the enormous trains of the Persian and other Asiatic armies. The greater part of the native soldiers are married, as well as the officers (Europeans); therefore, when the regiment marches, there are nearly as many women and children as soldiers. The women and children ride, two or three together, upon horses or oxen, or sit upon cars, or go on foot with bundles on their backs. They have all their effects packed upon cars, and drive their goats and cows before them. The officers follow, with their families, in European carriages, palanquins, or on horseback. Their tents, house furniture, etc., are packed upon camels and elephants, which generally bring up the rear. The camp is pitched on both sides of the road—on one side are the people, and on the other the animals.

Caunipoor is a strong military station, with four handsome barracks; there is also an important missionary society. The town possesses some handsome schools and private buildings, and a Christian church, in pure Gothic style.

12th January. Towards noon, we reached the small village of Beura. Here we found a bungalow; that is, a small house with two or four rooms barely furnished with the most necessary and plainest furniture. These bungalows stand upon the post-roads, and supply the place of hotels. They are built by government. One person pays one rupee (2s.) a day for a small room; a family, two rupees. The payment is the same in most bungalows, if the travellers remain twenty-four hours or only half an hour; it is only in a few that it is considered enough to pay half-price for staying a short time. At each bungalow, a native is placed as superintendent, who waits on the travellers, cooks for them, etc. The control is carried out by means of a book, in which each traveller writes his name. If there are no travellers, a person may remain as long as he chooses; when the contrary happens, he cannot stay more than twenty-four hours.

The villages which lie on the road are small, and appear very miserable and poor.

184

They are surrounded by high mud walls, which give them the appearance of a fortification.

After we had travelled three nights and two days and a half, we reached Agra on the 13th of January—the former residence of the Great Mogul of India.

The suburbs of Agra resemble, in poverty, the miserable villages before mentioned. They are composed of high walls of earth, within which are small dilapidated huts and barracks. A change was at once apparent when we had passed through a stately gateway. We then suddenly found ourselves in a large open square, surrounded by walls, from which four lofty gates led to the town, the fortress, and the suburbs. Agra, like most Indian towns, has no inn. A German missionary received me kindly; and, in addition to his hospitality, was obliging enough to show me personally whatever there was of interest in the town and neighbourhood.

Our first visit was to the beautiful mausoleum of the Sultan Akbar, at Secundra, four miles from Agra.

The porch which leads into the garden is a masterpiece. I stood before it for a long time amazed. The enormous building is raised upon a stone terrace, which is approached by broad steps; the gate is lofty, and is surmounted by an imposing dome. At the four corners are minarets of white marble three stories high; unfortunately, their upper parts are already somewhat dilapidated. On the front of the gate are the remains of a stone trellis-work.

The mausoleum stands in the centre of the garden; it is a square building four stories in height, each becoming narrower at the top, like a pyramid. The first sight of this monument is not very attractive, for the beauty of the gateway eclipses it; however, it improves on a more detailed examination.

The bottom story is surrounded by fine arcades; the rooms are plain, the walls covered with a brilliant white cement, intended as a substitute for marble. Several sarcophagi stand inside.

The second story consists of a large terrace, which covers the whole extent of the lower one; in its centre is an open airy apartment with a light arched roof, supported by columns. Several small kiosks at the corners and sides of the terrace give to the whole a somewhat bizarre though tasty appearance. The pretty domes of the kiosks must formerly have been very rich and splendid, for on many there are still to be seen beautiful remains of coloured glazed tiles and inlaid marble-work.

The third story resembles the second. The fourth and highest is the most handsome. It is constructed entirely of white marble, while the three lower ones are only of red sandstone. Broad-roofed arcades, whose exterior marble lattice-work is inimitably executed, form an open square, over which the most beautiful roof—the blue sky—spreads. Here stands the sarcophagus which contains the

185

bones of the sultan. On the arches of the arcades, texts from the Koran are inlaid in characters of black marble.

I believe this is the only Mahomedan monument in which the sarcophagus is placed at the top of the building in an uncovered space.

The palace of the Mongolian Sultan stands in the citadel. It is said to be one of the most remarkable buildings of Mongolian architecture. {177}

The fortifications are nearly two miles in extent, and consist of double and treble walls, the outer one of which is said to be seventy-five feet high.

The interior is divided into three principal courts. In the first live the guards; in the second, the officers and higher authorities; in the third, which occupies the side towards the Jumna, stands the palace, the baths, the harem, and several gardens. In this court, everything is made of marble. The walls of the rooms in the palaces are covered with such stones as agates, onyxes, jasper, cornelian, lapis-lazuli, etc., inlaid in mosaic work, representing flowers, birds, arabesques, and other figures. Two rooms without windows are exclusively destined to show the effects of illumination. The walls and the arched roof are covered with mica slate in small silvered frames; fountains splash over glass walls, behind which lights can be arranged, and jets of water are thrown up in the centre of the room. Even without lights, it glittered and sparkled most marvellously; what must be the effect when innumerable lamps throw back their rays a thousandfold! Such a sight enables one easily to understand the imaginative descriptions of the Eastern tales of "a thousand-and-one nights." Such palaces and rooms may be truly considered works of magic.

Near the palace stands a small mosque, which is also entirely constructed of white marble, richly and artistically furnished with arabesques, reliefs, etc.

Before leaving the fortress, I was led to a deep underground vault—the former scene of numerous secret executions. How much innocent blood may have been shed there!

The Jumna Mosque, which the erudite affirm to surpass that of Soliman's in Constantinople, stands outside the fortress, upon a high terrace near the river. It is of red sandstone, has the same wonderful domes, and was built by the Sultan Akbar. In the arches are to be seen remains of rich paintings in light and dark-blue, intermixed with gilding. It is to be regretted that this mosque is in a rather dilapidated condition; but it is hoped, however, that it will soon be completely restored, as the English government have already commenced repairing it.

From the mosque we returned again to the town, which is, for the most part, surrounded by rubbish. The principal street, "Sander," is broad and cleanly paved in the middle with square stones, and at the sides with bricks. At both extremities of this street stand majestic gateways. The houses of the town (from one to four stories high) are almost entirely of red sandstone; most of them are small, but many are surrounded by columns, pillars, and galleries. Several are distinguished by their handsome porches. The streets are narrow, crooked, and ugly; the bazaars unimportant. In India, as well as in the East, the more costly wares must be sought in the interior of the houses. The population of this town is said to have amounted formerly to 800,000; it is now scarcely 60,000.

The whole environs are full of ruins. Those who build can procure the materials at the mere cost of gathering them from the ground. Many Europeans inhabit half-ruinous buildings, which, at a small expense, they convert into pretty palaces.

Agra is the principal seat of two missionary societies—a Catholic and a Protestant. Here, as in Benares, they educate the offspring of the children they picked up in 1831. A little girl was pointed out to me that had recently been bought of a poor woman for two rupees (4s.)

At the head of the Catholic mission is a bishop. The present one, Mr. Porgi, is the founder of a tastefully-built church. In no similar establishment did I ever see so much order, or find the natives so well-behaved as here. On Sundays, after prayers, they amuse themselves with decorous and lively games; while in the Protestant establishments, after having worked all the week, they are compelled to pray all day long, and their greatest amusement consists in being allowed to sit for a few hours gravely before the house-doors. A person who passed a Sunday in this country among strict Protestants would imagine that God had forbidden the most innocent amusements.

These two religious societies, unfortunately, are not on very amicable terms, and censure and persecute every slight irregularity on the part of each other; by this means not setting the natives living round them a very good example.

My last visit was to the magnificent treasure of Agra, and, indeed, of all India—the famous Taj-Mehal.

I had read somewhere that this monument ought to be visited last, as the others would not be admired at all after seeing this. Captain Elliot says: "It is difficult to give a description of this monument; the architecture is full of strength and elegance."

The Taj-Mehal was erected by the Sultan Jehoe (Dschehoe), in memory of his favourite muntaza, Zemani. Its building is said to have cost £750,000. Properly speaking, the sultan's memory is more perpetuated by this building than that of his favourite, for every one who saw it would involuntarily ask who erected it. The names of the architect and builder are unfortunately lost. Many ascribe it to Italian masters; but when it is seen that there are so many other admirable works of Mahomedan architecture, either the whole must be considered foreign or this must be admitted to be native.

The monument stands in the centre of a garden, upon an open terrace of red sandstone, raised twelve feet above the ground. It represents a mosque of an octagon form, with lofty arched entrances, which, together with the four minarets that stand at the corners of the terrace, is entirely built of white marble. The principal dome rises to a height of 260 feet, and is surrounded by four smaller ones. Round the outside of the mosque extracts from the Koran are inlaid in characters of black marble.

In the principal apartment stand two sarcophagi, of which one contains the remains of the sultan, the other those of his favourite. The lower part of the walls of this apartment, as well as both sarcophagi, are covered with costly mosaic work of the most beautiful stones. A marble lattice-work, six feet high, surrounding the two sarcophagi, is a masterpiece of art. It is so delicate and finely worked, that it seems as if turned out of ivory. The graceful columns and the narrow cornices are also covered, above and below, with jasper, agate, etc. Among these, I was shown the so-called "goldstone," which has a perfect gold colour, and is said to be very costly, even more so than lapis-lazuli.

Two gateways and two mosques stand at a small distance from the Taj-Mehal. They are built of red sandstone and white marble. If they stood apart, each would be considered a master-work; as it is, however, they lose in attraction by their proximity to the Taj-Mehal, of which a traveller says, with full justice: "It is too pure, too sacred, too perfect, to have been constructed by men's hands—angels must have brought it from heaven; and one imagines there ought to be a glass shade over it, to protect it from every breath and every wind."

Although this mausoleum is more than 250 years old, it is as perfect as if it was only just finished.

Many travellers affirm that the Taj-Mehal produces a magical effect when lighted by the moon. I saw it during a full moonshine, but was so little pleased, that I much regretted, by this sight, having somewhat weakened my former impression of it. The moon's light gives a magical effect to old ruins or Gothic buildings, but not to a monument which consists of white brilliant marble. Moonlight makes the latter appear in indistinct masses, and as if partly covered with snow. Whoever first promulgated this opinion respecting the Taj-Mehal perhaps visited it in some charming company, so that he thought everything round him was heavenly and supernatural; and others may have found it more convenient, instead of putting it to the test themselves, to repeat the statement of their predecessors.

One of the most interesting excursions of my whole journey was to the ruins of the town of Fattipoor Sikri, eighteen miles from Agra, and six miles in circumference. We rode thither, and had ordered changes of horses, so as to be able to make the journey in one day.

On our way, we passed at times over extended heaths, on one of which we saw a small herd of antelopes. The antelope is a kind of deer, but smaller in size. It is extremely delicate and prettily formed, and is distinguished by narrow dark-brown

188

stripes along the back. The herd crossed the road before us without much timidity, passing over ditches and bushes, and leaping more than twenty feet at a time, with such graceful movements that they seemed as if dancing through the air. I was not less delighted by the sight of two wild peacocks. It afforded me peculiar pleasure to see these animals in a state of freedom, which we Europeans are accustomed to keep as rarities, like exotic plants.

The peacock is here somewhat larger than any I had seen in Europe; the display of colours also, and the general brilliancy of the plumage, struck me as being finer and brighter.

These birds are considered by the Indians almost as sacred as the cow. They appear to fully understand this kindness, for they are seen, like house-birds, walking about in the villages or quietly resting upon the roofs. In some districts, the Indians are so prejudiced in their favour, that no European can venture to shoot one of them without exposing himself to the greatest insults. Only four months since, two English soldiers fell victims to this neglect of Hindostanee customs. They killed several peacocks; the enraged people fell upon them and ill-used them in such a way that they shortly afterwards died.

Fattipoor Sikri stands upon a hill; the fortress walls, the mosque, and other buildings can therefore be seen from a distance. On both sides of the road, a short distance outside the walls, lie remains of houses or single apartments, fragments of handsome columns, etc. With great regret I saw the natives breaking many of them, and converting them into building materials for their houses.

The entrance to the fortress and town was through three handsome gates, and over masses of rubbish and fragments. The view which here presents itself is much more impressive than that at Pompeii, near Naples. There, indeed, everything is destroyed, but it is another and more orderly kind of destruction—streets and squares appear as clean as if they had only been abandoned yesterday. Houses, palaces, and temples are free from rubbish; even the track of the carriages remain uneffaced. Pompeii, moreover, stands on a plain, and it cannot, therefore, be seen at one glance; its extent, too, is scarcely half so great as that of Sikri; the houses are smaller, the palaces not so numerous, and inferior in splendour and magnitude. But here a larger space is covered with magnificent buildings, mosques, kiosks, columned halls, and arcades, with everything that was in the power of art to create; and no single object has escaped the destructive influence of time—all is falling into ruin. It is scarcely more than two hundred years since the town was in a flourishing state of wealth and magnificence, and it is hardly possible to divest the mind of the idea of a terrible earthquake having overwhelmed it. Unlike Pompeii, it was not covered by protecting ashes, but laid openly exposed to the weather. My sadness and astonishment increased at every step—sadness at the terrible destruction, astonishment at the still perceptible magnificence, the number of splendid buildings, the beautiful sculptures, and the rich ornaments. I saw some buildings whose interior and exterior were so covered with sculptures, that not the smallest space remained bare. The principal mosque exceeds in size and artistic construction even the Jumna Mosque in Agra. The entrance porch in the fore-court is said to be the loftiest in the world. The interior arch measures 72 feet, and the entire height amounts to 140 feet. The fore-court of the mosque is also one of the largest existing; its length is 436 feet, its breadth 408; it is surrounded by fine arabesques and small cells. This court is considered almost as sacred as the mosque itself, in consequence of the Sultan Akbar, "the just," having been accustomed to pay his devotions there. After his death, this spot was indicated by a kind of altar, which is of white marble, and of wonderful workmanship.

The mosque itself is built in the style of the Jumna Mosque, and has, like that, four enormous domes. The interior is filled with sarcophagi, in which lie the remains either of relations or favourite ministers of the Sultan Akbar. An adjoining court also contains a great number of sepulchral monuments.

The Sultan Akbar passed several hours every day in the Hall of Justice, and gave audience there to the meanest, as well as the most important of his subjects. A single column, standing in the centre of the hall, was the divan of the emperor. This column, the capital of which is marvellously executed, becomes broader towards the top, and is surrounded by a beautifully worked stone gallery, a foot high. Four broad stone passages or bridges lead into the adjoining apartments of the palace.

The sultan's palace is less remarkable for size than for its sculptures, columns, ornaments, etc. Every part is over-richly furnished with them.

I found less to admire in the famous Elephant gate. It is, indeed, loftily arched, but not so high as the entrance gate in the fore-court of the mosque; the two elephants, which were very beautifully executed in stone, are so much dilapidated, that it is scarcely possible to tell what they are intended to represent.

The so-called Elephant's Tower is in a better state of preservation. In some descriptions of this, it is stated that it is constructed only of elephants' tusks, and even of the tusks of those elephants only which were taken from enemies during Akbar's time, or had been captured by him in hunting. This is, however, not the case; the tower, which is sixty feet high, is built of stone, and the tusks are fastened on from top to bottom, so that they project out from it. The Sultan Akbar is said to have frequently sat upon the top of this tower, occupying himself by shooting birds.

All the buildings, even the enormous wall, are of red sandstone, and not, as many affirm, of red marble.

Many hundreds of small green birds have formed their nests in the holes and crevices of the buildings.

190

On the 19th of January I left the famous town of Agra, in the company of Mr. Law, in order to visit the still more celebrated city of Delhi, which is 122 miles from Agra. There is an excellent post-road all the way.

The country between Agra and Delhi continues tolerably unchanged; there is no elevation to be seen. Far and wide, cultivated land alternates with heaths and sandy moors, and the miserable villages or small towns which lie on the road, excite no desire to delay the journey even for a moment.

A long and handsome chain bridge crosses the Jumna near the town of Gassanger.

On the 20th of January, at 4 in the afternoon, we reached Delhi. Here I met with Dr. Sprenger, a very kind and amiable countryman. Dr. Sprenger, a Tyrolese, has won for himself, by his remarkable abilities and knowledge, a considerable reputation, not only among the English, but throughout the whole learned world. He holds the position of Director of the College in this place, and but a short time since was requested by the English government to go to Lucknau, for the purpose of examining the library of the Indian King of Lucknau, to make known the valuable works, and put the whole in order. He is a perfect master of the Sanscrit, the ancient and modern Persian, the Turkish, Arabic, and Hindostanee languages, and translates the most difficult of them into English and German. He has already made the most valuable and interesting contributions to literature, and will still continue to do so, as he is an extremely active man, and scarcely thirty-four years of age.

Although he was on the eve of his departure for Lucknau, he was, nevertheless, kind enough to become my Mentor.

We commenced with the great imperial town of Delhi; the town to which formerly the eyes not only of all India, but almost of all Asia, were directed. It was in its time to India what Athens was to Greece, and Rome to Europe. It also shares their fate—of all its greatness only the name remains.

The present Delhi is now called New Delhi, although it is already two hundred years old; it is a continuation of the old towns, of which there are said to have been seven, each of which were called Delhi. As often as the palaces, fortifications, mosques, etc., became dilapidated, they were left to fall into ruins, and new ones were built near the old ones. In this way, ruins upon ruins accumulated, which are said to have occupied a space more than six miles in breadth, and eighteen in length. If a great part of them were not already covered with a thin layer of earth, these ruins would certainly be the most extensive in the world.

New Delhi lies upon the Jumna; it contains, according to Brückner, a population of 500,000, {183} but I was informed that there was really only 100,000, among which are 100 Europeans. The streets are broader and finer than any I had yet seen in any Indian town. The principal street, Tchandni-Tschank, would do

191

honour to an European city: it is nearly three-quarters of a mile long, and about a hundred feet broad; a narrow canal, scant of water and half filled with rubbish, runs through its entire length. The houses in this street are not remarkable either for magnitude or splendour; they are at most one story high, and are furnished below with miserable porches or arcades, under which worthless goods are exposed for sale. I saw nothing of the costly shops, the numerous precious stones glittering in the evening with the lamps and lights, of which many travellers speak. The pretty houses and the rich shops must be sought for in the bye streets near the bazaar. The manufactures which I saw, consisted of gold and silver work, gold tissues and shawls. The natives execute the gold and silver wares so tastefully and artistically, that finer cannot be found even in Paris. The tissues woven in gold, the gold and silk embroideries and Cashmere shawls, are of the highest degree of perfection. The finest Cashmere shawls cost here as much as 4,000 rupees (£400). The dexterity of the workmen appears still more surprising after seeing the simple machines which they employ to produce their beautiful wares.

It is extremely interesting to walk about the principal streets of Delhi in the evening. There may be seen at once the modes of life of both the rich and the poor Indians. There is no town in which there are so many princes and nobles as in this. Besides the pensioned emperor and his relations, whose number amounts to several thousand, many other deposed and pensioned regents and ministers reside here. Their presence gives great animation to the town; they are fond of going out in public, frequently make greater or less parties, and ride (always on elephants) either in the neighbouring gardens, or in the evenings through the streets. In the day excursions, the elephants are decorated in the most costly manner with rugs and fine stuffs, gold lace, and fringe; the seats called the howdahs are even covered with Cashmere shawls; richly fringed canopies keep off the heat of the sun, or else servants hold enormous umbrellas for this purpose. The princes and nobles sit in these howdahs to the number of two or four, and are very gorgeously attired in Oriental costumes. These processions present a most beautiful appearance, and are even larger and more splendid than those of the Rajah of Benares, which I have described. Each procession consists frequently of as many as a dozen or more elephants, and fifty or sixty soldiers on foot and mounted, and as many servants, etc. In the evenings, on the contrary, they are not so pompous—one elephant, together with a few servants, suffices; they ride up and down the streets, coquetting with females of a certain class, who sit richly dressed and with unveiled faces at open windows or outside galleries. Others ride noble Arabian horses, whose stately appearance is still more increased by gold-embroidered trappings and bridles inlaid with silver. Between these riding parties, heavily laden camels from far distant regions walk deliberately along. There are, moreover, not a few bailis, drawn by beautiful white oxen, which the less wealthy people or the above mentioned women use. The bailis, as well as the oxen, are draped with scarlet cloths: the animals have their horns and the lower half of their feet painted brownish-red, and round their neck is a handsome collar, on which bells are fastened. The most beautiful women peep modestly out of the half-open bailis. If it were not known to what class unveiled women belong in India, it would be impossible to tell their position from their behaviour. Unfortunately, there are more of this class in India than in any other country: the principal cause of this is an unnatural law, a revolting custom. The girls of every family are generally betrothed when they are only a few months old; if, however, the bridegroom dies immediately, or at any time after the betrothal, the girl is considered as a widow, and as such cannot marry again. They then generally become dancers. The condition of widowhood is looked upon as a great misfortune, as it is believed that only those women are placed in this position, who have deserved it in a previous state of existence. An Indian can only marry a girl belonging to his own caste.

To the various objects of interest in the streets already noticed, must be added the jugglers, mountebanks, and serpent charmers, who wander about everywhere, and are always surrounded by a crowd of curious people.

I saw several tricks performed by the jugglers which were truly astonishing. One poured out fire and smoke from his mouth; then mixed white, red, yellow, and blue powders together, swallowed them, and then immediately spit out each one separately and dry; some turned their eyes downwards, and when they again raised them the pupils appeared as if of gold; they then bowed the head forward, and on again raising it, the pupils of their eyes had their natural colour, and their teeth were gold. Others made a small opening in their skin, and drew out of it yards of thread, silk cord, and narrow ribbons. The serpent charmers held the animals by their tails, and allowed them to twine round their arms, neck, and body; they took hold of large scorpions, and let them run over their hands. I also saw several battles between large serpents and ichneumons. These little animals, rather larger than a weasel, live, as is known, upon serpents and the eggs of crocodiles. They seize the former so dexterously by the neck that they always master them; the crocodile eggs they suck.

At the end of the principal street stands the imperial palace, which is considered one of the finest buildings in Asia. It occupies, together with its adjoining buildings, an extent of more than two miles, and is surrounded by a wall forty feet high.

At the principal entrance, a fine perspective view is obtained through several successive gateways, which is terminated in the background by a handsome hall. This hall is but small, and is inlaid with white marble and rare stones; the roof is arched over with mica, powdered over with small stars. Unfortunately, these will soon lose all their glittering brilliancy, as the greater portion of the mica has already fallen, and the remainder is likely to follow. At the back of the hall is a door of gilt metal, decorated with beautiful engraved work. In this hall the ex-monarch is accustomed to show himself to the people, who, from traditionary respect or curiosity, visit the palace. He also receives European visitors here.

The handsomest parts of the imperial palace are the universally admired and magnificent audience saloon and the mosque. The former stands in the centre of an open court; it is a long, square building; the roof is supported by thirty columns, and is open on all sides; several steps lead up to it, and a prettily decorated marble gallery, two feet high, surrounds it.

The present Great Mogul has so little taste, that he has had this divan divided into two parts by a very paltry partition wall. A similar wall adjoins both sides of the saloon, for what purpose I could not learn. In this divan is a great treasure: the largest crystal in the world. It is a block of about four feet in length, two and a half broad, and one foot thick; {185} it is very transparent. It was used by the emperors as a throne or seat in the divan. Now it is hidden behind the blank wall; and if I had not known of its existence from books, and been very curious to see it, it would not have been shown to me at all.

The mosque is indeed small, but, like the judgment-hall, it is of white marble, and with fine columns and sculptures.

Immediately adjoining the mosque is the garden "Schalinar," which is said to have been formerly one of the finest in India, but has now quite fallen to decay.

Heaps of dust and rubbish were laying in the court-yards; the buildings were almost like ruins; and miserable barracks stood against dilapidated walls. On account of the emperor's residence, it soon became necessary to build a new Delhi.

On my entrance to the palace, I had observed a group of men collected together in the court-yard. An hour afterwards, when we were returning from our visit, they were still seated there. We drew near to discover what it was that so attracted their attention, and saw a few dozen of tame birds seated upon perches quietly taking their food from the hands of attendants, or else fighting for it. The lookers-on were, as I was told, nearly all princes. Some were seated upon chairs, others stood round, together with their followers. In their home dresses, the princes are hardly to be distinguished from their servants, and in education and knowledge they are certainly not much in advance of them.

The emperor amuses himself with a diversion which is not more commendable. His troops consist of boys about eight or fourteen. They wear a miserable uniform, which in make and colour resembles the English; their exercises are conducted partly by old officers and partly by boys. I pitied the young soldiers from my heart, and wondered how it was possible for them to handle their heavy muskets and banners. The monarch generally sits for some hours every day in the small reception hall, and amuses himself by watching the manœuvres of his young warriors. This is the best time to get presented to his majesty. He is eighty-five, and at the time of my visit was so unwell, that I had not the good fortune to see him.

The emperor receives from the English government a yearly pension of fourteen lacs (1,400,000 rupees = £140,000). The revenues of his own possessions amount

194

to half as much more; but with all this, he is not so well off as the Rajah of Benares. He has too large a number of people to maintain: of the descendants of the imperial family alone more than three hundred, as well as a hundred women, and two thousand attendants. If to these are added the numerous elephants, camels, horses, etc., it may be easily understood why his exchequer is always empty.

He receives his pension on the first of every month. It has to be brought to him under the protection of the English military, or it would otherwise be seized by his creditors.

The emperor is said to be very discreet in raising his revenues by various means. For example, he confers honorary posts and appoints officials, for which he requires considerable sums of money; and—can it be believed!—he always finds fools enough to pay for such absurdities. Parents even buy appointments for their children. The present commander of the imperial troops is scarcely ten years old. The most remarkable fact, however, is that the vizier, who manages the emperor's income and expenditure, not only receives no salary, but pays the emperor annually 10,000 rupees for this office. What sums must be embezzled to make up for this!

The emperor issues a newspaper in his own palace, which is in the highest degree absurd and laughable. It does not treat of politics or the occurrences of the day, but exclusively of domestic incidents, conversation and relative affairs. It states, for example, "that the sultan's wife, A., owed the laundress, B., three rupees, and that the laundress came yesterday to ask for her money; that the lady had sent to her imperial husband to ask for the sum. The emperor referred her to the treasurer, who assured her, that as it was near the end of the month, he could not command a penny. The laundress was therefore put off until the next month." Or, "The Prince C. visited at such an hour the Prince D. or E.; he was received in such a room; stayed so long; the conversation was on this or that subject," etc.

Among the other palaces of the town, that in which the college is located is one of the handsomest. It is built in the Italian style, and is truly majestic; the columns are of uncommon height; the stairs, saloons, and rooms are very spacious and lofty. A fine garden surrounds the back of the palace, a large court-yard the front, and a high fortified wall encloses the whole. Dr. Sprenger, as director of the college, occupies a truly princely dwelling in it.

The palace of the Princess Begum, half in the Italian and half in the Mongolian style, is tolerably large, and is remarkable for its extremely handsome saloons. A pretty and hitherto well kept garden surrounds it on all sides.

The Princess Begum attracted great attention at the time before Delhi was under the English dominion, by her intelligence, enterprise, and bravery. She was a Hindoo by birth, and became acquainted in her youth with a German named Sombre, with whom she fell in love, and turned Christian in order to marry him.

195

Mr. Sombre formed a regiment of native troops, which, after they were well trained, he offered to the emperor. In the course of time, he so ingratiated himself with the emperor, that the latter presented him with a large property, and made him a prince. His wife is said to have supported him energetically in everything. After his death, she was appointed commander of the regiment, which post she held most honourably for several years. She died a short time since at the age of eighty.

Of the numerous mosques of New Delhi, I visited only two, the Mosque Roshun-ad-dawla, and the Jumna Mosque. The former stands in the principal street, and its pinnacles and domes are splendidly gilt. It is made famous through its connection with an act of cruelty on the part of Sheikh Nadir. This remarkable, but fearfully cruel monarch, on conquering Delhi in the year 1739, had 100,000 of the inhabitants cut to pieces, and is said to have sat upon a tower of this mosque to watch the scene. The town was then set fire to and plundered.

The Jumna Mosque, built by the Sheikh Djihan, is also considered a masterpiece of Mahomedan architecture; it stands upon an enormous platform, to which forty steps lead up, and rises in a truly majestic manner above the surrounding mass of houses. Its symmetry is astonishing. The three domes, and the small cupolas on the minarets, are of white marble; all the other parts, even the large slates with which the fine court-yard is paved, are of red sandstone. The inlaid ornamental work and stripes on the mosque, are also of white marble.

There are great numbers of caravansaries, frequently with very handsome portals. The baths are unimportant.

We devoted two days to making an excursion to the more distant monuments of Delhi. We first stopped at the still well-preserved "Purana Kale." All the handsome mosques resemble each other much. This one, however, is distinguished by its decoration, the richness and correctness of its sculptures, its beautiful inlaid work, and its size. Three lightly arched and lofty cupolas cover the principal building, small towers adorn the corners, and two high minarets stand at the sides. The entrance and the interior of the domes are inlaid with glazed tiles and painted, the colours are remarkably brilliant. The interior of every mosque is empty; a small tribune for speakers, and a few glass lustres and lamps, constitute the whole decoration.

The mausoleum of the Emperor Humaione, very much in the same style as the mosque, was commenced by this monarch himself. But as he died before it was completed, his son Akbar carried out his intentions. The high-arched temple, in the centre of which stands the sarcophagus, is inlaid with mosaic work of rare stones. Instead of window-panes, the openings are furnished with artistically worked stone lattices. In adjoining halls, under plain sarcophagi, rest the remains of several wives and children of the Emperor Humaione.

Not far from this is the monument of Nizam-ul-din, a very sacred and greatly

196

venerated Mahomedan. It stands in a small court, the floor of which is paved with marble. A square screen of marble, with four small doors, surrounds the sarcophagus. This screen is still more delicate and finely worked than that in the Taj-Mehal; it is scarcely conceivable how it was possible to execute such work in stone. The doors, pillars, and elegant arches are covered with the most chaste reliefs, as fine and perfect as any that I have seen in the most artistic towns of Italy. The marble used for them is of remarkable whiteness and purity, worthy, indeed, of these great works of art.

Adjoining this are several pretty monuments, all of white marble. They are passed by with some indifference when the most perfect of them all has been seen first.

A great deal has been said about a large water basin, which is surrounded on three sides by cells, already much dilapidated; the fourth side is open, and from it a beautiful stone staircase, forty feet broad, leads to the water basin, which is twenty-five feet deep. Every pilgrim would consider his pilgrimage of no account if he did not step in here immediately on his arrival.

Divers plunge from the terraces of the cells to the bottom of the basin, and fetch out the smallest pieces of money which have been thrown in. Some are dexterous enough to catch the coin even before it touches the bottom. We threw in several coins, which they succeeded in bringing up every time, but I can scarcely believe that they caught them before they reached the bottom. They remained long enough under water each time, not only to pick the coin up, but also to look for it. The feat was certainly surprising, but not, as some travellers affirm, so remarkable that similar ones might not be seen elsewhere.

Our last visit on this day was to the beautiful monument of the Vizier Sofdar-Dchang, which is also a mosque. In this monument I was especially struck by the inlaid work of white marble in red sandstone upon the four minarets, it was so diversified and so delicate; so chastely executed that the most expert draughtsman could not have produced it more correctly and delicately upon paper. The same may be said of the sarcophagi in the principal temple, which is hewn out of a block of fine white marble.

The monument is surrounded by a tolerably well-kept garden, laid out in the European style.

At the end of the garden, opposite the mausoleum, stands a small palace, principally belonging to the King of Lucknau. It is at present kept in good condition by the few European inhabitants of New Delhi. It contains a few articles of furniture, and serves for the accommodation of visitors to these ruins.

We remained here over night, and, thanks to the good-hearted and amiable Mrs. Sprenger, found every possible convenience we could desire. The first and most agreeable thing after our long wandering, was a well-furnished table. Such attentions are doubly deserving of thanks, when it is remembered at what a great amount of trouble they are procured. It is necessary on such excursions to take not only provisions and a cook, but also cooking utensils, table-services, bed-linen, and servants, enough in short for a small establishment. The train of baggage, which is always sent on before on these occasions, resembles a small emigration party.

On the following morning we went on to Kotab-Minar, one of the oldest and most beautiful buildings of the Patanas (from which people the Affghans derive their origin). The most wonderful part of this monument is the so-called "Giant's Column," a polygon with twenty-seven sides or half-round corners, and five stories or galleries, whose diameter at the basement is fifty-four feet, and whose height is twenty-six feet. A winding staircase of 386 steps, leads to the top. This building is said to belong to the thirteenth century, and to have been built by Kotab-ud-dun. The column is of red sandstone, and only the exterior is of white marble; decorations and wonderful sculptures are wound in broad stripes around the column; these are so finely and neatly chiselled as to resemble an elegant lace pattern. Any description of the delicacy and effect of this work would be far exceeded by the reality. The column is fortunately as well preserved as if it had only been standing about a hundred years. The upper part leans a little forwards (whether artificially, as in the tower at Bologna, is not decided); its top is flat, like a terrace, which does not correspond with the remainder of the architecture. It is not known whether anything formerly stood upon it. The column was in its present condition when the English conquered Delhi.

We mounted as far as the highest point, and a most charming view of the whole remains of Delhi, the Jumna, and the unbounded plain, opened itself here before us. The history of the people who once ruled Hindostan may here be studied in the ruins of imperial towns, lying one close beside the other. It was a great and imposing prospect.

Many places where magnificent palaces and monuments formerly stood are now cultivated fields. Wherever the ground is broken up, fragments of ruins show themselves.

Opposite the tower or column of Kotab-Minar stands a similar unfinished building, the base of which is considerably larger in circumference than that of the finished one. It is supposed that these two towers belonged to a magnificent mosque, {190} of which some courts, gateways, columns, and walls still remain.

These few remains of the mosque are remarkable for the perfect sculptures which covered the walls, gateways, etc., both outside and inside. The entrance-gateway has a considerable height. The columns in the courts are of Buddhist origin; the bell with long chain is sculptured on them in relief.

In the fore-court of the mosque stands a metal column similar to that at Allahabad, except that there is no lion upon its summit, and its height is not more than thirty-six feet. It is defaced by several marks and slight injuries, which are ascribed to the Mongolians, who, when they conquered Delhi, attempted in their destructive rage to pull down these columns; but they stood too firmly, and all their exertions were insufficient to destroy any of the inscriptions on them.

The remaining Patan or Affghan temples and monuments which lie dispersed among the other ruins, resemble each other as much as they differ from the Mahomedan and Hindoo buildings. The monuments of this kind generally consist of a small round temple, with a not very high cupola, surrounded by open arcades supported on pillars.

Here also, in the neighbourhood of Kotab-Minar, a hospitable dwelling is to be found. A ruined building is fitted up, and three of the rooms are furnished.

On the way homewards, we visited the observatory of the famous astronomer, Dey Singh. If that at Benares has been seen, this may well be passed by. Both were built by the same architect, and in the same style; but that at Benares is well preserved, while the one here is already much dilapidated. Some travellers consider this memorial as one of the most wonderful works of Indian art.

Near the observatory stands the old madrissa (school-house), a large building, with numerous rooms for teachers and pupils, and with open galleries and halls, in which the teachers sat surrounded by groups of youths. The building is rather neglected, but is partly inhabited by private persons.

Adjoining the madrissa stands a pretty mosque and a very handsome monument, both of white marble. The latter was erected by Aurang Zeb, in memory of his vizier Ghasy-al dyn Chan, the founder of the madrissa. It is as perfect in its execution as that of the saint Nizam-ul-din, and appears to have been erected by the same artist.

The palace of Feroze Schah is near New Delhi. It is indeed somewhat in ruins, but there is much to be seen in the existing remains of the building. The fore-court of the mosque was a short time since cleared with great labour of the rubbish and masses of stone which covered it, by the untiring zeal of Mr. Cobb, the esteemed editor of the English *Delhi News*. It is in very good preservation. In this palace stands the third metal column—Feroze-Schachs-Laht. The inscriptions upon it show that it existed a hundred years before the birth of Christ, and may therefore be considered as one of the oldest monuments of India. It was brought here from Lahore at the time this palace was built.

The Purana-Killa, or the old fortress of the palace of Babar, is much decayed. From the height and style of the remaining fragments of gateways and walls, an idea may be formed of the magnitude of the palace.

The ruins of Loglukabad are in an advanced state of dilapidation, and do not repay the trouble of a journey of seven miles.

The other numerous ruins are little more than mere repetitions of those already described, with which, however, they cannot be compared in size, elegance, and beauty. They may be of great interest to antiquarians and historians; but by myself, I candidly admit, they were not much valued.

I must not neglect to mention the English military station, which is situated upon some low hills near New Delhi. The peculiar formation of the ground renders a journey there extremely interesting: a district of enormous blocks of red sandstone, between which beautiful flowers were growing. There are numerous ruins here, much the same as in Delhi.

CHAPTER XIV. JOURNEY FROM DELHI TO BOMBAY.

THE THUGS OR STRANGLERS—DEPARTURE—CATTLE-MARKET— BARATPOOR—BIANA—WELLS AND PONDS—GOOD-NATURE OF THE INDIANS—POPPY PLANTATIONS—THE SUTTIS—NOTARA— KOTTAH—DESCRIPTION OF THE TOWN—THE ROYAL PALACE OF ARMORNEVAS—AMUSEMENTS AND DANCES—THE HOLY VILLAGE OF KESHO-RAE-PATUM.

In order to reach Bombay, I had two routes before me; the one leads past Simla to the foot of the Himalayas, the other to the famous rock temples of Adjunta and Elora. I would gladly have chosen the former, and have penetrated as far as the principal chain of the Himalayas—Lahore and the Indus; but my friends advised me not to make the attempt, for the simple reason, that these mountains were covered with deep snow, in which case I must have postponed my journey for at least three months. As I was unable to wait so long, I decided upon taking the latter road. In Calcutta, I had been recommended not to continue my journey beyond Delhi at all. They said the country was not under the control of the English government, and the people were far less civilized. People endeavoured more especially to excite my apprehension by terrible accounts of the Thugs or stranglers.

These Thugs form a singular sect, whose object is robbery and murder, and who, like the Italian banditti, are prepared to undertake any atrocity for which they are paid. They must not, however, in any case shed blood, and dare only make away with their victim by strangling. The act is not considered as very criminal, and the murderer absolves himself by a small present, which he gives to his priest; but, if he sheds only one drop of blood, he falls into the deepest disgrace, is expelled from his caste, and abandoned even by his own associates.

Many travellers affirm that the Thugs are a religious sect, and that they do not murder for the sake of plunder or of revenge, but in order, according to their belief, to ensure a meritorious action. I made many inquiries about this, and learnt from every one that it was no religious compulsion, but hatred, revenge, or desire of gain, which led to these acts. These stranglers are represented as possessing a most extraordinary dexterity in their abominable trade, united with the most untiring patience and perseverance; they frequently follow the victims they have selected for months, and strangle them either while sleeping, or by stealing behind them and throwing a twisted cloth or a cord round their necks, which they draw tight with such rapidity and force that death ensues instantaneously.

In Delhi, I gained more information. I was assured that all these dangers were exaggerated; that travellers were very rarely attacked in India, and that the Thugs were much reduced in numbers. Moreover, they did not make any attempt upon Europeans, as the English government instituted the strictest search for the culprits. With regard, therefore, to the danger, I was tolerably at ease, but I had still to anticipate privation and fatigue.

The first part of the journey was to Kottah, distant 290 miles. I had the choice of three modes of conveyance—palanquins, camels, or oxen bailis. None of them are expeditious; there are no highroads, and no organized accommodation for travelling; you must retain the same men and animals to the end of the journey, and, at the utmost, cannot go more than from twenty to twenty-two miles in one day. For a palanquin, it is necessary to engage eight bearers, besides several for the luggage. Although each does not receive more than eight rupees a-month, out of which he pays his own expenses; still the expense is heavy, because so many are required, and their return journey must be paid for. Travelling on camels is also expensive, and is the most inconvenient. I decided, therefore, on adopting the less costly mode of conveyance by oxen. As I travelled alone, Dr. Sprenger very kindly made all the necessary preparations; he drew up a written contract with the tschandrie (waggoner) in Hindostanee to the effect that I was to pay him the half of the fare, fifteen rupees (£1 10s.), immediately, and the other half when we arrived at Kottah, to which place he was to bring me in fourteen days; for every day over that time I had the right to deduct three rupees (6s.) Dr. Sprenger also sent one of his most trusty cheprasses {193} to accompany me, and his good wife furnished me with an excellent warm wrapper, and every kind of provision, so that my waggon would hardly hold all that I had.

With a sorrowful heart I parted from my good country people. God grant that I may see them yet again during my life!

On the morning of 30th of January, 1848, I left Delhi. The first day, we made very little progress, only eighteen miles, which brought us to Faridabad; the heavy awkward animals required to be first used to the draught. The first twelve miles of the journey afforded me some gratification, as along both sides of the road lay innumerable ruins, which I had visited with my friends only a few days previously.

This, as well as the following nights, were passed in caravansaries. I had no tent— no palanquins, and on this road there were no bungalows. Unfortunately, the caravansaries in the smaller villages are not to be compared with those in the larger towns; the cells are rudely constructed of clay, their length is scarcely seven feet, and the small opening, only four feet high, is without a door; but, to my astonishment, I found them always very cleanly swept, and I was also furnished with a low wooden stool, covered with network, upon which I threw my wrapper, and which served me for an excellent couch. The cheprasse laid himself, like Napoleon's Mameluke, before the entrance of my cell; but he slept much more soundly, for, even on the first night, he did not hear the least of a very sharp encounter which I had with an enormous dog that had been attracted by my well-filled provision basket.

31st January. Towards noon, we passed through the little town of Balamgalam, in which there is a small English military station, a mosque, and a very recently-erected Hindoo temple. We passed the night in the little town of Palwal.

In this neighbourhood, the peacocks are very tame. Every morning, I saw dozens of these beautiful birds on the trees; they come into the fields, and even into the towns, to fetch food from the good-natured natives.

1st February. Our night's station on this day was the small town of Cossi. We had already been overtaken during the last mile by a number of natives, who were busily hurrying into the town, in and outside of which a considerable cattle-market was being held. This market presented a picture of the greatest confusion; the animals stood on all sides between a multitude of trusses of hay and straw, the sellers crying and praising their wares without cessation, and leading the buyers here and there, partly by persuasion and partly by force, who also made no less noise than the former.

I was most struck by the innumerable cobblers, who set up their simple working implements between the piled-up bundles of hay and straw, consisting of small tables with thread, wire, and leather, and who were busily engaged at their trade, repairing the coverings for the feet. I remarked at this time, as well as on several other occasions, that the natives are by no means so indolent as they are generally represented to be, but, on the contrary, that they avail themselves of every favourable opportunity of earning money. All the caravansaries at the entrance of the town were crowded, and there was no other alternative except to pass through the whole town to the other side. The town-gate had a very promising appearance, rising proudly and boldly into the air; I hoped to see corresponding buildings, and saw instead wretched mud hovels and narrow lanes; so narrow, indeed, that the foot passengers were obliged to step under the entrances of the huts to allow our baili to pass them.

2nd February. A few miles distant from Matara, we turned out of the beaten road which leads from Delhi to Mutra, a town which still remains under English government. Matara is a pretty little town, with a very neat mosque, broad streets, and walled houses, many of which, indeed, are decorated with galleries, columns, or sculptures of red sandstone.

The appearance of the country here is of monotonous uniformity—boundless plains, on which orchards and meadows alternately present themselves, the latter apparently quite scorched up in consequence of the dry season. The corn was already a foot high; but such large quantities of yellow flowers were mixed with it, that there was great difficulty in telling whether corn or weeds had been sown. The cultivation of cotton is of very great importance here. The Indian plant does not, indeed, attain the height and thickness of the Egyptian; however, it is considered that the quality of the cotton does not depend upon the size of the plants, and that the cotton of this country is the finest and the best.

I observed upon these plains little houses here and there, built upon artificially-raised perpendicular mounds of clay, of from six to eight feet high. There are no steps leading to the tops of these mounds, the only means of access being by ladders, which can be drawn up at night. From what I could draw from the explanations of my servants, which, however, I only partially understood, they are used by families, who live in retired places, for security against the tigers, which are here very frequently seen.

3rd February. Baratpoor. We passed a place which was overgrown, in broad patches, with misshapen stunted bushes—a rare occurrence in this part of the country, where wood is scarce. My driver bestowed upon this tangled brushwood the high-sounding name of jungle. I should rather have compared them with the dwarfed bushes and shrubs of Iceland. The country beyond this woody district had a very remarkable appearance; the ground was in many places torn and fissured, as if in consequence of an earthquake.

In the caravansary at Baratpoor there were a great number of natives, soldiers, and particularly some very rough-looking men, of whom I felt inclined to be afraid: I was no longer in the English territories, and alone among all these people. However, they behaved themselves with the greatest civility, and greeted me in the evening and morning with a right hearty salaam. I think that a similar set of men in our own country would scarcely have shown me the same respect.

4th February. On the other side of the town, I saw two fine monuments before the door, round temples with lofty cupolas, and carved stone lattice work in the window openings. The fields and meadows were richly strewed with Indian fig-trees, a thing which I have scarcely met with anywhere else, except in Syria and Sicily; to the right of the road was a low rocky peak, whose highest point was crowned by a fortress. The dwelling-houses of the commanders, instead of being sheltered by the walls, rose high above them, and were tastily surrounded by verandahs; on the terrace of the principal building was a handsome pavilion, supported upon pillars. The outer walls of the fortress extended down into the valley below. We had proceeded about fourteen miles, when we came upon some monuments which had a very unique appearance. On a small spot, shaded by beautiful trees, was a round wall, formed of a number of flagstones of seven feet high and four feet wide; in the middle stood three monuments of a circular form, built of large square stones. The diameter of their tower part was about twelve feet, their height about six. They had no entrance.

203

I also saw a new species of bird today. It was very similar in size and form to the flamingo, with beautiful pinion feathers; its plumage was tinged with a rich whitish grey shade, the head was covered with deep red feathers. We rested this night at the somewhat large town of Hindon. The only object which attracted my notice here was a palace with such small windows, that they seemed more fitted for dolls than for men.

6th February. As I was about to leave the caravansary this morning, three armed men placed themselves before my waggon, and in spite of the exclamations of my people, prevented our starting. At last, I succeeded in understanding that the dispute was about a few pence, for having kept watch before the door of my sleeping-room during the night, which my people would not pay. The caravansary did not appear to the cheprasse very safe, and he had requested a guard in the evening from the *serdar* (magistrate). The people might have slept quite soundly in some corner of the court-yard, and, perhaps, have dreamt of watching, for although I had looked out several times during the night, there was not one of them to be seen; however, what can one expect for a few pence? I satisfied them with a small present, upon which they made a regular military movement, and allowed us to proceed.

If I had been inclined to be timid, I must have been in continual anxiety for several days from the appearance of the natives.

All of them were armed with sabres, bows and arrows, matchlocks, formidable clubs bound with iron, and even shields of ironplate. These arms were also carried by the cattle tenders in the fields. But nothing disturbed my equanimity, although ignorant of the language, and with only the old cheprasse with me; I always felt as though my last hours were not yet come. Nevertheless, I was glad that we had passed by clear daylight the dangerous ravines and deep gorges through which our road lay for several miles. From these we entered a large valley, at the entrance of which was an isolated mountain, surmounted by a fortress; four miles further on, we came to a small group of trees, in the middle of which was a stone terrace, five feet in height, upon which was a life-size statue of a horse carved in stone. By the side of this a well was dug out; a kind of cistern, built of large blocks of red sandstone, with steps leading up to the water.

Similar wells and cisterns, some of which are much larger, screened by beautiful mango and tamarind trees, are frequently met with in India, especially in districts where, as in the present one, good springs are scarce. The Hindoos and Mahomedans have the good belief that by the erection of works for general benefit, they may more easily attain future happiness. When such water reservoirs and groups of trees have been founded by Hindoos, several sculptured figures of their deities, or red painted stones, are commonly found placed on them. At many of the wells, and cisterns also, a man is placed, whose business it is to draw water for the weary travellers.

However agreeable the erection of these reservoirs may be in many respects, there is one circumstance which detracts from their value; the people always wash and bathe in the same ones from which they must procure their drinking water. But what objections will not thirst silence? I filled my jug as well as the others!

7th February. Dungerkamaluma is a small village at the foot of a low mountain. A short distance from the station lay a true Arabian sand desert, but which was fortunately not of very great extent. The sand plains of India are generally capable of being cultivated, as it is only necessary to dig a few feet deep to reach water, with which to irrigate the fields. Even in this little desert were a few fine-looking wheat fields.

This evening I thought that I should have been obliged to make use of my pistols. My waggoner always wanted every one to give him the road; if they did not do so, he abused them. Today we came upon half a dozen of armed traveller-waggoners, who took no notice of the calls of my driver, upon which he was enraged, and threatened to strike them with his whip. If it had come to blows, we should, no doubt, in spite of my aid, have come off the worst; but they contented themselves with mutual abuse and threats, and the fellows got out of the way.

I have everywhere remarked that the Indians jangle and threaten a great deal, but that they never go beyond that. I have lived a great deal among the people and observed them, and have often seen anger and quarrelling, but never fighting. Indeed, when their anger lasts long, they sit down together. The children never wrestle or pull each other about, either in sport or earnest. I only once saw two boys engaged in earnest quarrel, when one of them so far forgot himself as to give the other a box on the ear, but he did this as carefully as if he received the blow himself. The boy who was struck drew his sleeve over his cheek, and the quarrel was ended. Some other children had looked on from the distance, but took no part in it.

This good nature may partly depend upon the fact that the people eat so little flesh, and, according to their religion, are so extremely kind to all animals; but I think still that there is some cowardice at the bottom of it. I was told that a Hindoo could scarcely be persuaded to enter a dark room without a light; if a horse or ox makes the slightest start, both great and small run frightened and shrieking away. On the other side, again, I heard from the English officers that the sepoys were very brave soldiers. Does this courage come with the coat, or from the example of the English?

During the last day I saw a great many poppy plantations. They present a remarkable appearance; the leaves are fatty and shining, the flowers large and variegated. The extraction of the opium is performed in a very simple, but exceedingly tedious manner. The yet unripe poppy heads are cut in several places in the evening. A white tenacious juice flows out of these incisions, which quickly thickens by exposure to the air, and remains hanging in small tears. These tears are scraped off with a knife in the morning, and poured into vessels which have the form of a small cake. A second inferior quantity is obtained by pressing and

205

boiling the poppy heads and stems.

In many books, and, for instance, in Zimmerman's "Pocket-Book of Travels," I read under this head that the poppy plants reached a height of forty feet in India and Persia, and that the capsules were as large as a child's head, and held nearly a quart of seeds. This is not correct. I saw the finest plantations in India, and afterwards also in Persia, but found that the plants were never more than three, and, at the most, four feet high, and the capsule about as large round as a small hen's egg.

8th February. Madopoor, a wretched village at the foot of some low mountains. Today also we passed through terrible ravines and chasms, which like those of yesterday, were not near the mountains, but in the middle of the plains. The sight of some palms was, on the contrary, agreeable, the first I had seen since I left Benares; however, they bore no fruit. I was still more surprised to see, in a place so destitute of trees and shrubs, tamarind, and banyan or mango trees planted singly, which, cultivated with great care, flourish with incomparable splendour and luxuriance. Their value is doubled when it is known that under each there is either a well or a cistern.

9th February. Indergur, a small, unimportant town. We approached today very much nearer to the low mountains which we had already seen yesterday. We soon found ourselves in narrow valleys, whose outlets appeared to be closed with high, rocky wells. Upon some of the higher mountain peaks stood little kiosks, dedicated to the memory of the Suttis. The Suttis are those women who are burnt with the corpse of their husbands. According to the statement of the Hindoos, they are not compelled to do so, but their relations insult and neglect them when they do not, and they are driven out of society; consequently the poor women generally give their free consent. Upon the occasion, they are handsomely dressed and ornamented, and frequently stupefied with opium almost to madness; are led with music and singing to the place where the corpse of the husband, wrapped in white muslin, lies upon the funeral pile. At the moment that the victim throws herself upon the corpse, the wood is lighted on all sides. At the same time, a deafening noise is commenced with musical instruments, and every one begins to shout and sing, in order to smother the howling of the poor woman. After the burning, the bones are collected, placed in an urn, and interred upon some eminence under a small monument. Only the wives (and of these only the principal or favourite ones) of the wealthy or noble have the happiness to be burnt! Since the conquest of Hindostan by the English, these horrible scenes are not permitted to take place.

The mountain scenery alternated with open plains, and towards evening we came to still more beautiful mountains. A small fortress, which was situated upon the slope of a mountain, quite exposed, presented a very interesting appearance; the mosques, barracks, little gardens, etc., could be entirely overlooked. At the foot of this fortress lay our night-quarters.

10th February. Notara. We travelled a long distance through narrow valleys, upon roads which were so stony that it was scarcely possible to ride, and I thought every moment that the waggon must be broken to pieces. So long as the sun was not scorching on my head, I walked by the side, but I was soon compelled to seek the shade of the linen covering of the wagon. I bound up my forehead tightly, grasped both sides of the car, and submitted to my fate. The jungle which surrounded us resembled in beauty and luxuriance that near Baratpoor but it afforded me more amusement, as it was inhabited by wild apes. They were tolerably large, with yellowish, brown hair, black faces, and very long tails.

It was very pretty to see how anxious the mothers were about their young. When I startled them, she took one upon her back, the other clung to her breast, and with this double weight she not only sprung from branch to branch, but even from tree to tree.

If I had only possessed somewhat more imaginative power, I should have taken the forest for a fairy wood, for besides the merry monkeys, I saw many remarkable things. The rock sides and debris to the left of the road, for example, had the most singular and varied forms. Some resembled the ruins of temples and houses, others trees; indeed, the figure of a woman with a child in her arms, was so natural, that I could scarcely help feeling a regret at seeing it turned into this dismal lifelessness. Further on, lay a gate, whose noble artistic construction so deceived me, that I long sought for the ruins of the town to which it appeared to lead.

Not far distant from the jungle is the little town of Lakari, situated upon the almost perpendicular declivity of a mountain ridge, and also protected by fortifications. A beautiful pond, a large well with an artificial portico, terraces with Hindoo idols and Mahomedan funeral monuments, lie in very attractive disorder. Before Notara I found several altars, with the sacred bull carved in red stone. In the town itself stood a handsome monument, an open temple with columns upon a stone terrace, which was surrounded with fine reliefs, representing elephants and riders.

There was no caravansary at this place, and I was obliged to go about the streets with my cumbrous equipage in search of a lodging; but as no one would receive a Christian, not from any want of good nature, but in consequence of an erroneous religious opinion that a house which has been visited by an unbeliever is defiled. This opinion also extends to many other matters.

There was no alternative left for me except to pass the night in an open verandah.

In this town I saw a circumstance which proved the amiability of the people. A donkey, that was maimed either from its birth or by an accident, was dragging itself with great exertion across the street, a task which it required several minutes to accomplish. Several people who were coming that way with their loaded animals waited with great patience, without making a single murmur or raising a hand to drive the creature on. Many of the inhabitants came out of their houses and gave it fodder, and every passer-by turned out of the way for it. This feeling of sympathy touched me uncommonly.

11th February. On this, the thirteenth day of my journey, I reached Kottah. I was very well satisfied with my servants and driver, and indeed with the journey altogether! The owners of the caravansaries had not charged me more than a native; and had afforded me all the conveniences which the strict rules of religion allowed. I had passed the nights in open chambers, even under the open sky, surrounded by people of the poorest and lowest classes, and never received the slightest ill-treatment either by word or deed. I never had anything stolen, and when ever I gave any little trifle to a child, {200} such as a piece of bread, cheese, or the like, their parents always endeavoured to show their gratitude by other acts of kindness. Oh, that the Europeans only knew how easily these simple children of nature might be won by attention and kindness! But, unfortunately, they will continue to govern them by force, and treat them with neglect and severity.

Kottah is the chief city of the kingdom of Rajpootan. Here, as in all those provinces which the English government has left under the dominion of their native princes, there is an English official appointed, who bears the title of the "Resident." These residents might be properly called "kings," or at least the king's governors, since the real kings cannot do anything without their consent. These miserable shadows of kings dare not, for example, cross the boundaries of their own states without permission of the resident. The more important fortresses of the country have English garrisons, and here and there small English military stations are established.

This control is in some respects beneficial to the people, in others injurious. The custom of burning widows is done away with, and strictly forbidden; as well as the horrible punishment of being trodden to death by elephants, or dragged along, tied to their tails. On the other hand, the taxation is increased, for the king is obliged to pay a considerable tribute for the right of ruling according to the will of the resident. This naturally comes out of the pockets of the people. The King of Rajpootan pays annually 300,000 rupees (£30,000) to the English government.

The resident at Kottah, Captain Burdon, was an intimate friend of Dr. Sprenger's, who had previously acquainted him with my speedy arrival. But, unfortunately, he was at that time inspecting the different military stations; however, he had before his departure made arrangements for my reception, and requested Dr. Rolland to see them carried out. He carried his attentions so far as to send on books, newspapers, and servants, to the last station, which, however, I missed, as my driver had turned off from the main road, during the last two days, into a shorter one. I reached the handsome bungalow of the resident, and found the house quite vacant; Mrs. Burdon, together with her children, had accompanied her husband, as is generally the case in India, where frequent change of air is very necessary for Europeans. The house, the servants, and sepoys which were left, and the captain's

208

palanquin and equipage, were placed entirely at my disposal; and in order to complete my happiness, Dr. Rolland was so good as to accompany me in all my excursions.

12th February. This morning, the king, Ram-Singh, who had been immediately informed of my arrival, sent me a quantity of fruits and sweetmeats in large baskets, his own riding elephant, handsomely caparisoned, an officer on horseback, and some soldiers. I was very soon seated with Dr. Rolland in the howdah, and trotted to the neighbouring town. Kottah contains about 30,000 inhabitants, and lies on the river Chumbal, in a far stretching and, in some places, very rocky plain, 1,300 feet above the level of the sea. The town, which is conspicuously situated, is surrounded by strong fortified works, upon which are placed fifty pieces of cannon. The immediate neighbourhood is rocky, naked, and barren. The interior of the town is separated into three parts by as many gates. The first part is inhabited by the poorer classes, and appeared very wretched. In the two other parts the tradespeople and the gentry reside; they have an incomparably better aspect. The principal street, although uneven and stony, is sufficiently wide to allow carriages, and ponderous beasts of burden, to pass without hindrance.

The architecture of the houses is in the highest degree original. The smallness of the windows had already attracted my notice in Benares, here they are so narrow and low that it is hardly possible to put the head out; they are for the most part closed with finely worked stone lattice, instead of glass. Many of the houses have large alcoves; in others there are spacious saloons on the first floor, which rest on pillars and occupy the whole front of the house; many of these halls were separated by partition walls into smaller open saloons. At both corners of the hall were decorated pavilions, and at the further end, doors leading to the interior of the house. These halls are generally used as shops and places of business; also as the resort of idlers, who sit upon mats and ottomans, smoking their hookas and watching the bustle in the streets. In other houses, again, the front walls were painted in fresco, with terrible-looking dragons, tigers, lions, twice or thrice as large as life, stretching their tongues out, with hideous grimaces; or with deities, flowers, arabesques, etc., without sense or taste grouped together, miserably executed, and bedaubed with the most glaring colours.

The numerous handsome Hindoo temples, all built upon lofty stone terraces, form an agreeable feature of the town. They are higher, more capacious, and finer buildings than those of Benares, with the exception of the Bisvishas. The temples here stand in open halls, intersected by colonnades, ornamented with several quadrangular towers, and surmounted by a cupola of from twenty to forty feet in height. The sanctuary is in the middle; it is a small, carefully enclosed building, with a door leading into it. This door, as well as the pillars and friezes, is covered with beautiful sculptures; the square towers are quite as carefully constructed as those at Benares. Hideous statues and fanciful figures stand under the halls, some of which are painted in bright red colours. On the side walls of the terraces are

209

arabesques, elephants, horses, etc., carved in relief.

The royal palace lies at the extremity of the third part of the town, and forms a town within a town, or rather a fortress in a fortress, as it is surrounded by immense fortified walls, which command the town as well as the country round it; many large and small buildings are enclosed within these walls, but do not present anything remarkable beyond their handsome halls. Had the resident been in Kottah I should have been presented to the king, but as it was not etiquette in his absence, I was compelled to put up with my disappointment.

From the town we proceeded to Armornevas, one of the neighbouring palaces of the king's. The road to it was indescribably bad, full of rocks and large stones. I was astonished to see with what dexterity our elephant set his plump feet between them, and travelled on as quickly as if he was going over the levellest road.

When I expressed my surprise to Dr. Rolland that the king should not have a good road made to his residence, which he so often visited, he informed me that it was a maxim with all Indian monarchs not to make roads, for, according to their opinion, in case of a war, they offered too great facilities to the invasion of the enemy.

The castle is small and unimportant. It lies on the river Chumbal, which has here hollowed out for itself a remarkably deep bed in the rock. Picturesque ravines and groups of rock form its shores.

The garden of the castle is so thickly planted with orange, citron, and other trees, that there is not room for even the smallest flowering plant or shrub.

The few flowers which the Indian gardens contain, are placed at the entrances. The paths are raised two feet, as the ground is always muddy and damp in consequence of the frequent watering. Most of the Indian gardens which I afterwards saw resembled these.

The king frequently amuses himself here with tiger-hunting. Somewhat higher up the river small towers are erected upon slight eminences; the tigers are driven gradually towards the water, and always more and more hemmed in, until they are within shot of the towers; the king and his friends sit securely upon the tops of the towers, and fire bravely upon the wild beasts.

Near the castle was a small wooden temple, which had just been built; the principal part, however, the amiable idols, was awanting. It was owing to this fortunate circumstance that we were allowed to enter the sanctuary, which consisted of a small marble kiosk standing in the centre of the hall. The temple and the columns were covered with bad paintings in the most brilliant colours. It is strange that neither the Hindoos nor the Mahometans should have applied themselves to painting, for there are neither good pictures nor drawings to be seen among any of these people, although they have displayed such proficiency in architecture, carving in relief, and in mosaic work.

We lastly visited a remarkably fine wood of tamarind and mango trees, under the shadows of which the ashes of a number of kings are preserved in handsome monuments. These monuments consist of open temples, with broad flights of ten or twelve steps leading up to them. At the bottom of the steps, on each side, stand stone figures of elephants. Some of the temples are ornamented with beautiful sculptures.

The evening was passed in all kinds of amusements. The good doctor would have made me acquainted with all the arts of the Hindoos; however, the greater number of them were no longer new to me. A snake-charmer exhibited his little society, which performed very clever tricks, and also allowed the most poisonous serpents to twine themselves round his body, and the largest scorpions ran over his arms and legs. Afterwards, four elegant female dancers appeared dressed in muslin, ornamented with gold and silver, and loaded with jewellery,—ears, forehead, neck, breast, loins, hands, arms, feet, in short, every part of the body was covered with gold, silver, and precious stones; even the toes were ornamented with them, and from the nose, a large ring with three stones hung over the mouth. Two of the dancers first commenced. Their dance consisted of the same winding movements which I had already seen in Benares, only they were far more animated, and twisted their fingers, hands, and arms about in every conceivable manner. They might well be said to dance with their arms but not with their feet. They danced for ten minutes without singing, then they began to scream, without however keeping time, and their motions became more violent and wild, until in about half an hour both strength and voice failed, they stopped quite exhausted, and made way for their sisters, who repeated the same spectacle. Dr. Rolland told me that they represented a love story, in which every virtue and passion, such as truth, self-devotion, hate, persecution, despair, etc., played a part. The musicians stood a little behind the dancers, and followed all their movements. The whole space which such a company requires, is at the most ten feet in length and eight broad. The good Hindoos amuse themselves for hours together with these tasteless repetitions.

I remember having read in books that the Indian female dancers were far more graceful than the European, that their songs were highly melodious, and that their pantomime was tender, inspiring, and attractive. I should scarcely think the authors of such books could have been in India! Not less exaggerated are the descriptions of others, who affirm that there are no dances more indelicate than those of the Indians. I might again ask these people if they had ever seen the Sammaquecca and Refolosa in Valparaiso, the female dancers of Tahiti, or even our own in flesh-coloured leggings? The dresses of the females in Rajpootan and some parts of Bundelkund are very different from those of other parts of India. They wear long, coloured, many-folded skirts, tight bodies, which are so short that they scarcely cover the breasts; and, over this, a blue mantle, in which they envelop the upper part of the body, the head, and the face, and allow a part to hang down in front like a veil. Girls who do not always have the head covered, nearly resemble our own peasant girls. Like the dancers, they are overloaded with jewellery; when they cannot afford gold and silver, they content themselves with some other metals. They wear also rings of horn, bone, or glass beads, on the fingers, arms, and feet. On the feet they carry bells, so that they are heard at a distance of sixty paces; the toes are covered with broad heavy rings, and they have rings hanging from their noses down to the chin, which they are obliged to tie up at meal time. I pitied the poor creatures, who suffered not a little from their finery! The eyebrows and eyelids are dyed black while the children are very young, and they frequently paint themselves with dark-blue streaks of a finger's breadth over the eyebrows, and with spots on the forehead. The adult women tattoo their breasts, foreheads, noses, or temples with red, white, or yellow colours, according as they are particularly attached to one or the other deity. Many wear amulets or miniatures hung round their necks, so that I at first thought they were Catholics, and felt gratified at the brilliant successes of the missionaries. But, when I came nearer to one of the people, that I might see these pictures better, what did I discover there? Perhaps a beautiful Madonna!—a fair-haired angel's head!—an enthusiastic Antonio of Padua! Ah no! I was met by the eight-armed god Shiva grinning at me, the ox's head of Vishnu, the long-tongued goddess Kalli. The amulets contained, most probably, some of the ashes of one of their martyrs who had been burned, or a nail, a fragment of skin, a hair of a saint, a splinter from the bone of a sacred animal, etc.

13th February. Dr. Rolland conducted me to the little town of Kesho-Rae-Patum, one of the most sacred in Bunda and Rajpootan. It lies on the other side of the river, six miles from Kottah. A great number of pilgrims come here to bathe, as the water is considered particularly sacred at this spot. This belief cannot be condemned, when it is remembered how many Christians there are who give the preference to the Holy Maria at Maria-Zell, Einsiedeln, or Loretto, which, nevertheless, all represent one and the same.

Handsome steps lead from the heights on the banks down to the river, and Brahmins sit in pretty kiosks to take money from believers for the honour of the gods. On one of the flights of steps lay a very large tortoise. It might quietly sun itself there in safety—no one thought of catching it. It came out of the sacred river; indeed, it might, perhaps, be the incarnation of the god Vishnu himself. {204} Along the river stood numbers of stone altars, with small bulls, and other emblematical figures, also cut in stone. The town itself is small and miserable, but the temple is large and handsome.

The priests were here so tolerant as to admit us to all parts of the temple. It is open on all sides, and forms an octagon. Galleries run round the upper part, one-half of which are for women, the other for the musicians. The sanctuary stands at the back of the temple; five bells hang before it, which are struck when women enter the temple; they rung out also at my entrance. The curtained and closed doors were then opened, and afforded us a full view of the interior. We saw there a little group of idols carved in stone. The people who followed us with curiosity commenced a gentle muttering upon the opening of the doors. I turned round, somewhat startled, thinking that it was directed against us and indicated anger, but it was the prayers, which they repeated in a low voice and with a feeling of devotion. One of the Brahmins brushed off the flies from the intelligent countenances of the gods.

Several chapels join the large temple, and were all opened to us. They contained red-painted stones or pictures. In the front court sits a stone figure of a saint under a covering, completely clothed, and with even a cap on the head. On the opposite bank of the river, a small hill rises, upon which rests the figure of a large and rather plump ox hewn in stone. This hill is called the "holy mountain."

Captain Burdon has built a very pretty house near the holy mountain, where he sometimes lives with his family. I saw there a fine collection of stuffed birds, which he had brought himself from the Himalayas. I was particularly struck by the pheasants, some of which shone with quite a metallic lustre; and there were some not less beautiful specimens of heathcocks.

I had now seen all, and therefore asked the doctor to order me a conveyance to Indor, 180 miles distant, for the next day. He surprised me with the offer, on the part of the king, to provide me with as many camels as I required, and two sepoys on horseback as attendants. I asked for two; the one for myself, the other for the driver and the servants which Dr. Rolland sent with me.

CHAPTER XV. JOURNEY FROM DELHI TO BOMBAY CONTINUED.

TRAVELLING ON INDIAN CAMELS—MY MEETING WITH THE BURDON FAMILY—THE DIFFERENT CLASSES OF WOMEN AMONG THE NATIVE POPULATION IN INDIA—UDJEIN—CAPTAIN HAMILTON—INTRODUCTION AT COURT—MANUFACTURE OF ICE— THE ROCK TEMPLES OF ADJUNTA—A TIGER HUNT—THE ROCK TEMPLES OF ELORA—THE FORTRESS OF DOWLUTABAD.

14TH February. The camels were ordered at 5 o'clock in the morning, but it was not until towards noon that they came, each with a driver. When they saw my portmanteau (twenty-five pounds in weight), they were quite puzzled to know what to do with it. It was useless my explaining to them how the luggage is carried in Egypt, and that I had been accustomed to carry very little with me on my own animal: they were used to a different plan, and would not depart from it.

Travelling on camels is always unpleasant and troublesome. The jolting motion of the animal produces in many people the same ill effects as the rocking of a ship on the sea; but in India it is almost unbearable, on account of the inconvenience of the arrangements. Here each animal has a driver, who sits in front and takes the best place; the traveller has only a little space left for him on the hinder part of the animal.

Dr. Rolland advised me at once to put up with the inconvenience as well as I could. He told me that I should fall in with Captain Burdon in the next day or two, and it would be easy to obtain a more convenient conveyance from him. I followed his advice, allowed my luggage to be carried, and patiently mounted my camel.

We passed through extensive plains, which were most remarkable for some considerable flax plantations, and came to a beautiful lake, near to which lay a very pretty palace. Towards evening, we reached the little village of Moasa, where we stayed for the night.

In those countries which are governed by native princes, there are neither roads nor arrangements for travelling; although in every village and town there are people appointed whose business it is to direct travellers on their way and carry their luggage, for which they are paid a small fee. Those travellers who have a guard from the king or aumil (governor), or a cheprasse with them, do not pay anything for this attendance; others give them a trifle for their services, according as the distance is greater or less.

When I reached Moasa, every one hastened to offer me their services—for I travelled with the king's people, and in this part of the country a European woman is a rarity. They brought me wood, milk, and eggs. My table was always rather frugally furnished: at the best I had rice boiled in milk or some eggs, but generally only rice, with water and salt. A leathern vessel for water, a little saucepan for boiling in, a handful of salt, and some rice and bread, were all that I took with me.

15th February. Late in the evening I reached Nurankura, a small place surrounded by low mountains. I found here some tents belonging to Captain Burdon, a maid, and a servant. Terribly fatigued, I entered one of the tents directly, in order to rest myself. Scarcely had I taken possession of the divan, than the maid came into the tent, and, without any observation, commenced kneading me about with her hands. I would have stopped her, but she explained to me that when a person was fatigued it was very refreshing. For a quarter of an hour she pressed my body from head to foot vigorously, and it certainly produced a good effect—I found myself much relieved and strengthened. This custom of pressing and kneading is very common in India, as well as in all Oriental countries, especially after the bath; and Europeans also willingly allow themselves to be operated upon.

The maid informed me, partly by signs, partly by words, that I had been expected since noon; that a palanquin stood ready for me, and that I could sleep as well in it as in the tent. I was rejoiced at this, and again started on my journey at 11 o'clock at night. The country was indeed, as I knew, infested with tigers, but as several torch-bearers accompanied us, and the tigers are sworn enemies of light, I could composedly continue my uninterrupted sleep. About 3 o'clock in the morning, I was set down again in a tent, which was prepared for my reception, and furnished with every convenience.

16th February. This morning I made the acquaintance of the amiable family of the Burdons. They have seven children, whom they educate chiefly themselves. They live very pleasantly and comfortably, although they are wholly thrown on their own resources for amusement, as there are, with the exception of Dr. Rolland, no Europeans in Kottah. It is only very rarely that they are visited by officers who may be passing through, and I was the first European female Mrs. Burdon had seen for four years.

I passed the most delightful day in this family circle. I was not a little astonished to find here all the conveniences of a well-regulated house; and I must take this opportunity of describing, in few words, the mode of travelling adopted by the English officers and officials in India.

In the first place, they have tents which are so large, that they contain two or three rooms; one which I saw was worth more than 800 rupees (£80). They take with them corresponding furniture, from a footstool to the most elegant divan; in fact, nearly the whole of the house and cooking utensils. They have also a multitude of servants, every one of whom has his particular occupation, which he understands exceedingly well. The travellers, after passing the night in their beds, about 3 o'clock in the morning either lie or sit in easy palanquins, or mount on horseback, and after four or five hours' ride, dismount, and partake of a hot breakfast under tents. They have every household accommodation, carry on their ordinary occupations, take their meals at their usual hours, and are, in fact, entirely at home.

The cook always proceeds on his journey at night. As soon as the tents are vacated, they are taken down and quickly removed, and as quickly re-erected: there is no scarcity of hands or of beasts of burden. In the most cultivated countries of Europe, people do not travel with so much luxury and ease as in India.

In the evening, I was obliged to take my departure again. Captain Burdon very kindly offered me the use of his palanquin and the necessary bearers as far as Indos, but I pitied the people too much, and declared that I did not find travelling on camels unpleasant; that in fact, on account of the open view, that mode was to be preferred to palanquins. However, on account of my little portmanteau, I took a third camel. I left the sepoys behind here. This evening we went eight miles towards the little town Patan.

17th February. It was not till this morning that I saw Patan was situated on a romantic chain of hills, and possesses several remarkably handsome temples, in the open halls belonging to which are placed sculptured stone figures, the size of life. The arabesques and figures on the pillars were sharply executed in relief. In

215

the valleys which we passed through, there was a large quantity of basaltic rock and most beautifully crystallized quartz. Towards evening, we reached Batschbachar, a miserable little town.

18th February. Rumtscha is somewhat larger and better. I was obliged to put up my bed in the middle of the bazaar under an open verandah. Upon this road there were no caravansaries. Half of the inhabitants of the town gathered round me, and watched all my motions and doings with the greatest attention. I afforded them an opportunity of studying the appearance of an angry European female, as I was very much displeased with my people, and, in spite of my slight knowledge of the language, scolded them heartily. They allowed the camels to go so lazily, that although we had travelled since early in the morning until late in the evening, we had not gone more than twenty or twenty-two miles, not faster than an ox-waggon would have gone. I made them understand that this negligence must not happen again. I must now take occasion to contradict those persons who affirm that the camel can travel on the average eighty miles daily, and that even when they go slowly, their steps are very long. I examine every circumstance very accurately, and then form an opinion from my own experience, without allowing myself to be misled by what has been written about it. Before commencing a journey, I observe not only the principal distances, but also those between the individual places, arrange a plan of my journey with the help of friends who are acquainted with the subject, and by this means have the advantage over my driver, who cannot persuade me that we have gone forty or sixty miles, when we have not gone more than half this distance. Moreover, I was able, while travelling from Delhi to Kottah by the ox-waggon, to observe several camel equipages, which I fell in with every evening at the same night station. It is true that I had most excellent oxen, and that the camels were ordinary; but in this journey, with good camels, I did not go more than thirty, or at the utmost, thirty-two miles in the day, and travelled from 4 o'clock in the morning until 6 in the evening, without any other stoppage than two hours at noon. A camel which is able to travel eighty miles in a day is an exception to the general rule, and would scarcely perform such a feat the second or third time.

19th February. Ranera is an unimportant place. I was here offered a cow-stall to sleep in. It was indeed kept very clean; but I preferred sleeping in the open air.

Till a late hour of the night this town was very lively: processions of men and a number of women and children followed the noise of the tam-tam, which they accompanied with a wild, howling song, and proceeded to some tree, under which an image of an idol was set up.

We had on this day to cross several ranges of low hills. The uncultivated ground was everywhere scorched up by the sun; {209} nevertheless, the plantations of poppies, flax, corn, and cotton, etc., grew very luxuriantly. Water-dykes were let into the fields on every side, and peasants, with their yokes of oxen, were engaged in bringing water from the wells and streams. I did not see any women at work.

216

In my numerous journeys, I had an opportunity of observing that the lot of the poorer classes of women in India, in the East, and among coloured people generally, was not so hard as it is believed to be. In the towns where Europeans reside, for example, their linen is washed and prepared by men; it is very seldom that it is necessary for women to take part in out-door labour; they carry wood, water, or any other heavy burdens only in their own houses. At harvest time, indeed, the women are seen in the fields, but there also they only do the lighter kind of work. If carriages with horses or oxen are seen, the women and children are always seated upon them, and the men walk by the side, often laden with bundles. When there are no beasts of burden with the party, the men carry the children and baggage. I also never saw a man ill use his wife or child. I heartily wish that the women of the poorer classes in my own country were treated with only half the consideration which I saw in all other parts of the world.

20th February. Udjein on the Seepa, one of the oldest and best built towns of India, is the capital of the kingdom of Sindhia, with a population of more than 100,000 souls.

The architecture of this town is quite peculiar: the front walls of the houses, only one story high, are constructed of wood, and furnished with large regular window openings in the upper part, which are securely closed by beams, instead of glass. In the interior, the apartments are built very lofty and airy: they have the full height from the level of the ground to the roof, without the interruption of an intermediate arch. The outer walls and beams of the houses are painted with a dark brown oil colour, which gave to the town an indescribably dusky appearance.

Two houses were remarkable for their size and the uncommonly fine execution of the wood carvings. They contained two stories, and were very tastefully ornamented with galleries, pillars, friezes, niches, etc. As far as I could learn from the answers I received to my questions, and the numerous servants and soldiers walking about before them, they were the palaces of the aumil and the Queen Widow of Madhadji-Sindhia.

We passed through the entire town; the streets were broad, the bazaars very extensive, and so overcrowded with men, that we were frequently compelled to stop; it happened to be a large market. Upon such occasions in India, as well as at great festivals and meetings of people, I never once saw any one intoxicated, although there was no lack of intoxicating drinks. The men here are temperate, and restrain themselves, yet without forming into societies.

Outside the town I found an open verandah, in which I took up my quarters for the night.

I was here a witness of a deplorable scene, a consequence of an erroneous religious belief of the otherwise amiable Hindoos. Not far from the verandah lay a fakir, outstretched upon the earth, without any signs of life; many of the passers-by stopped, looked at him, and then went on their way. No one spoke to

217

or helped him. The poor man had sunk exhausted on this spot, and was no longer capable of saying to what caste he belonged. I took heart, approached him, and raised the head-cloth, which had fallen over a part of his face; two glassy eyes stared at me. I felt the body; it was stiff and cold. My help came too late.

The next morning the corpse still lay in the same place. I was informed that they waited to see if any relations would come to carry it away, if not it would be removed by the pariahs.

21st February. In the afternoon I reached Indor, the capital of the kingdom of Holkar.

As I approached the dwelling of the Europeans, I found them just about to ride out. The equipage of the resident, Mr. Hamilton, to whom I had letters, was distinguishable from the others by its greater splendour. Four beautiful horses were harnessed to an open landau, and four servants, in Oriental liveries, ran by the side of the carriage. The gentlemen had scarcely perceived my approach, when they stopped, and sent a servant towards me; they, perhaps, wished to know what chance had thrown a solitary European female into this remote country. My servant, who already had the letter to Mr. Hamilton in his hand, hastened to him directly, and gave it to him. Mr. Hamilton read it hastily through, alighted from his carriage immediately, came and received me very cordially. My shabby clothes, faded by the sun, were of no account to him, and he did not treat me with less respect, because I came without much baggage, and without a train of attendants.

He conducted me himself to the bungalow, set apart for strangers, offered me several rooms, and remained until he saw that the servants had properly provided all conveniences. After he had given me a servant for my own exclusive use, and had ordered a guard before the bungalow, in which I was about to live alone, he took his departure, and promised to send for me to dinner in an hour.

A few hundred paces distant from the bungalow is the palace of the resident; it is a building of very great beauty, constructed of large, square stones, in a pure Italian style of architecture. Broad flights of steps led up into halls which are peculiarly remarkable for their magnitude and beautifully arched roofs, the latter being finer than any that I had yet seen. The saloons, rooms, and internal arrangements corresponded to the high expectations which the sight of the outside raised.

It was a Sunday, and I had the pleasure of finding the whole European society of Indor assembled at the house of the resident. It consisted of three families. My astonishment at the magnificence surrounding me, at the luxuries at table, was yet more increased when a complete, well-trained band of musicians commenced playing fine overtures and some familiar German melodies. After dinner Mr. Hamilton introduced the chaplain to me, a Tyrolese, named Näher. This active man had established his chapel in the space of three years, the congregation consisting chiefly of young natives.

I was invited to be present on the following morning at the first operation performed here, by a European surgeon, on a patient under the influence of ether. A large tumour was to be extracted from the neck of a native. Unfortunately the inhalation did not turn out as was expected: the patient came to again after the first incision, and began shrieking fearfully. I hastily left the room, for I pitied the poor creature too much to bear his cries. The operation indeed was successful, but the man suffered considerable pain.

During breakfast, Mr. Hamilton proposed that I should exchange my apartments in the bungalow for a similar one in his palace, because the going backwards and forwards at each meal time was very fatiguing. He placed at my disposal the rooms of his wife, who was deceased, and appointed me a female servant.

After tiffen (lunch) I was to see the town, and be presented at court. I employed the intermediate time in visiting Mr. and Mrs. Näher. The latter, who was also a German, was moved even to tears when she saw me: for fifteen years she had not spoken with a fellow-countrywoman.

The town of Indor contains nearly 25,000 inhabitants; it is not fortified; the houses are built in the same manner as those in Udjein.

The royal palace stands in the centre of the town, and forms a quadrangle. The middle of the front rises in the form of a pyramid, to the height of six stories. A remarkably lofty and very handsome gateway, flanked on both sides by round and somewhat projecting towers, leads into the court-yard. The exterior of the palace is completely covered with frescoes, for the most part representing elephants and horses, and from a distance they present a good appearance. The interior is separated into several courts. In the first court, on the ground floor, is situated a saloon, surrounded by two rows of wooden pillars. The Durwar (ministerial council) is held here. In the first story of the same building a fine open saloon is appropriated to the use of some sacred oxen.

Opposite this cattle-stall is the reception-room. Dark stairs, which require to be lighted in broad daylight, lead to the royal apartments. The stairs are said to be equally dark in almost all the Indian palaces; they believe it is a security against enemies, or, at least, that it makes their entrance more difficult. In the reception saloon sat the queen, Jeswont-Rao-Holcar, an aged, childless widow; at her side her adopted son, Prince Hury-Rao-Holcar, a youth of fourteen years, with very good-natured features and expressive eyes. Seats, consisting of cushions, were placed for us by their side. The young prince spoke broken English, and the questions which he put to me proved him to be well acquainted with geography. His mundsch, {212a} a native, was represented as a man of intelligence and learning. I could not find an opportunity, after the audience, of complimenting him upon the progress which the prince had made. The dress of the queen and of the prince consisted of white Dacca muslin; the prince had several precious stones and pearls upon his turban, breast, and arms. The queen was not veiled, although Mr. Hamilton was present.

219

All the apartments and passages were crowded with servants, who, without the slightest ceremony, came into the audience-hall, that they might observe us more closely; we sat in a complete crowd.

We were offered sweetmeats and fruits, sprinkled with rosewater, and some attar of roses was put upon our handkerchiefs. After some time areca nuts and betel leaves were brought on silver plates, which the queen herself handed to us; this is a sign that the audience is at an end, and visitors cannot leave until it is made. Before we got up to go, large wreaths of jasmine were hung round our necks, and small ones round our wrists. Fruits and sweetmeats were also sent home to us.

The queen had given the mundsch directions to conduct us round the whole of the palace. It is not very large, and the rooms, with the exception of the reception-saloon, are very simple, and almost without furniture; in each, cushions covered with white muslin lie upon the floor.

As we stood upon the terrace of the house, we saw the prince ride out. Two servants led his horse, and a number of attendants surrounded him. Several officers accompanied him upon elephants, and mounted soldiers closed the procession. The latter wore wide white trousers, short blue jackets, and handsome round caps; they looked very well. The people raised a low murmur when they saw the prince, as an indication of their pleasure.

The mundsch was good enough to show me the mode adopted for making ice. The proper time for this is during the months of December and January; although, even in the month of February, the nights, and especially the early hours of the morning before sun-rise, are so cold, that small quantities of water are covered with a thin sheet of ice. For this purpose, either shallow pits are dug in earth rich in saltpetre, {212b} and small shallow dishes of burnt porous clay are filled with water, and placed in these pits, or when the soil does not contain any saltpetre, the highest terraces on the houses are covered with straw, and the little dishes of water are placed up there. The thin crusts of ice thus obtained are broken into small pieces, a little water is poured over them, and the whole is put into the ice-houses, which are also lined with straw. This mode of obtaining ice is already practised in Benares.

Mr. Hamilton was so obliging as to make the arrangements for the continuance of my journey. I could have had the royal camels again, but preferred a car with oxen, as the loss of time was inconsiderable, and the trouble far less. Mr. Hamilton himself made the contract with the driver, pointed out the stations at which we should stop between this and Auranjabad (230 miles), gave me an excellent servant and sepoy, furnished me with letters, and even asked me if I had sufficient money. This excellent man did all this with so much amiability, that, in fact, I scarcely knew whether the kindnesses or the way in which they were offered, were most to be admired. And not only in Indor, but everywhere else that he was known, I heard his name always mentioned with the most profound respect.

On the 23rd of February I left Indor on my way to the little village of Simarola. The road led through delightful groves of palm-trees and richly cultivated land. In Simarola, I found a pretty and comfortably furnished tent, which Mr. Hamilton had sent on, in order to surprise me with a good night station. I silently thanked him most heartily for his care.

24th February. From Simarola the country was truly picturesque. A narrow ledge of rock, in some places scarcely broad enough for the road, led down a considerable declivity {213} into small valleys, on the sides of which beautiful mountains towered up. The latter were thinly wooded; among the trees I was particularly struck by two species, the one with yellow, the other with red flowers; both of them, very singularly, were quite destitute of leaves.

On this side of Kottah the camel trains were less frequent, in consequence of the very stony state of the road; instead of these, we met trains of oxen. We passed some today of incredible extent. I do not exaggerate when I affirm that I have seen trains of several thousand head of cattle, on whose backs, corn, wool, salt, etc., were conveyed. I cannot imagine where the food for so many animals is obtained; there are nowhere any meadows, for, with the exception of the plantations, the ground is scorched up, or at most covered with thin, parched, jungle grass, which I never saw any animal eat.

The industry of the women and children in the villages through which these trains pass is great beyond measure; they provide themselves with baskets, and follow the train for a considerable distance, collecting the excrement of the oxen, which they work up into flat bricks, and dry them in the sun to use as fuel. Late in the evening, we entered the village of Burwai, which lies on the river Nurbuda, in the midst of a storm of thunder and lightning. I was told that there was a public bungalow here, but as the darkness of the night prevented our finding it, I contented myself with the balcony of a house.

25th February. We had this morning to cross the river Nurbuda, which, with the preparations for doing so, occupied two hours.

26th February. Rostampoor. Between this place and Simarola, the land is rather barren, and also very thinly inhabited; we often travelled several miles without seeing a village.

27th February. Today we were gratified with the prospect of a fertile country and beautiful mountains. On an isolated mountain was situated the famous old fortress of Assergur, from which arose two half-decayed minarets. Towards evening we passed between many ruins; amongst which I observed another handsome mosque, the fore-court, the minarets, and side walls of which were standing. Adjoining this district of ruins, lay the very flourishing town of Berhampoor, which still numbers 60,000 inhabitants, but I was told that it was formerly much larger.

An aumil resides in the town, and also an English officer, who keeps an eye on his

221

proceedings. We were obliged to pass through the whole town, through the deep river Taptai, up and down hill, and over shocking roads, to reach the bungalow of the latter, so that we did not arrive there till late at night. Captain Henessey and his family were already supping: they received me with true cordiality, and, although worn out with fatigue, and much travel-stained, I took my place at their hospitable table, and continued a conversation with this amiable family until a late hour of the night.

28th February. Unfortunately I was obliged to proceed on my journey again this morning. Between Berhampoor and Ichapoor, there were the most beautiful and varied plantations—corn, flax, cotton, sugar-cane, poppies, dahl, etc. The heat had already began to be oppressive (towards 108° Fah.) I was at the same time continually on the road from 4 o'clock in the morning, till 5 or 6 in the evening, and only seldom made a short halt on the banks of some river, or under a tree. It was altogether impossible to travel at night, as the heaths and jungles were frequently of great extent, and moreover, somewhat infested with tigers, the presence of which we experienced on the following day; besides all this, my people were unacquainted with the road.

29th February. Today's stage was one of the most considerable; we therefore started as early as 3 o'clock in the morning; the road passed through terrible wastes and wild jungles. After we had proceeded for some time quietly, the animals stopped short and remained as if fixed to the ground, and began to tremble; their fear soon communicated itself to my people, who shouted, without intermission, the words "*Bach! bach!*" which means "Tiger! tiger!" I ordered them to continue making as much noise as possible, in order to scare away the animals if they really were near. I had some jungle grass gathered and made a fire, which I kept constantly blazing. However, I heard no howling, and observed no other indication of our dreaded neighbour than the terror of my people and cattle. Nevertheless, I awaited the sunrise this time with great anxiety, when we continued our journey. We afterwards learnt that scarcely a night passes in this neighbourhood without an ox, horse, or goat being carried off by tigers. Only a few days previously, a poor woman who was late in returning from gathering jungle grass, had been torn to pieces. All the villages were surrounded with high stone and mud walls, whether from fear of the wild beasts, or from any other cause, I could not learn with certainty. These fortified villages extend as far as Auranjabad, over a distance of 150 miles.

March 1st. Bodur is an unimportant village. Upon the road from Indor to Auranjabad, there are no bungalows with rooms, and it is very seldom that even an open one is to be found—that is, a building with three wooden walls, over which a roof is thrown. We found one of these bungalows in Bodur. It was indeed already taken possession of by about a dozen Indian soldiers, but they withdrew unasked, and gave up to me half of the airy chamber. During the whole night they remained still and quiet, and were not the slightest annoyance.

222

2nd March. Furdapoor, a small village at the foot of beautiful mountains. As the poor oxen began to be wearied with travelling, the driver rubbed them down every evening from head to foot.

3rd March. Adjunta. Before coming to this place we passed a terrible rocky pass which might be easily defended. The road was very narrow, and so bad that the poor animals could scarcely make any way with the empty cars. On the heights of the pass, a strongly fortified gate was placed, which closed the narrow road; it was, however, left open in time of peace. The low ground and the heights on the sides were rendered inaccessible by strong and lofty walls.

The view became more delightful at every step: romantic valleys and ravines, picturesque masses and walls of rock lay on both sides, immeasurable valleys spread themselves out behind the mountains, while in front the view swept over an extensive open plain, at the commencement of which lay the fortress of Adjunta. We had already reached it at about 8 o'clock in the morning. Captain Gill resides in Adjunta, and I had letters of introduction to him from Mr. Hamilton. When I expressed a wish, after the first greeting was over, to visit the famous rock temples of Adjunta, he deeply regretted that he had not received a letter from me four-and-twenty hours sooner, as the temples were nearer to Furdapoor than to Adjunta. What was to be done? I was resolved upon seeing them, and had but little time to lose, so I decided upon retracing my way. I only provided myself with a small stock of provisions, and immediately mounted one of the horses from the captain's stable, which brought me past the rocky pass in a good hour. The road towards the temples here turns off to the right into desolate, barren mountain valleys, whose death-like stillness was unbroken by the breathing of an animal, or the song of a bird. This place was well calculated to raise and excite expectations.

The temples, twenty-seven in number, are excavated in tall perpendicular cliffs, which form a semicircle. In some of the cliffs there are two stories of temples, one over the other; paths lead to the top, but these are so narrow and broken, that one is frequently at a loss where to set the foot. Beneath are terrible chasms, in which a mountain stream loses itself; overhead, the smooth rocky surface extends several hundred feet in height. The majority of the temples are quadrangular in form, and the approach to the interior is through verandahs and handsome gateways, which, from being supported on columns, appear to bear the weight of the whole mass of rock. These temples are called "Vihara." In the larger one I counted twenty-eight, in the smallest eight pillars. On one, and sometimes on both side-walls, there is a very small dark cell, in which most probably the priest lived. In the background, in a large and lofty cell, is the sanctuary. Here are gigantic figures in every position; some measure more than eighteen feet, and nearly reach to the roof of the temple, which is about twenty-four feet high. The walls of the temples and verandahs are full of idols and statues of good and evil spirits. In one of the temples, a battle of giants is represented. The figures are above life size, and the whole of the figures, columns, verandahs and gateways,

223

are cut out of the solid rock. The enormous number and remarkable beauty of the sculptures and reliefs on the columns, capitals, friezes, gateways, and even on the roof of the temples, is indeed most astonishing; the variety in the designs and devices is inexhaustible. It appears incredible that human hands should have been able to execute such masterly and gigantic works. The Brahmins do, indeed, ascribe their origin to supernatural agencies, and affirm that the era of their creation cannot be ascertained.

Remains of paintings are found on the walls, ceiling, and pillars, the colours of which are brighter and fresher than those of many modern works of art.

The second class of temples have an oval form, and have majestic lofty portals leading immediately into the interior; they are called *chaitya*. The largest of these temples has on each side a colonnade of nineteen pillars—the smallest, one of eight; in these there are no verandahs, no priest's cells, and no sanctuaries. Instead of the latter, a high monument stands at the extremity of the temple. Upon one of these monuments an upright figure of the deity Buddha is sculptured in a standing position. On the walls of the larger temple gigantic figures are hewn out of the solid rock, and under these a sleeping Buddha, twenty-one feet in length.

After I had wandered about here for some hours, and had seen enough of each of the temples, I was led back to one of them, and saw there a small table well covered with eatables and drinkables, inviting me to a welcome meal. Captain Gill had been so kind as to send after me a choice tiffen, together with table and chairs, into this wilderness. Thus refreshed and invigorated, I did not find the return fatiguing. The house in which Captain Gill lives at Adjunta is very remarkably situated: a pleasant little garden, with flowers and shrubs, surrounds the front, which commands a view of a fine plain, while the back stands upon the edge of a most fearful precipice, over which the dizzy glance loses itself among steep crags and terrible gorges and chasms.

As Captain Gill had learnt that I wished to visit the famous fortress of Dowlutabad, he told me that no one was admitted without the permission of the commander of Auranjabad; but, to spare my going out of my way (as the fortress lies on this side of Auranjabad), he offered to send a courier there immediately, and order him to bring the card of admission to me at Elora. The courier had to travel altogether a distance of 140 miles—70 there and as many back. I looked upon all these attentions as the more obliging, as they were shown to me—a German woman, without distinction or attractions—by English people.

4th March. At 4 o'clock in the morning, the good captain joined me at the breakfast table; half an hour later, I was seated in my waggon and travelling towards the village of Bongeloda, which I reached the same day.

5th March. Roja is one of the most ancient towns of India. It has a gloomy aspect; the houses are one story high, and built of large square stones, blackened by age; the doors and windows are few in number and irregularly situated.

Outside the town lay a handsome bungalow with two rooms; but, as I was informed that it was occupied by Europeans, I decided upon not going there, and took up my quarters for the night under the eaves of a house.

The country between this and Adjunta is a flat plain; the parched heaths and poor jungles are interspersed with beautiful plantations. The land near Pulmary was especially well cultivated.

6th March. Early in the morning, I mounted a horse for the purpose of visiting the equally-renowned rock temples of Elora (ten miles from Roja). But, as it frequently happens in life that the proverb, "man proposes and God disposes," proves true, such was the case in the present instance—instead of the temples, I saw a tiger-hunt.

I had scarcely left the gates of the town behind, when I perceived a number of Europeans seated upon elephants, coming from the bungalow. On meeting each other, we pulled up, and commenced a conversation. The gentlemen were on the road to search for a tiger-lair, of which they had received intimation, and invited me, if such a sport would not frighten me too much, to take part in it. I was greatly delighted to receive the invitation, and was soon seated on one of the elephants, in a howdah about two feet high, in which there were already two gentlemen and a native—the latter had been brought to load the guns. They gave me a large knife to defend myself with, in case the animal should spring too high and reach the side of the howdah.

Thus prepared, we approached the chain of hills, and, after a few hours, were already pretty near the lair of the tigers, when our servants cried out quite softly, "Bach, bach!" and pointed with their fingers to some brushwood. I had scarcely perceived the flaming eyes which glared out of one of the bushes before shots were fired. Several balls took effect on the animal, who rushed, maddened, upon us. He made such tremendous springs, that I thought every moment he must reach the howdah and select a victim from among us. The sight was terrible to see, and my apprehensions were increased by the appearance of another tiger; however, I kept myself so calm, that none of the gentlemen had any suspicion of what was going on in my mind. Shot followed shot; the elephants defended their trunks with great dexterity by throwing them up or drawing them in. After a sharp contest of half an hour, we were the victors, and the dead animals were triumphantly stripped of their beautiful skins. The gentlemen politely offered me one of them as a present; but I declined accepting it, as I could not postpone my journey sufficiently long for it to be dried. They complimented me on my courage, and added, that such sport would be extremely dangerous if the elephants were not particularly well trained; above all, they must not be afraid of the tigers, nor even stir from the spot; for, if they ran away, the hunters would be upset by the branches of the trees, or be left hanging upon them, when they would certainly become the victims of the bloodthirsty animals. It was too late to visit the temples today, and I therefore waited till the next morning.

The temples of Elora lie on that kind of table-land which is peculiar to India. The principal temple, Kylas, is the most wonderful of all those which are hewn out of the rock. It surpasses, in magnitude and finish, the best specimens of Indian architecture; it is, indeed, affirmed to have claims to precedence over the marvellous buildings of the ancient Egyptians. The Kylas is of conical form, 120 feet in height and 600 in circumference. For the construction of this masterwork, a colossal block was separated from the solid rock by a passage 240 feet long and 100 broad. The interior of the temple consists of a principal hall (66 feet long by 100 broad), and several adjoining halls, which are all furnished with sculptures and gigantic idols; but the real magnificence consists in the rich and beautiful sculptures on the exterior, in the tastefully-executed arabesques, and in the fine pinnacles and niches, which are cut out on the tower. The temple rests on the backs of numerous elephants and tigers, which lie next to each other in peaceful attitudes. Before the principal entrance, to which several flights of steps lead, stand two figures of elephants above life-size. The whole is, as has been said before, hewn from a single mass of rock. The cliff from which this immense block was separated surrounds the temple, on three sides, at a distance of 100 feet, forming colossal perpendicular walls, in which, as at Adjunta, enormous colonnades, larger and smaller temples, from two to three stories high, are excavated. The principal temple is called Rameswur, and somewhat exceeds in size the largest vichara at Adjunta; its breadth is ninety-eight feet, it extends into the rock 102 feet, and the height of the ceiling is twenty-four feet; it is supported by twenty-two pilasters, and covered with the most beautiful sculptures, reliefs, and colossal gods, among which the principal group represents the marriage of the god Ram and the goddess Seeta. A second vichara, nearly as handsome as this last, is called Laoka; the principal figure in this is Shiva.

Not far distant, a number of similar temples are excavated in another rock. They are much more simple, with unattractive portals and plain columns; therefore, not to be compared with those at Adjunta. This task would have been impossible if the rock had been granite or a similar primitive foundation; unfortunately, I could not ascertain what the rock was, I only examined the pieces which were here and there chipped off, and which were very easily broken. It is not with the less astonishment that one contemplates these surprising works, which will always be considered as inimitable monuments of human ingenuity.

The temple of Kylas is, unfortunately, somewhat decayed from age and the destructive action of the weather. It is a sad pity that the only monument of this kind in the world will, by-and-bye, fall into ruins. Towards 11 o'clock in the morning I returned to Roja, and immediately continued my journey to the famous fortress Dowlutabad, having safely received the admission in Roja.

The distance was only eight miles; but the roads were execrably bad, and there was a mountain-pass to cross similar to that near Adjunta. The fortress, one of the oldest and strongest in India, is considered as the most remarkable of its kind, not only in the Deccan but in all India. It presents a most imposing aspect, and is situated upon a peak of rock 600 feet high, which stands isolated in a beautiful plain, and appears to have been separated from the adjoining mountains by some violent natural convulsion. The circumference of this rock amounts to about a mile. It is cut round perpendicularly to a height of 130 feet and thirty feet below the top of the moat by which it is surrounded, which cutting is equally perpendicular, so that the whole height of the escarpment is 160 feet, and the rock, consequently, inaccessible. There is no pathway leading to the fortress, and I was, therefore, extremely curious to know by what means the summit was reached. In the side of the rock itself was a very low iron door, which is only visible in time of peace, as the ditch can be filled a foot above its level when required. Torches were lighted, and I was carefully conducted through narrow low passages, which led with numerous windings upwards through the body of the rock. These passages were closed in many places by massive iron gates. Some considerable distance above the precipitous part of the rock, we again emerged into the open air; narrow paths and steps, protected by strongly-fortified works, led from this place to the highest point. The latter was somewhat flattened, (140 feet in diameter), completely undermined, and so contrived, that it could be heated red-hot. A cannon, twenty-three feet long, was planted here.

At the foot of this fortress are scattered numerous ruins, which, I was told, were the remains of a very important town; nothing is left of it now except the fortified walls, three or four feet deep, which must be passed to reach the peak of rock itself.

In the same plain, but near to the range of mountains, standing on a separate elevation, is a considerably larger fortress than Dowlutabad, but of far inferior strength.

The numerous fortresses, as well as the fortified towns, were, as I here learned, the remnants of past times, when Hindostan was divided into a great number of states, continually at war with each other. The inhabitants of the towns and villages never went out unarmed; they had spies continually on the watch; and to secure themselves from sudden attacks, drove their herds inside the walls every night, and lived in a continual state of siege. In consequence of the unceasing warfare which prevailed, bands of mounted robbers were formed, frequently consisting of as many as ten or twelve thousand men, who too often starved out and overcame the inhabitants of the smaller towns, and completely destroyed their young crops. These people were then compelled to enter into a contract with these wild hordes, and to buy themselves off by a yearly tribute.

Since the English have conquered India, peace and order have been everywhere established; the walls decay and are not repaired; the people indeed frequently wear arms, but more from habit than necessity.

The distance from Dowlutabad to Auranjabad was eight miles. I was already much fatigued, for I had visited the temples, ridden eight miles over the mountain pass, and mounted to the top of the fortress during the greatest heat; but I looked forward to the night, which I preferred passing in a house and a comfortable bed, rather than under an open verandah; and, seating myself in my waggon, desired the driver to quicken the pace of his weary oxen as much as possible.

CHAPTER XVI. CONTINUATION OF JOURNEY AND SOJOURN.

AURANJABAD—PUNA—EAST INDIAN MARRIAGES—THE FOOLISH WAGGONER—BOMBAY—THE PARSEES, OR FIRE-WORSHIPPERS— INDIAN BURIAL CEREMONIES—THE ISLAND OF ELEPHANTA— THE ISLAND OF SALSETTE.

On the 7th of March, late in the evening, I reached Auranjabad. Captain Stewart, who lived outside the town, received me with the same cordiality as the other residents had done.

8th March. Captain Stewart and his wife accompanied me this morning to the town to show me its objects of interest, which consisted of a monument and a sacred pool. Auranjabad is the capital of the Deccan, has 60,000 inhabitants, and is partly in ruins.

The monument, which is immediately outside the town, was built more than two hundred years since by the Sultan Aurung-zeb-Alemgir, in memory of his daughter. It by no means deserves to be compared to the great Tadsch at Agra. It is a mosque, with a lofty arched dome and four minarets. The building is covered all round—the lower part of the outside with a coating of white marble five feet high; the upper portion is cased with fine white cement, which is worked over with ornamental flowers and arabesques. The entrance doors are beautifully inlaid with metal, on which flowers and ornamental designs are engraved in a highly artistic manner. Unfortunately, the monument is already much decayed; one of the minarets is half fallen in ruins. In the mosque stands a plain sarcophagus, surrounded by a marble trellis-work. Both have nothing in common with the great Tadsch beyond the white marble of which they are constructed; in richness and artistic execution, they are so much inferior, that I could not understand how any one could be led to make so incredible a comparison.

Near the mosque lies a pretty marble hall, surrounded by a neglected garden.

The reigning king would have removed the marble from this monument for use in some building in which he was to be interred! He requested permission to do so from the English government. The answer was to the effect, that he could do so if he wished, but he should remember, that if he had so little respect for the monuments of his predecessors, his own might experience a similar fate. This answer induced him to relinquish his intentions.

The pool considered sacred by the Mahomedans is a large basin, constructed of square stones. It is full of large pikes, none of which, however, are allowed to be taken; in fact, there is an attendant appointed to supply them with food. The fish are consequently so tame and familiar, that they will eat turnips, bread, etc., out of the hand. The rainy season causes the death of many of them: were it not for this fortunate circumstance, the pool would before long contain more fish than water. Since the English have come here, the attendants are said not to be so conscientious, and very often smuggle fish out of the pool into the English kitchens, for the sake of a little ready money.

After spending a very agreeable day, I took a hearty farewell of my friendly hostess, and continued my journey in a fresh waggon towards Puna, 136 miles distant.

9th March. Toka. The roads here began to be better, and there were bungalows to be had on payment of the ordinary fees.

10th March. Emanpoor, a small village situated on the summit of a chain of hills. I found here the handsomest bungalow I had seen during the whole journey from Benares to Bombay.

11th March. We passed the whole day in travelling through a barren country, over naked hills and mountains: the majestic solitary trees with the wells had already ceased at Auranjabad.

Towards noon we passed the very flourishing town of Ahmednugger, in the neighbourhood of which a large English military station is established.

12th March. The bungalow at Serur was too near, that at Candapoor too distant. I therefore decided upon taking up my quarters for the night under the eaves of a house.

13th March. In Candapoor there are some handsome Hindoo temples and several small Mahomedan monuments. Near Lony is a large English military station. I also found an obelisk erected there in memory of a battle won by 1,200 English against 20,000 natives.

14th March. Puna. I had endless trouble here to find Mr. Brown, to whom I had an introduction from Mr. Hamilton. The Europeans reside in all parts of the town, for the most part miles apart, and I had the misfortune to meet with some who were not the most polite, and did not consider it worth taking the trouble to give me information. Mr. Brown, on the contrary, received me as kindly as I could desire.

His first inquiry was whether any accident had happened to me on the road. He told me that, only a short time since, an officer was robbed between Suppa and Puna, and as he attempted to defend himself, was murdered; but he added that such instances were extraordinarily rare.

I had arrived about noon. After dinner, Mr. Brown conducted me to the town, which belongs to the East India Company. It contains 15,000 inhabitants, and is situated at the junction of the rivers Mulla and Mutta, over both of which handsome bridges are thrown. The streets are broad and kept clean; the houses, like those in Udjein, are furnished with false wooden walls. Some were painted all over, and belonged mostly, as I was informed, to fakirs, with whom the town swarmed.

It was the month in which the Hindoos prefer to celebrate their marriages, and we met in several streets merry processions of that kind. The bridegroom is enveloped in a purple mantle, his turban dressed out with gold tinsel, tresses, ribbons, and tassels, so that from a distance it appears like a rich crown. The depending ribbons and tassels nearly cover the whole face. He is seated upon a horse; relatives, friends, and guests surround him on foot. When he reaches the house of the bride, the doors and windows of which are securely closed, he seats himself quietly and patiently on the threshold. The female relations and friends also gather together here, without conversing much with the bridegroom and the other men. This scene continues unchanged until nightfall. The bridegroom then departs with his friends; a closely covered waggon, which has been held in readiness, is drawn up to the door; the females slip into the house, bring out the thickly-veiled bride, push her into the waggon, and follow her with the melodious music of the tam-tam. The bride does not start until the bridegroom has been gone a quarter of an hour. The women then accompany her into the bridegroom's house, which, however, they leave soon afterwards. The music is kept up in front of the house until late in the night. It is only the marriages of the lower classes that are celebrated in this manner.

There is a road leading from Puna to Pannwell, a distance of seventy miles, and travellers can post all the way. From Pannwell to Bombay the journey is made by water. I adhered to the cheaper baili, and Mr. Brown was so obliging as to procure one for me, and to lend me a servant.

On the 15th of March I again set out, and on the same day arrived at Woodgown, a village with one of the dirtiest bungalows in which I ever made up my bed.

16th March. Cumpuily. The country between this place and Woodgown is the most beautiful that I saw in India; the view from a mountain some miles on this side of Kundalla, was particularly striking. The spectator stands here in the midst of an extensive mountainous district: peaks of the most diversified forms are piled in numerous rows above and alongside of each other, presenting the most beautiful and variegated outlines.

There are, also, enormous terraces of rock, flattened cones of peaks, with battlements and pinnacles, which at first sight might be taken for ruins and fortresses. In one place the lofty roof of a majestic building presents itself—in another, a gigantic Gothic tower rises aloft. The volcanic form of the Tumel mountain is the most uncommon object which meets the eye. Beyond the

230

mountains extends a wide plain, at the extremity of which lies the polished surface of the long wished-for ocean. The greater part of the mountains is covered with beautiful green woods. I was so much delighted with the extreme beauty of the prospect, that I congratulated myself for the first time on the slow pace of my sleepy oxen.

The village of Karly lies between Woodgown and Kundalla; it is famous on account of its temples, which are about two miles distant. I did not visit them, because I was assured that they were not half so interesting as those at Adjunta and Elora.

Kundalla lies upon a mountain plateau. There are several pretty country-houses here, to which many European families, from the neighbourhood of Bombay, resort during the hot weather.

In the Deccan, and the province of Bombay, I found the natives were less handsome than in Bengal and Hindostan; their features were much coarser, and not so open and amiable.

For several days we have again met very large trains of oxen, some of the drivers of which had their families with them. The females of these people were very ragged and dirty, and at the same time loaded with finery. The whole body was covered with coloured woollen borderings and fringes, the arms with bracelets of metal, bone, and glass beads; even to the ears large woollen tassels were hung, in addition to the usual ornaments, and the feet were loaded with heavy rings and chains. Thus bedecked, the beauties sat on the backs of the oxen, or walked by the side of the animals.

17th March. Since the attack of the negroes in Brazil, I had not been in such a fright as I was today. My driver had appeared to me, during the whole journey, somewhat odd in his manner, or rather foolish: sometimes abusing his oxen, sometimes caressing them, shouting to the passers-by, or turning round and staring at me for some minutes together. However, as I had a servant with me who always walked by the baili, I paid little attention to him. But this morning my servant had gone on, without my consent, to the next station, and I found myself alone with this foolish driver, and on a rather secluded road. After some time he got down from the waggon, and went close behind it. The bailis are only covered over at the sides with straw matting, and are open at the front and back; I could therefore observe what he was doing, but I would not turn round, as I did not wish to make him think that I suspected him. I, however, moved my head gradually on one side to enable me to watch his proceedings. He soon came in front again, and, to my terror, took from the waggon the hatchet which every driver carries with him, and again retired behind. I now thought nothing less than that he had evil intentions, but I could not fly from him, and dare not, of course, evince any fear. I very gently and unobserved drew my mantle towards me, rolled it together, so that I might, at least, protect my head with it, in case he made a blow at me with the hatchet.

He kept me for some time in this painful state of suspense, then seated himself on his place and stared at me, got down again, and repeated the same proceedings several times. It was not until after a long hour that he laid the hatchet on one side, remained sitting on the waggon, and contented himself with gaping vacantly at me every now and then. At the end of a second hour we reached the station where my servant was, and I did not allow him to leave my side again.

The villages through which we passed today were of the most wretched description; the walls of the huts were constructed of rushes, or reeds, covered with palm leaves; some had no front wall.

These villages are chiefly inhabited by Mahrattas, a race which were, at one period, rather powerful in India, and indeed in the whole peninsula. They were, however, expelled from Hindostan by the Mongols, in the eighteenth century, and fled into the mountains which extend from Surata to Goa. During the present century, the majority of these people were compelled to place themselves under the protection of the English. The only Mahratta prince who still maintains, in any degree, his independence, is the Scindiah; the others receive pensions.

The Mahrattas are adherent to the religion of Brahma. They are powerfully built; the colour of their skin varies from dirty black to clear brown; their features are repulsive and ill-formed. They are inured to all manner of hardships, live chiefly upon rice and water, and their disposition is represented as being morose, revengeful, and savage. They excite themselves to fighting by means of opium, or Indian hemp, which they smoke like tobacco.

In the afternoon, I reached the little town of Pannwell. Travellers embark, towards the evening, in boats, and proceed down the river Pannwell to the sea, reaching Bombay about morning.

I had safely completed the long and tedious journey from Delhi to Pannwell in seven weeks. For having accomplished it I was especially indebted to the English officials, who afforded me both advice and assistance; their humanity, their cordial friendliness I shall ever remember. I again offer them my most sincere and warmest thanks; and the greatest compliment which I can pay them is the wish that my own countrymen, the Austrian consuls and ambassadors, resembled them!

At Bombay I stayed at the country-house of the Hamburgh consul, Herr Wattenbach, intending only to draw upon his hospitality for a few days, and to leave as soon as possible, in order to take advantage of the monsoon {225} in my passage through the Arabian and Persian seas. Days, however, grew into weeks, for the favourable time was already past, and the opportunity of meeting with ship conveyance was there very rare.

Herr Wattenbach made my stay in Bombay very agreeable; he showed me everything worth seeing, and accompanied me in excursions to Elephanta and Salsette.

Bombay lies on a small but remarkably pretty island, which is separated from the mainland by a very narrow arm of the sea; its extent is about five square miles, and it is inhabited by 250,000 souls. Bombay is the principal town of Western India, and as its harbour is the best and safest on the whole west coast, it is the chief seat of commerce for the produce and manufactures of India, the Malay country, Persia, Arabia, and Abyssinia. In a commercial respect, it stands only second to Calcutta. In Bombay, every language of the civilized world is to be heard, and the costumes and habits of every nation are to be seen. The finest view of the whole island and town of Bombay, as well as the neighbouring islands of Salsette, Elephanta, Kolabeh, Caranjah, and the mainland, is to be had from the Malabar point. The country, at some distance from the town, consists chiefly of low hills, which are covered with beautiful woods of cocoa-nut and date-trees; in the plain surrounding the town there are also many such groves divided into gardens by walls. The natives are very fond of building their dwellings under the dark shadows of these trees; while, on the contrary, the Europeans seek for as much light and air as possible. The country-houses of the latter are handsome and convenient, but not to be compared with those of Calcutta, either in size or magnificence. The town lies on a level, along the sea-shore.

The active life of the rich inland and European commercial population must be sought for in the fortified parts of the town, which constitute a large quadrangle. Here is to be found merchandise from all parts of the world. The streets are handsome, the large square called The Green especially so. The buildings most remarkable for their architectural beauty are the Town-hall, whose saloon has no equal, the English Church, the Governor's Palace, and the Mint.

The Open Town and the Black Town {226} adjoin the fortified portions, and are considerably larger. In the Open Town, the streets are very regular and broad, more so than any other Indian city that I saw; they are also carefully watered. I observed many houses decorated with artistically-carved wooden pillars, capitals, and galleries. The bazaar is an object of great interest; not, as many travellers affirm, on account of the richness of the merchandise, of which there is not more to be seen than in other bazaars—in fact, there is not even any of the beautiful wood mosaic work of which Bombay produces the finest—but from the diversity of people, which is greater here than anywhere else. Three parts, indeed, are Hindoos, and the fourth Mahomedans, Persians, Fire-worshippers, Mahrattas, Jews, Arabs, Bedouins, Negroes, descendants of Portuguese, several hundred Europeans, and even some Chinese and Hottentots. It requires a long time to be able to distinguish the people of the different nations by their dress and the formation of their faces.

The most wealthy among people owning property here are the Fire-worshippers, called also Gebers, or Parsees. They were expelled from Persia about 1,200 years since, and settled down along the west coast of India. As they are remarkably industrious and hard-working, very well disposed and benevolent, there are no poor, no beggars to be found among them—all appear to be prosperous. The handsome houses in which the Europeans reside mostly belong to them; they are the largest owners of land, ride out in the most beautiful carriages, and are surrounded by innumerable servants. One of the richest of them—Jamsetize-Jeejeebhoy—built, at his own expense, a handsome hospital in the Gothic style, and provides European medical men and receives the sick of every religious denomination. He was knighted by the English government, and is certainly the first Hindoo who could congratulate himself on such a distinction.

While speaking of the Fire-worshippers, I will relate all that I myself saw of them, as well as what I learnt from Manuckjee-Cursetjee, one of the most cultivated and distinguished among them.

The Fire-worshippers believe in one Supreme Being. They pay the greatest reverence to the four elements, and especially to the element of fire, and to the sun, because they look upon them as emblems of the Supreme Being. Every morning they watch for the rising sun, and hasten out of their houses, and even outside of the town, to greet it immediately with prayers. Besides the elements, the cow is considered sacred by them.

Soon after my arrival, I went one morning upon the esplanade of the town for the purpose of seeing the great number of Parsees {227} who, as I had read, assembled themselves there waiting for the first rays of the sun, on the appearance of which, as if at a given signal, they throw themselves on the ground, and raise a loud cry of joy. I, however, merely saw several Parsees, not in groups, but standing separately here and there, reading silently from a book, or murmuring a prayer to themselves. These did not even come at the same time, for many arrived as late as 9 o'clock.

It was precisely the same with the corpses which are stated to be exposed upon the roofs for the birds of prey to feed upon. I saw not a single one. In Calcutta, Mr. V---, who had but recently come from Bombay, assured me that he had himself seen many. I cannot believe that the English government would permit such a barbarous proceeding, and one so prejudicial to health. But I must resume my narrative. My first question, after I had been introduced to Manuckjee, was as to the manner in which the Parsees bury their dead. He conducted me to a hill outside the town, and pointed out a wall, four-and-twenty feet high, enclosing a round space of about sixty feet in diameter. He told me that within this wall there was a bier, with three partitions, built up, and near to it a large pit excavated. The bodies of the deceased are placed upon the bier, the men on the first, the women on the second, and children on the third compartment, and are fastened down with iron bands; and, according to the commands of their religion, are left exposed to the action of the element of air. The birds of prey, which always gather in large swarms round such places, fall upon the bodies ravenously, and in a few minutes devour the flesh and skin; the bones are gathered up and thrown into the cave. When this becomes full, the place is abandoned and another erected.

234

Many wealthy people have private burial-places, over which they have fine wire gauze stretched, so that the deceased members of their family may not be stripped of their flesh by birds of prey.

No one is allowed to enter the burial-ground except the priests, who carry the bodies; even the door is rapidly closed, for only one glance into it would be a sin. The priests, or rather bearers, are considered so impure that they are excluded from all other society, and form a separate caste. Whoever has the misfortune to brush against one of these men, must instantly throw off his clothes and bathe.

The Parsees are not less exclusive with respect to their temples; no one of any other belief is allowed to enter them, or even to look in. The temples which I saw here, of course only from the outside, are very small, extremely plain, and destitute of the slightest peculiarity of architecture; the round entrance-hall surrounds a kind of fore-court, enclosed by a wall. I was only allowed to go as far as the entrance of the wall leading to the fore-court. The handsomest temple in Bombay {228} is a small unimportant building, and I must again contradict those descriptions which make so much of the beautiful temples of the Fire-worshippers.

As I was informed by Manuckjee, the fire burns in a kind of iron vase, in a completely empty, unornamented temple or apartment. The Parsees affirm that the fire which burns in the principal temple, and at which all the others are lighted, originates from the fire which their prophet, Zoroaster, lighted in Persia 4,000 years since. When they were driven out of Persia they took it with them. This fire is not fed with ordinary wood alone; more costly kinds, such as sandal, rose-wood, and such like, are mixed with it.

The priests are called magi, and in each temple there is a considerable number of them. They are distinguished, as regards their dress, from the other Parsees, only by a white turban. They are allowed to marry.

The women visit the temple generally at different hours from the men. They are not forbidden to go there at the same time as the latter; but they never do so, and, indeed, very seldom go at all. A pious Parsee is supposed to pray daily four times, and each time for an hour; for this purpose, however, it is not necessary that he should go to the temple; he fixes his eyes upon fire, earth, or water, or stares into the open air. Whoever finds four hours of prayer daily too much, ingratiates himself with the priests, who are humane and considerate, like the priests of other religions, and willingly release applicants from their cares for the consideration of a moderate gift.

The Parsees prefer offering up their prayers in the morning in the presence of the sun, which they honour the most, as the greatest and most sacred fire. The worship of fire is carried to such an extent by them that they do not pursue any trades which require the use of fire, neither will they fire a gun, or extinguish a light. They let their kitchen-fires burn out. Many travellers even affirm that they will not assist in extinguishing a conflagration; but this is not the case. I was assured that on such an occasion, some years since, many Parsees had been seen giving their help to put the fire out.

Manuckjee was so obliging as to invite me to his house, that I might become acquainted in some degree with the mode of life of Parsee families; he also conducted me to the houses of several of his friends.

I found the rooms furnished in the European manner, with chairs, tables, sofas, ottomans, pictures, mirrors, etc. The dress of the women was little different from that of the more wealthy Hindoos; it was more decorous, as it was not made of transparent muslin, but of silk; and they had, moreover, trousers. The silk was richly embroidered with gold, which luxury is extended to three-year old children. The younger ones, and even the newly-born infants, are wrapped in plain silk stuff. The children wore little caps, worked with gold and silver. The Parsee women consider gold ornaments, pearl and precious stones as necessary a part of their dress as the Hindoos; even in the house they wear a great quantity, but when visiting, or on the occasion of any festival, the jewellery of a wealthy Parsee woman is said to exceed in value 100,000 rupees (£10,000). Children of only seven or eight months old, wear finger-rings and bracelets of precious stones or pearls.

The dress of the men consists of wide trousers and long kaftans. The shirts and trousers are chiefly made of white silk, the jacket of white muslin. The turban differs greatly from that of the Mahomedans; it is a cap of pasteboard, covered with coloured stuff or waxed cloth, ten or twelve inches high.

Both men and women wear round their waists, over the shirt, a girdle passing twice round, which they take off during prayers and hold in their hands; with this exception, they are never seen without it. The law is so strict with regard to the point, that whoever does not wear the girdle is driven out of society. No agreement or contract is valid if the girdle is not worn when it is made. The children begin to wear it when they reach their ninth year. Before this ceremony, they do not belong to the community; they may even eat of food prepared by Christians, and the girls can accompany their fathers in a public place. The girdle changes all; the son eats at his father's table, the girls remain at home, etc.

A second religious ordinance relates to the shirt; this must be cut of a certain length and breadth, and consist of nine seams, which are folded over each other on the breast in a peculiar manner.

A Parsee is allowed to have only one wife. If the wife has no children, or only girls, during a period of nine years, he can, if she consents, be divorced from her, and marry another; he must, however, still provide for her. She can also marry again. According to the religious belief of the Parsee, he is certain to enjoy perfect happiness in a future state of existence if he has a wife and a son in this life.

The Parsees are not divided into castes. In the course of time the Parsees have acquired many of the customs of the Hindoos. For example, the women are not allowed to show themselves in public places; in the house they are separated from the men, take their meals alone, and are, upon the whole, considered more as mere property. The girls are promised when children, and betrothed to the man when in their fourteenth year; if, however, the bridegroom dies, the parents can seek for another. It is considered by the Parsees to be a disgrace if the father does not find a husband for his daughter.

The Parsee women, however, enjoy far more freedom in their houses than the unfortunate Hindoos: they are allowed to sit even at the front windows, and sometimes be present when their husbands receive visits from their male friends, and on both occasions without being veiled.

The Parsees may be easily distinguished from all other Asiatic people by their features, and especially by the lighter colour of their skin. Their features are rather regular, but somewhat sharp, and the cheekbones are broad. I did not think them so handsome as the Mahomedans and Hindoos.

Manuckjee is a great exception to his country people. He is, perhaps, the first who has visited Paris, London, and a considerable part of Italy. He was so well pleased with European manners and customs, that on his return he endeavoured to introduce several reforms among the people of his sect. Unfortunately, he was unsuccessful. He was decried as a man who did not know what he would be doing, and many withdrew from him their friendship and respect in consequence.

He allows his family to go about the house with freedom; but even there he cannot depart much from established custom, as he does not wish to separate entirely from his sect. His daughters are educated in the European method; the eldest plays a little on the piano, embroiders, and sews. She wrote a small paragraph in English in my album very well. Her father did not engage her as a child, but wished that her own inclinations might correspond with his selection of a husband. I was told that she would probably not meet with one, because she is educated too much in the European style; she is already fourteen years of age, and her father has not yet provided her with a bridegroom.

When I first visited this house, the mother and daughters were seated in a drawing-room, engaged with needlework. I remained during their meal-time, a liberty which an orthodox Parsee would not have afforded to me; I was not, however, allowed to join them at table. It was first laid for me, and I ate alone. Several dishes were placed before me, which, with slight deviations, were prepared in the European manner. Everyone, with the exception of the master of the house, watched with surprise the way in which I used a knife and fork; even the servants stared at this, to them, singular spectacle. When I had sufficiently appeased my appetite in this public manner, the table was as carefully brushed as if I had been infected with the plague. Flat cakes of bread were then brought and laid upon the uncovered table, instead of plates, and six or seven of the same dishes which had been served to me. The members of the family each washed their hands and faces, and the father said a short grace. All except the youngest child, who was only six years of age, sat at the table, and reached with their right hands into the different dishes. They tore the flesh from the bones, separated the fish into pieces, and then dipped the pieces into the various soups and sauces, and threw them with such dexterity into the mouth, that they did not touch their lips with their fingers. Whoever accidentally does, must immediately get up and wash his hand again, or else place before him the dish into which he has put his unwashed hand, and not touch any other one. The left hand is not used during the whole meal time.

This mode of eating appears, indeed, very uninviting; but it is, in fact, not at all so; the hand is washed, and does not touch anything but the food. It is the same in drinking; the vessel is not put to the lips, but the liquid is very cleverly poured into the open mouth. Before the children have acquired this dexterity in eating and drinking, they are not permitted, even when they wear the girdle, to come to the table of the adults.

The most common drink in Bombay is called sud or toddy, a kind of light spirituous beverage which is made from the cocoa and date-palm. The taxes upon these trees are very high; the latter are, as in Egypt, numbered and separately assessed. A tree which is only cultivated for fruit, pays from a quarter to half a rupee (6d. to 1s.); those from which toddy is extracted, from three-quarters to one rupee each. The people here do not climb the palm-trees by means of rope-ladders, but they cut notches in the tree, in which they set their feet.

During my stay here, an old Hindoo woman died near to Herr Wattenbach's house, which circumstance gave me an opportunity of witnessing an Indian funeral. As soon as she began to show signs of death, the women about her every now and then set up a horrible howling, which they continued at short intervals after her decease. Presently, small processions of six or eight women approached, who also commenced howling as soon as they discovered the house of the mourners. These women all entered the house. The men, of whom there were a great number present, seated themselves quietly in front of it. At the expiration of some hours, the dead body was enveloped in a white shroud, laid upon an open bier, and carried by the men to the place where it was to be burnt. One of them carried a vessel with charcoal and a piece of lighted wood, for the purpose of igniting the wood with the fire of the house.

The women remained behind, and collected in front of the house in a small circle, in the middle of which was placed a woman who was hired to assist in the lamentations. She commenced a wailing song of several stanzas, at the end of each of which the whole joined in chorus; they kept time also by beating their breasts with the right hand and bowing their heads to the ground. They executed this movement as quickly and regularly as if they had been dolls worked by a wire.

After this had been carried on for a quarter of an hour, there was a short pause,

238

during which the women struck their breasts with both their fists so violently, that the blows could be heard at some considerable distance. After each blow, they stretched their hands up high and bowed their heads very low, all with great regularity and rapidity. This proceeding seemed even more comical than the first. After much exertion, they seated themselves round in a ring, drank toddy, and smoked tobacco.

On the following morning, both men and women repeated their visit. The former, however, did not enter the house; they lit a fire and prepared a plain meal. As often as a party of women came, one of the men went to the house-door and announced them, upon which the principal mourner came out of the house to receive them. She threw herself with such violence on the ground before them, that I thought she would not be able to rise up again; the women struck themselves with their fists once on their breasts, and then drew their hands to their heads. The widow raised herself in the meantime, threw herself impetuously round the necks of each of the women, throwing, at the same time, her head-dress over the head of her consoler, and both endeavoured to out-do each other in howling. All these evolutions were very rapidly performed; a dozen embraces were gone through in a moment. After the reception, they went into the house and continued howling at intervals. It was not until sun-set that all was still, and a supper concluded the whole affair. The women ate in the house—the men in the open air.

Funerals and marriages always cost the Hindoos a great deal. The one here described was that of a woman of the poorer class. Nevertheless, it is considered essential that there should be no want of toddy during two days, or of provisions for meals, at which there are an abundance of guests. In addition to this, there is the wood, which also costs a considerable sum, even when it is only common wood. The rich, who use on such occasions the most costly wood, frequently pay more than a thousand rupees (£100).

I once met the funeral procession of a Hindoo child. It lay upon a cushion, covered with a white sheet, and was strewed with fresh and beautiful flowers. A man carried it on both his arms as gently and carefully as if it was sleeping. In this instance, also, there were only men present.

The Hindoos have no particular festival-day in the week, but festivals at certain times, which last for some days. I was present at one of these during my stay, Warusche-Parupu, the New-Year's festival, which took place on the 11th of April. It was a kind of fast-night celebration. The principal amusement consisted in throwing yellow, brown, and red colours over each other, and painting themselves with the same on their cheeks and foreheads. The noisy tam-tam, or a couple of violins, headed the procession, and greater or less followed, who, laughing and singing, danced from house to house, or from one place to another. Several, indeed, on this occasion, found the toddy rather too exciting, but not so much as to lose their consciousness or to exceed the bounds of decorum. The women do

239

not take part in these public processions; but, in the evening, both sexes assemble in the houses, where the festivities are said not to be carried on in the most decorous manner.

Martyrs' festivals are no longer celebrated with full splendour. I did not see any; their time is past. I was, however, so fortunate as to see a martyr, to whom great numbers of people flocked. This holy man had, for three-and-twenty years, held one of his arms raised up with the hand turned back so far that a flower-pot could stand upon it. The three-and-twenty years were passed, and the flower-pot was removed; but neither hand nor arm were to be brought into any other position, for the muscles had contracted, the arm was quite withered, and presented a most repulsive appearance.

The Island of Elephanta is about six or eight miles distant from Bombay. Herr Wattenbach was so kind as to take me there one day. I saw some rather high mountains, which, however, we did not ascend; we visited only the temples, which are very near to the landing-place.

The principal temple resembles the larger viharas at Adjunta, with the single exception, that it is separated on both sides from the solid rock, and is connected with it only above, below, and at the back. In the sanctuary stands a gigantic three-headed bust. Some believe that it represents the Hindoo Trinity; one of the heads is full-faced, the two others in profile, one right, the other left. The bust, including the head-dress, measures certainly as much as eight feet. On the walls and in the niches, there are a number of giant statues and figures; in fact, whole scenes of the Hindoo mythology. The female figures are remarkable; they all have the left hip turned out, the right turned inwards. The temple appears to be devoted to the god Shiva.

In the neighbourhood of the large temple stands a smaller one, whose walls are also covered with deities. Both temples were much injured by the Portuguese, who, when they conquered the island, in their noble religious zeal planted cannon before them, in order to destroy the shocking Pagan temples; in which attempt they succeeded much better than in the conversion of the Pagans. Several columns are quite in ruins; nearly all are more or less damaged, and the ground is covered with fragments. None of either the gods or their attendants escaped uninjured.

There is a most enchanting view across the sea of the extensive town, and the delightful hills surrounding it, from the façade of the large temple. We passed a whole day here very agreeably. During the hot hours of noon, we amused ourselves by reading in the cool shadows of the temple. Herr Wattenbach had sent on several servants previously; among others, the cook, together with tables, chairs, provisions, books, and newspapers. In my opinion, this was rather superfluous; but what would my countrywomen have said could they have seen the English family which we accidentally met with here; they carried several couches, easy chairs, enormous foot-stools, a tent, etc., with them. That is what I call a simple country party!

Salsetta (also called Tiger Island) is united to Bombay by means of a short artificial dam. The distance from the fort to the village, behind which the temples are situated, is eighteen miles, which we travelled, with relays of horses, in three hours. The roads were excellent, the carriage rolled along as if on a floor.

The natural beauty of this island far exceeds that of Bombay. Not mere rows of hills, but magnificent mountain chains here raise their heads, covered even to their summits with thick woods, from which bare cliffs here and there project; the valleys are planted with rich fields of corn, and slender green palms.

The island does not appear to be densely populated. I saw only a few villages and a single small town inhabited by Mahrattas, whose appearance is as needy and dirty as those near Kundalla.

From the village where we left the carriage we had still three miles to go to the temples.

The principal temple alone is in the style of a chaitza; but it is surrounded by an uncommonly high porch, at both extremities of which idols one-and-twenty feet high stand in niches. Adjoining to the right is a second temple, which contains several priests' cells, allegorical figures of deities, and reliefs. Besides these two, there are innumerable other smaller ones in the rocks, which extend on both sides from the principal temple; I was told there were more than a hundred. They are all viharas with the exception of the principal temple; the greater number, however, are scarcely larger than ordinary small chambers, and are destitute of any peculiarity.

The rock temples of Elephanta and Salsetta rank, in respect to magnitude, grandeur, and art, far below those of Adjunta and Elora, and are of interest only to those who have not seen the latter.

It is said that the temples at Salsetta are not much visited, because there is considerable danger attending it; the country is represented to be full of tigers, and so many wild bees are said to swarm round the temples that it is impossible to enter them; and moreover the robbers, which are known by the name of bheels, live all round here. We fortunately met with none of these misfortunes. Later, indeed, I wandered about here alone. I was not satisfied with a single sight, and left my friends privately while they were taking their noon rest, and clambered from rock to rock as far as the most remote temple. In one I found the skin and horns of a goat that had been devoured, which sight somewhat frightened me; but trusting to the unsociability of the tiger, who will rather fly from a man in broad day than seek him out, I continued my ramble. We had, as I have said, no danger to resist; it was different with two gentlemen who, some days later, nearly fell victims, not indeed to wild beasts, but to wild bees. One of them knocked upon an opening in the side of the rock, when an immense swarm of bees rushed out upon them, and it was only by the greatest exertion that they escaped,

241

miserably stung on the head, face, and hands. This occurrence was published in the newspapers as a warning for others.

The climate of Bombay is healthier than that of Calcutta; even the heat is more tolerable on account of the continual sea-breezes, although Bombay lies five degrees further south. The mosquitoes here, as in all hot countries, are very tormenting. A centipede slipped into my bed one evening, but I fortunately discovered it in time.

I had already decided upon taking my passage in an Arabian boat, which was to leave for Bassora on the 2nd of April, when Herr Wattenbach brought the news that on the 10th a small steamer would make its first voyage to Bassora. This afforded me great pleasure—I did not suspect that it would happen with a steamer as with a sailing vessel, whose departure is postponed from day to day; nevertheless, we did not leave the harbour of Bombay until the 23rd of April.

CHAPTER XVII. FROM BOMBAY TO BAGHDAD.

DEPARTURE FROM BOMBAY—SMALL-POX—MUSCAT—BANDR-ABAS —THE PERSIANS—THE KISHMA STRAITS—BUSCHIR—ENTRANCE INTO THE SCHATEL-ARAB—BASSORA—ENTRANCE INTO THE TIGRIS—BEDOUIN TRIBES—CTESIPHON AND SELEUCIA—ARRIVAL AT BAGHDAD.

The steamer "Sir Charles Forbes" (forty horse-power, Captain Lichfield) had only two cabins, a small and a large one. The former had already been engaged for some time by an Englishman, Mr. Ross; the latter was bespoken by some rich Persians for their wives and children. I was, therefore, obliged to content myself with a place upon deck; however, I took my meals at the captain's table, who showed me the most extreme attention and kindness during the whole voyage.

The little vessel was, in the fullest sense of the word, overloaded with people; the crew alone numbered forty-five; in addition to that there were 124 passengers, chiefly Persians, Mahomedans, and Arabs. Mr. Ross and myself were the only Europeans. When this crowd of persons were collected, there was not the smallest clear space on the deck; to get from one place to another it was necessary to climb over innumerable chests and boxes, and at the same time to use great caution not to tread upon the heads or feet of the people.

In such critical circumstances I looked about immediately to see where I could possibly secure a good place. I found what I sought, and was the most fortunate of all the passengers, more so than even Mr. Ross, who could not sleep any night in his cabin on account of the heat and insects. My eye fell upon the under part of the captain's dinner-table, which was fixed upon the stern deck; I took possession of this place, threw my mantle round me, so that I had a pretty secure position, and no cause to fear that I should have my hands, feet, or indeed my head trodden upon.

I was somewhat unwell when I left Bombay, and on the second day of the voyage a slight attack of bilious fever came on. I had to contend with this for five days. I crept painfully from my asylum at meal times to make way for the feet of the people at table. I did not take any medicine (I carried none with me), but trusted to Providence and my good constitution.

A much more dangerous malady than mine was discovered on board on the third day of the voyage. The small-pox was in the large cabin. Eighteen women and seven children were crammed in there. They had much less room than the negroes in a slave-ship; the air was in the highest degree infected, and they were not allowed to go on the deck, filled as it was with men; even we deck passengers were in great anxiety lest the bad air might spread itself over the whole ship through the opened windows. The disease had already broken out on the children before they were brought on board; but no one could suspect it, as the women came late at night, thickly veiled, and enveloped in large mantles, under which they carried the children. It was only on the third day, when one of the children died, that we discovered our danger.

The child was wrapped in a white cloth, fastened upon a plank, which was weighted by some pieces of coal or stone, and lowered into the sea. At the moment that it touched the water, the waves closed over it, and it was lost to our sight.

I do not know whether a relation was present at this sad event; I saw no tears flow. The poor mother might, indeed, have sorrowed, but she dare not accompany her child; custom forbade it.

Two more deaths occurred, the other invalids recovered, and the contagion happily did not spread any further.

30th April. Today we approached very near to the Arabian coast, where we saw a chain of mountains which were barren and by no means attractive. On the following morning (1st of May) small forts and watch-towers made their appearance, here and there, upon the peaks of beautiful groups of rock, and presently, also, a large one was perceptible upon an extensive mountain at the entrance of a creek.

We came to anchor off the town of Muscat, which lies at the extremity of the creek. This town, which is subject to an Arabian prince, is very strongly fortified, and surrounded by several ranges of extraordinarily formed rocks, all of which are also occupied by forts and towers. The largest of these excites a sad reminiscence: it was formerly a cloister of Portuguese monks, and was attacked by the Arabs one night, who murdered the whole of its inmates. This occurrence took place about two centuries since.

243

The houses of the town are built of stone, with small windows and terraced roofs. Two houses, distinguished from the others only by their larger dimensions, are the palaces of the mother of the reigning prince, and of the sheikh (governor). Some of the streets are so narrow that two persons can scarcely walk together. The bazaar, according to the Turkish custom, consists of covered passages, under which the merchants sit cross-legged before their miserable stalls.

In the rocky valley in which Muscat lies the heat is very oppressive (124° Fah. in the sun), and the sunlight is very injurious to the eyes, as it is not in the slightest degree softened by any vegetation. Far and wide there are no trees, no shrubs or grass to be seen. Every one who is in any way engaged here, go as soon as their business is finished to their country-houses situated by the open sea. There are no Europeans here; the climate is considered fatal to them.

At the back of the town lies a long rocky valley, in which is a village containing several burial-places, and, wonderful to say, a little garden with six palms, a fig, and a pomegranate-tree. The village is larger and more populous than the town; containing 6,000 inhabitants, while the latter has only 4,000. It is impossible to form any conception of the poverty, filth, and stench in this village; the huts stand nearly one over the other, are very small, and built only of reeds and palm-leaves; every kind of refuse was thrown before the doors. It requires considerable self-denial to pass through such a place, and I wonder that plague, or some other contagion, does not continually rage there. Diseases of the eyes and blindness are, however, very frequent.

From this valley I passed into a second, which contains the greatest curiosity of Muscat, a rather extensive garden, which, with its date-palms, flowers, vegetables, and plantations, constitutes a true picture of an oasis in the desert. The vegetation is only kept up, for the most part, by continual watering. The garden belongs to the Arabian prince. My guide seemed to be very proud of this wonderful garden, and asked me whether there were such beautiful gardens in my country!

The women in Muscat wear a kind of mask of blue stuff over the face, fastened upon springs or wires, which project some distance beyond the face; a hole is cut in the mask between the forehead and nose, which allows something more than the eyes to be seen. These masks are worn by the women only when they are at some distance from home; in and near their houses they are not used. All the women that I saw were very ugly; the men, also, had not the fine, proud features which are so frequently met with among the Arabians. Great numbers of negroes are employed here as slaves.

I made this excursion at the time of the greatest heat (124° Fah. in the sun), and rather weakened by my illness, but did not experience the slightest ill consequences. I had been repeatedly warned that in warm countries the heat of the sun was very injurious to Europeans who were not accustomed to it, and frequently caused fever and sometimes even sun-stroke. If I had attended to every advice, I should not have seen much. I did not allow myself to be led astray—

244

went out in all weathers, and always saw more than my companions in travel.

On the 2nd of May we again set sail, and on the 3rd of May entered the Persian Sea, and passed very near to the island of Ormus. The mountains there are remarkable for a variegated play of colours; many spots shine as if they were covered with snow. They contain large quantities of salt, and numbers of caravans come annually from Persia and Arabia to procure it. In the evening we reached the small Persian town of Bandr-Abas, off which we anchored.

May 4th. The town is situated on low hills of sand and rocks, which are separated from higher mountains by a small plain. Here also the whole country is barren and wild; solitary groups of palms are found only in the plains.

I looked wistfully towards the land,—I would gladly have visited Persia. The captain, however, advised me not to do so in the dress I wore; because, as he informed me, the Persians were not so good-natured as the Hindoos, and the appearance of a European woman in this remote district was too uncommon an event; I might probably be greeted with a shower of stones.

Fortunately there was a young man on board who was half English and half Persian (his father, an Englishman, had married an Armenian from Teheran), and spoke both languages equally well. I asked him to take me on shore, which he very readily did. He conducted me to the bazaar, and through several streets. The people indeed flocked from all sides and gazed at me, but did not offer me the slightest annoyance.

The houses here are small, and built in the Oriental style, with few windows, and terraced roofs. The streets are narrow, dirty, and seemingly uninhabited; the bazaar only appeared busy. The bakers here prepare their bread in the most simple manner, and, indeed, immediately in the presence of their customers: they knead some meal with water into a dough, in a wooden dish, separate this into small pieces, which they squeeze and draw out with their hands, until they are formed into large thin flakes, which are smeared over with salt water, and stuck into the inner side of a round tube. These tubes are made of clay, are about eighteen inches in diameter, and twenty-two in length; they are sunk one half in the ground, and furnished with an air-draft below. Wood-charcoal is burnt inside the tube at the bottom. The cakes are baked on both sides at once; at the back by the red-hot tube, and in front by the charcoal fire. I had half-a-dozen of such cakes baked—when eaten warm, they are very good.

It is easy to distinguish the Persians from the Arabs, of whom there are many here. The former are larger, and more strongly built; their skin is whiter, their features coarse and powerful, and their general appearance rude and wild. Their dress resembles that of the Mahomedans. Many wear turbans, others a conical cap of black Astrachan, from a foot to one and a half high.

I was told of so great an act of gratitude of the young man, Mr. William Hebworth, who accompanied me to Bandr-Abas, that I cannot omit to mention it.

245

At the age of sixteen he went from Persia to Bombay, where he met with the kindest reception in the house of a friend of his father's, by whom he was assisted in every way, and even obtained an appointment through his interest. One day his patron, who was married, and the father of four children, had the misfortune to be thrown from his horse, and died from the effects of the fall. Mr. Hebworth made the truly noble resolve of marrying the widow, who was much older than himself, and, instead of property, possessed only her four children, that he might in this way pay the debt of gratitude which he owed to his deceased benefactor.

In Bandr-Abas we hired a pilot to take us through the Straits of Kishma. About noon we sailed.

The passage through these straits is without danger for steamers, but is avoided by sailing vessels, as the space between the island Kishma and the mainland is in parts very narrow, and the ships might be driven on to the shore by contrary winds.

The inland forms an extended plain, and is partially covered with thin underwood. Great numbers of people come from the neighbouring mainland to fetch wood from here.

The captain had spoken very highly of the remarkable beauty of this voyage, the luxuriance of the island, the spots where the sea was so narrow that the tops of the palms growing on the island and mainland touched each other, etc. Since the last voyage of the good captain, a very unfrequent phenomenon would seem to have taken place—the lofty slender palms were transformed into miserable underwood, and, at the narrowest point, the mainland was at least half a mile from the island. Strange to say, Mr. Ross afterwards gave the same description of the place; he believed the captain in preference to his own eyes.

At one of the most considerable contractions stands the handsome fort Luft. Fifteen years since the principal stronghold of the Persian pirates was in this neighbourhood. A severe battle was fought between them and the English, near Luft, in which upwards of 800 were killed, many taken prisoners, and the whole gang broken up. Since that event, perfect security has been restored.

5th May. We left the straits, and three days later came to anchor off Buschir.

There are considerable quantities of sea-weeds and molluscæ in the Persian Gulf; the latter had many fibres, were of a milk-white colour, and resembled a forest agaric in form; others had a glistening rose colour with small yellow spots. Conger eels of two or three feet in length were not uncommon.

8th May. The town of Buschir is situated on a plain six miles from the mountains, whose highest peak, called by the Persians Hormutsch, by the English Halala, is 5,000 feet high.

The town contains 15,000 inhabitants, and has the best harbour in Persia; but its appearance is very dirty and ugly.

The houses stand quite close together, so that it is easy to pass from one to the other over the terraces, and it requires no great exertion to run over the roofs, as the terraces are enclosed only by walls one or two feet high. Upon some houses, square chambers (called wind-catchers), fifteen or twenty feet high, are erected, which can be opened above and at the sides, and serve to intercept the wind and lead it into the apartments.

The women here cover up their faces to such a degree that I cannot imagine how they find their way about. Even the smallest girls imitate this foolish custom. There is also no lack of nose-rings, bracelets, sandals, etc.; but they do not wear nearly so many as the Hindoos. The men are all armed; even in the house they carry daggers or knives, and besides these, pistols in the streets.

We remained two days in Buschir, where I was very well received by Lieutenant Hennelt, the resident.

I would gladly have left the ship here to visit the ruins of Persepolis, and travel by land from thence to Shiraz, Ispahan, Teheran, and so onwards; but serious disturbances had broken out in these districts, and numerous hordes of robbers carried on their depredations. I was in consequence compelled to alter my plan, and to go straight on to Baghdad.

10th May. In the afternoon we left Buschir.

11th May. Today I had the gratification of seeing and sailing on one of the most celebrated rivers in the world, the Schatel-Arab (river of the Arabs), which is formed by the junction of the Euphrates, Tigris, and Kaurun, and whose mouth resembles an arm of the sea. The Schatel-Arab retains its name as far as the delta of the Tigris and Euphrates.

12th May. We left the sea and the mountains behind at the same time, and on both shores immense plains opened before us whose boundaries were lost in the distance.

Twenty miles below Bassora we turned off into the Kaurun to set down some passengers at the little town of Mahambrah, which lies near the entrance of that river. We immediately turned back again, and the captain brought the vessel round in the narrow space in an exceedingly clever way. This proceeding caused the uninitiated some anxiety; we expected every moment to see either the head or stern run a-ground, but it succeeded well beyond all measure. The whole population of the town was assembled on the shore; they had never before seen a steamer, and took the most lively interest in the bold and hazardous enterprise.

About six years ago, the town Mahambrah experienced a terrible catastrophe; it was at that time under Turkish rule, and was surprised and plundered by the Persians; nearly all the inhabitants, amounting to 5,000, were put to death. Since that period it has been retained by the Persians.

Towards noon we arrived at Bassora. Nothing is visible from the river but some fortified works and large forests of date-trees, behind which the town is situated far inland.

The journey from Bombay to this place had occupied eighteen days, in consequence of the unfavourable monsoon, and was one of the most unpleasant voyages which I ever made. Always upon deck in the midst of a dense crowd of people, with a heat which at noon time rose to 99° 5' Fah., even under the shade of a tent. I was only once able to change my linen and dress at Buschir, which was the more annoying as one could not prevent the accumulation of vermin. I longed for a refreshing and purifying bath.

Bassora, one of the largest towns of Mesopotamia, has among its inhabitants only a single European. I had a letter to the English agent, an Armenian named Barseige, whose hospitality I was compelled to claim, as there was no hotel. Captain Lichfield presented my letter to him and made known my request, but the polite man refused to grant it. The good captain offered me accommodation on board his ship, so that I was provided for for the present.

The landing of the Persian women presented a most laughable spectacle: if they had been beauties of the highest order, or princesses from the sultan's harem, there could not have been more care taken to conceal them from the possibility of being seen by men.

I was indebted to my sex for the few glimpses which I caught of them in the cabin; but among the whole eighteen women I did not see a single good-looking one. Their husbands placed themselves in two rows from the cabin to the ship's ladder, holding large cloths stretched before them, and forming in this way a kind of opaque moveable wall on both sides. Presently the women came out of the cabin; they were so covered with large wrappers that they had to be led as if they were blind. They stood close together between the walls, and waited until the whole were assembled, when the entire party, namely, the moveable wall and the beauties concealed behind it, proceeded step by step. The scrambling over the narrow ship's ladders was truly pitiable; first one stumbled, and then another. The landing occupied more than an hour.

13th May. The captain brought me word that a German missionary was accidentally at Bassora, who had a dwelling with several rooms, and could probably give me shelter. I went to him immediately, and he was so obliging as to provide me with a room in which, at the same time, I found a fireplace. I took leave of the good captain with sincere regret. I shall never forget his friendliness and attentions. He was a truly good-hearted man, and yet the unfortunate crew, mostly Hindoos and negroes, were treated worse on board his ship than I had observed elsewhere. This was the fault of the two mates, who accompanied nearly every word with pushes and blows of the fist. In Muscat three of the poor fellows ran away.

The Christian Europeans excel the pagan Hindoos and Musselmen in learning and science; might they not also at least equal the latter in kindness and humanity?

A small English war-steamer was expected at Bassora in the course of a few days, which carried letters and dispatches between this place and Baghdad, and whose captain was so good as to take European travellers (of whom there are not many that lose themselves here) with him.

I availed myself of the few days of my stay to look about the town, and see what still remains of its ancient celebrity.

Bassora, or Bassra, was founded in the reign of the Caliph Omar, in the year 656. Sometimes under Turkish, sometimes under Persian dominion, it was at last permanently placed under the latter power. There are no vestiges of antiquity remaining; neither ruins of handsome mosques nor caravansaries. The fortified walls are much dilapidated, the houses of the town small and unattractive, the streets crooked, narrow, and dirty. The bazaar, which consists of covered galleries with wretched stalls, cannot show a single good stock of goods, although Bassora is the principal emporium and trading port for the Indian wares imported into Turkey. There are several coffee-stalls and a second-rate caravansary in the bazaar. A large open space, not very remarkable for cleanliness, serves in the day as a corn-market; and in the evening several hundred guests are to be seen seated before a large coffee-stall, drinking coffee and smoking nargillies.

Modern ruins are abundant in Bassora, the result of the plague which in the year 1832 carried off nearly one half of the inhabitants. Numbers of streets and squares consist only of forsaken and decaying houses. Where, a few years back, men were busily engaged in trade, there is now nothing left but ruins and rubbish and weeds, and palms grow between crumbling walls.

The position of Bassora is said to be particularly unhealthy: the plain surrounding it is intersected at one extremity with numerous ditches filled with mud and filth, which give off noxious exhalations, at the other it is covered with forests of date trees, which hinders the current of air. The heat is so great here, that nearly every house is furnished with an apartment, which lies several feet below the level of the street, and has windows only in the high arches. People live in these rooms during the day.

The inhabitants consist for the most part of Arabs; the rest are Persians, Turks, and Armenians. There are no Europeans. I was advised to wrap myself in a large cloth and wear a veil when I went out; the former I did, but I could not endure the veil in the excessive heat, and went with my face uncovered. The cloth (isar) I carried so clumsily that my European clothes were always visible; nevertheless I was not annoyed by any one.

On the 16th of May, the steamer Nitocris arrived. It was small (forty horse power), but very handsome and clean; the captain, Mr. Johns, declared himself ready to take me, and the first officer, Mr. Holland, gave up his cabin to me. They would not take any compensation either for passage or board.

249

The journey from Bassora to Baghdad would have been very fatiguing and inconvenient if I had not met with this opportunity. With a boat it would have required forty or fifty days, as the distance is 500 English miles, and the boat must have been for greater part of the distance drawn by men. The distance by land amounts to 390 miles; but the road is through deserts, which are inhabited by nomadic tribes of Bedouins, and over-run with hordes of robbers, whose protection must be purchased at a high price.

17th May. We weighed anchor in the morning at 11 o'clock, and availed ourselves of the current which extends 120 miles up the stream.

In the afternoon we reached the point Korne, also called the Delta (fifty miles from Bassora). The Tigris and Euphrates join here. Both rivers are equally large, and as it could not, probably, be decided which name should be retained, both were given up, and that of Schatel-Arab adopted.

Many learned writers attempt to give increased importance to this place, by endeavouring to prove by indubitable evidence that the garden of Eden was situated here. If this was the case, our worthy progenitor made a long journey after he was driven out of Paradise, to reach Adam's Peak in Ceylon.

We now entered the Tigris. For a distance of three miles further, we were gratified by the sight of beautiful forests of date-trees, which we had already enjoyed, almost without intermission, from the mouth of the Schatel-Arab; they now suddenly terminated. Both sides of the river were still covered with a rich vegetation, and beautiful orchards, alternated with extended plots of grass, which were partially covered with bushes or shrub-like trees. This fruitfulness, however, is said to extend only a few miles inland: more distant from the river the country is a barren wilderness.

We saw in several places large tribes of Bedouins, who had pitched their tents in long rows, for the most part close to the banks. Some of these hordes had large closely-covered tents; others again had merely a straw mat, a cloth, or some skins stretched on a pair of poles, scarcely protecting the heads of those lying under them from the burning rays of the sun. In winter, when the temperature frequently falls to freezing point, they have the same dwellings and clothing as in summer: the mortality among them is then very great. These people have a wild appearance, and their clothing consists of only a dark-brown mantle. The men have a part of this drawn between the legs, and another part hung round them; the women completely envelop themselves in it; the children very commonly go quite naked until the twelfth year. The colour of their skin is a dark brown, the face slightly tattooed: both the men and women braid their hair into four plaits, which hang down upon the back of the head and temples. The weapons of the men are stout knotted sticks; the women are fond of adorning themselves with glass beads, mussel-shells, and coloured rags; they also wear large nose-rings.

They are all divided into tribes, and are under the dominion of the Porte, to whom they pay tribute; but they acknowledge allegiance only to the sheikh elected by themselves, many of whom have forty or fifty thousand tents under their control. Those tribes who cultivate land have fixed dwellings; the pastoral tribes are nomadic.

Half-way between Bassora and Baghdad, the lofty mountain chain of Luristan becomes visible. When the atmosphere is clear, the summits, 10,000 feet high, and covered with perpetual snow, may be seen.

Every step in advance leads to the scene of the great deeds of Cambyses, Cyrus, Alexander, etc.: every spot of ground has historical associations. The country is the same; but what has become of its towns and its powerful empires? Ruined walls and heaps of earth and rubbish are the only remains of the most beautiful cities; and where firmly established empires formerly existed, are barren steppes overrun by robber hordes.

The Arabs engaged in agriculture are themselves exposed to the depredations of their nomadic countrymen, especially in harvest time. In order to avoid this evil as much as possible, they bring their crops into small fortified places, of which I observed many between Bassora and Baghdad.

We took in wood several times during the passage, and on these occasions I could approach the inhabitants without fear, as they were inspired with respect for the well-manned and armed vessel. In one instance, I was led far into the underwood in pursuit of some beautiful insects, when I found myself on a sudden surrounded by a swarm of women and children, so that I thought it advisable to hasten back again to the ship's people—not that any one offered me any violence; but they crowded round me, handled my dress, wanted to put on my straw bonnet; and this familiarity was far from pleasant on account of their extreme dirtiness. The children seemed shockingly neglected; many were covered with pimples and small sores; and both great and small had their hands constantly in their hair.

At the places where we stopped they generally brought sheep and butter, both of which were singularly cheap. A sheep cost at the utmost five krans (4s. 6d.). They were very large and fat, with long thick wool, and fat tails of about fifteen inches long and eight inches broad. Our crew had a better diet than I had ever noticed on board any ship. What pleased me even more was the equal good treatment of the natives, who were not in any particular less thought of than the English. I never met with greater order and cleanliness than here—a proof that blows and thumps are not indispensably necessary, as I had so often been assured.

In the districts where the ground was covered with underwood and grass, I saw several herds of wild swine; and there were said to be lions here, who come from the mountains, especially during the winter time, when they carried off cows and sheep: they very seldom attacked men. I was so fortunate as to see a pair of lions, but at such a distance, that I cannot say whether they exceeded in beauty and size those in European menageries. Among the birds, the pelicans were so polite as to make their respects to us by scraping.

21st May. Today we saw the ruins of the palace of Khuszew Anushirwan at Ctesiphon. Ctesiphon was formerly the capital of the Parthian, and afterwards of the new Persian empire: it was destroyed by the Arabs in the seventeenth century. Nearly opposite, on the right bank of the Tigris, lay Seleucia, one of the most celebrated towns of Babylon, and which, at the time of its prosperity, had a free independent government and a population of 600,000 souls. The chief portion were Greeks.

One obtained two views of Ctesiphon in passing, in consequence of the river winding considerably—almost running back again several miles. I made a trip there from Baghdad, and therefore reserve my account of it.

The old caliphate appears in marvellous magnificence and extent from a distance, but unfortunately loses this on nearer approach. The minarets and cupolas, inlaid with variegated earthenware tiles, glitter in the clear sunlight; palaces, gateways, and fortified works, in endless succession, bound the yellow, muddy Tigris; and gardens, with date and other fruit trees, cover the flat country for miles round.

We had scarcely anchored, when a number of natives surrounded the ship. They made use of very singular vehicles, which resemble round baskets: these are formed of thick palm leaves, and covered with asphalt. They are called "guffer;" are six feet in diameter and three feet in height; are very safe, for they never upset, and may be travelled in over the worst roads. Their invention is very ancient.

I had a letter to the English resident, Major Rawlinson; but as Mr. Holland, the first officer of the ship, offered me the use of his house, I took advantage of this, on account of his being a married man, which Mr. Rawlinson was not. I found Mrs. Holland a very pretty, amiable woman (a native of Baghdad), who, though only three-and-twenty, had already four children, the eldest of whom was eight years old.

CHAPTER XVIII. MESOPOTAMIA, BAGHDAD, AND BABYLON.

Baghdad, the capital of Assyria, was founded during the reign of the Caliph Abu-Jasar-Almansor. A century later, in the reign of Haroun-al-Raschid, the best and most enlightened of all the caliphs, the town was at its highest pitch of prosperity; but at the end of another century, it was destroyed by the Turks. In the sixteenth century it was conquered by the Persians, and continued to be a perpetual source of discord between them and the Turks, although it at length became annexed to the Ottoman Empire. Nadir Schah again endeavoured to wrest it from the Turks in the eighteenth century.

The present population, of about 60,000 souls, consists of about three-fourths Turks, and the remainder of Jews, Persians, Armenians, and Arabs. There are only fifty or sixty Europeans living there.

The town is partly situated on both sides of the Tigris, but chiefly on the east. It is surrounded by fortified walls of brick, with numerous towers at regular intervals; both walls and towers, however, are weak, and even somewhat dangerous, and the cannons upon them are not in good condition.

The first thing that it was necessary for me to provide myself with here, was a large linen wrapper, called *isar*, a small fez, and a kerchief, which, wound round the fez, forms a little turban; but I did not make use of the thick, stiff mask, made of horse-hair, which covers the face, and under which the wearer is nearly suffocated. It is impossible to imagine a more inconvenient out-door dress for our sex than the one worn here. The isar gathers the dust from the ground, and it requires some dexterity to hold it together in such a way as to envelop the whole body. I pitied the poor women greatly, who were often obliged to carry a child, or some other load, or perhaps even to wash linen in the river. They never came from this work, except dripping with water. Even the smallest girls here are clothed in this way whenever they go out.

In my Oriental dress I could walk about without any covering on my face, perfectly uninterrupted. I first examined the town, but there was not much to see, as there are no remains of the old Caliphate buildings. The houses are of burnt bricks, and are only one story high; the backs are all turned towards the streets, and it is but rarely that a projecting part of the house is seen with narrow latticed windows. Those houses only whose façades are towards the Tigris make an exception to this rule; they have ordinary windows, and are sometimes very handsome. I found the streets rather narrow, and full of dirt and dust. The bridge of boats over the Tigris, which is here 690 feet broad, is the most wretched that I ever saw. The bazaars are very extensive. The old bazaar, a relic of the former town, still shows traces of handsome columns and arabesques, and Chan Osman is distinguished by its beautiful portal and lofty arches. The principal passages are so broad, that there is room for a horseman and two foot passengers, to go through side by side. The merchants and artisans here, as in all eastern countries, live in separate streets and passages. The better shops are to be found in private houses, or in the chans at the bazaars. Miserable coffee-stalls are everywhere numerous.

The palace of the pascha is an extensive building, but neither tasteful nor costly; it is imposing only from a distance. There are but few mosques, and those present nothing costly or artistic, except the inlaid tiles.

To be able to overlook the whole of Baghdad, I mounted, with great difficulty, the exterior of the dome of the Osman Chan, and was truly astounded at the extent and beautiful position of the town. It is impossible to form any idea of an Oriental town by passing through the narrow and uniform streets, no matter how often, as these are all alike, and, one with the other, resemble the passages of a jail. But, from above, I looked down over the whole town, with its innumerable houses, many of which are situated in pretty gardens. I saw thousands and thousands of terraces spread at my feet, and before all, the beautiful river, rolling on through dark orchards and palm groves, to the town, which extends along its banks for five miles.

All the buildings are, as already remarked, constructed of unburnt bricks, of which the greater part are stated to have been brought down the Euphrates, from the ruins of the neighbouring city of Babylon. By a close examination, traces of the old architecture are to be found on the fortifications; the bricks of which they are built are about two feet in diameter, and resemble fine slabs of stone.

The houses are prettier inside than out; they have clean plastered courts, numerous windows, etc. The rooms are large and lofty, but not nearly so magnificently furnished as those in Damascus. The summer is so hot here, that people find it necessary to change their rooms three times a-day. The early part of the morning is passed in the ordinary rooms; towards 9 o'clock they retire, during the remainder of the day, into the underground rooms, called sardab, which, like cellars, are frequently situated fifteen or twenty feet below the surface; at sunset they go up on to the terraces, where they receive visits, gossip, drink tea, and remain until night. This is the most pleasant time, as the evenings are cool and enlivening. Many affirm the moonlight is clearer here than with us, but I did not find this to be the case. People sleep on the terraces under mosquito nets, which surround the whole bed. The heat rises in the rooms, during the day, as high as 99°; in the sun, to 122° or 131° Fah.; it seldom exceeds 88° 25' in the sardabs. In winter, the evenings, nights, and mornings are so cold, that fires are necessary in the rooms.

The climate of this place is considered very healthy, even by Europeans. Nevertheless, there is a disease here of which the young females are terribly afraid, and which not only attacks the natives, but strangers, when they remain several months here. This is a disgusting eruption, which is called the Aleppo Boil, or Date-mark.

This ulcer, which is at first no larger than a pin's head, gradually increases to the size of a halfcrown piece, and leaves deep scars. It generally breaks out on the face; there is scarcely one face among a hundred, to be seen without these disfiguring marks. Those who have only one have reason to consider themselves fortunate; I saw many with two or three of them. Other parts of the body are also not exempt. The ulcers generally appear with the ripening of the dates, and do not go away until the next year, when the same season returns again. This disease does not occur more than once in a lifetime; it attacks children for the most part during their infancy. No remedy is ever applied, as experience has shown that it cannot be prevented; the Europeans have tried inoculation, but without success.

This disease is met with in several districts on the Tigris; there are no traces of it to be found at a distance from the river. It would appear, therefore, to be, in some way, connected with the evaporation from the stream, or the mud deposited on its banks; the former seems less probable, as the crews of the English steamers, which are always on the river, escape, while all the Europeans who live on land fall victims to it. One of the latter had forty such boils, and I was told that he suffered horribly. The French consul, who expected to remain here for several years, would not bring his wife with him, to expose her face to the danger of these ineradicable marks. I had only been here some weeks, when I discovered slight indications of a boil on my hand, which became large, but did not penetrate very deep, and left no permanent scar. I exulted greatly at escaping so easily, but my exultation did not continue long; only six months afterwards, when I had returned to Europe, this disease broke out with such violence that I was covered with thirteen of those boils, and had to contend with them more than eight months.

On the 24th of May I received an invitation from the English resident, Major Rawlinson, to an entertainment in honour of the queen's birthday. There were only Europeans present at dinner, but in the evening, all denominations of the Christian world were admitted—Armenians, Greeks, etc. This entertainment was given upon the handsome terraces of the house. The floor was covered with soft carpets; cushioned divans invited the fatigued to rest, and the brilliant illumination of the terraces, courts, and gardens diffused a light almost equal to that of day. Refreshments of the most delicate kind made it difficult for Europeans to remember that they were so far from their native country. Less deceptive were two bands of music, one of which played European, the other native pieces, for the amusement of the guests. Fire-works, with balloons and Bengal lights, were followed by a sumptuous supper, which closed the evening's entertainments. Among the women and girls present, there were some remarkably beautiful, but all had most bewitching eyes, which no young man could glance at with impunity. The art of dyeing the eyelids and eyebrows principally contributes to this. Every hair on the eyebrows which makes its appearance in an improper place, is carefully

255

plucked out, and those which are deficient have their place most artistically supplied by the pencil. The most beautiful arched form is thus obtained, and this, together with the dyeing of the eyelids, increases uncommonly the brightness of the eye. The desire for such artificial beauty extends itself even to the commonest servant girls.

The fair sex were dressed in Turkish-Greek costume; they wore silk trousers, gathered together round the ankles, and over these, long upper garments, embroidered with gold, the arms of which were tight as far as the elbow, and were then slit open, and hung down. The bare part of the arm was covered by silk sleeves. Round their waists were fastened stiff girdles of the breadth of the hand, ornamented in front with large buttons, and at the sides with smaller ones. The buttons were of gold, and worked in enamel. Mounted pearls, precious stones, and gold coins, decorated the arms, neck, and breast. The head was covered with a small, pretty turban, wound round with gold chains, or gold lace; numerous thin tresses of hair stole from underneath, falling down to the hips. Unfortunately, many of them had the bad taste to dye their hair, by which its brilliant black was changed into an ugly brown-red.

Beautiful as this group of women were in appearance, their society was very uninteresting, for an unbroken silence was maintained by these members of our garrulous sex, and not one of their pretty faces expressed an emotion or sentiment. Mind and education, the zests of life, were wanting. The native girls are taught nothing; their education is completed when they are able to read in their mother tongue (Armenian or Arabian), and then, with the exception of some religious books, they have no other reading.

It was more lively at a visit which I made, some days later, to the harem of the pasha; there was then so much chatting, laughing, and joking, that it was almost too much for me. My visit had been expected, and the women, fifteen in number, were sumptuously dressed in the same way that I have already described; with the single exception, that the upper garment (kaftan) was shorter, and made of a more transparent material, and the turbans ornamented with ostrich feathers.

I did not see any very handsome women here; they had only good eyes, but neither noble nor expressive features.

The summer harem, in which I was received, was a pretty building, in the most modern style of European architecture, with lofty, regular windows. It stood in the middle of a small flower-garden, which was surrounded by a large fruit-garden.

After I had been here rather more than an hour, a table was laid, and chairs placed round it. The principal woman invited me to join them, and leading the way, seated herself at the table, when, without waiting till we were seated, she hastily picked out her favourite morsels from the various dishes with her hands. I was also compelled to help myself with my hands, as there was no knife and fork in the whole house, and it was only towards the end of the meal that a large gold teaspoon was brought for me.

The table was profusely covered with excellent meat-dishes, with different pilaus, and a quantity of sweet-meats and fruits. I found them all delicious, and one dish so much resembled our fritters, that I almost thought it was meant for them.

After we had finished, those who had not room to sit down with us took their seats together with some of the principal attendants: after them came, in succession, the inferior slaves, among whom were some very ugly negresses; these also seated themselves at the table, and ate what remained.

After the conclusion of the meal, strong coffee was handed round in small cups, and nargillies brought. The cups stood in little golden bowls, ornamented with pearls and turquoises.

The pasha's women are distinguished from their attendants and slaves only by their dress and jewellery; in demeanour I found no difference. The attendants seated themselves without hesitation upon the divans, joined, uninvited, in the conversation, smoked, and drank coffee as we did. Servants and slaves are far better and more considerately treated by the natives than by the Europeans. Only the Turks hold slaves here.

Although such strict decorum is observed in all public places, there is an utter disregard of it in the harems and baths. While a part of the women were engaged in smoking and drinking coffee, I slipped away, and went into some of the adjoining apartments, where I saw enough, in a few minutes, to fill me with disgust and commiseration for these poor creatures; from slothfulness and the want of education, morality appeared to be so degraded as to profane the very name of humanity.

I was not less grieved by a visit to a public female bath. There were young children, girls, women, and mothers; some having their hands, feet, nails, eyebrows, hair, etc., washed and coloured: others were being bathed with water, or rubbed with fragrant oils and pomades, while the children played about among them. While all this was going on, the conversation that prevailed was far from being remarkable for its decency. Poor children! how are they to acquire a respect for modesty, when they are so early exposed to the influence of such pernicious examples.

Among the other curiosities of Baghdad, I saw the funeral monument of Queen Zobiedé, the favourite wife of Haroun-al-Raschid. It is interesting, because it differs very much from the ordinary monuments of the Mahomedans. Instead of handsome cupolas and minarets, it consists of a moderate sized tower, rising from an octagon building; the tower has a considerable resemblance to those of the Hindoo temples. In the interior stand three plainly built tombs, in one of which the queen is buried; in the other two, relations of the royal family. The whole is constructed of bricks, and was formerly covered with handsome cement, coloured tiles, and arabesques, of which traces still remain.

Mahomedans consider all such monuments sacred; they frequently come from great distances to offer up their devotions before them. They think it equally desirable to erect a burial-place near such a monument, which they show with pride to their friends and relations. Round this monument there were large spaces covered with tombs.

On the return from this monument, I went a little out of my way to see that part of the town which had fallen into ruins, and been desolated by the last plague. Herr Swoboda, an Hungarian, gave me a dreadful picture of the state of the town at that time. He had shut himself closely up with his family and a maid servant, and being well furnished with provisions, received nothing from outside but fresh water. He carefully plastered up the doors and windows, and no one was allowed to go out upon the terraces, or, indeed, into the air at all.

These precautions were the means of preserving his whole family in health, while many died in the neighbouring houses. It was impossible to bury all the dead, and the bodies were left to decompose where they died. After the plague had ceased, the Arabs of the desert made their appearance for the purpose of robbing and plundering. They found an easy spoil, for they penetrated without resistance into the empty houses, or without difficulty overpowered the few enfeebled people who remained. Herr Swoboda, among the rest, was obliged to make an agreement with the Arabs, and pay tribute.

I was glad to leave this melancholy place, and directed my steps towards some of the pleasant gardens, of which there are great numbers in and round Baghdad. None of these gardens, however, are artificial; they consist simply of a thick wood of fruit-trees, of all species (dates, apple, apricot, peach, fig, mulberry, and other trees), surrounded by a brick wall. There is, unfortunately, neither order nor cleanliness observed, and there are neither grass plots nor beds of flowers, and not a single good path; but there is a considerable number of canals, as it is necessary to substitute artificial watering for rain and dew.

I made two long excursions from Baghdad; one to the ruins of Ctesiphon, the other to those of Babylon. The former are eighteen, the latter sixty miles distant from Baghdad. On both occasions, Major Rawlinson provided me with good Arabian horses, and a trusty servant.

I was obliged to make the journey to Ctesiphon and back again in one day, to avoid passing the night in the desert; and, indeed, had to accomplish it between sunrise and sunset, as it is the custom in Baghdad, as in all Turkish towns, to close the gates towards sunset, and to give up the keys to the governor. The gates are again opened at sunrise.

My considerate hostess would have persuaded me to take a quantity of provisions with me; but my rule in travelling is to exclude every kind of superfluity. Wherever I am certain to find people living, I take no eatables with me, for I can content myself with whatever they live upon; if I do not relish their food, it is a sign that I have not any real hunger, and I then fast until it becomes so great that any kind of dish is acceptable. I took nothing with me but my leathern water flask, and even this was unnecessary, as we frequently passed creeks of the Tigris, and sometimes the river itself, although the greater part of the road lay through the desert.

About half-way, we crossed the river Dhyalah in a large boat. On the other side of the stream, several families, who live in huts on the bank, subsist by renting the ferry. I was so fortunate as to obtain here some bread and buttermilk, with which I refreshed myself. The ruins of Ctesiphon may already be seen from this place, although they are still nine miles distant. We reached them in three hours and a half.

Ctesiphon formerly rose to be a very powerful city on the Tigris; it succeeded Babylon and Seleucia; the Persian viceroys resided in the summer at Ecbatania, in the winter at Ctesiphon. The present remains consist only of detached fragments of the palace of the Schah Chosroes. These are the colossal arched gate-porch, together with the gate, a part of the principal front, and some side walls, all of which are so strong that it is probable that travellers may still continue to be gratified with a sight of them for centuries. The arches of the Tauk-kosra gate is the highest of the kind that is known; it measures ninety feet, and is therefore about fifteen feet higher than the principal gate at Fattipore-Sikri, near Agra, which is erroneously represented by many as being the highest. The wall rises sixteen feet above the arch.

On the façade of the palace, small niches, arches, pillars, etc., are hewn out from the top to bottom; the whole appears to be covered with fine cement, in which the most beautiful arabesques are still to be seen. Opposite these ruins on the western shore of the Tigris, lie a few remains of the walls of Seleucia, the capital of Macedonia.

On both banks, extensive circles of low mounds are visible in every direction; these all contain, at a slight depth, bricks and rubbish.

Not far from the ruins stands a plain mosque, which holds the tomb of Selamam Pak. This man was a friend of Mahomet's, and is on that account honoured as a saint. I was not allowed to enter the mosque, and was obliged to content myself with looking in through the open door. I saw only a tomb built of bricks, surrounded by a wooden lattice, painted green.

I had already observed a number of tents along the banks of the Tigris on first reaching the ruins; my curiosity induced me to visit them, where I found everything the same as among the desert Arabs, except that the people were not so savage and rough; I could have passed both day and night among them without apprehension. This might be from my having been accustomed to such scenes.

A much more agreeable visit was before me. While I was amusing myself among the dirty Arabs, a Persian approached, who pointed to a pretty tent which was pitched at a short distance from us, and said a few words to me. My guide explained to me that a Persian prince lived in this tent, and that he had politely invited me by this messenger. I accepted the invitation with great pleasure, and was received in a very friendly manner by the prince, who was named Il-Hany-Ala-Culy-Mirza.

The prince was a handsome young man, and said that he understood French; but we soon came to a stop with that, as his knowledge of it did not extend beyond "*Vous parlez Français!*" Luckily, one of his people had a better acquaintance with English, and so we were able to carry on some conversation.

The interpreter explained to me that the prince resided in Baghdad, but on account of the oppressive heat, he had taken up his residence here for some time. He was seated upon a low divan under an open tent, and his companions reclined upon carpets. To my surprise, he had sufficient politeness to offer me a seat by his side upon the divan. Our conversation soon became very animated, and his astonishment when I related to him my travels increased with every word. While we were talking, a nargilly of most singular beauty was placed before me; it was made of light-blue enamel on gold, ornamented with pearls, turquoises, and precious stones. For politeness' sake, I took a few puffs from it. Tea and coffee were also served, and afterwards the prince invited me to dinner. A white cloth was spread upon the ground, and flat cakes of bread, instead of plates, laid upon it: an exception was made for me, as I had a plate and knife and fork. The dinner consisted of a number of dishes of meat, among which was a whole lamb with the head, which did appear very inviting; besides these, several pilaus, and a large roast fish. Between the eatables stood bowls of curds and whey, and sherbet: in each bowl was a large spoon. The lamb was carved by a servant with a knife and the hand; he distributed the parts among the guests, placing a piece upon the cake of bread before each one. They ate with their right hand. Most of them tore off small morsels of meat or fish, dipped them in one of the pilaus, kneaded them into a ball, and put them into their mouths. Some, however, ate the fat dishes without pilau; after each mouthful they wiped off the fat, which ran over their fingers, on the bread. They drank a great deal while eating, all using the same spoons. At the conclusion of the meal, the prince, in spite of the strict prohibition of wine, ordered some to be brought (my presence serving as an excuse). He then poured out a glass for me, and drank a couple himself—one to my health and one to his own.

When I told him that I intended to go to Persia, and in particular to Teheran, he offered to give me a letter to his mother, who was at court, and under whose protection I could be introduced there. He wrote immediately, using his knee for want of a table, pressed his signet ring upon the letter, and gave it to me; but told me laughingly not to say anything to his mother about his having drank wine.

After meal time, I asked the prince whether he would allow me to pay a visit to his wife,—I had already learned that one of his wives was with him. My request was granted, and I was led immediately into a building, near which had formerly been a small mosque.

I was here received in a cool arched apartment by a remarkably handsome young creature. She was the most beautiful of all the women I had ever yet seen in harems. Her figure, of middling proportions, was most exquisitely symmetrical; her features were noble and truly classical; and her large eyes had a melancholy expression: the poor thing was alone here, and had no society but an old female servant and a young gazelle. Her complexion, probably not quite natural, was of dazzling whiteness, and a delicate red tinted her cheeks. The eyebrows only, in my opinion, were very much deformed by art. They were in the form of a dark-blue streak, an inch wide, which extended in two connected curves from one temple to the other, and gave the face a somewhat dark and very uncommon appearance. The principal hairs were not dyed; her hands and arms, however, were slightly tattooed. She explained to me that this shocking operation was performed upon her when she was only a child, a custom which is also practised by the Mahomedan women in Baghdad.

The dress of this beauty was like that of the women in the pasha's harem, but instead of the small turban, she wore a white muslin cloth lightly twisted round the head, which she could also draw over her face as a veil.

Our conversation was not very lively, as the interpreter was not allowed to follow me into this sanctum. We were therefore obliged to content ourselves with making signs and looking at one another.

When I returned to the prince, I expressed to him my wonder at the rare beauty of his young wife, and asked him what country was the cradle of this true angel. He told me the north of Persia, and assured me, at the same time, that his other wives, of whom he had four in Baghdad and four in Teheran with his mother, very much excelled this one in beauty.

When I would have taken my leave of the prince to return home, he proposed to me that I should remain a little while longer and hear some Persian music. Two minstrels presently appeared, one of whom had a kind of mandolin with five strings; the other was a singer. The musician preluded very well, played European as well as Persian melodies, and handled his instrument with great facility; the singer executed roulades, and, unfortunately, his voice was neither cultivated nor pure; but he seldom gave false notes, and they both kept good time. The Persian music and songs had considerable range of notes and variations in the melody; I had not heard anything like them for a long time.

I reached home safely before sunset, and did not feel very much fatigued, either by the ride of thirty-six miles, the terrible heat, or the wandering about on foot. Only two days afterwards, I set out on my road to the ruins of the city of Babylon. The district in which these ruins lie is called Isak-Arabia, and is the seat of the ancient Babylonia and Chaldea.

I rode, the same evening, twenty miles, as far as the Chan Assad. The palms and fruit-trees gradually decreased in number, the cultivated ground grew less and less, and the desert spread itself before me, deadening all pleasure and animation. Here and there grew some low herbage scarcely sufficient for the frugal camel; even this ceases a few miles before coming to Assad, and from thence to Hilla the desert appeared uninterruptedly in its sad and uniform nakedness.

We passed the place where the town of Borossippa formerly stood, and where it is said that a pillar of Nourhwan's palace is yet to be seen; but I could not discover it anywhere, although the whole desert lay open before me and a bright sunset afforded abundance of light. I therefore contented myself with the place, and did not, on that account, remember with less enthusiasm the great Alexander, here at the last scene of his actions, when he was warned not to enter Babylon again. Instead of the pillar, I saw the ruins of one large and several smaller canals. The large one formerly united the Euphrates with the Tigris, and the whole served for irrigating the land.

31st May. I had never seen such numerous herds of camels as I did today; there might possibly have been more than 7,000 or 8,000. As most of them were unloaded and carried only a few tents, or women and children, it was probably the wandering of a tribe in search of a more fruitful dwelling-place. Among this enormous number, I saw only a few camels that were completely white. These are very highly prized by the Arabians; indeed, almost honoured as superior beings. When I first saw the immense herd of these long-legged animals appearing in the distant horizon, they looked like groups of small trees; and I felt agreeably surprised to meet with vegetation in this endless wilderness. But the wood, like that in Shakspere's Macbeth, shortly advanced towards us, and the stems changed into legs and the crowns into bodies.

I also observed a species of bird today to which I was a complete stranger. It resembled, in colour and size, the small green papagien, called paroquets, except that its beak was rather less crooked and thick. It lives, like the earth-mouse, in small holes in the ground. I saw flocks of them at two of the most barren places in the desert, where there was no trace of a blade of grass to be discovered, far and wide.

Towards 10 o'clock in the morning, we halted for two hours only at Chan Nasri, as I was resolved to reach Hilla today. The heat rose above 134° Fah.; but a hot wind, that continually accompanied us, was still more unbearable, and drove whole clouds of hot sand into the face. We frequently passed half-ruined canals during the day.

The chans upon this road are among the best and the most secure that I have ever met with. From the exterior, they resemble small fortresses; a high gateway leads into a large court-yard, which is surrounded on all sides by broad, handsome halls built with thick brick walls. In the halls, there are niches arranged in rows; each one being large enough to serve three or four persons as a resting-place. Before the niches, but also under the halls, are the places for the cattle. In the court-yard, a terrace is also built five feet high for sleeping in the hot summer nights. There are likewise a number of rings and posts for the cattle in the court, where they can be in the open air during the night.

These chans are adapted for whole caravans, and will contain as many as 500 travellers, together with animals and baggage; they are erected by the government, but more frequently by wealthy people, who hope by such means to procure a place in heaven. Ten or twelve soldiers are appointed to each chan as a guard. The gates are closed in the evening. Travellers do not pay anything for staying at these places.

Some Arabian families generally live outside the chans, or even in them, and they supply the place of host, and furnish travellers with camel's milk, bread, coffee, and sometimes, also, with camel's or goat's flesh. I found the camel's milk rather disagreeable, but the flesh is so good that I thought it had been cow-beef, and was greatly surprised when my guide told me that it was not.

When travellers are furnished with a pasha's firman (letter of recommendation), they can procure one or more mounted soldiers (all the soldiers at the chans have horses) to accompany them through dangerous places, and at times of disturbances. I had such a firman, and made use of it at night.

In the afternoon we approached the town of Hilla, which now occupies a part of the space where Babylon formerly stood. Beautiful woods of date-trees indicated from afar the inhabited country, but intercepted our view of the town.

Four miles from Hilla we turned off the road to the right, and shortly found ourselves between enormous mounds of fallen walls and heaps of bricks. The Arabs call these ruins Mujellibe. The largest of these mounds of bricks and rubbish is 2,110 feet in circumference, and 141 feet in height.

Babylon, as is known, was one of the greatest cities of the world. With respect to its founder there are various opinions. Some say Ninus, others Belus, others Semiramis, etc. It is said that, at the building of the city (about 2,000 years before the birth of Christ), two million of workmen, and all the architects and artificers of the then enormous Syrian empire, were employed. The city walls are described as having been 150 feet high, and twenty feet thick. The city was defended by 250 towers; it was closed by a hundred brazen gates, and its circumference was sixty miles. It was separated into two parts by the Euphrates. On each bank stood a beautiful palace, and the two were united by an artistic bridge, and even a tunnel was constructed by the Queen Semiramis. But the greatest curiosities were the temples of Belus and the hanging gardens. The tower of the temple was ornamented with three colossal figures, made of pure gold, and representing gods. The hanging gardens (one of the seven wonders of the world) are ascribed

263

to Nebuchadnezar, who is said to have built them at the wish of his wife Amytis.

Six hundred and thirty years before Christ, the Babylonian empire was at the highest point of its magnificence. At this time it was conquered by the Chaldeans. It was afterwards subject in succession to the Persians, Osmans, Tartars, and others, until the year A.D. 1637, since which time it has remained under the Osman government.

The temple of Belus or Baal was destroyed by Xerxes, and Alexander the Great would have restored it; but as it would have required 10,000 men for two months (others say two years) merely to remove the rubbish, he did not attempt it.

One of the palaces is described as having been the residence of the king, the other a castle. Unfortunately they are so fallen to decay, that they afford no means of forming a satisfactory opinion even to antiquarians. It is supposed, however, that the ruins called Mujellibe are the remains of the castle. Another large heap of ruins is situated about a mile distant, called El Kasir. According to some, the temple of Baal stood here, according to others the royal palace. Massive fragments of walls and columns are still to be seen, and in a hollow a lion in dark grey granite, of such a size that at some distance I took it for an elephant. It is very much damaged, and, to judge from what remains, does not appear to have been the work of a great artist.

The mortar is of extraordinary hardness; it is easier to break the bricks themselves, than to separate them from it. The bricks of all the ruins are partly yellow and partly red, a foot long, nearly as broad, and half an inch thick.

In the ruins El Kasir stands a solitary tree, which belongs to a species of firs which is quite unknown in this district. The Arabs call it Athalé, and consider it sacred. There are said to be several of the same kind near Buschir—they are there called Goz or Guz.

Many writers see something very extraordinary in this tree; indeed they go so far as to consider it as a relic of the hanging gardens, and affirm that it gives out sad melancholy tones when the wind plays through its branches, etc. Everything, indeed, is possible with God; but that this half-stunted tree which is scarcely eighteen feet high, and whose wretched stem is at most only nine inches in diameter, is full 3,000 years old, appears to me rather too improbable!

The country round Babylon is said to have been formerly so flourishing and fruitful, that it was called the Paradise of Chaldea. This productiveness ceased with the existence of the buildings.

As I had seen everything completely, I rode on as far as Hilla, on the other side of the Euphrates. A most miserable bridge of forty-six boats is here thrown across the river, which is four hundred and thirty feet broad. Planks and trunks of trees are laid from one boat to the other, which move up and down at every step; there is no railing at the side, and the space is so narrow that two riders can scarcely pass. The views along the river are very charming; I found the vegetation here still rich, and several mosques and handsome buildings give life to the blooming landscape.

In Hilla I was received by a rich Arab. As the sun was already very near setting, I was shown to a beautiful terrace instead of a room. A delicious pilau, roast lamb, and steamed vegetables were sent to me for supper, with water and sour milk.

The terraces here were not surrounded by any walls, a circumstance which was very agreeable to me, as it gave me an opportunity of observing the mode of life and customs of my neighbours.

In the court-yards I saw the women engaged in making bread, and in the same way as at Bandr-Abas. The men and children meanwhile spread straw mats upon the terraces, and brought dishes with pilaus, vegetables, or some other eatables. As soon as the bread was ready, they began their meal. The women also seated themselves, and I thought that the modern Arabs were sufficiently advanced in civilization to give my sex their place at table. But to my regret I saw the poor women, instead of helping themselves from the dishes, take straw fans to keep off the flies from the heads of their husbands. They may have had their meal afterwards in the house, for I did not see them eat anything, either upon the terraces or in the courts. They all slept upon the terraces. Both men and women wrapped themselves in rugs, and neither the one nor the other took off any of their clothing.

1st June. I had ordered for this morning two fresh horses and Arabs as a guard, that I might proceed with some safety to the ruins of Birs Nimroud. These ruins are situated six miles distant from Hilla, in the desert or plain of Shinar, near the Euphrates, upon a hill 265 feet high, built of bricks, and consist of the fragments of a wall twenty-eight feet long, on one side thirty feet high, and on the other thirty-five. The greater part of the bricks are covered with inscriptions. Near this wall lie several large blackish blocks which might be taken for lava, and it is only on closer examination that they are found to be remains of walls. It is supposed that such a change could only have been brought about by lightning.

People are not quite unanimous in their opinions with respect to these ruins. Some affirm that they are the remains of the Tower of Babel, others that they are those of the Temple of Baal.

There is an extensive view from the top of the hill over the desert, the town of Hilla with its charming palm-gardens, and over innumerable mounds of rubbish and brick-work. Near these ruins stands an unimportant Mahomedan chapel, which is said to be on the same spot where, according to the Old Testament, the three youths were cast into the furnace for refusing to worship idols.

In the afternoon I was again in Hilla. I looked over the town, which is said to contain 26,000 inhabitants, and found it built like all Oriental towns. Before the Kerbela gates is to be seen the little mosque Esshems, which contains the remains

265

of the prophet Joshua. It completely resembles the sepulchre of the Queen Zobiedé near Baghdad.

Towards evening the family of my obliging host, together with some other women and children, paid me a visit. Their natural good sense had deterred them from visiting me on the day of my arrival, when they knew I was fatigued by the long ride. I would willingly have excused their visit today also, for neither the rich nor poor Arabs have much idea of cleanliness. They, moreover, would put the little dirty children into my arms or on my lap, and I did not know how to relieve myself of this pleasure. Many of them had Aleppo boils, and others sore eyes and skin diseases. After the women and children had left, my host came. He was, at least, clean in his dress, and conducted himself with more politeness.

On the 2nd of July I left Hilla at sunrise, and went on, without stopping, to the Khan Scandaria (sixteen miles), where I remained some hours; and then went the same day as far as Bir-Zanus, sixteen miles further. About an hour after midnight I again halted, and took a soldier to accompany me. We had scarcely proceeded four or five miles from the khan when we perceived a very suspicious noise. We stopped, and the servant told me to be very quiet, so that our presence might not be detected. The soldier dismounted, and crept rather than walked in the sand to reconnoitre the dangerous spot. My exhaustion was so great that, although alone in this dark night on the terrible desert, I began to doze upon the horse, and did not wake up till the soldier returned with a cry of joy, and told us that we had not fallen in with a horde of robbers, but with a sheikh, who, in company with his followers, were going to Baghdad. We set spurs to our horses, hastened after the troop, and joined them. The chief greeted me by passing his hand over his forehead towards his breast; and, as a sign of his good will, offered me his arms, a club with an iron head, covered with a number of spikes. Only a sheikh is allowed to carry such a weapon.

I remained in the sheikh's company until sunrise, and then quickened my horse's pace, and at about 8 o'clock was again seated in my chamber at Baghdad, after having, in the short space of three days and a half, ridden 132 miles and walked about a great deal. The distance from Baghdad to Hilla is considered to be sixty miles, and from Hilla to Birs Nimroud six.

I had now seen everything in and around Baghdad, and was desirous of starting on my journey towards Ispahan. Just at this time the Persian prince, Il-Hany-Ala-Culy-Mirza, sent me a letter, informing me that he had received very bad news from his native country; the governor of Ispahan had been murdered, and the whole province was in a state of revolt. It was therefore impossible to enter Persia by this route. I decided in this case to go as far as Mósul, and there determine my further course according to circumstances.

Before concluding my account of Baghdad, I must state that at first I was greatly afraid of scorpions, as I had heard that there were great numbers there; but I never saw one, either in the sardabs or on the terraces, and during my stay of four weeks only found one in the court.

CHAPTER XIX. MÓSUL AND NINEVEH.

JOURNEY OF THE CARAVAN THROUGH THE DESERT—ARRIVAL AT MÓSUL—CURIOSITIES—EXCURSION TO THE RUINS OF NINEVEH AND THE VILLAGE OF NEBBI YUNUS—SECOND EXCURSION TO THE RUINS OF NINEVEH—TEL-NIMROUD— ARABIAN HORSES—DEPARTURE FROM MÓSUL.

In order to travel from Baghdad to Mósul safely, and without great expense, it is necessary to join a caravan. I requested Herr Swoboda to direct me to a trustworthy caravan guide. I was indeed advised not to trust myself alone among the Arabs, at least to take a servant with me; but with my limited resources this would have been too expensive. Moreover, I was already pretty well acquainted with the people, and knew from experience that they might be trusted.

A caravan was to have left on the 14th of June, but the caravan guides, like the ship captains, always delay some days, and so we did not start until the 17th instead of the 14th.

The distance from Baghdad to Mósul is 300 miles, which occupy in travelling from twelve to fourteen days. Travellers ride either horses or mules, and in the hot months travel during the night.

I had hired a mule for myself and my little baggage, for which I paid the low price of fifteen krans (12s. 6d.), and had neither fodder nor anything else to provide.

Every one who intends proceeding with the caravan is obliged to assemble before the city gate about 5 o'clock in the evening. Herr Swoboda accompanied me there, and particularly recommended me to the care of the caravan guide, and promised him in my name a good bachshish if he saved me all the trouble he could during the journey.

In this way I entered upon a fourteen days' journey through deserts and steppes, a journey full of difficulties and dangers, without any convenience, shelter, or protection. I travelled like the poorest Arab, and was obliged, like him, to be content to bear the most burning sun, with no food but bread and water, or, at the most, a handful of dates, or some cucumbers, and with the hot ground for a bed.

I had, while in Baghdad, written out a small list of Arabian words, so that I might procure what was most necessary. Signs were easier to me than words, and by the aid of both, I managed to get on very well. I became in time so used to the signs that, in places where I could make use of the language, I was obliged to take some

267

pains to prevent myself from using my hands at the same time.

While I was taking leave of Herr Swoboda, my little portmanteau, and a basket with bread and other trifles, had already been put into two sacks, which were hung over the back of the mule. My mantle and cushion formed a comfortable soft seat, and everything was in readiness—only the mounting was rather difficult, as there was no stirrup.

Our caravan was small. It counted only twenty-six animals, most of which carried merchandise, and twelve Arabs, of whom five went on foot. A horse or mule carries from two to three and a half hundredweight, according to the state of the road.

About 6 we started. Some miles outside the town several other travellers joined us, chiefly pedlars with loaded animals, so that presently our party increased in numbers to sixty. But our numbers changed every evening, as some always remained behind, or others joined us. We often had with us some shocking vagabonds, of whom I was more afraid than robbers. It is, moreover, said not to be uncommon for thieves to join the caravan, for the purpose of carrying on their depredations, if there should be an opportunity of doing so.

I should, on the whole, have no great faith in the protection which such a caravan is capable of affording, as the people who travel in this way are principally pedlars, pilgrims, and such like, who probably have never in their lives used a sword or fired a gun. A few dozen well-armed robbers would certainly get the better of a caravan of even a hundred persons.

On the first night we rode ten hours, until we reached Jengitsché. The country around was flat and barren, uncultivated and uninhabited. Some few miles outside Baghdad cultivation appeared to be suddenly cut off, and it was not until we came to Jengitsché that we saw again palms and stubble fields, showing that human industry is capable of producing something everywhere.

Travelling with caravans is very fatiguing: although a walking pace is never exceeded, they are on the road from nine to twelve hours without halting. When travelling at night the proper rest is lost, and in the day it is scarcely possible to get any sleep, exposed in the open air to the excessive heat, and the annoyances of flies and mosquitoes.

18th June. In Jengitsché we met with a chan, but it was by no means equal in appearance and cleanliness to that on the road to Babylon; its chief advantage was being situated near the Tigris.

The chan was surrounded by a small village, to which I proceeded for the purpose of satisfying my hunger. I went from hut to hut, and at last fortunately succeeded in obtaining some milk and three eggs. I laid the eggs in the hot ashes and covered them over, filled my leathern flask from the Tigris, and thus loaded returned proudly to the chan. The eggs I ate directly, but saved the milk for the evening.

After this meal, procured with such difficulty, I certainly felt happier, and more contented than many who had dined in the most sumptuous manner.

During my search through the village, I noticed, from the number of ruined houses and huts, that it seemed to have been of some extent formerly. Here, also, the last plague had carried off the greater part of the inhabitants; for, at the present time, there were only a few very poor families.

I here saw a very peculiar mode of making butter. The cream was put into a leathern bottle, and shaken about on the ground until the butter had formed. When made, it was put into another bottle filled with water. It was as white as snow, and I should have taken it for lard if I had not seen it made.

We did not start this evening before 10 o'clock, and then rode eleven hours without halting, to Uesi. The country here was less barren than that between Baghdad and Jengitsché. We did not, indeed, see any villages on the road; but small groups of palms, and the barking of dogs, led us to conclude that there were some very near. At sun-rise we were gratified by the sight of a low range of mountains, and the monotony of the plain was here and there broken at intervals, by small rows of hills.

19th June. Yesterday I was not quite satisfied with the chan at Jengitsché; but I should have been very thankful for a far worse one today, that we might have found any degree of shelter from the pitiless heat of the sun; instead, we were obliged to make our resting place in a field of stubble, far removed from human habitations. The caravan guide endeavoured to give me some little shade by laying a small cover over a couple of poles stuck into the ground; but the place was so small, and the artificial tent so weak, that I was compelled to sit quietly in one position, as the slightest movement would have upset it. How I envied the missionaries and scientific men, who undertake their laborious journeys furnished with horses, tents, provisions, and servants. When I wished, shortly afterwards, to take some refreshments, I had nothing but lukewarm water, bread so hard that I was obliged to sop it in water to be able to eat it, and a cucumber without salt or vinegar! However, I did not lose my courage and endurance, or regret, even for a moment, that I had exposed myself to these hardships.

We set out again about 8 o'clock in the evening, and halted about 4 in the morning at Deli-Abas. The low range of mountains still remained at our side. From Deli-Abas we crossed the river Hassei by a bridge built over it.

20th June. We found a chan here; but it was so decayed that we were obliged to encamp outside, as there is danger of snakes and scorpions in such ruins. A number of dirty Arab tents lay near the chan. The desire for something more than bread and cucumber, or old, half-rotten dates, overcame my disgust, and I crept into several of these dwellings. The people offered me buttermilk and bread. I noticed several hens running about the tents with their young, and eagerly looking for food. I would gladly have bought one, but as I was not disposed to kill and prepare it myself, I was obliged to be contented with the bread and buttermilk.

Some plants grow in this neighbourhood which put me in mind of my native country—the wild fennel. At home I scarcely thought them worth a glance, while here they were a source of extreme gratification. I am not ashamed to say, that at the sight of these flowers the tears came into my eyes, and I leant over them and kissed them as I would a dear friend.

We started again today, as early as 5 in the evening, as we had now the most dangerous stage of the journey before us, and were desirous of passing it before nightfall. The uniformly flat sandy desert in some degree altered in character. Hard gravel rattled under the hoofs of the animals; mounds, and strata of rock alternated with rising ground. Many of the former were projecting from the ground in their natural position, others had been carried down by floods, or piled over each other. If this strip had not amounted to more than 500 or 600 feet, I should have taken it to be the former bed of a river; but as it was, it more resembled the ground left by the returning of the sea. In many places saline substances were deposited, whose delicate crystals reflected the light in all directions.

This strip of ground, which is about five miles long, is dangerous, because the hills and rocks serve as a favourable ambush for robbers. Our drivers constantly urged the poor animals on. They were obliged to travel here over hills and rocks quicker than across the most convenient plains. We passed through in safety before darkness came on, and then proceeded more leisurely on our journey.

21st June. Towards 1 in the morning, we came up with the town Karatappa, of which, however, we saw only the walls. A mile beyond this we halted in some stubble fields. The extensive deserts and plains end here, and we entered upon a more cultivated and hilly country.

On the 22nd of June, we halted in the neighbourhood of the town Küferi.

Nothing favourable can be said of any of the Turkish towns, as they so much resemble each other in wretchedness, that it is a pleasure not to be compelled to enter them. The streets are dirty, the houses built of mud or unburnt bricks, the places of worship unimportant, miserable stalls and coarse goods constitute the bazaars, and the people, dirty and disgusting, are of a rather brown complexion. The women increase their natural ugliness, by dyeing their hair and nails reddish brown with henna, and by tattooing their hands and arms. Even at twenty-five years old, they appear quite faded.

On the 23rd of June, we halted not far from the town of Dus, and took up our resting-place for the day.

In this place, I was struck by the low entrances of the houses; they were scarcely three feet high, so that the people were obliged to crawl rather than walk into them.

On the 25th of June, we came to Daug, where I saw a monument which resembled that of Queen Zobiedé in Baghdad. I could not learn what great or holy man was buried under it.

25th June. At 4 this morning we came to the place where our caravan guide lived, a village about a mile from Kerku. His house was situated, with several others, in a large dirty court-yard, which was surrounded by a wall with only one entrance. This court-yard resembled a regular encampment: all the inhabitants slept there; and, besides these, there was no want of mules, horses, and asses. Our animals immediately went to their stalls, and trod so near to the sleepers, that I was quite anxious for their safety; but the animals are cautious, and the people know that, and remain perfectly quiet.

My Arab had been absent three weeks, and now returned only for a very short time; and yet none of his family came out to greet him except an old woman. Even with her, whom I supposed to be his mother, he exchanged no kind of welcome. She merely hobbled about here and there, but gave no help, and might as well have remained where she was lying, as the others.

The houses of the Arabs consist of a single, lofty, spacious apartment, separated into three parts by two partition walls, which do not extend quite across to the front wall. Each of these compartments is about thirty feet in length by nine in breadth, and serves as a dwelling for a family. The light fell through the common door-way and two holes, which were made in the upper part of the front wall. A place was set apart for me in one of these compartments, where I could pass the day.

My attention was first directed to the nature of the relationships between the several members of the family. At first this was very difficult, as it was only towards the very young children that any kind of attachment or love was shown. They appeared to be a common property. At last, however, I succeeded in ascertaining that three related families lived in the house—the patriarch, a married son, and a married daughter.

The patriarch was a handsome, powerful old man, sixty years of age, and the father of my guide, which I had learnt before, as he was one of our travelling party; he was a terrible scold, and wrangled about every trifle; the son seldom contradicted him, and gave way to all that his father wished. The caravan animals belonged, in common, to both, and were driven by themselves, and by a grandson fifteen years old, and some servants. When we had reached the house, the old man did not attend to the animals much, but took his ease and gave his orders. It was easy to see that he was the head of the family.

The first impression of the Arab character is that it is cold and reserved; I never saw either husband and wife, or father and daughter, exchange a friendly word; they said nothing more than was positively necessary. They show far more feeling towards children. They allow them to shout and make as much noise as they like, no one vexes or contradicts them, and every misconduct is overlooked. But as soon as a child is grown up, it becomes his duty to put up with the infirmities of his parents, which he does with respect and patience.

To my great astonishment, I heard the children call their mothers máma or nána, their fathers bàba, and their grandmothers eté or eti.

The women lie lazily about during the whole day, and only in the evening exert themselves to make bread. I thought their dress particularly awkward and inconvenient. The sleeves of their shirts were so wide that they stuck out half a yard from the arms; the sleeves of the kaftan were still larger. Whenever they do any work, they are obliged to wind them round their arms, or tie them in a knot behind. Of course they are always coming undone, and causing delay and stoppage of their work. In addition to this, the good folks are not much addicted to cleanliness, and make use of their sleeves for blowing their noses on, as well as for wiping their spoons and plates. Their head coverings are not less inconvenient: they use first a large cloth, twice folded; over this two others are wound, and a fourth is thrown over the whole.

Unfortunately, we stayed here two days. I had a great deal to undergo the first day: all the women of the place flocked round me to stare at the stranger. They first commenced examining my clothes, then wanted to take the turban off my head, and were at last so troublesome, that it was only by force that I could get any rest. I seized one of them sharply by the arm, and turned her out of the door so quickly, that she was overcome before she knew what I was going to do. I signified to the others that I would serve them the same. Perhaps they thought me stronger than I was, for they retired immediately.

I then drew a circle round my place and forbade them to cross it, an injunction they scrupulously attended to.

I had now only to deal with the wife of my guide. She laid siege to me the whole day, coming as near to me as possible, and teasing me to give her some of my things. I gave her a few trifles, for I had not much with me, and she then wanted everything. Fortunately her husband came out of the house just then; I called him and complained of his wife, and at the same time threatened to leave his house, and seek shelter somewhere else, well knowing that the Arabs consider this a great disgrace. He immediately ordered her harshly out, and I at last had peace. I always succeeded in carrying out my own will. I found that energy and boldness have a weight with all people, whether Arabs, Persians, Bedouins, or others.

Towards evening I saw, to my great delight, a cauldron of mutton set on the fire. For eight days I had eaten nothing but bread, cucumber, and some dates; and, therefore, had a great desire for a hot and more nutritious meal. But my appetite was greatly diminished when I saw their style of cookery. The old woman (my guide's mother) threw several handsful of small grain, and a large quantity of onions, into a pan full of water to soften. In about half an hour she put her dirty

272

hands into the water, and mixed the whole together, now and then taking a mouthful, and, after chewing it, spitting it back again into the pan. She then took a dirty rag, and strained off the juice, which she poured over the flesh in the pot.

I had firmly made up my mind not to touch this food; but when it was ready it gave out such an agreeable odour, and my hunger was so great, that I broke my resolution, and remembered how many times I had eaten of food the preparation of which was not a whit cleaner. What was so bad in the present instance was that I had seen the whole process.

The broth was of a bluish black in colour, and with a rather strongly acid taste—both the result of the berries. But it agreed with me very well, and I felt as strong and well as if I had undergone no hardships during my journey from Baghdad.

I hoped soon to have had a similar dainty meal, but the Arab does not live so extravagantly; I was obliged to remain satisfied with bread and some cucumbers, without salt, oil, or vinegar.

26th June. We left the village and passed Kerkü. At sunrise, we ascended a small hill, from the summit of which I was astonished by a beautiful prospect: a majestic lofty chain of mountains extended along an enormous valley, and formed the boundary between Kurdistan and Mesopotamia.

In this valley there were the most beautiful flowers, mallows, chrysanthemums, and thistly plants. Among the latter, there was one which frequently occurs in Germany, but not in such richness and magnificence. In many places these thistles cover large spaces of ground. The country people cut them down, and burn them instead of wood, which is here a great luxury, as there are no trees. We saw, today, some herds of gazelles, which ran leaping past us.

On the 27th of June we made our encampment near the miserable little town Attum-Kobri. Before reaching it, we crossed the river Sab (called by the natives Altum-Su, golden water), by two old Roman bridges. I saw several similar bridges in Syria. In both instances they were in good preservation, and will apparently long remain as evidences of the Roman power. Their wide and lofty arches rested upon massive pillars, and the whole was constructed of large square blocks of stone; the ascent of bridges of this kind is so steep that the animals are obliged to scramble up like cats.

On the 28th of June we reached the town of Erbil (formerly Arbela), where, to my great chagrin, we remained until the evening of the following day. This little town, which is fortified, is situated upon an isolated hill in the centre of a valley. We encamped, fortunately, near some houses outside the town, at the foot of the hill. I found a hut, which was tenanted by some men, two donkeys, and a number of fowls. The mistress, for a small acknowledgment, provided me a little place, which at least sheltered me from the burning heat of the sun. Beyond that, I had not the slightest convenience. As this hut, in comparison with the others, was a complete palace, the whole of the neighbours were constantly collected here.

273

From early in the morning till late in the evening, when it is the custom to recline upon the terraces, or before the huts, there was always a large party; one came to gossip, others brought meal with them, and kneaded their bread meanwhile, so as not to miss the conversation. In the background, the children were being washed and freed from vermin, the asses were braying, and the fowls covering everything with dirt. These, altogether, made the stay in this place more unbearable than even hunger and thirst. Still, I must say, to the credit of these people, that they behaved with the greatest propriety towards me, although not only women, but a great number of men of the poorest and lowest class, were coming backwards and forwards continually; even the women here left me in quiet.

In the evening, some mutton was cooked in a vessel which just before was full of dirty linen steeped in water. This was emptied out, and, without cleaning the pot, it was used to prepare the food in the same manner as at the house of my guide.

On the 30th of June we halted at the village of Sab. We here crossed the great river Sab by means of rafts, the mode of constructing which is certainly very ancient. They consist of leathern bottles, filled with air, fastened together with poles, and covered with planks, reeds, and rushes. Our raft had twenty-eight wind-bags, was seven feet broad, nearly as long, and carried two horse-loads and six men. As our caravan numbered thirty-two loaded animals, the crossing of the river occupied half a day. Four or five of the animals were tied together and drawn over by a man seated across an air-bag. The weaker animals, such as the donkeys, had a bag half filled with air tied on their backs.

The night of the 30th of June, the last of our journey, was one of the most wearisome: we travelled eleven hours. About half-way, we came to the river Hasar, called Gaumil by the Greeks, and made remarkable by the passage of Alexander the Great. It was broad, but not deep, and we therefore rode through. The chain of mountains still continued at the side at some considerable distance, and here and there rose low, sterile hills, or head-lands. The total absence of trees in this part of Mesopotamia is striking: during the last five days I did not see a single one. It is, therefore, easy to imagine that there are many people here who have never seen such a thing. There were spaces of twenty miles in extent, upon which not a single branch was to be seen. However, it is fortunate that there is no scarcity of water; every day we came once or twice to rivers of various sizes.

The town of Mósul did not become visible until we were within about five miles. It is situated upon a slight elevation in a very extensive valley, on the west bank of the Tigris, which is already much narrower here than near Baghdad. We arrived about 7 o'clock in the morning.

I was fresh and active, although during these fifteen days I had only twice had a hot meal—the ink-coloured lamb soup at Kerkü and Ervil; although I had been obliged to remain day and night in the same clothes, and had not even an opportunity of once changing my linen, not to say anything of the terrific heat, the continual riding, and other fatigues.

274

I first dismounted at the caravansary, and then procured a guide to the English Vice-consul, Mr. Rassam, who had already prepared a room for me, as he had been previously informed of my coming by a letter from Major Rawlinson, at Baghdad.

I first visited the town, which, however, does not present any very remarkable features. It is surrounded by fortified works, and contains 25,000 inhabitants, among which there are scarcely twelve Europeans. The bazaars are extensive, but not in the least degree handsome; between them lie several coffee-stalls and some chans. I found the entrances to all the houses narrow, low, and furnished with strong gates. These gates are relics of former times, when the people were always in danger from the attacks of enemies. In the interiors, there are very beautiful court-yards, and lofty, airy rooms, with handsome entrances and bow-windows. The doors and window-frames, the stairs and walls of the ground-floor rooms, are generally made of marble; though the marble which is used for these purposes is not very fine, yet it still looks better than brick walls. The quarry lies close to the town.

Here also the hot part of the day is passed in the sardabs. The heat is most terrible in the month of July, when the burning simoom not unfrequently sweeps over the town. During my short stay at Mósul, several people died very suddenly; these deaths were ascribed to the heat. Even the sardabs do not shelter people from continual perspiration, as the temperature rises as high as 97° 25' Fah.

The birds also suffer much from the heat: they open their beaks wide, and stretch their wings out far from their bodies.

The inhabitants suffer severely in their eyes; but the Aleppo boils are not so common as in Baghdad, and strangers are not subject to them.

I found the heat very oppressive, but in other respects was very well, especially as regards my appetite: I believe that I could have eaten every hour of the day. Probably this was in consequence of the hard diet which I had been obliged to endure on my journey.

The principal thing worth seeing at Mósul is the palace, about half a mile from the town. It consists of several buildings and gardens, surrounded with walls which it is possible to see over, as they lie lower than the town. It presents a very good appearance from a distance, but loses on nearer approach. In the gardens stand beautiful groups of trees, which are the more valuable as they are the only ones in the whole neighbourhood.

During my stay at Mósul, a large number of Turkish troops marched through. The Pasha rode out a short distance to receive them, and then returned to the town at the head of the foot regiments. The cavalry remained behind, and encamped in tents along the banks of the Tigris. I found these troops incomparably better clothed and equipped than those which I had seen, in 1842, at Constantinople. Their uniform consisted of white trousers, blue cloth spencers, with red facings, good shoes, and fez.

As soon as I was in some degree recovered from the fatigue of my late journey, I requested my amiable host to furnish me with a servant who should conduct me to the ruins of Nineveh; but instead of a servant, the sister of Mrs. Rassam and a Mr. Ross accompanied me. One morning we visited the nearest ruins on the other side of the Tigris, at the village Nebbi Yunus opposite the town; and, on another day, those called Tel-Nimroud, which are situated at a greater distance, about eighteen miles down the river.

According to Strabo, Nineveh was still larger than Babylon. He represents it as having been the largest city in the world. The journey round it occupied three days. The walls were a hundred feet high, broad enough for three chariots abreast, and defended by fifteen hundred towers. The same authority states that the Assyrian king Ninus was the founder, about 2,200 years before the birth of Christ.

The whole is now covered with earth, and it is only when the peasants are ploughing, that fragments of brick or marble are here and there turned up. Long ranges of mounds, more or less high, extending over the immeasurable plain on the left bank of the Tigris, are known to cover the remains of this town.

In the year 1846, the Trustees of the British Museum sent the erudite antiquarian, Mr. Layard, to undertake the excavations. It was the first attempt that had ever been made, and was very successful. {268}

Several excavations were made in the hills near Nebbi Yunus, and apartments were soon reached whose walls were covered with marble slabs wrought in relief. These represented kings with crowns and jewels, deities with large wings, warriors with arms and shields, the storming of fortifications, triumphal processions, and hunting parties, etc. They were unfortunately deficient in correct drawing, proportions, or perspective; the mounds and fortifications were scarcely three times as high as the besiegers; the fields reached to the clouds; the trees and lotus flowers could scarcely be distinguished from each other; and the heads of men and animals were all alike, and only in profile. On many of the walls were found those wedge-shaped characters, or letters, which constitute what are called cuneiform inscriptions, and are found only on Persian and Babylonian monuments.

Among all the rooms and apartments which were brought to light, there was only one in which the walls were covered with fine cement and painted; but, notwithstanding the greatest care, it was not possible to preserve this wall. When it came in contact with the air, the cement cracked and fell off. The marble also is partially converted into lime, or otherwise injured, in consequence of the terrible conflagration which laid the city in ruins. The bricks fall to pieces when they are dug out.

From the number of handsome apartments, the abundance of marble, and the

276

paintings and inscriptions upon it, the inference is drawn that this spot contains the ruins of a royal palace.

A considerable quantity of marble slabs, with reliefs and cuneiform inscriptions, were carefully detached from the walls and sent to England. When I was at Bassora, a whole cargo of similar remains lay near the Tigris, and among others a sphynx.

On our return we visited the village Nebbi Yunus, which is situated on a slight eminence near the ruins. It is remarkable only on account of a small mosque, which contains the ashes of the prophet Jonas, and to which thousands of devotees make annual pilgrimages.

During this excursion we passed a number of fields, in which the people were engaged in separating the corn from the straw in a very peculiar manner. For this purpose, a machine was employed, consisting of two wooden tubs, between which was fastened a roller, with from eight to twelve long, broad, and blunt knives or hatchets. This was drawn by two horses or oxen over the bundles of corn laid on the ground, until the whole of the corn was separated from the straw. It was then thrown up into the air by means of shovels, so that the chaff might be separated from the grain by the wind.

We finally visited the sulphur springs, which lie close to the walls of Mósul. They are not warm, but appear to contain a large quantity of sulphur, as the smell is apparent at a considerable distance. These springs rise in natural basins, which are surrounded by walls eight feet in height. Every one is allowed to bathe there without any charge, for people are not so niggardly and sparing of nature's gifts as in Europe. Certain hours are set apart for women, and others for the men.

On the following day we rode to the Mosque Elkosch, near the town. Noah's son Shem has found a resting-place here. We were not allowed to enter this mosque, but certainly did not lose much by that, as all these monuments are alike, and are not remarkable either for architecture or ornament.

The Nineveh excavations are carried on most extensively at Tel-Timroud, a district where the mounds of earth are the most numerous. Tel-Nimroud is situated about eighteen miles from Mósul down the Tigris.

We took our seats one moonlight evening upon a raft, and glided down between the dull banks of the Tigris. After seven hours, we landed, about 1 o'clock in the morning, at a poor village, bearing the high sounding name Nimroud. Some of the inhabitants, who were sleeping before their huts, made us a fire and some coffee, and we then laid down till daybreak upon some rugs we had brought with us.

At daybreak we took horses (of which there are plenty in every village), and rode to the excavations, about a mile from Nimroud. We found here a great number of places which had been dug up, or rather, uncovered mounds of earth, but not, as at Herculaneum, whole houses, streets, squares, indeed, half a town. Nothing beyond separate rooms has been brought to light here, or at the utmost, three or four adjoining ones, the exterior walls of which are not, in any case, separated from the earth, and have neither windows nor doors visible.

The objects which have been discovered exactly resemble those in the neighbourhood of Mósul, but occur in greater numbers. Besides these, I saw several idols and sphynxes in stone. The former represented animals with human heads; their size was gigantic—about that of an elephant. Four of these statues have been found, two of which were, however, considerably damaged. The others were not indeed in very good preservation, although sufficiently so to show that the sculptors did not particularly excel in their profession. The sphynxes were small, and had unfortunately suffered more damage than the bulls.

Shortly before my arrival, an obelisk of inconsiderable height, a small and uninjured sphynx, together with other remains, had been sent to England.

The excavations near Tel-Nimroud have been discontinued about a year, and Mr. Layard has been recalled to London. An order was afterwards given to cover in the places which had been dug open, as the wandering Arabs had begun to do a great deal of injury. When I visited the spot, some places were already covered in, but the greater part remained open.

The excavations near Nebbi Yunus are still being carried on. An annual grant is made by the British government for this purpose.

The English resident at Baghdad, Major Rawlinson, had made himself perfectly master of the cuneiform character. He reads the inscriptions with ease, and many of the translations are the results of his labours.

We returned to Mósul on horseback in five hours and a half. The power of endurance of the Arabian horses is almost incredible. They were allowed only a quarter of an hour's rest in Mósul, where they had nothing but water, and then travelled the eighteen miles back again during the hottest part of the day. Mr. Ross told me that even this was not equal to the work done by the post horses: the stations for these are from forty-eight to seventy-two miles distant from each other. It is possible to travel from Mósul by Tokat to Constantinople in this way. The best Arabian horses are found round Baghdad and Mósul.

An agent of the Queen of Spain had just purchased a stud of twelve magnificent horses (eight mares and four stallions), the dearest of which had cost on the spot £150 sterling. They stood in Mr. Rassam's stable. Their handsome, long, slender heads, their sparkling eyes, slight bodies, and their small delicately formed feet, would have filled any admirer of horses with delight.

I could now venture, not, indeed, without considerable risk, although with the possibility of some insult, upon the desired journey into Persia. I sought a caravan to Tebris. Unfortunately, I could not find one which went direct there, and I was, therefore, compelled to make this journey in separate stages, a circumstance which was so much the worse for me, as I was told that I should not find any Europeans on the way.

Nevertheless I took the chance. Mr. Rassam arranged for me the journey as far as Ravandus, and furnished me with a letter of recommendation to one of the natives there. I wrote out a small lexicon of Arabian and Persian words, and took leave of this hospitable family at sunset, on the 8th of July. I started on this journey with some feelings of anxiety, and scarcely dared to hope for a fortunate termination. On that account I sent my papers and manuscripts from here to Europe, so that in case I was robbed or murdered my diary would at least come into the hands of my sons. {270}

CHAPTER XX. PERSIA.

JOURNEY OF THE CARAVAN TO RAVANDUS—ARRIVAL AT AND STAY IN RAVANDUS—A KURDISH FAMILY—CONTINUATION OF THE JOURNEY—SAUH-BULAK—OROMIA—AMERICAN MISSIONARIES—KUTSCHIÉ—THREE GENEROUS ROBBERS— PERSIAN CHANS AND ENGLISH BUNGALOWS—ARRIVAL AT TEBRIS.

On the 8th of July the caravan guide called for me in the evening. His appearance was so unfavourable that I should scarcely have ventured to travel a mile with him had I not been assured that he was a man well known in the place. His dress consisted of rags and tatters, and his countenance resembled that of a robber. Ali, that was his name, told me that the travellers and goods had already gone on and were encamped in the chan near Nebbi-Yunus, where they were to pass the night. The journey was to be commenced before sunrise. I found three men and some pack-horses; the men (Kurds) were no better in appearance than Ali, so that I could not promise myself much gratification from their society. I took up my quarters for the night in the dirty court-yard of the chan, but was too much frightened to sleep well.

In the morning, to my astonishment, there were no indications of starting. I asked Ali what was the cause of this, and received as answer that the travellers were not all assembled yet, and that, as soon as they were, we should proceed immediately. In the expectation that this might soon happen, I dared not leave the miserable shelter to return to Mósul, from which we were only a mile distant. The whole day was spent in waiting; these people did not come until evening. There were five of them: one, who appeared to be a wealthy man, with his two servants, was returning from a pilgrimage. We started at last about 10 o'clock at night. After

279

travelling for four hours we crossed several ranges of hills, which form the boundaries of Mesopotamia and Kurdistan. We passed several villages, and reached Secani on the morning of the 10th of July. Ali did not halt at the village which lies on the pretty river Kasir, but on the other side of the river near a couple of deserted, half-ruined huts. I hastened directly into one of the best to make sure of a good place, where the sun did not come through the sieve-like roof, which I fortunately found but the pilgrim, who hobbled in directly after me, was inclined to dispute its possession. I threw my mantle down, and seating myself upon it, did not move from the place, well knowing that a Mussulman never uses force towards a woman, not even towards a Christian one. And so it turned out; he left me in my place and went grumbling away. One of the pedlars behaved himself in a very different manner: when he saw that I had nothing for my meal but dry bread, while he had cucumbers and sweet melons, he gave me a cucumber and a melon, for which he would not take any money. The pilgrim also ate nothing else, although he had only to send one of his servants to the village to procure either fowls or eggs, etc. The frugality of these people is really astonishing.

About 6 in the evening we again proceeded on our journey, and for the first three hours went continually up-hill. The ground was waste and covered with boulders, which were full of shallow holes, and resembled old lava.

Towards 11 at night we entered an extensive and beautiful valley, upon which the moon threw a brilliant light. We purposed halting here, and not continuing our journey further during the night, as our caravan was small, and Kurdistan bears a very bad name. The road led over fields of stubble near to stacks of corn. Suddenly half a dozen powerful fellows sprung out from behind, armed with stout cudgels, and seizing our horses' reins, raised their sticks, and shouted at us terribly. I felt certain that we had fallen into the hands of a band of robbers, and was glad to think that I had left my treasures which I had collected at Babylon and Nineveh, together with my papers, at Mósul; my other effects might have been easily replaced. During the time this was passing in my mind, one of our party had sprung from his horse and seized one of the men by the breast, when he held a loaded pistol before his face and threatened to shoot him. This had an immediate effect; the waylayers relinquished their hold, and soon entered into a peaceful conversation with us; and at last, indeed, showed us a good place to encamp, for which, however, they requested a small bachshish, which was given to them by a general collection. From me, as belonging to the female sex, they required nothing. We passed the night here, though not without keeping guard.

11th July. About 4 o'clock we were again upon the road, and rode six hours, when we came to the village of Selik. We passed through several villages, which, however, had a very miserable appearance. The huts were built of reeds and straw; the slightest gust of wind would have been sufficient to have blown them over. The dress of the people approaches in character to the Oriental; all were very scantily, dirtily, and raggedly clothed.

Near Selik I was surprised by the sight of a fig-tree and another large tree. In this country trees are rare. The mountains surrounding us were naked and barren, and in the valleys there grew at most some wild artichokes or beautiful thistles and chrysanthemums.

The noble pilgrim took upon himself to point out my place under the large tree, where the whole party were encamped. I gave him no reply, and took possession of one of the fig-trees. Ali, who was far better than he looked, brought me a jug of buttermilk, and altogether today passed off tolerably pleasantly.

Several women from the village visited me and begged for money, but I gave them none, as I knew from experience that I should be attacked by all if I gave to one. I once gave a child a little ring, and not only the other children, but their mothers and grandmothers, crowded round me. It cost me some trouble to keep them from forcibly emptying my pockets. Since that time I was more cautious. One of the women here changed her begging manner into one so threatening, that I was heartily glad at not being alone with her.

We left this village at 4 in the afternoon. The pilgrim separated from us, and the caravan then consisted of only five men. In about an hour and a half we reached an eminence from which we obtained a view of an extensive and well cultivated hill country. The land in Kurdistan is without comparison better than in Mesopotamia, and the country is consequently better inhabited; we were, therefore continually passing through different villages.

Before nightfall we entered a valley which was distinguished for fresh rice plantations, beautiful shrubs, and green reeds: a brisk stream murmured at our side, the heat of the day was now succeeded by the evening shadows, and, at this moment we had nothing to wish for. This good fortune, however, did not last long; one of the pedlars was suddenly taken so ill that we were obliged to stop. He nearly fell off his mule, and remained motionless. We covered him with rugs, but beyond that we could not do anything for him, as we had neither medicines nor other remedies with us. Fortunately, he fell asleep after a few hours, and we squatted down on the ground and followed his example.

12th July. This morning our patient was well again; a doubly fortunate circumstance, as we had to pass a terribly rocky and stony road. We were obliged to scramble up and down the mountainous side of a valley, as the valley itself was completely occupied by the irregular course of the river Badin, which wound in a serpentine direction from side to side. Pomegranates and oleanders grew in the valley, wild vines twined themselves round the shrubs and trees, and larches covered the slopes of the hills.

After a difficult and dangerous ride of six hours, we came to a ford of the river Badin. Our raft turned out to be so small that it would carry only two men, and very little baggage; and we were, in consequence, four hours in crossing. We stayed for the night not far from the ferry of Vakani.

281

13th July. The road still continued bad; we had to ascend an immense pile of mountains. Far and wide, nothing was to be seen but rock and stone, although, to my astonishment, I observed that in many places the stones had been gathered on one side, and every little spot of earth made use of. A few dwarf ash-trees stood here and there. The whole has the character of the country near Trieste.

Although there were no villages on the road, there appeared to be some near, for on many of the heights I observed large burial-places, especially on those which are overshadowed by ash-trees. It is the custom throughout Kurdistan to establish the burial-places on high situations.

We did not travel more than seven hours today, and halted in the valley of Halifan. This little valley has an uncommonly romantic situation; it is surrounded by lofty and beautiful mountains, which rise with a gentle slope on one side, and on the other are steep and precipitous. The whole valley was covered with a rich vegetation; the stubble-fields were interspersed with tobacco and rice plantations, and meadows. Poplar-trees surrounded the village, which was pleasantly situated at the foot of a hill, and a stream of crystalline clearness rushed forcibly out of a mountain chasm, and flowed calmly and still through this delightful valley. Towards evening, numerous herds of cows, sheep, and goats came from the mountain-slopes towards the village.

We encamped at some distance from the village; I could not procure any relish for my dry bread, and had no other bed than the hard ground of a stubble-field. Nevertheless I should include this evening among the most agreeable; the scenery round compensated me sufficiently for the want of every other enjoyment.

14th July. Ali allowed us to rest only half the night; at 2 o'clock we were again mounted. A few hundred paces from our resting-place was the entrance of a stupendous mountain-pass. The space between the sides of the rocks afforded only sufficient room for the stream and a narrow pathway. Fortunately the moon shone out brilliantly, otherwise it would have been scarcely possible for the most practised animal to ascend the narrow and extremely dangerous road between the fallen masses of rock and rolling stones. Our hardy animals scrambled like chamois along, over the edges of the steep precipices, and carried us with safety past the terrible abyss, at the bottom of which the stream leapt, with a frightful roaring, from rock to rock. This night-scene was so terrible and impressive that even my uncultivated companions were involuntarily silent—mute, and noiseless, we went on our way, nothing breaking the death-like stillness but the rattling steps of our animals.

We had proceeded about an hour in this way, when the moon was suddenly obscured; thick clouds gathered round from all sides, and the darkness soon became so great that we could scarcely see a few steps before us. The foremost man continually struck fire, so as to light up the path somewhat by the sparks. But this did not help us much, the animals began to slip and stumble. We were compelled to halt, and stood quiet and motionless, one behind the other, as if suddenly changed to stone by magic. Life returned again with daybreak, and we spurred our animals briskly forwards.

We were in an indescribably beautiful circle of mountains; at our side lay high cliffs; before and behind, hills and mountains crowded over each other, and in the far distance an enormous peak, covered with snow, completed the romantic picture. This mountain-pass is called Ali-Bag. For three hours and a half we continued going up hill, without intermission.

A short distance before reaching the plateau, we observed, in several places, small spots of blood, of which nobody at first took much notice, as they might have been caused by a horse or mule that had injured itself. But shortly we came to a place which was entirely covered with large blood-spots. This sight filled us with great horror; we looked round anxiously for the cause of these marks and perceived two human bodies far down below. One hung scarcely a hundred feet down on the declivity of the rock, the other had rolled further on, and was half-buried under a mass of rock. We hastened from this horrible scene as quickly as we could; it was several days before I could free myself from the recollection of it.

All the stones on the plateau were full of holes, as if other stones had been stuck in. This appearance ceased as we went further up. In the valley, at the other side of the plateau, there were vines, which, however, did not rise far above the ground, as they were not supported in any way.

Our road continued on through the mountains. We frequently descended, but again had to cross several heights, and, finally, came out upon a small elevated plain, which, on both sides, was bounded by steep declivities. A village of huts, made of branches, was situated on this plain, and on the summits of two neighbouring rocks fortified works were erected.

My travelling companions remained behind here; but Ali went with me to the town of Ravandus, which only becomes visible from this side at a very short distance.

The situation and view of this town is most charming; not indeed from its beauty, for it is not more remarkable in that respect than other Turkish towns, but on account of its peculiarity. It is situated upon a steep, isolated cone, surrounded by mountains. The houses are built in the form of terraces, one above another, with flat roofs, which are covered with earth, stamped down hard, so as to resemble narrow streets, for which they serve to the upper houses, and it is frequently difficult to tell which is street and which roof. On many of the terraces, walls, formed of the branches of trees, are erected, behind which the people sleep. Lower down, the hill is surrounded by a fortified wall.

When I first caught hold of this eagle's nest, I feared that I had not much probability of finding any conveniences for travellers, and every step further confirmed this opinion. Ravandus was one of the most miserable towns I ever

283

saw. Ali conducted me over a beggarly bazaar to a dirty court, which I took for a stable, but was the chan; and, after I had dismounted, took me into a dark recess, in which the merchant, to whom I had a letter, sat upon the ground before his stall. This merchant was the most considerable of his class in Ravandus. Mr. Mansur, that was the merchant's name, read over the letter which I had brought, for full a quarter of an hour, although it only consisted of a few lines, and then greeted me with a repeated salaam, which means "you are welcome."

The good man must have concluded that I had not tasted any food today, for he very hospitably ordered breakfast immediately, consisting of bread, sheep's cheese, and melons. These were eaten all together. My hunger was so great that I found this plan excellent. I ate without ceasing. The conversation, on the contrary, was not so successful; my host did not understand any European language, nor I any Asiatic language. We made use of signs, and I took pains to make him understand that I was desirous of going on further as soon as possible. He promised to do his utmost for me, and also explained that he would see to me during my stay; he was not married, and therefore could not receive me into his own house, but would take me to one of his relations.

After breakfast was ended he took me to a house resembling those of the Arabs at Kerkil, except that the court-yard was very small, and completely filled with rubbish and puddles. Under the door-way, four ugly women with half-ragged clothes, were seated upon a dirty rug, playing with some little children. I was obliged to sit down with them, and undergo the usual curious examination and staring. For some time I put up with it, but then left this charming society, and looked about for a place where I could arrange my toilette a little. I had not changed my clothes for six days, having been exposed, at the same time, to a heat which was far greater than that under the line. I found a dirty and smutty room, which, in addition to the disgust it excited, made me fear the presence of vermin and scorpions; of the latter I had a particular dread. I thought at first that they were to be found in every place, as I had read in many descriptions of travels that they were innumerable in these countries. My fear lessened afterwards, as I did not meet with any, even in the dirtiest places; in ruins, court-yards, or sardabs. Altogether I only saw two during my whole journey, but I suffered a great deal from other vermin, which are only to be removed by burning the clothes and linen.

I had scarcely taken possession of this beggarly room, when one woman after the other came in; the women were followed by the children, and then by several neighbours, who had heard of the arrival of an *Inglesi*; I was worse off here than under the gateway.

At last, one of the women luckily thought of offering me a bath, and I accepted the proposal with great joy. Hot water was prepared, and they made a sign for me to follow them, which I did, and found myself in the sheep-stall, which, perhaps, had not been cleaned for years, or indeed as long as it had stood. In this place

284

they pushed two stones together, upon which I was to stand, and in the presence of the whole company, who followed me like my shadow, allow myself to be bathed with water. I made signs to them to go out, as I wished to perform this office myself; they did indeed leave me, but as misfortune had it, the stall had no door, and they were all able to look in just the same.

I passed four days among these people, the day time in dark recesses, the evenings and nights upon the terraces. I was obliged, like my hostess, constantly to squat down on the ground, and when I wanted to write anything I had to make use of my knees instead of a table. Every day they told me there was a caravan going away to-morrow. Alas! they said so only to quiet me, they saw, perhaps, how disagreeable the stay was to me. The women lounged about the whole day sleeping or chattering, playing with, or scolding the children. They preferred going about in dirty rags to mending and washing them, and they allowed their children to tyrannize over them completely.

When the latter wanted anything and did not get it, they threw themselves on the ground, struck about with their hands and feet, howling and shrieking until they obtained what they desired.

They had no fixed meal-times during the day, but the women and children were constantly eating bread, cucumbers, melons and buttermilk. In the evenings they bathed very much, and every one washed their hands, faces, and feet, which ceremony was frequently repeated three or four times before prayers; but there was a great want of real devotion: in the middle of the prayers they chattered right and left. However, there is not much difference with us.

Notwithstanding all these glaring and gross defects I found these people very amiable: they willingly permitted themselves to be taught, admitted their failings, and always allowed me to be right when I said or explained anything to them. For example, the little Ascha, a girl seven years of age was very intractable. If she was denied anything she threw herself on the ground, crying miserably, rolling about in the filth and dirt, and smearing with her dirty hands the bread, melons, etc. I endeavoured to make the child conscious of her misbehaviour, and succeeded beyond all expectation. I, in fact, imitated her. The child looked at me astounded, upon which I asked if it had pleased her. She perceived the offensiveness of her conduct, and I did not often need to imitate her. It was just the same with regard to cleanliness. She immediately washed herself carefully, and then came running joyfully to me showing her hands and face. During the few days I was here the child became so fond of me that she would not leave my side, and sought in every way to make friends with me.

I was not less fortunate with the women; I pointed out their torn clothes, brought needles, and thread, and taught them how to sew and mend. They were pleased with this, and I had in a short time a whole sewing school round me.

How much good might be done here by any one who knew the language and had the inclination, only the parents must be taught at the same time as the children.

What a fine field is here open to the missionaries if they would accustom themselves to live among these people, and with kindness and patience to counteract their failings! As it is, however, they devote at the utmost only a few hours in the day to them, and make their converts come to them, instead of visiting them in their own houses.

The women and girls in the Asiatic countries receive no education, those in the towns have little or no employment, and are left to themselves during the whole day. The men go at sunrise to the bazaars, where they have their stalls or workshops, the bigger boys go to school or accompany their fathers, and neither return home before sunset. There the husband expects to find the carpets spread out on the terraces, the supper ready, and the nargilly lighted, he then plays a little with the young children, who, however, during meal-time are obliged to keep away with their mothers. The women in the villages have more liberty and amusement, as they generally take part in the housekeeping. It is said that the people in the country here are, as among ourselves, more moral than in the towns.

The dress worn by the richer Kurds is the Oriental, that of the common people differs slightly from it. The men wear wide linen trousers, over them a shirt reaching to the hips, and fastened round the waist by a girdle. They frequently draw on, over the shirt, a jacket without sleeves, made of coarse brown woollen stuff, which is properly cut into strips of a hand's breath, and joined together by broad seams. Others wear trousers of brown stuff instead of white linen; they are, however, extremely ugly, as they are really nothing more than a wide shapeless sack with two holes, through which the feet are put. The coverings for the feet are either enormous shoes of coarsely woven white sheeps' wool, ornamented with three tassels, or short, very wide boots of red or yellow leather, reaching only just above the ankle and armed with large plates an inch thick. The head-dress is a turban.

The women wear long wide trousers, blue shirts, which frequently reach half a yard over the feet, and are kept up by means of a girdle; a large blue mantle hangs from the back of the neck, reaching down to the calves. They wear the same kind of plated boots as the men. On their heads they wear either black kerchiefs wound in the manner of a turban, or a red fez, the top of which is very broad, and covered with silver coins arranged in the form of a cross. A coloured silk kerchief is wound round the fez, and a wreath made of short black silk fringe is fastened on the top. This wreath looks like a handsome rich fur-trimming, and is so arranged that it forms a coronet, leaving the forehead exposed. The hair falls in numerous thin tresses over the shoulders, and a heavy silver chain hangs down behind from the turban. It is impossible to imagine a head dress that looks better than this.

Neither women or girls cover their faces, and I saw here several very beautiful girls with truly noble features. The colour of the skin is rather brown, the

286

eyebrows and lashes were black, and the hair dyed reddish-brown with henna. Among the lower orders small nose rings are sometimes worn here.

Mr. Mansur furnished me with a very good table in the morning, I had buttermilk, bread, cucumber, and on one occasion dates roasted in butter, which, however, was not very palatable; in the evening mutton and rice, or a quodlibet of rice, barley, maize, cucumber, onions and minced meat. I found it all very good as I was healthy, and had a good appetite. The water and buttermilk are taken very cold, and a piece of ice is always put into them. Ice is to be met with in abundance not only in the towns, but also in every village. It is brought from the mountains in the neighbourhood, the people eat large pieces of it with great relish.

In spite of the endeavours of Mr. Mansur and his relations to render my stay bearable, or perhaps, indeed, pleasant, according to their ideas, I was agreeably surprised when Ali came one morning bringing the news that he had met with a small freight to Sauh-Bulak (seventy miles) a place which laid on my road. That same evening I went to the caravansary, and the next morning, 18th July, was on the road before sunrise.

Mr. Mansur was to the last very hospitable. He not only gave me a letter to a Persian living in Sauh-Bulak, but also provided me with bread for the journey, some melons, cucumbers, and a small bottle of sour milk. The latter was particularly acceptable to me, and I would advise every traveller to remember this nourishing and refreshing drink.

Sour milk is put into a small bag of thick linen, the watery part filters through, and the solid part can be taken out with a spoon, and mixed with water as desired. In the hot season, indeed, it dries into cheese on the fourth or fifth day, but this also tastes very well, and in four or five days you come to places where the supply may be renewed.

On the first day we passed continually through narrow valleys between lofty mountains. The roads were exceedingly bad, and we were frequently obliged to cross over high mountains to pass from one valley into another. These stony valleys were cultivated as much as was possible. We halted at Tschomarichen.

19th July. The road and country was the same as those of yesterday, except that we had more hilly ground to ascend. We very nearly reached the height of the first snow region.

Towards evening, we came to Raid, a miserable place with a half-ruined citadel. Scarcely had we encamped, when several well-armed soldiers, headed by an officer, made their appearance. They spoke for some time with Ali, and at last the officer introduced himself to me, took his place at my side, showed me a written paper, and made several signs. As far as I could understand, he meant to say that I was now in Persia, and that he wanted to see my passport. However, I did not wish to take it out of my portmanteau in the presence of the whole of the villagers, who were already assembled round me, and, therefore, explained to him that I did not understand him. With this assurance he left me, saying to Ali: "What shall I do with her? She does not understand me, and may go on further." {279} I do not think that I should have been so leniently dealt with in any European state!

In almost every village, a great part of the people immediately assembled round me. The reader may imagine what a crowd had gathered together during this discussion. To be continually stared at in this way was one of the greatest inconveniences of my journey. Sometimes I quite lost my patience, when the women and children pressed round me, handling my clothes and head. Although quite alone among them, I gave them several slight blows with my riding-whip. This always had the desired effect; the people either went away altogether or drew back in a ring. But here, a boy about sixteen was inclined to punish my boldness. As usual, I went to the river to fill my leathern flask, to wash my hands and face, and bathe my feet. This boy slipped after me, picked up a stone, and threatened to throw it at me. I dare not, of course, evince any fear; and I went, therefore, quite composedly into the river. The stone came flying, although I observed, by the way in which it was thrown, that he was more desirous of frightening than hitting me; it was not thrown with force, and fell several feet away. After throwing a second and third, he went away; perhaps because he saw that I did not heed him.

20th July. Immediately outside Raid, we had to ascend a rather considerable mountain by a bad and dangerous road, and then came out upon an extensive elevated plain. We left the high mountains further behind, the headlands were covered with short grass, but there was again a great deficiency of trees. We met great numbers of herds of goats and sheep. The latter were very large, with thick wool and fat tails; the wool is said to be particularly good and fine.

My apprehensions on this journey were not quite groundless, as it was seldom that a day passed in undisturbed quiet. Today, for instance, a circumstance occurred which frightened me not a little: our caravan consisted of six men and fourteen pack animals; we were quietly pursuing our way, when suddenly a troop of mounted men came dashing down upon us at full gallop. There were seven well-armed, and five unarmed. The former carried lances, sabres, daggers, knives, pistols, and shields; they were dressed like the common people, with the exception of the turban, which was wound round with a simple Persian shawl. I thought they had been robbers. They stopped and surrounded us, and then inquired where we came from, where we were going to, and what kind of goods we carried? When they had received an explanation, they allowed us to go on. At first I could not understand the meaning of the proceeding at all; but, as we were stopped several times in the course of the day in a similar manner, I concluded that these men were soldiers on duty.

We remained at Coromaduda over night.

21st July. The roads and prospects very similar to those of yesterday. We were again stopped by a troop of soldiers, and this time the affair seemed likely to be of more consequence. Ali must have made some incorrect statements. They took possession of both of his pack animals, threw their loads down on the ground, and one of the soldiers was ordered to lead them away. Poor Ali begged and entreated most pitifully. He pointed to me, and said that everything belonged to me, and requested that they should have some compassion with me as a helpless woman. The soldier turned to me and asked if it was true. I did not think it advisable to give myself out as their owner, and therefore appeared not to understand him, but assumed an air of great concern and trouble. Ali, indeed, began to cry. Our position would have been most desperate; for, what could we have done with the goods in this barren uninhabited district without our animals. At last, however, the leader of the party relented, sent after the animals, and returned them to us.

Late in the evening, we reached the little town of Sauh-Bulak. As it was not fortified, we could still enter; however, the chans and bazaars were all closed, and we had much trouble to get the people of one of the chans to receive us. It was very spacious and handsome; in the centre was a basin of water, and round it small merchants' stalls and several niches for sleeping. The people—all men— were mostly retired to rest; only a few remained at their devotions. Their astonishment may be imagined when they saw a woman enter with a guide. It was too late to give my letter today, and I therefore seated myself composedly against the luggage, in the belief that I should have to pass the night so; but a Persian came to me and pointed out a niche to sleep in, carried my luggage there, and, after a little while, brought me some bread and water. The kindness of this man was the more admirable, as it is known how much the Mahomedans hate the Christians. May God reward him for it. I was truly in want of this refreshment.

22nd July. Today I presented my letter, and the Persian merchant received me with a welcome. He conducted me to a Christian family, and promised to make arrangements for the continuation of my journey as soon as possible. In this instance, also, the conversation was carried on more by the means of signs than words.

There were twenty Christian families in this town, who are under the care of a French missionary and have a very pretty church. I looked forward with pleasure to conversing again in a language with which I was familiar, but learnt that the missionary was on a journey, so that I was not better off than at Ravandus, as the people with whom I lived spoke only Persian.

The man, whose trade was that of a carpenter, had a wife, six children, and an apprentice. They all lived in the same room, in which they gave me a place with great readiness. The whole family were uncommonly good and obliging towards me, were very open-hearted, and if I bought fruit, eggs, or anything of the kind, and offered them any, they accepted it with great modesty. But it was not only towards myself that they were so kind, but also towards others; no beggar went away from their threshold unrelieved; and yet this family was terrible, and made my stay a complete purgatory. The mother, a very stupid scolding woman, bawled and beat her children the whole day. Ten minutes did not pass without her dragging her children about by the hair, or kicking and thumping them. The children were not slow in returning it; and, besides that, fought among themselves; so that I had not a moment's quiet in my corner, and was not unfrequently in danger of coming in for my share, for they amused themselves by spitting and throwing large blocks of wood at each other's heads. The eldest son several times throttled his mother in such a way that she became black and blue in the face. I always endeavoured, indeed, to establish peace; but it was very seldom that I succeeded, as I was unfortunately not sufficient master of the language to make them understand the impropriety of their conduct.

It was only in the evening, when the father returned, that there was any order of peace; they dare not quarrel then, much less fight.

I never met with such conduct among any people—even the poorest or lowest classes of the so-called heathens or unbelievers; I never saw their children attempt to strike their parents. When I left Sauh-Bulak, I wrote a letter for the missionary, in which I directed his attention to the failings of this family, and besought him to counteract them, by teaching them that religion does not consist merely in prayers and fasts, in bible-reading, and going to church.

My stay here was far less bearable than at Ravandus. I daily entreated the Persian merchant to help me to go on further, even if the journey should be attended with some danger. He shook his head and explained to me, that there was no caravan going, and that if I travelled alone I might expect either to be shot or beheaded.

I bore it for five days, but it was impossible to do so any longer. I begged the merchant to hire me a horse and a guide, and made up my mind at least to go as far as Oromia, fifty miles, in spite of all dangers or other circumstances. I knew that I should find American missionaries there, and that I should then have no more anxiety about proceeding on further.

The merchant came on the following day, accompanied by a wild-looking man, whom he introduced to me as my guide. I was obliged, in consequence of the danger of travelling without a caravan, to pay four times as much; but I was willing to accede to anything to be able to get away. The bargain was made, and the guide pledged himself to start the next morning, and to bring me to Oromia in three days. I paid him half of the money in advance, and retained the other half until we came to our journey's end, so as to be able to fine him in case he did not keep his agreement.

I was partly glad and partly afraid when the contract was concluded, and to overcome my apprehensions, I went into the Bazaars, and walked about outside the town.

290

This town is situated in a small treeless valley near a range of hills. Although I did not wear anything but the isar, I was never annoyed out of doors. The bazaars are less beggarly than those at Ravandus, the chan is large and comfortable. I found the appearance of the common people very repulsive. Tall and strongly built, with marked features, which were still more disfigured by an expression of wildness and ferocity, they all appeared to me like robbers or murderers.

In the evening I put my pistols in proper order, and made up my mind not to sell my life cheaply.

28th July. Instead of leaving Sauh-Bulak at sunrise, I did not start until towards mid-day. I travelled on with my guide through desolate roads between treeless hills, and trembled involuntarily when any one met us. However, thank God, there were no adventures to go through. We had to fight indeed, but only with tremendous swarms of large grasshoppers which flew up in some places in clouds. They were about three inches long, and were furnished with large wings of a red or blue colour. All the plants and grass in the district were eaten away. I was told that the natives catch these grasshoppers and dry and eat them. Unluckily I never saw any such dish.

After a ride of seven hours we came to a large fruitful and inhabited valley. Today's journey seemed to promise a favourable termination, for we were now in an inhabited neighbourhood, and frequently passed villages. Some peasants were still working here and there in the fields, their appearance greatly amused me: they wore the high black Persian caps, which were comically contrasted with their ragged dress.

We remained in this valley, over night, at the village Mahomed-Jur. If I had not been too idle I might have had an excellent meal of turtle. I saw several of them on the road by the brooks, and even in the fields, and had only to pick them up. But then to hunt for wood, make a fire, and cook! No; I preferred eating a crust of bread and a cucumber in quiet.

29th July. This morning we reached, in three hours, the village of Mahomed-Schar. To my astonishment my driver made preparations for stopping here. I urged him to continue the journey, but he explained to me that he could not go any further without a caravan, as the most dangerous part of the journey was now before us. At the same time he pointed to some dozens of horses in an adjoining stubble field, and endeavoured to make me understand that in a few hours a caravan was going our way. The whole day passed, and the caravan did not appear. I thought that my guide was deceiving me; and was exceedingly irritated when, in the evening, he arranged my mantle on the ground for me to sleep. It was now necessary that I should make a strenuous effort to show the fellow that I would not be treated like a child, and remain here as long as he thought fit. Unfortunately I could not scold him in words, but I picked up the mantle and threw it at his feet, and explained to him that I would keep the remainder of the fare if he did not bring me to Oromia to-morrow on the third day. I then turned my back to him (one of the greatest slights), seated myself on the ground, and, resting my head in my hands, gave myself up to the most melancholy reflections. What should I have done here if my guide had left me, or had thought fit to remain until a caravan happened to pass by.

During my dispute with the guide, some women had come up from the village. They brought me some milk and some hot food, seated themselves by me, and inquired what I was so troubled about.

I endeavoured to explain the whole affair. They understood me and took my part. They were vexed with my guide, and endeavoured to console me. They did not stir from me, and pressed me so heartily to partake of their food, that I found myself compelled to eat some. It consisted of bread, eggs, butter, and water, which were boiled up together. Notwithstanding my trouble, I enjoyed it very much. When I offered the good people a trifle for this meal they would not take it. They seemed gratified that I was more at ease.

30th July. About 1 o'clock at night my guide began to stir himself, saddled my horse, and called me to mount. Still I was at a loss to understand his proceedings, for I saw no signs of a caravan. Could he mean to take his revenge on me? Why did he travel at night through a country which he ought to have chosen day-time for? I did not understand enough Persian to be able to obtain an explanation, and did not wish to say anything more to the fellow about not keeping his contract, so I was obliged to go—and I did go.

With great anxiety I mounted my horse and ordered my guide, who was inclined to ride behind, to go on in front. I had no mind to be attacked from behind, and kept my hand constantly on my pistols. I listened to every sound, watched every movement of my guide, even the shadow of my own horse sometimes scared me; however, I did not turn back.

After a sharp ride of about half-an-hour, we came up with a large caravan train, which was guarded by half a dozen well-armed peasants. It really appeared that the place was very dangerous, and that my guide had been acquainted with the passing of a caravan. Nothing caused me more surprise on this occasion, than the indolence of these people. As they are accustomed to travel in the night during the hot season, they also continue the custom at other times, and pass through the most dangerous places, although the danger would be much less during the day.

After some hours we came to the Lake Oromia, which henceforth continued on our right side; on the left lay barren hills, ravines and mountains, extending for some miles, forming a most dreaded place. Morning brought us into another beautiful fruitful valley, studded with villages, the sight of which gave me courage to leave the caravan, and hasten on.

The Lake Oromia, from which the town takes its name, is more than sixty miles long, and in many places more than thirty wide. It appears closely surrounded by lofty mountains, although considerable levels intervene. Its water contains so

292

much salt, that neither fish nor mollusca can live in it. It is a second Dead Sea—it is said that a human body cannot sink in it. Large patches of the shore are covered with thick, white saline incrustations, so that the people have only to separate the salt they want from the ground. Although the lake, and the country round it are very beautiful, they do not present a very attractive prospect, as the surface of the lake is not enlivened by any boats.

Since I had left the sandy deserts round Baghdad, I had not seen any camels, and thought that I should not see this animal again, as I was travelling northwards. To my astonishment, we met several trains of camels, and I learnt afterwards, that these animals were used as beasts of burden by the Kurds, as well as the Arabs. This is a proof that they are able to bear a colder climate; for in winter the snow drifts to a depth of several feet in the valleys. The camels in these districts are somewhat more robust, their feet are thicker, their hair closer and longer, their necks longer, and not nearly so slender, and their colour darker. I did not see any light-coloured ones.

The Kurds of the valleys employ beasts of burden for carrying their crops, as well as waggons, which are however very simple and clumsy. The body is formed of several long thin stems of trees bound together; the axles of shorter stems, with disks of thick board for wheels, of which each waggon has generally only two. Four oxen are yoked to these, each pair being led by a guide, who sits very oddly on the shaft between the yoke, with his back towards them.

Late in the evening, we reached Oromia safely, after a hard ride of more than sixteen hours. I had no letters to any of the missionaries, and with the exception of Mr. Wright, they were all absent. They lived with their wives and children in the country. However, Mr. Wright received me with true Christian friendship, and after many disagreeable days I again found comfort.

The first evening I laughed heartily when Mr. Wright told me in what manner the servant had informed him of my arrival. As I did not know enough of Persian to be able to tell the servant to announce me, I merely pointed to the stairs. He understood this, and went up to his master, saying that there was a woman below who could not speak any language. Afterwards I asked a servant for a glass of water, in English; he rushed up stairs as if he had been possessed, not, as I thought, to get what I wanted, but to tell his master that I spoke English.

Mr. Wright acquainted the other missionaries of my presence, and they were so good as to come and visit me. They also invited me to spend a few days with them in the country, but I accepted their friendly invitation for one day only, as I had already lost so much time on the road. They all advised me not to go any further alone; although they admitted that the most dangerous part of the journey was past, and recommended me to take with me some armed peasants when passing the mountains near Kutschié.

Mr. Wright was so good as to look out for a courageous and trusty guide. I paid

293

double fare, in order to reach Tebris in four, instead of six days. In order to make the guide think that I was a poor pilgrim, I gave Mr. Wright the half of the agreed price, and begged him to pay it instead of myself, and also to say that he would be paid the other half by Mr. Stevens, the English consul.

I made as good use as possible of the day which I passed at Oromia. In the morning I visited the town, and afterwards I visited, with Mrs. Wright, several rich and poor families, in order to observe their mode of life.

The town contains 22,000 inhabitants, is surrounded by walls, but not closed by gates; it is possible to pass in and out at any hour of the night. It is built like all Turkish towns, with this exception—that the streets are rather broad, and kept clean. Outside the town are numerous large fruit and vegetable gardens, which are surrounded by very high walls; pretty dwelling-houses stand in the centre of the gardens.

The women here go closely veiled. They cover over their heads and breast with a white kerchief, in which thick impenetrable network is inserted, at the places opposite the eyes.

In the houses of the poorer classes two or three families live under one roof. They possess little more than straw mats, blankets, pillows, and a few cooking utensils, not to forget a large wooden box in which the meal, their chief property, is kept. Here as everywhere else where corn is cultivated, bread is the principal food of the common people. Every family bake twice daily, morning and evening.

Many of the small houses have very pretty courts, which are planted with flowers, vines, and shrubs, and looked like gardens.

The dwellings of the wealthy are lofty, airy, and spacious; the reception rooms have a large number of windows, and are covered with carpets. I saw no divans, people always lie upon the carpets. As we made the visits without being invited, we found the women in very plain coloured cotton dresses, of course, made in their own fashion.

In the afternoon I rode with the missionaries to their large country-house, which is situated about six miles from the town, on some low hills. The valley through which we rode was very large, and altogether well cultivated and delightful. Although it is said to lie about 4,000 feet above the level of the sea, cotton, castor-oil plants, vines, tobacco, and every kind of fruit grow here as in South Germany. The castor-oil plant, indeed, is not more than four feet high, and the cotton but one foot; they produce, however, rather abundantly. Several villages are half hid in orchards. I came into this country at a fortunate time: there were beautiful peaches, apricots, apples, grapes, etc., true fruits of my native country, of which I had long been deprived.

The house of the missionary society is most charmingly situated; it commands a view of the whole valley, the town, the low range of hills, and the mountains. The

294

house itself is large, and furnished with every possible convenience, so that I thought I was in the country-house of wealthy private people, and not under the roof of simple disciples of Christ. There were four women here, and a whole troop of children, great and small. I passed several very pleasant hours among them, and was heartily sorry that I was obliged to take leave of them at 9 in the evening.

Several native girls were also introduced to me who were educated by the wives of the missionaries. They spoke and wrote a little English, and were well acquainted with geography. I cannot avoid, on this occasion, making some observations with regard to the missionaries, whose mode of life and labours I had frequent opportunities of observing during my journey. I met with missionaries in Persia, China, and India, and everywhere found them living in a very different manner to what I had imagined.

In my opinion the missionaries were almost, if not complete martyrs, and I thought that they were so absorbed with zeal and the desire to convert the heathen, that, like the disciples of Christ, quite forgetting their comforts and necessaries, they dwelt with them under one roof, and ate from one dish, etc. Alas! these were pictures and representations which I had gathered out of books; in reality the case was very different. They lead the same kind of life as the wealthy: they have handsome dwellings, which are fitted up with luxurious furniture, and every convenience. They recline upon easy divans, while their wives preside at the tea-table, and the children attack the cakes and sweetmeats heartily; indeed their position is pleasanter and freer from care than that of most people; their occupation is not very laborious, and their income is certain, whatever may be the national or political condition of their country.

In places where several missionaries reside meetings are held three or four times a week. These meetings or assemblies are supposed to be for the transaction of business; but are not much other than soirées, at which the ladies and children make their appearance in elegant full dress. One missionary receives his friends at breakfast, a second at dinner, the third at tea, several equipages and a number of servants stand in the court-yard.

Business is also attended to: the gentleman generally retire for half an hour or so; but the greater part of the time is passed in mere social amusement.

I do not think that it can be easy to gain the confidence of the natives in this way. Their foreign dress, and elegant mode of life, make the people feel too strongly the difference of rank, and inspire them with fear and reserve rather than confidence and love. They do not so readily venture to look up to people of wealth or rank, and the missionaries have consequently to exert themselves for some time until this timidity is overcome. The missionaries say that it is necessary to make this appearance, in order to create an impression and command respect; but I think that respect may be inspired by noble conduct, and that virtue will attract men more than external splendour.

Many of the missionaries believe that they might effect a great deal by preaching and issuing religious tracts in the native language in the towns and villages. They give the most attractive report of the multitude of people who crowd to hear their preaching and receive their tracts, and it might reasonably be thought that, according to their representations, at least half of their hearers would become converts to Christianity; but unfortunately the listening and receiving tracts is as good as no proof at all. Would not Chinese, Indian, or Persian priests have just as great troops of hearers if they appeared in their respective national costume in England or France, and preached in the language of those countries? Would not people flock round them? would they not receive the tracts given out gratis, even if they could not read them?

I have made the minutest inquiries in all places respecting the results of missions, and have always heard that a baptism is one of the greatest rarities. The few Christians in India, who here and there form villages of twenty or thirty families, have resulted principally from orphan children, who had been adopted and brought up by the missionaries; but even these require to be supplied with work, and comfortably attended to, in order to prevent them from falling back into their superstitions.

Preaching and tracts are insufficient to make religious doctrine understandable, or to shake the superstitions which have been imbibed in infancy. Missionaries must live among the people as fathers or friends, labour with them—in short, share their trials and pleasures, and draw them towards them by an exemplary and unpretending mode of life, and gradually instruct them in a way they are capable of understanding. They ought not to be married to Europeans for the following reasons:—European girls who are educated for missionaries frequently make this their choice only that they be provided for as soon as possible. If a young European wife has any children, if she is weak or delicate, they are then unable to attend any longer to their calling, and require a change of air, or even a journey to Europe. The children also are weak, and must be taken there, at latest in their seventh year. Their father accompanies them, and makes use of this pretext to return to Europe for some time. If it is not possible to undertake this journey, they go to some mountainous country, where it is cooler, or he takes his wife and family to visit a Mela. {287} At the same time, it must be remembered that these journeys are not made in a very simple manner: as mine has been, for instance; the missionary surrounds himself with numerous conveniences; he has palanquins carried by men, pack-horses, or camels, with tents, beds, culinary, and table utensils; servants and maids in sufficient number. And who pays for all this? Frequently poor credulous souls in Europe and North America, who often deny themselves the necessaries of life, that their little savings may be squandered in this way in distant parts of the world.

If the missionaries were married to natives, the greater part of these expenses and requirements would be unnecessary; there would be few sick wives, the children would be strong and healthy, and would not require to be taken to Europe.

296

Schools might be established here and there for their education, although not in such a luxurious manner as those at Calcutta.

I hope that my views may not be misunderstood; I have great respect for missionaries, and all whom I have known were honourable men, and good fathers; I am also convinced that there are many learned men among them, who make valuable contributions to history and philosophy, but whether they thus fulfil their proper object is another question. I should consider that a missionary has other duties than those of a philosopher.

For my own part, I can only express my obligations to the missionaries; everywhere they showed me the greatest kindness and attention. Their mode of life certainly struck me, because I involuntarily associate with the name "missionary" those men who at first went out into the world, without support, to diffuse the doctrines of Christ, taking nothing with them but a pilgrim's staff.

Before concluding my description of Oromia, I must remark that this neighbourhood is considered to be the birth-place of Zoroaster, who is said to have lived 5,500 years before the birth of Christ, and was the founder of the sect of Magi, or fire-worshippers.

On the 1st of August, I rode ten hours to the village of Kutschié, which lies near the Lake Oromia; we seldom caught sight of the lake, although we were always very near to it all day. We passed through large, fertile villages, which would have presented a charming prospect if they had not been situated between barren and naked hills and mountains.

I had not enjoyed so pleasant a day during the whole journey from Mósul, or from Baghdad. My guide was a remarkably good fellow, very attentive to me, and provided everything carefully when we reached Kutschié; he took me to a very cleanly peasant's cottage, among some excellent people; they immediately laid down a nice carpet for me on a small terrace, brought me a basin of water to wash, and a quantity of large black mulberries on a lacquered plate. Afterwards I had some strong soup with meat, fat, sour milk, and good bread, all in clean vessels; but what was better than all, the people retired as soon as they had set the food before me, and did not stare at me as if I was a strange animal. When I offered to pay these good people, they would not take anything; I had no opportunity of rewarding them until the following morning, when I took two men of the family as guard across the mountains, and gave them twice as much as they are generally paid; they thanked me, with touching cordiality, and wished me safety and good fortune on my journey.

2nd August. It occupied three hours to pass the most dangerous part of these desolate mountains. My two armed men would not, indeed, have afforded me much protection against a band of robbers, although they were the means of making the journey less terrible than it would have been if I had gone with my old guide alone. We met several large caravans, but all going towards Oromia.

297

When we had crossed the mountains, the two men left us. We entered into enormous valleys, which seemed to have been forgotten by nature, and deserted by man. In my opinion, we were not in any degree out of the danger, and I was right; for, as we were passing three ruined cottages in this barren valley, several fellows rushed out upon us, laid hold of our horses' reins, and commenced rummaging my luggage. I expected nothing but an order to dismount, and already saw my little property lost. They talked with my guide, who told them the tale which I had imposed upon him—that I was a poor pilgrim, and that the English consuls or missionaries paid all my travelling expenses. My dress, the smallness of my baggage, and being alone, agreed perfectly with this; they believed him, and my silent supplicative look, and let me go; they even asked me if I would have some water, of which there is a scarcity in these villages. I begged them for a draught, and so we parted good friends. Nevertheless I was for some time fearful that they might repent their generosity and follow us.

We came to the shores of the lake again today, and continued to travel for some time at its side. After a ride of fourteen hours, we rested at a chan in the village of Schech-Vali.

3rd August. The oppressive sense of fear was now at an end. We passed through peaceful inhabited valleys, where the people were working in the fields, carrying home corn, tending cattle, etc.

During the hot noon hours we rested at Dise-halil, a rather considerable town, with very clean streets; the principal street is intersected by a clear brook, and the court-yards of the houses resemble gardens. Here also I saw outside the town a great number of very large gardens surrounded by high walls.

From the number of chans, this town would appear to be very much visited. In the small street through which we passed, I counted more than half a dozen. We dismounted at one of them, and I was quite astonished at the conveniences which I found there. The stalls were covered; the sleeping-places for the drivers were on pretty walled terraces; and the rooms for travellers, although destitute of all furniture, were very clean, and furnished with stoves. The chans were open to every one, and there is nothing to pay for using them; at the utmost, a small trifle is given to the overseer, who provides the travellers' meals.

In this respect, the Persians, Turks, and the so-called uncultivated people, are much more generous than we are. In India, for example, where the English build bungalows, travellers must pay a rupee per night, or even for an hour, which does not include any provision for the driver or the animals: they are obliged to take their rest in the open air. The travellers who are not Christians are not allowed to come into most of the bungalows at all; in a few they are admitted, but only when the rooms are not required by a Christian; if, however, one should arrive at night, the poor unbeliever is obliged to turn out for him without pity. This humane custom extends also to the open bungalows, which consist only of a roof and three wooden walls. In the countries of the unbelievers, however, those who come first have the place, whether they are Christians, Turks, or Arabs; indeed, I am firmly convinced, that if all the places were occupied by unbelievers, and a Christian was to come, they would make room for him.

In the afternoon, we went as far as Ali-Schach, a considerable place, with a handsome chan.

We here met with three travellers, who were also going to Tebris. My guide agreed to travel with them, and that we should start at night. Their society was not very agreeable to me, for they were well armed, and looked very savage. I should have preferred waiting until daybreak, and going without them, but my guide assured me that they were honest people; and trusting more to my good fortune than his word, I mounted my horse about 1 o'clock at night.

4th August. I soon lost my fear, for we frequently met small parties of three or four persons, who would scarcely have ventured to travel at night if the road had been dangerous. Large caravans also, of several hundred camels, passed us and took up the road in such a way, that we were obliged to wait for half an hour to allow them to pass.

Towards noon we entered a valley in which lay a town, which was certainly large, but of such an unpretending appearance, that I did not at once inquire what was its name. The nearer we approached the more ruined it appeared. The walls were half fallen, the streets and squares full of heaps of rubbish, and many of the houses were in ruins; it seemed as if a pestilence or an enemy had destroyed it. At last I asked its name, and could hardly believe that I had understood it rightly when I was told that it was Tebris.

My guide conducted me to the house of Mr. Stevens, the English consul, who, to my vexation, was not in the town, but ten miles away in the country. A servant, however, told me that he would go directly to a gentleman who could speak English. In a very short time he came, and his first questions were: "How did you come here, *alone?* Have you been robbed? Have you parted from your company and only left them in the town?" But when I gave him my pass, and explained everything to him, he appeared scarcely to believe me. He thought it bordered upon the fabulous that a woman should have succeeded, without any knowledge of the language, in penetrating through such countries and such people. I also could not be too thankful for the evident protection which Providence had afforded me. I felt myself as happy and lively as if I had taken a new lease of my life.

Doctor Cassolani showed me to some rooms in Mr. Stevens's house, and said that he would immediately send a messenger to him, and I might meanwhile make known my wants to him.

When I expressed to him my astonishment at the miserable appearance and ugly entrance to this town, the second in the country, he told me that the town could not be well seen from the side at which I came in, and that the part which I saw was not considered the town, but was chiefly old and, for the most part, deserted.

CHAPTER XXI. SOJOURN IN TEBRIS.

*DESCRIPTION OF THE TOWN—THE TOWN—PERIOD OF FASTING—
BEHMEN MIRZA—ANECDOTES OF THE PERSIAN GOVERNMENT—
INTRODUCTION TO THE VICEROY AND HIS WIFE—BEHMEN
MIRZA'S WIVES—VISIT TO A PERSIAN LADY—PERSECUTION OF
THE LOWER CLASSES, OF THE CHRISTIANS, AND OF THE JEWS—
DEPARTURE.*

Tebris, or Tauris, is the capital of the province of Aderbeidschan, and the
residence of the successor to the throne of Persia, who bears the title of Viceroy.
It is situated in a treeless valley on the rivers Piatscha and Atschi, and contains
160,000 inhabitants. The town is handsomer than Teheran or Ispahan, possesses a
number of silk looms and leather manufactories, and is said to be one of the
principal seats of Asiatic commerce.

The streets are tolerably broad, and are also kept clean, there is in each an
underground water canal with openings at regular intervals for the purpose of
dipping out water.

There is no more to be seen of the houses than in any other Oriental town. Lofty
walls with low entrances, without windows, and with the fronts always facing the
court-yards, which are planted with flowers and small trees, and generally
adjoining a beautiful garden. The reception rooms are large and lofty, with whole
rows of windows, forming a complete wall of glass. The decoration of the rooms
is not elegant, generally nothing beyond some few carpets; European furniture
and articles of luxury are rare.

There are no handsome mosques, palaces, or monuments, either ancient or
modern, with the exception of the partly ruined mosque of Ali-Schach, which,
however, will not bear comparison in any respect with those in India.

The new bazaar is very handsome, its lofty, broad covered streets and passages
forcibly called to my remembrance the bazaar at Constantinople; but it had a
more pleasant appearance as it is newer. The merchant's stalls also are larger, and
the wares, although not so magnificent and rich as some travellers represent, are
more tastefully displayed and can be more easily overlooked, especially the
carpets, fruits, and vegetables. The cookshops also looked very inviting, and the
various dishes seemed so palatable and diffused such a savoury odour, that I could
have sat down with pleasure and partaken of them. The shoe department, on the
contrary, presented nothing attractive; there were only goods of the plainest
description exposed; while in Constantinople the most costly shoes and slippers,

300

richly embroidered with gold, and even ornamented with pearls and precious stones, are to be seen under glass cases.

I had arrived at Tebris at a rather unfavourable time—namely, the fast month. From sunrise to sunset nothing is eaten, nobody leaves the house, there are neither visits nor company—indeed, nothing but praying. This ceremony is so strictly observed that invalids frequently fall victims to it, as they will take neither medicine nor food during the day; they believe that if they were to eat only a mouthful, they would forfeit the salvation to be obtained by fasting. Many of the more enlightened make an exception to this custom in cases of illness; however, in such an instance the physician must send a written declaration to the priest, in which he explains the necessity of taking medicine and food. If the priest puts his seal to this document, pardon is obtained. I am not aware whether this granting of indulgences was taken by the Mahomedans from the Christians, or the reverse. Girls are obliged to keep these fasts after their tenth year, and boys after their fifteenth.

It was to the courteousness of Dr. Cassolani, and his intimacy with some of the principal families in Tebris, that I was indebted for my introduction to them, and even for my presentation at court, notwithstanding the strict observance of the fast.

There was no viceroy in Tebris until about six months since, but only a governor; the present reigning schach, Nesr-I-Din, raised the province of Aderbeidschan to a vice-royalty, and decreed that every eldest son of the future inheritor of the empire should reside here as viceroy until he came to the throne.

The last governor of Tebris, Behmen Mirza, the schach's brother, was a remarkably intelligent and just man. He brought the province of Aderbeidschan into a flourishing condition in a few years, and everywhere established order and security. This soon excited the envy of the prime minister Haggi-Mirza-Aagassi; he urged the schach to recall his brother, and represented to him that he would engage the affections of the people too much, and that he might at last make himself king.

For a long time the schach paid no attention to these insinuations, for he loved his brother sincerely; but the minister did not rest until he had attained his wishes. Behmen Mirza, who knew all that was going on at court, hastened to Teheran for the purpose of exculpating himself before the schach. The latter assured him of his love and confidence, and told him, candidly, that he might retain his office if the minister would consent to it, and recommended him to endeavour to gain his favour.

Behmen Mirza learnt, however, through his friends, that the minister entertained an inveterate hatred towards him, and that he ran the risk of being deprived of his sight, or even made away with altogether. They advised him to lose no time, but quit the country immediately. He followed their advice, returned quickly to Tebris, gathered his valuables together, and fled with a part of his family to the neighbouring Russian dominions. Having arrived there, he appealed to the Emperor of Russia by letter, soliciting his protection, which was magnanimously afforded to him. The emperor wrote to the schach declaring that the prince was no longer a Persian subject, and that therefore every persecution of himself or his family must cease; he also provided him with a pretty palace near Tiflis, sent him costly presents, and, as I was informed, allowed him a yearly pension of 20,000 ducats.

It may be seen from this circumstance that the minister completely governed the schach; indeed he succeeded to such an extent, that the schach honoured him as a prophet, and unconditionally carried out all his suggestions. He was, on one occasion, desirous of effecting some very important object. He told the schach, at a morning visit, that he woke in the night and felt himself being carried upwards. He went up higher and higher, and finally entered heaven, where he saw and spoke with the king's father, who requested him to describe the government of his son. The deceased king was greatly rejoiced to hear of his good conduct, and recommended that he should continue to go on thus. The delighted king, who had cordially loved his father, did not cease from asking further questions, and the artful minister always contrived to bring in at the end of his answers—"It was only this or that thing that the father wished to see done," and of course the good son fulfilled his father's wishes, not for one moment doubting the assertions of his minister.

The king is said to be rather passionate, and when in such a state of mind, will order the immediate execution of an offender. The minister, on the other hand, possesses at least enough sense of justice to endeavour to stay the sentence of death upon men whom he does not fear. He has, therefore, given orders that when such a circumstance occurs, he is to be sent for immediately, and that the preparations for the execution are to be delayed until he comes. He makes his appearance then as if accidentally, and asks what is going on. The enraged sovereign tells him that he is about to have an offender executed. The minister agrees with him completely, and steps to the window to consult the sky, clouds, and sun. Presently he cries out that it would be better to postpone the execution until the following day, as the clouds, sun, or sky at the present moment are not favourable to it, and that some misfortune to the king might probably result from it. In the meanwhile, the king's rage abates, and he consents that the condemned should be taken away, and generally, that he shall be set free; the next morning the whole affair is forgotten.

The following circumstance is also interesting; the king had once a particular hatred for one of his town governors, and ordered him to the capital, with the intention of having him strangled. The minister, who was a friend of the governor, was desirous of saving him, and did so in the following manner. He said to the king, "Sire, I bid you farewell, I am going to Mecca." The king, greatly grieved at the prospect of losing his favourite for so long (the journey to Mecca

302

takes at least a year), hastily asked the reason of his making this journey. "You know, sire, that I am childless, and that I have adopted the governor whom you wish to have executed; I shall then lose my son, and I wish to fetch another from Mecca." The king answered that he knew nothing of this, but as such was the case he would not have him executed, but allow him to retain his office.

The king has a great affection for his mother. When she visited him, he always rose and continued standing, while she sat down. The minister was much annoyed at this mark of respect, and said to him, "You are king, and your mother must stand before you." And he ultimately succeeded according to his wish. If, however, the king's mother comes at a time when the minister is not present, her son pays her this respect. He then gives strict orders to his people not to say anything of it to the minister.

I was told these and other things by a very trustworthy person, and they may serve to give my readers some slight idea of the system of government in Persia.

I was presented to the viceroy a few days after my arrival. I was conducted one afternoon by Dr. Cassolani to one of the royal summer-houses. The house was situated in a small garden, which was surrounded by another larger one, both enclosed by very high walls. In the outer garden there were, besides meadows and fruit trees, nothing deserving of much notice, except a number of tents, in which the military were encamped. The soldiers wore the usual Persian dress, with the single exception that the officers on duty had a sword, and the soldiers a musket. They only appear in uniform on the most rare occasions, and then they are, in some respects, like European soldiers.

Several eunuchs received us at the entrance of the small garden. They conducted us to an unpretending looking house, one story high, at the end of a field of flowers. I should never have looked for the country seat of the successor to the Persian throne in this house; but such it was. At the narrow entrance of the little house were two small flights of stairs, one of which led to the reception-room of the viceroy, the other to that of his wife. The doctor entered the former and several female slaves took me to the viceroy's wife. When I reached the top of the stairs, I took off my shoes, and entered a small, comfortable room, the walls of which consisted almost entirely of windows. The viceroy's wife, who was only fifteen years of age, sat upon a plain easy chair, not far from her stood a middle-aged woman, the duenna of the harem, and an easy chair was placed for me opposite the princess.

I was fortunate enough to be remarkably well received. Dr. Cassolani had described me as an authoress, adding that I intended to publish the experiences of my journey. The princess inquired whether I should mention her also, and when she was answered in the affirmative, she determined to show herself in full dress, in order to give me an idea of the gorgeous and costly dress of her country.

The young princess wore trousers of thick silk, which were so full of plaits that they stood out stiff, like the hooped petticoats of our good old times. These trousers are from twenty to five and twenty yards wide, and reach down to the ankle. The upper part of the body was covered as far as the hips by a bodice, which, however, did not fit close to the body. The sleeves were long and narrow. The corset resembled that of the time of the hooped petticoats; it was made of thick silk, richly and tastefully embroidered round the corners with coloured silk and gold. A very short white silk chemise was to be seen under the corset. On her head she wore a three-cornered white kerchief, extending in front round the face, and fastened under the chin; behind, it fell down as far as the shoulders. This kerchief was also very handsomely embroidered with gold and silk. The jewellery consisted of precious stones and pearls of great purity and size; but they had not much effect, as they were not set in gold, but simply perforated and strung upon a gold thread, which was fastened above the head kerchief, and came down under the chin.

The princess had on black silk open-worked gloves, over which were several finger rings. Round the wrists sparkled costly bracelets of precious stones and pearls. On her feet she wore white silk stockings.

She was not remarkably beautiful; her cheek bones were rather too prominent; but altogether her appearance was very attractive. Her eyes were large, handsome, and intellectual, her figure pretty, and her age—fifteen years.

Her face was a very delicate white and red; and the eyebrows were covered with blue streaks, which, in my opinion, rather disfigured than adorned them. On the temple a little of her brilliant black hair was to be seen.

Our conversation was carried on by signs. Dr. Cassolani, who spoke Persian very well, was not allowed to cross the threshold today, and the princess had received me, consequently, unveiled. During this stupid interview, I found time enough to look at the distant view from the windows. It was here that I first saw how extensive the town was, and what an abundance of gardens it possessed. The latter are, indeed, its peculiar ornament, for it contains no fine buildings; and the large valley in which it lies, together with the mountains round, are naked and barren, and present no attractions. I expressed my surprise at the great size of the town and the number of the gardens.

Towards the end of the audience, a quantity of fruits and sweetmeats were brought, of which, however, I alone partook—it being fast time.

Leaving the princess, I was conducted to her husband, the viceroy. He was seventeen, and received me seated upon an easy chair at a bow-window. I had to thank my character of authoress, that a chair was placed ready for me. The walls of the large room were panelled with wood, and ornamented with several mirrors, gilt-work, and oil-paintings of heads and flowers. In the middle of the saloon stood two large empty bedsteads.

The prince wore a European dress: trousers of fine white cloth, with broad gold lace; a dark blue coat, the collar, facings, and corners of which were richly embroidered with gold; white silk gloves and stockings. His head was covered by a Persian fur cap nearly a yard high. This is not, however, his ordinary dress; he is said to change his mode of dressing oftener than his wife, and sometimes to wear the Persian costume, sometimes to envelop himself in cashmere shawls, as his fancy may be.

I should have supposed that he was at least twenty-two. He has a pale, tawny complexion, and, altogether, no attractive, amiable, or intellectual expression; never looks straightforward and openly at you, and his glance is savage and repulsive. I pitied, in my mind, all those who were his subjects. I would rather be the wife of a poor peasant than his favourite princess.

The prince put several questions to me, which Dr. Cassolani, who stood a few paces from us, interpreted. They were nothing remarkable, chiefly common-places about my journey. The prince can read and write in his mother tongue, and has, as I was told, some idea of geography and history. He receives a few European newspapers and periodicals from which the interpreter has to make extracts, and read to him. His opinion of the great revolutions of the time was, that the European monarchs might have been very good, but they were most remarkably stupid to allow themselves to be so easily driven from the throne. He considered that the result would have been very different if they had had plenty of people strangled. As far as regards execution and punishment, he far exceeds his father; and, unfortunately, has no controlling minister at his side. His government is said to be that of a child; one moment he orders something to be done, and an hour afterwards countermands it. But what can be expected from a youth of seventeen, who has received little or no education; was married at fifteen, and, two years afterwards, takes the unlimited control of a large province with a revenue of a million tomans (£500,000), and with every means of gratifying his desires.

The prince has at present only one regular wife, although he is allowed to have four; however, he has no scarcity of handsome female friends. It is the custom in Persia, that when the king, or the successor to the throne, hears that any one of his subjects has a handsome daughter or sister, he demands her. The parents or relations are greatly rejoiced at this command, for if the girl is really handsome, she is, in any case, well provided for. If, after some time, she no longer pleases the king or prince, she is married to some minister or rich man; but, if she has a child, she is immediately considered as the king's or prince's acknowledged wife, and remains permanently at court. When, on the contrary, a girl does not please the regent at first sight, her family are very much disappointed, and consider themselves unfortunate. She is, in this case, sent home again immediately, her reputation for beauty is lost, and she has not, after this, much chance of making a good match.

The princess is already a mother, but, unfortunately, only of a daughter. She is, for the present, the chief wife of the prince, because no other female has given birth

305

to a son; but whoever brings the first son into the world will then take her place: she will be honoured as the mother of the heir to the throne. In consequence of this custom, the children are unfortunately liable to the danger of being poisoned; for any woman who has a child excites the envy of all those who are childless; and this is more particularly the case when the child is a boy. When the princess accompanied her husband to Tebris, she left her little daughter behind, under the protection of its grandfather, the Schach of Persia, in order to secure it from her rivals.

When the viceroy rides out, he is preceded by several hundred soldiers. They are followed by servants with large sticks, who call upon the people to bow before the powerful ruler. The prince is surrounded by officers, military, and servants, and the procession is closed by more soldiers. The prince only is mounted, all the rest are on foot.

The prince's wives are also permitted to ride out at times, but they are obliged to be thickly veiled, and entirely surrounded by eunuchs, several of whom hasten on before, to tell the people that the wives of the monarch are on the road. Every one must then leave the streets, and retire into the houses and bye-lanes.

The wives of the banished prince, Behmen, who were left behind, learnt, through Dr. Cassolani, that I thought of going to Tiflis. They requested me to visit them, that I might be able to tell the prince that I had seen them and left them well. The doctor conducted me into their presence. He had been the friend and physician of the prince, who was not one of the fanatic class, and allowed him the *entrée* to the females.

Nothing very worthy of notice took place at this visit. The house and garden were plain, and the women had wrapped themselves in large mantles, as the doctor was present, some, indeed, covered a part of their faces while speaking with him. Several of them were young, although they all appeared older than they really were. One, who was twenty-two, I should have taken to be at least thirty. A rather plump dark beauty of sixteen was also introduced to me as the latest addition to the harem. She had been bought at Constantinople only a short time since. The women appeared to treat her with great good-nature; they told me that they took considerable pains to teach her Persian.

Among the children there was a remarkably beautiful girl of six, whose pure and delicate countenance was fortunately not yet disfigured by paint. This child, as well as the others, was dressed in the same way as the women; and I remarked that the Persian dress was really, as I had been told, rather indecorous. The corset fell back at every quick movement; the silk or gauze chemise, which scarcely reached over the breast, dragged up so high that the whole body might be seen as far as the loins. I observed the same with the female servants, who were engaged in making tea or other occupations; every motion disarranged their dress.

My visit to Haggi-Chefa-Hanoum, one of the principal and most-cultivated women in Tebris, was far more interesting. Even at the entrance of the court-yard and house, the presence of a well-regulating mind might be perceived. I had never seen so much cleanliness and taste in any Oriental house. I should have taken the court-yard for the garden, if I had not afterwards seen the latter from the windows. The gardens here are, indeed, inferior to ours, but are magnificent when compared with those at Baghdad. They have flowers, rows of vines and shrubs, and between the fruit-trees pleasant basins of water and luxuriant grass-plots.

The reception-room was very large and lofty; the front and back (of which the former looked out into the court-yard, the latter into the garden), consisted of windows, the panes of which were in very small six and eight-sided pieces, framed in gilded wood; on the door-posts there was also some gilding. The floor was covered with carpeting; and at the place where the mistress of the house sat, another piece of rich carpet was laid over. In Persia, there are no divans, but only thick round pillows for leaning upon.

Intimation had previously been given of my visit. I found a large party of women and young girls assembled, who had probably been attracted here by their curiosity to see a European woman. Their dress was costly, like that of the princess, but there was a difference in the jewellery. Several among them were very handsome, although they had rather broad foreheads, and too prominent cheek-bones. The most charming features of the Persians are their eyes, which are remarkable, as well for their size as their beautiful form and animated expression. Of course, there was no want of paint on their skins and eye-brows.

This party of women was the most agreeable and unconstrained that I ever found in Oriental houses. I was able to converse in French with the mistress of the house, by the help of her son, of about eighteen, who had received an excellent education in Constantinople. Not only the son, but also the mother and the other women, were read and well-informed. Dr. Cassolani, moreover, assured me that the girls of rich families could nearly all read and write. They are, in this respect, far in advance of the Turks.

The mistress of the house, her son, and myself, sat upon chairs, the rest squatted down on carpets round us. A table, the first that I had seen in a Persian house, was covered with a handsome cloth, and set out with the most magnificent fruits, sherbets, and various delicacies, which had been prepared by my host herself; among the sweetmeats were sugared almonds and fruits, which not only appeared inviting, but tasted deliciously.

The sweet melons and peaches were just in their prime during my stay at Tebris. They were so delicious, that it may well be said Persia is their native country. The melons have more frequently a whitish, or greenish, than a yellow pulp. They may be eaten entirely, with the exception of the outermost thin rind; and, if it were possible for anything to exceed sugar in sweetness, it would be these melons. The peaches are also juicy, sweet, and aromatic.

Before leaving Tebris, I must say a few words about the people. The complexion of the common men is rather more than sunburnt; among the upper classes, white is the prevailing colour of the skin. They all have black hair and eyes. Their figures are tall and powerful, the features very marked—especially the nose—and the look rather wild. The women, both of the upper and lower classes, are uncommonly thickly veiled when they go out. The better-dressed men wear, out of doors, a very long mantle of dark cloth with slashed sleeves, which reach to the ground; a girdle or shawl surrounds their waist, and their head-dress consists of a pointed black fur cap more than a foot high, which is made of the skins of unborn sheep. The women of the labouring class do not appear to have much to do; during my journey, I saw only a few at work in the fields, and I noticed also in the town that all the hard work is done by the men.

In Tebris, as well as throughout the whole of Persia, the Jews, semi-Mahomedans, and Christians, are intolerably hated. Three months since, the Jews and Christians in Tebris were in great danger. Several crowds of people gathered together and marched through the quarter where these people dwelt, when they commenced plundering and destroying the houses, threatening the inhabitants with death, and, in some cases, even putting their threats into execution. Fortunately, this horrible proceeding was immediately made known to the governor of the town; and he, being a brave and determined man, lost not a moment's time even to throw his kaftan over his house-dress, but hastened out into the midst of the crowd, and succeeded, by means of a powerful speech, in dispersing the people.

On arriving at Tebris, I expressed my desire to continue my journey from here to Tiflis by way of Natschivan and Erivan. It appeared at first that there was not much hope of its possibility, as, since the late political disturbances in Europe, the Russian government, like the Chinese, had strictly prohibited the entrance of any foreigners; however, Mr. Stevens promised to make use of all his power with the Russian consul, Mr. Anitschow, in my favour. I was indebted to this, together with my sex and age, for being made an exception. I received from the Russian consul not only the permission, but also several kind letters of introduction to people at Natschivan, Erivan, and Tiflis.

I was advised to ride from Tebris to Natschivan with post-horses, and to take a servant with me as far as that place. I did so, and commenced my journey at 9 o'clock in the morning of the 11th of August. Several gentlemen, whose acquaintance I had made in Tebris, accompanied me about a mile out of the town, and we encamped on the bank of a beautiful little river, and partook of a cold breakfast. Then I began my journey alone, indeed, but composedly and with good courage, for now I thought I was entering a Christian country, beneath the sceptre of a civilized, European, law and order-loving monarch.

CHAPTER XXII. ASIATIC RUSSIA—ARMENIA, GEORGIA, AND MINGRELIA.

SOPHIA—MARAND—THE RUSSIAN FRONTIER—NATSCHIVAN— JOURNEY OF THE CARAVAN—A NIGHT'S IMPRISONMENT— CONTINUATION OF THE JOURNEY—ERIVAN—THE RUSSIAN POST —THE TARTARS—ARRIVAL IN TIFLIS—SOJOURN THERE— CONTINUATION OF THE JOURNEY—KUTAIS—MARAND—TRIP ON THE RIBON—REDUTKALE.

11th August. The stations between Tebris and Natschivan are very irregular; one of the longest, however, is the first—namely, to the village of Sophia, which occupied us six hours. The road lay through valleys, which were, for the most part, barren and uninhabited.

As it was already 3 o'clock when we reached Sophia, the people there endeavoured to prevent me from going any further. They pointed to the sun, and at the same time signified that I might be attacked by robbers, plundered, and even murdered; but such statements had no influence with me; and after I had with great trouble ascertained that it would only require four hours to reach the next station, I determined to continue my journey; and to the vexation of my servant, whom I had engaged as far as Natschivan, ordered him to saddle fresh horses.

Immediately after leaving Sophia, we entered barren, rocky valleys, which my guide represented as being very dangerous, and which I should not have liked to pass at night; but as the sun was shining in full splendour, I urged on my horse, and amused myself by looking at the beautiful colours and grouping of the rocks. Some were of a glittering pale green; others covered with a whitish, half transparent substance; others again terminated in numerous oddly formed angles, and from the distance looked like beautiful groups of trees. There was so much to see that I really had no time to think of fear.

About half-way lay a pretty little village in a valley, and beyond it rose a steep mountain, on the summit of which a charming prospect of mountain country kept me gazing for a long while.

We did not reach Marand till nearly 8 o'clock; but still with our heads, necks, and baggage, all safe.

Marand lies in a fertile valley, and is the last Persian town which I saw, and one of the most agreeable and handsome. It has broad, clean streets, houses in good repair, and several small squares with beautiful springs, which are, moreover, surrounded by trees.

My shelter for the night was not so good as the town promised: I was obliged to share the court with the post-horses. My supper consisted of some roasted and very salt eggs.

12th August. Our journey for today was as far as Arax, on the Russian frontier. Although only one stage, it took us eleven hours. We followed the course of a small brook, which wound through barren valleys and ravines; not a single village lay on our road; and with the exception of some little mills and the ruins of a mosque, I saw no more buildings in Persia. Persia is, on the whole, very thinly populated, on account of the scarcity of water. No country in the world has more mountains, and fewer rivers, than Persia. The air is, on this account, very dry and hot.

The valley in which Arax is situated is large, and the extraordinary formation of the mountains and rocks renders it very picturesque. In the extreme distance rise lofty mountains, of which Ararat is more than 16,000 feet in height, and in the valley itself there are numerous rocky elevations. The principal of these, a beautiful sharp rocky cone, of at least 1,000 feet in height, is called the Serpent Mountain.

The river Aras flows close to the headland. It separates Armenia from Media, has a terrible fall, and high waves. It here forms the boundary between the Russian and Persian dominions. We crossed in a boat. On the opposite side of the river were several small houses where travellers are obliged to stop and prove that they are not robbers, and especially that they are not politically dangerous. Occasionally they are detained in quarantine for some time, when the plague or cholera happens to be prevalent in Persia.

A letter from the Russian consul at Tebris ensured me a very courteous reception; from the quarantine I was saved, as there was no plague or cholera. I had, however, scarcely set my foot upon Russian ground, when the impudent begging for drink-money began. The officer had among his people a Cossack, who represented himself as understanding German, and he was sent to me to ask what I wished for. The rogue knew about as much German as I did Chinese—hardly three or four words. I therefore signified to him that I did not require his services, in spite of which he held out his hand, begging for money.

13th August. I left Arax betimes in the morning, in company with a customs' officer, and rode to the town of Natschivan, which lies in a large valley, surrounded by the lofty mountains of Ararat. The country here is fertile, but there are very few trees.

I never had so much trouble to obtain shelter in any place as in this. I had two letters, one to a German physician, the other to the governor. I did not wish to go to the latter in my travelling dress, as I was again among cultivated people, who are accustomed to judge of you by your dress, and there was no inn. I therefore intended to ask accommodation in the doctor's house. I showed the address, which was written in the native language, to several people to read, that they might point out the house to me; but they all shook their heads, and let me go on.

At last I came to the custom-house, where my little luggage was immediately taken possession of, and myself conducted to the inspector. He spoke a little German, but paid no regard to my request. He told me to go into the custom-house, and unlock my portmanteau.

The inspector's wife and sister accompanied me. I was much astonished at this politeness, but found, however, too soon that other reasons had induced them to come—both the ladies wished to see what I had brought with me. They had chairs brought, and took their places before my portmanteau, which was opened, when three pair of hands were thrust in. A number of papers folded together, coins, dried flowers, and other objects, obtained from Nineveh, were instantly seized hold of, and thrown about; every ribbon, every cap, was taken out; and it was clearly perceptible that the inspector's wife had some difficulty in parting with them again.

After this was sufficiently examined, a common box, which contained my greatest treasure, a small relief from Nineveh, was brought forward. One of the men took hold of a heavy wooden axe, for the purpose of striking off the lid. This was rather too much for me, and I would not allow it. To my great satisfaction, a German woman came in just at this moment. I told her what was in the box, and that I did not object to its being opened, although I wished them to do it carefully with a chisel and pincers; but, strange to say, there were no such tools in the place, although they were wanted daily. I at last succeeded in persuading them to break off the lid with care. Notwithstanding the anxiety I was in, I could not help laughing at the foolish faces which both the women and the customs' officer made when they saw the fragments of brick from Babylon, and the somewhat damaged Ninevite head. They could not at all comprehend why I should carry such objects with me.

The German woman, Henriette Alexandwer, invited me to take coffee with her; and when she heard of my perplexity with respect to a lodging, she offered me a room in her house. On the following day, I visited the governor, who received me very politely, and overpowered me with favours,—I was obliged to move into his house directly. He attended to my passport, and obtained all the necessary *visés*, of which I required half a dozen since entering the Christian dominions, and made an agreement for me with some Tartars, whose caravan was going to Tiflis. I then looked round the miserable half-ruined town with the good Mrs. Alexandwer, and saw Noah's monument.

According to Persian accounts, Natschivan is said to have been one of the largest and handsomest towns of Armenia; and Armenian writers affirm that Noah was the founder. The modern town is built quite in the Oriental style; only a few of the houses have the windows and doors turned towards the streets; generally the front faces the small garden. The dress of the people is also rather like the Persian, but the officials, merchants, etc., wear European costume.

Nothing more remains of Noah's sepulchre than a small arched chamber, without a cupola. It appears to have been formerly covered with one, but it is not possible to decide from the few ruins that now remain. In the interior, neither a sarcophagus nor grave are to be seen; a single brick pillar stands in the centre, and supports the roof. The whole is surrounded by a low wall. Many pilgrims come here, Mahomedans as well as Christians; and both sects entertain the remarkable belief, that if they press a stone into the wall while thinking of something at the same time, and the stone remains sticking to the wall, that their thoughts are either true or will come to pass, and the reverse when the stone does not adhere. The truth of the matter is, however, simply this: the cement or mortar is always rather moist, and if a smooth stone is pushed a little upwards while being pressed, it remains hanging; if it is only pressed horizontally, it falls off again.

Not far from Noah's tomb stands another very handsome monument; unfortunately I could not learn to whose memory it was erected, or to what age it belonged. It consists of a high building, resembling a tower with twelve angles; the walls between the angles are covered, from top to bottom, with the most artistic mathematical figures in triangles and sexagons, and some places are inlaid with glazed tiles. The monument is surrounded by a wall, forming a small court-yard; at the entrance-gates stand half-ruined towers, like minarets.

17th August. I felt very unwell today, which was the more unpleasant, as the caravan started in the evening. For several days I had been unable to take any food, and suffered from excessive lassitude. Nevertheless I left my rest, and mounted my caravan nag; I thought that change of air would be the best restorative.

Fortunately we went only a short distance beyond the city gate, and remained there during the night and the following day. We did not proceed any further until the evening of the 18th of August. The caravan only conveyed goods, and the drivers were Tartars. The journey from Natschivan to Tiflis is generally made in from twelve to fourteen days; but with my caravan, to judge from the progress we made at the commencement, it would have occupied six weeks, for on the first day we went scarcely any distance, and on the second, very little more than the first; I should have travelled quicker on foot.

19th August. It is really unbearable. During the whole day we lay in waste stubble-fields, exposed to the most scorching heat, and did not mount our horses until 9 o'clock in the evening; about an hour afterwards we halted, and encamped. The only thing good about this caravan was the food. The Tartars do not live so frugally as the Arabs. Every evening an excellent pillau was made with good-tasting fat, frequently with dried grapes or plums. Almost every day beautiful water and sugar-melons were brought to us to buy. The sellers, mostly Tartars, always selected a small lot and offered it to me as a present.

The road led continually through large, fertile valleys round the foot of Ararat. Today I saw the majestic mountain very clearly, and in tolerable proximity. I should think we were not more than two or three miles from it. It seemed, from its magnitude, as if separated from the other mountains, and standing alone; but it is in fact, connected with the chain of Taurus by a low range of hills. Its highest summit is divided in such a way that between two peaks there is a small plain, on which it is said that Noah's ark was left after the deluge. There are people who affirm that it would still be found there if the snow could be removed.

In the more recent treatises on geography, the height of Ararat is given as 16,000 feet; in the older ones, as 11,000. The Persians and Armenians call this mountain Macis; the Grecian writers describe it as a part of the Taurus range. Ararat is quite barren, and covered above with perpetual snow; lower down lies the cloister, Arakilvank, at the place where Noah is said to have taken up his first abode.

20th August. We encamped in the neighbourhood of the village Gadis. Many commentators of the Scriptures place the garden of Eden in the Armenian province of Ararat. In any case, Armenia has been the scene of most important events. Nowhere have so many bloody battles taken place as in this country, as all the great conquerors of Asia have brought Armenia under their control.

21st August. We still continued near Ararat; meanwhile we passed by Russian and German colonies, the houses in the latter had exactly the appearance of those in German mountain villages. The road was, throughout, very uneven and stony, and I cannot imagine how the post can travel upon it.

Today I met with another very unpleasant adventure. My caravan encamped in the neighbourhood of the station Sidin, about fifty paces from the side of the post-road. Towards 8 in the evening I walked out as far as the road, and as I was about to return I heard the sound of post-horses coming; I remained in the road to see the travellers, and noticed a Russian, seated in an open car, and by his side a Cossack, with a musket. When the vehicle had passed, I turned quietly round; but, to my astonishment, heard it stop, and felt myself, almost at the same moment, seized forcibly by the arms. It was the Cossack who held me, and endeavoured to drag me to the car. I tried to release myself, pointed to the caravan, and said that I belonged to it. The fellow immediately stopped my mouth with his hand, and threw me into the car, where I was tightly held by the other man. The Cossack immediately jumped up, and the driver urged his horses on as quickly as they could go. The whole was done so quickly that I scarcely knew what had happened to me. The men held me tightly by the arms, and my mouth was kept covered up until we were so far from the caravan that the people belonging to it could no longer have heard my cries.

Fortunately I was not frightened; I thought at once that these two amiable Russians might, in their zeal, have taken me for a very dangerous person, and have supposed they had made a very important capture. When they uncovered my mouth, they commenced questioning me as to my native country, name, etc. I understood enough Russian to give them this information, but they were not satisfied with that, and required to see my passport; I told them that they must send for my portmanteau, and then I would show them that I had permission to travel.

We came, at last, to the post-house, where I was taken into a room; the Cossack placed himself with his musket under the open door, so as to keep his eye continually on me; and the other man, who, from his dark-green velvet facings, I supposed to be one of the Emperor's officers, remained some time in the room. At the end of half an hour, the post-master, or whoever he was, came to examine me, and to hear an account of the achievements of my captors, who hastened, with laughing countenances, to give a complete statement of what had happened.

I was obliged to pass the night, under strict guard, upon a wooden bench, without either a wrapper or a mantle with me, and suffering from hunger and thirst. They neither gave me a coverlet nor a piece of bread; and when I merely rose from the bench to walk up and down the room, the Cossack rushed in immediately, seized my arms, and led me back to the bench, telling me, at the same time, that I must remain there quietly.

Towards morning they brought me my luggage, when I showed them my papers, and was set at liberty. Instead, however, of apologizing for having treated me in such a way, they laughed at me; and when I came out into the court, every one pointed at me with their fingers, and joined my gaolers in their laughter. Oh! you good Turks, Arabs, Persians, Hindoos, or whatever else you may be called, such treatment was never shown to me amongst you! How pleasantly have I always taken leave of all your countries; how attentively I was treated at the Persian frontiers, when I would not understand that my passport was required, and here, in a Christian empire, how much incivility have I had to bear during this short journey!

On the 22nd of August I rejoined my caravan, where I was received with cordiality.

23rd August. The country still presented the same features; one large valley succeeding another. These valleys are less cultivated than those in Persia; today, however, I saw one which was tolerably well planted, and in which the villagers had even planted trees before their huts.

24th August. Station Erivan. I was happy to have reached this town, as I hoped to meet with some of my country-people here, and, by their help, to find a quicker mode of conveyance to Tiflis. I was determined to leave the caravan, since we did not go more than four hours a day.

I had two letters; one to the town physician, the other to the governor. The latter was in the country; Dr. Müller, however, received me so well that I could not possibly have been better taken care of.

Erivan {305} is situated on the river Zengui, and is the capital of Armenia; it contains about 17,000 inhabitants, and is built upon low hills, in a large plain, surrounded on all sides with mountains. The town has some fortified walls.

314

Although the European mode of architecture already begins to predominate greatly, this town is by no means to be reckoned among either the handsome or cleanly ones. I was most amused by the bazaars, not on account of their contents, for these do not present any remarkable features, but because I always saw there different, and for the most part unknown, national costumes. There were Tartars, Cossacks, Circassians, Georgians, Mingrelians, Turkonians, Armenians, etc.; chiefly powerful, handsome people, with fine expressive features—particularly the Tartars and Circassians. Their dress partly resembled the Persian; indeed that of the Tartars differed from it only by points to the boots, and a less lofty cap. The points on the boots are frequently as much as four inches long, and turned inward and towards the end; the caps are also pointed, and made of black fur, but not more than half as high. Very few of the women of these tribes are seen in the streets, and those are enveloped in wrappers; nevertheless, they do not veil their faces.

The Russians and the Cossacks have stupid coarse features, and their behaviour corresponds completely to what their appearance indicates; I never met with a people so covetous, coarse, and slavish as they are. When I asked about anything, they either gave me a surly answer, or none at all, or else laughed in my face. This rudeness would not, perhaps, have appeared so remarkable if I had come from Europe.

It had already been my intention in Natschivan to travel with the Russian post; but I had been dissuaded from doing so, as I was assured that, as a solitary woman, I should not be able to agree with the people. However, here I was determined to do so, and I requested Dr. Müller to make the necessary preparations for me.

In order to travel in Russia by the post, it is necessary to procure a padroschne (certificate of permission), which is only to be had in a town where there are several grades of officials, as this important document requires to be taken to six of the number. 1st, to the treasurer; 2nd, to the police (of course with the passport, certificate of residence, etc.); 3rd, to the commandant; 4th, again to the police; 5th, again to the treasurer; and 6th, to the police again. In the padroschne an accurate account must be given of how far the traveller wishes to go, as the postmaster dare not proceed a single werst beyond the station named. Finally, a half kopec (half kreutzer), must be paid per werst for each horse. This at first does not appear much; but is, nevertheless, a considerable tax, when it is remembered that seven wersts are only equal to a geographical mile, and that three horses are always used.

On the 26th of August, about 4 in the morning, the post was to have been at the house; but it struck 6, and there was still no appearance of it. If Dr. Müller had not been so kind as to go there, I should not have started until the evening. About 7, I got off—an excellent foretaste of my future progress.

We travelled certainly with speed; but any one who had not a body of iron, or a well-cushioned spring carriage, would not find this very agreeable, and would certainly prefer to travel slower upon these uneven, bad roads.

The post carriage, for which ten kopecs a station is paid, is nothing more than a very short, wooden, open car, with four wheels. Instead of a seat, some hay is laid in it, and there is just room enough for a small chest, upon which the driver sits. These cars naturally jolt very much. There is nothing to take hold of, and it requires some care to avoid being thrown out. The draught consists of three horses abreast; over the centre one a wooden arch is fixed, on which hang two or three bells, which continually made a most disagreeable noise. In addition to this, imagine the rattling of the carriage, and the shouting of the driver, who is always in great activity urging on the poor animals, and it may be easily understood that, as is often the case, the carriage arrives at the station without the travellers.

The division of the stations is very irregular, varying from fourteen to thirty wersti. Between the second and third stations, I passed over a very short space of ground, where I found a kind of lava, exactly resembling the beautiful, brilliant, glassy lava of Iceland (black agate, also called obsidian), which was stated to be found in that island only. The second stage led through a newly-erected Russian village, extending to Lake Liman.

August 27th. Today I had another evidence of the pleasure of travelling by the Russian post. On the previous evening I had ordered and paid for everything before-hand; yet I was obliged in the morning to awaken the post officers myself, as well as to see after the driver, and to be constantly about among the people, in order to get away. At the third station I was kept waiting three hours for the horses; at the fourth they gave me none, and I was obliged to stay all night, although I had gone only fifty-five wersti the whole day.

The character of the country changes before reaching Delischan: the valleys contract to narrow gorges, and the mountains seldom leave space for small villages and plots of ground. The naked masses of rock cease, and luxuriant woods cover the heights.

Near Pipis, the last stage that I went today, beautiful cliffs and rocks rose close to the post-road, many of them presenting the appearance of enormous columns.

August 28th. Continual trouble with the post people. I am the greatest enemy of scolding and harsh treatment; but I should have best liked to have spoken to these people with a stick. No idea can be formed of their stupidity, coarseness, and want of feeling. Officers, as well as servants, are frequently found at all hours of the day sleeping or drunk. In this state they do as they please, will not stir from their places, and even laugh in the faces of the unfortunate travellers. By the aid of much quarrelling and noise, one is at last induced to drag out the car, a second to grease it, another baits the horses, which have often to be harnessed, then the straps are not in order, and must be first fastened and repaired; and innumerable other things of this kind, which are done with the greatest tardiness. When, afterwards, in the towns I expressed my disapprobation of these wretched post

316

establishments, I received as answer that these countries had been too short a time under Russian dominion, that the imperial city was too far distant, and that I, as a single woman without servants, might consider myself fortunate in having got through as I had.

I did not know what reply to make to this, except that in the most recently acquired colonial possessions of the English, which are still farther from the capital, everything is excellently arranged; and that there a woman without servants was as quickly attended to as a gentleman, since they find her money not less acceptable than that of the latter. The case is very different, however, at a Russian post station; when an official or officer comes, every one is active enough, cringing round the watering-place for fear of flogging or punishment. Officers and officials belong, in Russia, to the privileged class, and assume all kinds of despotism. If, for example, they do not travel on duty, they should not, according to the regulations, have any greater advantages than private travellers. But, instead of setting a good example, and showing the mass of the people that the laws and regulations must be observed, it is precisely these people who set all laws at defiance. They send a servant forward or borrow one from their fellow-travellers, to the station to announce that on such a day they shall arrive, and will require eight or twelve horses. If any hindrance occurs during this time—a hunt or a dinner—or if the wife of the traveller has a headache or the cramp, they postpone the journey without any ado to another day or two; the horses stand constantly ready, and the postmaster dare not venture to give them to private travellers. {308} It may so happen that travellers have in such a case to wait one or even two days at a station, and do not get through their journey quicker by the post than by a caravan. In the course of my journey by the Russian post, I several times went only a single stage during a whole long day. When I saw an uniform I was always in dread, and made up my mind that I should have no horses.

In each post-house, there are one or two rooms for travellers, and a married Cossack in charge, who, together with his wife, attends to strangers, and cooks for them. No charge is made for the room, the first comer is entitled to it. These attendants are as obliging as the stable people, and it is often difficult to procure with money a few eggs, milk, or anything of the kind.

The journey through Persia was dangerous; that through Asiatic Russia, however, was so troublesome, that I would prefer the former under any circumstances.

From Pipis the country again diminishes in beauty: the valleys expand, the mountains become lower, and both are frequently without trees, and barren.

I met, today, several nomadic parties of Tartars. The people sat upon oxen and horses, and others were loaded with their tents and household utensils; the cows and sheep, of which there were always a great number, were driven by the side. The Tartar women were mostly richly clothed, and also very ragged. Their dress consisted almost entirely of deep red silk, which was often even embroidered with gold. They wore wide trousers, a long kaftan, and a shorter one over that; on the

317

head a kind of bee-hive, called *schaube*, made of the bark of trees, painted red and ornamented with tinsel, coral, and small coins. From the breast to the girdle their clothes were also covered with similar things, over the shoulders hung a cord with an amulet in the nose, they wore small rings. They had large wrappers thrown round them; but left their faces uncovered.

Their household goods consisted of tents, handsome rugs, iron pots, copper coins, etc. The Tartars are mostly of the Mahomedan religion.

The permanent Tartars have very peculiar dwellings, which may be called enormous mole-hills. Their villages are chiefly situated on declivities, and hills, in which they dig holes of the size of spacious rooms. The light falls only through the entrance, or outlet. This is broader than it is high, and is protected by a long and broad portico of planks, resting either upon beams or the stems of trees. Nothing is more comical than to see such a village, consisting of nothing but these porticoes, and neither windows, doors, nor walls.

Those who dwell in the plains make artificial mounds of earth, and build their huts of stone or wood. They then throw earth over them, which they stamp down tightly, so that the huts themselves cannot be seen at all. Until within the last sixty years, it is said that many such dwellings were to be seen in the town of Tiflis.

29th August. This morning I had still one stage of twenty-four wersti ere I reached Tiflis. The road was, as everywhere else, full of holes, ruts and stones. I was obliged always to tie a handkerchief tightly round my head, to ease the jolting; and still, I was every day attacked with headache. Today, however, I learnt the full nuisance of these carriages. It had rained, not only during the whole night, but still continued so. The wheels threw up such masses of mud, that I soon sat in a thick puddle, I was covered even over the head, and my face did not escape. Small boards hanging over the wheels would have easily remedied this inconvenience; but none trouble themselves in this country about the comfort of travellers.

Tiflis comes in sight during the latter half of the stage. The prospect of the town charmed me much; as, with the exception of a few church towers, it was built in the European style; and, since Valparaiso, I had not seen any town resembling the European. Tiflis contains 50,000 inhabitants, it is the capital of Georgia, {309} and is situated tolerably near the mountains. Many of the houses are built on hills, on high steep rocks. From some of the hills there is a beautiful view of the town and valley. The latter, at the time of my visit, was not very attractive, as the harvest had deprived it of all the charms of colour; there were also but few gardens, etc. On the other hand, the river Kurry (generally called Cyrus) winds in graceful curves through the town and valley, and in the far distance sparkle the snow-crowned summits of the Caucasus. A strong citadel, Naraklea, is situated upon steep rocks, immediately before the town.

The houses are large, and tastefully ornamented with façades and columns, and covered with sheet iron or bricks. The Erivanski Place is very handsome. Among the buildings the Palace of the governor, the Greek and Armenian seminaries, and several barracks are conspicuous. The large theatre, in the centre of the Erivanski Place, was not then finished. It is evident that the old town must give place to the new one. Everywhere houses are being pulled down, and new ones built; the narrow streets will soon only be known by tradition, and the only remains of the Oriental architecture, are the Greek and Armenian houses. The churches are far inferior in splendour and magnitude to the other buildings; the towers are low, round, and generally covered with green glazed tiles. The oldest Christian church stands upon a high rock in the fortress, and is used only for the prisoners.

The bazaars and chan present no features worthy of notice; moreover, there are already here, as in all European towns, shops and stores in all the streets. Several wide bridges are thrown over the Kurry. The town contains numerous warm sulphuretted springs, from which, indeed, it derives its name: Tiflis or Ibilissi, meaning "warm town." Unfortunately, the greater number of the many baths are in the worst condition. The buildings, within which the springs are enclosed, are surmounted by small cupolas with windows. The reservoirs, the floor, and walls, are for the most part covered with large stone slabs; very little marble is to be seen. There are private and public baths, and men are not allowed to enter the buildings where the women assemble; however, they are not nearly so strict here as in the East. The gentleman who was so kind as to accompany me to one of these baths, was permitted to come into the anteroom, although it was separated from the bathing-place only by a simple wooden partition.

Not far from the baths lies the Botanic Garden, which has been laid out, at great expense, on the declivity of a mountain. The terraces, which had to be artificially cut, are supported by masonry and filled with earth. Why such an unsuitable place was chosen I cannot imagine; the less so as I saw only a few rare plants and shrubs, and everywhere nothing but grape-vines; I fancied myself in a vineyard. The most remarkable things in this garden are two vine-stocks, whose stems were each a foot in diameter. They are so extended in groves and long rows that they form pleasant walks. More than a thousand flasks of wine are annually obtained from these two vines.

A large grotto has been excavated in one of the upper terraces whose whole front side is open, and forms a high-arched hall. In the fine summer evenings there is music, dancing, and even theatrical performances.

On Sundays and festivals the pretty gardens of the governor are opened to the public. There are swings and winding-paths, and two bands of music. The music executed by the Russian military was not so good as that which I heard by the blacks in Rio Janeiro.

When I visited the Armenian Church, the corpse of a child had just been laid out. It was in a costly open bier, covered with red velvet and richly ornamented with gold lace. The corpse was strewed over with flowers, decorated with a crown, and covered with fine white gauze. The priests, in sumptuous robes, conducted the funeral ceremonies, which were very similar to the Catholic. The poor mother, at whose side I accidentally happened to kneel, sobbed loudly when preparations were made to carry away the dear remains. I also could not restrain my tears: I wept not for the death of the child, but for the deep grief of the afflicted parent.

Leaving this place of mourning, I visited some Greek and Armenian families. I was received in spacious rooms, which were fitted up in the most simple manner. Along the walls stood painted wooden benches partly covered with rugs. On these benches the people sit, eat, and sleep. The women wear Grecian dresses.

European and Asiatic costumes are seen so frequently together in the streets, that neither the one nor the other appears peculiar. The greatest novelty to me, in this respect, was the Circassian dress. It consists of wide trousers, short coats full of folds, with narrow sashes, and breast pockets for from six to ten cartridges; tight half-boots, with points turned inwards, and close-fitting fur caps. The more wealthy wore coats of fine dark-blue cloth, and the edges were ornamented with silver.

The Circassians are distinguished from all other Caucasian people by their beauty. The men are tall, have very regular features and great ease in their motions. The women are of a more delicate build; their skin is whiter, their hair dark, their features regular, their figures slender, with their busts well developed: in the Turkish harems they are considered the greatest beauties. I must confess, however, that I have seen many handsomer women in the Persian harems than in the Turkish, even when they contained Circassians.

The Asiatic women, when in the streets here, wrap themselves in large white mantles; many cover the mouth as well, and some few the remainder of the face.

Of the domestic life of the Russian officials and officers I cannot say much. I had, indeed, a letter to the chancellor director, Herr von Lille, and to the governor, Herr von Jermaloff; but both gentlemen were not much pleased with me—my free expression of opinion, perhaps, did not suit them. I made no scruple of speaking my mind with regard to the ill-regulated posting establishments, and the miserable roads. I, moreover, related my imprisonment, with a few comments; and, what crowned all, I said that I had intended to have gone on from here across the Caucasus to Moscow and Petersburgh, but that I had been completely deterred from doing so by my short experience of travelling in the country, and would take the shortest road to get beyond the frontier as soon as possible. If I had been a man and had spoken so, I should probably have been treated with a temporary residence in Siberia.

Herr von Lille, however, always received me with politeness when I called on him for the purpose of having my passport prepared. The governor did not treat me with a like consideration; first he put me off from one day to another, then it pleased the mighty man to pass two days in the country. When he came back, it was a Sunday; on which day such a great work could not possibly be done, and so

I did not obtain my passport until the sixth day.

Thus it fared with me, who was provided with letters to the chief officers,—how do poor people come off? I heard, indeed, that they are often kept waiting two or three weeks.

The viceroy, Prince Woronzou, was unfortunately not in Tiflis at the time. I regretted his absence the more, as I everywhere heard him represented as an educated, just, and extremely amiable man.

Far pleasanter than these visits to the Russian governor was that to the Persian Prince Behmen Mirza, to whom I brought letters and intelligence from his family, who were remaining in Tebris. Although he was ill at the time, nevertheless he received me. I was conducted into a large saloon, a complete hospital for eight sick persons: the prince, four of his children, and three wives, laid there upon rugs and cushions. They all suffered from fever. The prince was a remarkably handsome and powerful man of five and thirty; his full eyes were expressive of intelligence and goodness. He spoke with great regret of his fatherland; a smile of painful delight played round his features when I mentioned his children, {312} and related how safely and well I had travelled through those provinces which, but a short time before, had been under his control. What a happiness would it be for Persia if such a man as this was to come to the throne instead of the young viceroy.

The most interesting, and, at the same time, useful acquaintance which I made was that of Herr Salzmann, a German. This gentleman possesses considerable knowledge of agriculture, and more than all, a singularly good heart; he interests himself for all kinds of people, and more especially his own countrymen. Wherever I mentioned his name, people spoke of him with true respect. He had just received a decoration from the Russian government, although he was not in their service.

Herr Salzmann has built a very handsome house, with every possible convenience for the reception of travellers; besides this he owns a large fruit-garden, ten wersti distant from the town, in the neighbourhood of which are some naphtha springs. When he found that I wished to see these he immediately invited me to join a party to visit them. The springs are situated very near to the Kurry. Square pits, about twenty-five fathoms deep, are dug, and the naphtha is dipped out by means of wooden buckets. This naphtha, however, is of the commonest kind, of a dark brown colour, and thicker than oil. Asphalte, cart-grease, etc., are made from it. The fine white naphtha, which can be used for lighting and fuel, is peculiar to the Caspian Sea.

A walk to the Chapel of David, which lies upon a hill immediately in front of the town, repays the trouble. Besides the lovely country, there is to be seen here a fine monument erected in memory of the Russian ambassador, Gribojetof, who was murdered in Persia on the occasion of a revolt. A cross, at the foot of which lies

321

his mourning wife, is very artistically cast in metal.

On Monday, the 5th of September, I received my passport, about 11 o'clock; I ordered the post carriage an hour afterwards. Herr Salzmann proposed that I should visit some German settlements, which were situated at about ten or twenty wersti from Tiflis, and offered to accompany me there; but I had not much inclination to do so, more particularly as I had heard everywhere that the settlers had already much degenerated, and that idleness, fraud, dirt, drunkenness, etc., was not less frequent among them than in the Russian colonies.

I left Tiflis about 3 in the afternoon. Just outside the town stands, by the roadside, a cross cast in metal, with the eye of Providence upon a pedestal of polished granite, surrounded by an iron railing. An inscription states that, on the 12th of October, in the year 1837, his imperial majesty was upset here, but that he had escaped without injury. "Erected by his grateful subjects."

This incident appears, therefore, to have been one of the most remarkable in the life of this powerful ruler, as it has been commemorated by a monument. It has, certainly, not been erected without the approval of the emperor. I am by no means certain which is the most to be wondered at, the people who placed it here, or the monarch who permitted it.

I went only one stage today, but it was so long, that I had to continue my journey into the evening. To go any further was not to be thought of, as the country, not only here, but in the greater part of this province, is so unsafe that it is impossible to travel in the evening or night without the protection of Cossacks, for which purpose a small company is placed at each station.

The scenery was rather agreeable; pretty hills enclosed pleasant looking valleys, and on the tops of some mountains stood ruins of castles and fortified places. There were times in the history of this kingdom as well as the German when one noble made war upon the others, and no man was safe of his life and property. The nobles lived in fortified castles upon hills and mountains, went out mailed and harnessed like knights, and when threatened by hostile attacks, their subjects fled to the castles. There are still said to be people who wear, either over or under the clothes, shirts of mail, and helmets instead of caps. I did not, however, see anything of the kind. The river Kurry continued to run along by our road. Not far from the station a long handsome bridge led across, but it was so awkwardly placed that it was necessary to go out of the way a whole werst to reach it.

6th September. The journey became still more romantic. Bushes and woods covered the hills and valleys, and the tall-stemmed, rich, green Turkish corn waved in the fields. There were also numbers of old castles and fortresses. Towards evening, after having with great exertion travelled four stages, I reached the little town of Gory, whose situation was exceedingly charming. Wooded mountains surrounded it in wide circles, while nearer at hand rose pretty groups of hills. Nearly in the centre of the mass of houses a hill was to be seen, whose summit was crowned by a citadel. The little town possesses some pretty churches, private houses, barracks, and a neat hospital. Both towns and villages here lose the Oriental character entirely.

When the atmosphere is clear the Caucasian mountains are to be seen rising in three ranges between the Caspian and Black seas, forming the boundary between Asia and Europe. The highest points are the Elberus and the Kasbeck; these, according to a new geography, are of the respective heights of 16,800 and 14,000 feet. The mountains were covered with snow far down their sides.

7th September. Today I travelled one stage as far as Suram: I could not proceed any further, as twelve horses were ordered for an officer who was returning from a bathing-place, with his wife and friends.

Suram lies in a fruitful valley, in the centre of which rises a beautiful mountain with the ruins of an old castle. In order to dispel my bad humour I took a walk to this old castle. Although it was considerably ruined, the lofty arches, stately walls, and extensive fortifications showed that the noble knight had lived tolerably sumptuously. On the return nothing astonished me more than the number of animals yoked to the ploughs. The fields lay in the finest plains, the ground was loose and free from stones, and yet each plough was drawn by twelve or fourteen oxen.

8th September. The mountains drew nearer and nearer together, the prospect became more beautiful; climbing plants, wild hops, vines, etc., twined round the trees to their highest branches, and the underwood grew so thick and luxuriantly, that it called to my mind the vegetation of the Brazils.

The third stage was for the greater part of the way along the banks of the river Mirabka through a narrow valley. The road between the river and the mountain side was so narrow, that in many places there was only room for one carriage. We had frequently to wait ten or twenty minutes to allow the cars loaded with wood, of which we met a great number, to pass us, and yet this was called a post-road.

Georgia has been for fifty year under Russian dominion, and only within a recent time have roads been commenced here and there. Fifty years hence, they may, perhaps, be finished, or fallen again into decay. Bridges are as scarce as roads. The rivers, such as the Mirabka are crossed in miserable ferry boats, those which are shallower must be forded. In time of rain, or sudden thaw in the snow mountains, the rivers are overflowed, and travellers must then either wait some days or risk their lives. What a tremendous difference between the colonies of Russia and England!

Late in the evening, I arrived, wet through and covered with mud, at the station, two wersti from Kutais. It is remarkable that the post-houses are generally one or two wersti from the villages or towns. A traveller, in consequence of this custom, is exposed to the inconvenience of making a special journey if he has anything to attend to in those places.

9th September. Kutais contains 10,000 inhabitants, and lies in a natural park; all round is the most luxuriant vegetation. The houses are neat and ornamental; the green painted church towers and barracks peep invitingly from between. The large river Ribon {314} separates the town from the large citadel which very picturesquely occupies a neighbouring hill.

The dresses of the people are as various as round Tiflis; the headgear of the Mingrelian peasants appears truly comic. They wear round black felt caps, in the shape of a plate, fastened by a string under the chin. The women frequently wear the Tartarian schaube, over which they throw a veil, which, however, is put back so that the face is seen. The men wear, in the mornings, and in rainy weather, large black collars (called burki) of sheep's wool, or felt, which reach below the knees. I must here mention that the beauty for which the Georgians are so famous must not be sought for among the common people. I did not find them particularly handsome.

The carts which the peasants use are remarkable, the front part rests upon curved pieces of wood, or sledge-bars; the hinder part upon two small thick discs of wood.

My stay in Kutais was caused by the want of horses; it was not till 2 o'clock in the afternoon that I could continue my journey. I had two stages to reach the village of Marand, which lies on the river Ribon, where the post-cars are changed for a boat, by which the journey to Redutkale, on the Black Sea, is made.

The first stage passes chiefly through fine woods, the second presents an open view over fields and meadows; the houses and huts are quite buried beneath bushes and trees. We met a number of peasants who, although they had only a few fowls, eggs, fruits, etc., to carry to the town for sale, were nevertheless on horseback. There was abundance of grass and willow trees, and consequently of horses and horned cattle.

At Marand I stopped, for want of an inn, with a Cossack. These people, who also live here as settlers, have pretty wooden cottages, with two or three rooms, and a piece of land which they use as field and garden. Some of them receive travellers, and know how to charge enough for the miserable accommodation they afford. I paid twenty kopecs (8d.) for a dirty room without a bed, and as much for a chicken. Beyond that I had nothing, for the people are too lazy to fetch what they have not by them. If I wanted bread, or anything that my hosts had not got, I might seek for it myself. As I have said before, it is only for an officer that they will make any exertion.

I had left Tiflis about 3 in the afternoon of the 5th of September, and reached this place in the evening of the 9th, five days to travel 274 wersti (195 miles). I call that a respectable Russian post!

The boat did not start for Redutkale, a distance of eighty wersti, until the morning of the 11th. It was bad weather; and the Ribon, otherwise a fine river, cannot be navigated during a strong wind, on account of the projecting trunks of trees and logs. The scenery still continued beautiful and picturesque. The stream flows between woods, maize, and millet fields, and the view extends over hills and mountains to the distant and gigantic Caucasus. Their singular forms, peaks, sunken plateaus, split domes, etc. appear sometimes on the right, sometimes on the left, in front, and behind, according to the ever-changing windings of the river. We frequently halted and landed, every one running to the trees. Grapes and figs were abundant, but the former were as sour as vinegar, and the latter hard and small. I found a single one ripe, and that I threw away when I had tasted it. The fig-trees were of a size such as I had never seen, either in India or Sicily. I believe the whole sap is here converted into wood and leaves. In the same way, the great height of the vines may be the cause of the grapes being so small and bad. There must certainly be a great field for improved cultivation here.

12th September. Our boat did not go far. There was a smart breeze, and as we were already near the Black Sea, we were obliged to remain at anchor.

13th September. The wind had dropped, and we could, without danger, trust ourselves on the sea, upon which we had to sail for some hours, from the principal arm of the Ribon to that on which Redutkale was situated. There was indeed a canal leading from the one to the other, but it can only be passed at very high water, as it is much filled with drift sand.

In Redutkale, a speculating Cossack host also received me, who had three little rooms for guests.

According to the Russian calendar, this was the last day of August. On the 1st of September, the steamer was to come, and sail again after two hours. I therefore hastened to the commandant of the town to have my passport signed, and to request admittance to the ship. Government steamers ply twice every month, on the 1st and 15th, from Redutkale to Odessa, by way of Kertsch. Sailing vessels rarely offer an opportunity of passage. These steamers always keep close into the coast; they touch at eighteen stations (fortresses and military posts), carry military transports of all kinds, and convey all passengers free. Travellers must, however, be content with a deck place: the cabins are few, and belong to the crew and higher officers, who frequently travel from one station to another. No places can be had by paying for them.

The commandant prepared my passport and ticket directly. I cannot avoid remarking in this place that the prolixity of writing by the Russian government officials far exceeds that of the Austrians, which I had formerly considered impossible. Instead of a simple signature, I received a large written sheet, of which several copies were taken, the whole ceremony occupying more than half an hour.

The steamer did not arrive until the 5th (Russian calendar). Nothing is more tedious than to wait from hour to hour for a conveyance, especially when it is necessary, in addition, to be ready to start at any moment. Every morning I packed up. I did not venture to cook a fowl or anything else, for fear I should be called away from it as soon as ready; and it was not until the evening that I felt a little safer, and could walk out a little.

From what I could see of the neighbourhood of Redutkale and Mingrelia altogether, the country is plentifully furnished with hills and mountains, large valleys lie between, and the whole are covered with rich woods. The air is on that account moist and unhealthy, and it rains very frequently. The rising sun draws up such dense vapours, that they float like impenetrable clouds, four or five feet above the earth. These vapours are said to be the cause of many diseases, especially fever and dropsy. In addition to this, the people are so foolish as to build their houses in among the bushes and under thick trees, instead of in open, airy, and sunny places. Villages are frequently passed, and scarcely a house is to be seen. The men are remarkably idle and stupid; they are tawny and lean. The natives seldom reach the age of sixty; and it is said that the climate is even more unhealthy for strangers.

Still I believe that much might be done in this country by industrious settlers and agriculturists. There is abundance of land, and three-fourths of it certainly lies uncultivated. By thinning the woods and draining the land, the badness of the climate would be lessened. It is already, even without cultivation, very fruitful; and how much this might be increased by a proper and rational mode of treatment. Rich grass grows everywhere, mixed with the best herbs and clover. Fruit grows wild; the vines run up to the tops of the highest trees. It is said that in time of rain the ground is so soft, that only wooden ploughs are used. Turkish corn is most generally grown, and a kind of millet, called gom.

The inhabitants prepare the wine in the most simple manner. They hollow out the trunk of a tree, and tread the grapes in it; they then pour the juice into earthen vessels, and bury these in the ground.

The character of the Mingrelians is said to be altogether bad, and they are generally looked upon as thieves and robbers; murders are said not to be unfrequent. They carry off one another's wives, and are much addicted to drunkenness. The father trains the children to stealing, and the mother to obscenity.

Colchis or Mingrelia lies at the end of the Black Sea, and towards the north on the Caucasian mountains. The neighbouring people were formerly known under the name of Huns and Alani. The Amazons are said to have dwelt in the country between the Caucasus and the Caspian Sea.

The little town of Redutkale may contain about 1,500 inhabitants. The men are so indolent that, during the five days that I passed here, I could not procure a few grapes or figs for love or money. I went daily to the bazaar, and never found any for sale. The people are too lazy to bring wood from the forest; they work only when the greatest necessity compels them, and require to be paid exorbitantly. I paid as much, if not more, for eggs, milk, and bread as I would have done in Vienna. It might well be said that the people are here in the midst of plenty, and yet almost starve.

I was not better pleased by the thoughtless and meaningless performance of religious ceremonies among these people. On all occasions, they cross themselves before eating or drinking, before entering a room, before putting on an article of clothing, etc. The hands have nothing else to do but to make crosses. But the most provoking thing of all is, that they stand still before every church they pass, bow half a dozen times, and cross themselves without end. When they are travelling, they stop their carriages to perform this ceremony.

While I was at Redutkale a vessel sailed. The priests were brought on board, and were obliged to go all over the ship, and pronounce a blessing upon it on every corner of the sails. They crept into every cabin or hole, and at last blessed the sailors, who laughed at them for their trouble.

I constantly found that there was less real religion in those places where there was the most parade made of it.

CHAPTER XXIII. EUROPEAN RUSSIA.

DEPARTURE FROM REDUTKALE—ATTACK OF CHOLERA—ANAPKA —SUSPICIOUS SHIP—KERTSCH—THE MUSEUM—TUMULI— CONTINUATION OF THE JOURNEY—THEODOSIA (CAFFA)—PRINCE WORONZOFF'S PALACE—THE FORTRESS OF SEWASTOPOL— ODESSA.

On the 17th of September, at 9 in the morning, the steamer arrived, and an hour afterwards I was seated on the deck. The vessel was called Maladetz; it was 140 horse power, and the commandant's name was Zorin.

The distance from Redutkale to Kertsch is only 420 miles in a straight line, but for us, who continually kept close to the shore, it amounted to nearly 580.

The view of the Caucasus—the hills and headlands—the rich and luxuriant country remains fresh in my memory to this day. In a charming valley lies the village Gallansur, the first station, at which we stopped for a short time.

Towards 6 o'clock in the evening, we reached the fortified town Sahun, which lies partly on the shore, and partly on a broad hill. Here I saw, for the first time, Cossacks in full uniform; all those I had previously seen were very badly dressed, and had no military appearance; they wore loose linen trousers, and long ugly coats, reaching down to their heels. These, however, wore close-fitting spencers with breast-pockets, each of which was divided for eight cartridges, wide trousers, which sat in folds upon the upper part of the body, and dark blue cloth caps, trimmed with fur. They rowed a staff officer to the ship.

18th September. We remained the whole day in Sahun. The coal-boats, from some inconceivable negligence, had not arrived; the coals were taken on board after we had been some time at anchor, and our supply was not completed until 6 o'clock in the evening, when we again started.

19th September. During the night there was much storm and rain. I begged permission to seat myself on the cabin steps, which I received; but, after a few minutes, an order came from the commandant to take me under cover. I was much surprised and pleased at this politeness, but I was soon undeceived when I was led into the large sailors' cabin. The people smelt horribly of brandy, and some of them had evidently taken too much. I hastened back on to the deck, where, in spite of the raging of the elements, I felt more comfortable than among these well-bred Christians.

In the course of the day we stopped at Bambur, Pizunta, Gagri, Adlar, and other places. Near Bambur I observed majestic groups of rocks.

20th September. The Caucasian mountains were now out of sight, and the thick woods were also succeeded by wide open spaces. We were still troubled with wind, storm, and rain.

The engineer of the ship, an Englishman, Mr. Platt, had accidentally heard of my journey (perhaps from my passport, which I had to give up on entering the ship); he introduced himself to me today, and offered me the use of his cabin during the day-time; he also spoke to one of the officers for me, and succeeded in obtaining a cabin for me, which, although it joined the sailors' cabin, was separated from it by a door. I was very thankful to both the gentlemen for their kindness, which was the greater, as the preference was given to me, a stranger, over the Russian officers, of whom at least half a dozen were on deck.

We remained a long time at Sissassé. This is an important station; there is a fine fortress upon a hill—round it stand pretty wooden houses.

21st September. This was a terrible night! One of the sailors, who was healthy and well the day before, and had taken his supper with a good appetite, was suddenly attacked with cholera. The cries of the poor fellow disturbed me greatly, and I went upon deck, but the heavy rain and piercing cold were not less terrible. I had nothing but my mantle, which was soon wet through; my teeth chattered; the frost made me shake throughout; so there was nothing to be done but to go below again—to stop my ears, and remain close to the dying man. He was, in spite of all help, a corpse before the end of eight hours. The dead body was landed in the morning, at Bschada; it was packed in a heap of sail-cloth, and kept secret from the travellers. The cabin was thoroughly washed with vinegar, and scoured, and no one else was attacked.

I did not at all wonder that there was sickness on board, only I had expected it would be among the poor soldiers, who were day and night upon the deck, and had no further food than dry, black bread, and had not even mantles or covering; I saw many half-frozen from cold, dripping with rain, gnawing a piece of bread: how much greater suffering must they have to undergo in the winter time! The passage from Redutkale to Kertsch, I was told, then frequently occupied twenty days. The sea is so rough that it is difficult to reach the stations, and sometimes the ship lies for days opposite them. If it should happen that a poor soldier has to proceed the whole distance, it is really a wonder that he should reach the place of his destination alive. According to the Russian system, however, the common man is not worthy of any consideration.

The sailors are indeed better, but, nevertheless, not well provided for; they receive bread and spirits, a very small quantity of meat, and a soup made of sour cabbage, called bartsch, twice a day.

The number of officers, their wives, and soldiers on the deck, increased at every station, very few being landed from the ship.

The deck was soon so covered with furniture, chests, and trunks, that there was scarcely a place to sit down, except on the top of a pile of goods. I never saw such an encampment on board a ship.

In fine weather, this life afforded me much amusement; there was always something new to see; every one was animated and happy, and appeared to belong to the same family; but if a heavy rain came on suddenly, or a wave washed over the deck, the passengers began to shout and cry, and the contents of every chest became public. One cried, "How shall I shelter my sugar-loaves?" another, "Oh, my meal will be spoiled." There a woman complained that her bonnet would be full of spots; here, another, that the uniform of her husband would certainly be injured.

At some of the smaller stations, we had taken on board sick soldiers, in order to carry them to the hospital at Kertsch. This was done, as I was told, less on account of nursing them than as a measure of safety. The former they would have received at the place they came from; but all the small villages between Redutkale and Anapka are still frequently disturbed by the Circassian-Tartars, who undauntedly break out from the mountains and rob and murder. Very lately they were reported to have fired a cannon at one of the government steamers. The Circassians {320a} are as partial to the Russians as the Chinese are to the English!

The poor invalids were also laid on the deck, and but little attention was shown to

329

them, beyond stretching a sail-cloth over them, to keep the wind partially off; but when it rained heavily, the water ran in on all sides, so that they lay half in the wet.

22nd September. We saw the handsome town and fortress Nowa Russiska, which contains some very pretty private houses, hospitals, barracks, and a fine church. The town and fortress lie upon a hill, and were founded only ten years since.

In the evening, we reached Anapka, which place was taken by the Turks in 1829. Here the finely wooded mountains and hills, and the somewhat desolate steppes {320b} of the Crimea commence.

In the course of the day I had an opportunity of observing the watchfulness and penetration of our commandant. A sailing-vessel was quietly at anchor in a small creek. The commandant, perceiving it, immediately ordered the steamer to stop, ordered out a boat, and sent an officer to see what it was doing there. So far everything had gone correctly; for in Russia, where the limits of every foreign fly is known, what a whole ship is about, must also be seen to. But now comes the comical part of the affair. The officer went near the ship, but did not board it, and did not ask for the ship's papers, but merely called out to the captain to know what he was about there? The captain answered that contrary winds had compelled him to anchor there, and that he waited for a favourable one to sail to this place and that. This answer satisfied the officer and the commandant completely. To me it seemed just as if any one was asked whether he was an honourable man or a rogue, and then trusted to his honour when he gave himself a good character.

23rd September. Another bad night; nothing but wind and rain. How I pitied the poor, sick fellows, and even those who were well, exposed to this weather on the deck.

Towards noon we arrived at Kertsch; the town can be seen very well from the sea, as it stretches out in a semi-circle on the shore, and rises a little up the hill Mithridates {321}, which lies behind. Higher up the hill is the museum, in the style of a Grecian temple—circular, and surrounded with columns. The summit of the mountain ends in a fine group of rocks, between which stand some obelisks and monuments, which belong to the old burial-place. The country round is a steppe, covered with artificial earth-mounds, which make the graves of a very remote period. Besides the Mithridates, there is no hill or mountain to be seen.

Kertsch lies partly on the spot where Pantikapäum formerly stood. It is now included in the government of Tauria; it is fortified, has a safe harbour, and rather considerable commerce. The population amounts to 12,000. The town contains many fine houses, which are chiefly of modern date; the streets are broad, and furnished with raised pavements for foot passengers. There is much gaiety in the two squares on Sundays and festivals. A market of every possible thing, but especially provisions, is held there. The extraordinary vulgarity and rudeness of the common people struck me greatly; on all sides I heard only abuse, shouting, and cursing. To my astonishment I saw dromedaries yoked to many loaded carts.

The Mithridates is 500 feet high, and beautiful flights of stone steps and winding paths lead up its sides, forming the only walks of the towns' people. This hill must formerly have been used by the ancients as a burial-place, for everywhere, if the earth is only scraped away, small narrow sarcophagi, consisting of four stone slabs, are found. The view from the top is extensive, but tame; on three sides a treeless steppe, whose monotony is broken only by innumerable tumuli; and on the fourth side, the sea. The sight of that is everywhere fine, and here the more so, as one sea joins another, namely, the Black Sea and the Sea of Asoph.

There was a tolerable number of ships in the roads, but very far short of four or six hundred, as the statements in the newspapers gave out, and as I had hoped to see.

On my return, I visited the Museum, which consists of a single apartment. It contains a few curiosities from the tumuli, but everything handsome and costly that was found was taken to the Museum at St. Petersburgh. The remains of sculptures, bas-reliefs, sarcophagi, and epitaphs are very much decayed. What remains of the statues indicates a high state of art. The most important thing in the Museum is a sarcophagus of white marble, which, although much dilapidated, is still very beautiful. The exterior is full with fine reliefs, especially on one side, where a figure, in the form of an angel, is represented holding two garlands of fruit together over its head. On the lid of the sarcophagus are two figures in a reclining posture. The heads are wanting; but all the other parts, the bodies, their position, and the draping of the garments, are executed in a masterly manner.

Another sarcophagus of wood, shows great perfection in the carving and turning of the wood.

A collection of earthen jars, water jugs and lamps, called to my mind those in the museum at Naples. The jars, burnt and painted brown, have a form similar to those discovered at Herculaneum and Pompeii. The water jugs are furnished with two ears, and are so pointed at the bottom, that they will not stand unless rested against something. This form of vessel is still used in Persia. Among other glass-ware, there were some flasks which consisted almost entirely of long necks, bracelets, rings and necklaces of gold; some small four-cornered embossed sheets, which were worn either on the head or chest, and some crowns, made of laurel wreaths, were very elegant. There were chains and cauldrons in copper, and ugly grotesque faces and ornaments of various kinds, which were probably fixed on the exterior of the houses. I saw some coins which were remarkably well stamped.

I had now to visit the tumuli. I sought long and in vain for a guide: very few strangers come to this place, and there are consequently no regular guides. At last there was nothing left for me but to apply to the Austrian Vice-consul, Herr Nicolits. This gentleman was not only willing to comply with my wish, but was even so obliging as to accompany me himself.

The tumuli are monuments of an entirely peculiar character; they consist of a passage about sixty feet long, fourteen broad, and twenty-five high, and a very small chamber at the end of the passage. The walls of the passage are sloping, like the roof of a house, and contract so much at the top, that at the utmost one foot is left between. They are built of long and very thick stone slabs, which are placed over each other in such a way that the upper row projects about six or seven inches beyond the under one. Upon the opening at the top are placed massive slabs of stone. Looking down from the entrance, the walls appear as if fluted. The room, which is a lengthened quadrangle, is spanned by a small arched roof, and is built in the same manner as the passage. After the sarcophagus was deposited in the room, the whole monument was covered with earth.

The fine marble sarcophagus which is in the Museum, was taken from a tumulus which was situated near the quarantine house, and is considered to be that of King Bentik.

The greater number of the monuments were opened by the Turks; the remainder were uncovered by the Russian government. Many of the bodies were found ornamented with jewels and crowns of leaves, like those in the Museum; an abundance of coins was also found.

The 26th of September was a great festival among the Russians, who celebrated the finding of the cross. The people brought bread, pastry, fruit, etc., to the church, by way of sacrifice. The whole of these things were laid up in one corner. After the service, the priest blessed them, gave some few morsels to the beggars round him, and had the remainder packed into a large basket and sent to his house.

In the afternoon, nearly the whole of the people went to the burial-ground. The common people took provisions with them, which were also blessed by the priests, but were hastily consumed by the owners.

I saw only a few people in the Russian dress. This consists, both for men and women, of long wide blue cloth coats; the men wear low felt hats, with broad brims, and have their hair cut even all round; the women bind small silk kerchiefs round their heads.

Before finishing my account of Kertsch, I must mention that there are naphtha springs in the neighbourhood; but I did not visit them, as they were described to me as precisely similar to those at Tiflis.

The next part of my journey was to Odessa. I could go either by sea or land. The latter was said to present many objects of beauty and interest; but I preferred the former, as I had in the first place no great admiration of the Russian post; and, secondly, I was heartily anxious to turn my back upon the Russian frontiers.

On the 27th of September, at 8 in the morning, I went on board the Russian steamer Dargo, of 100 horse power. The distance from Odessa to Constantinople amounts to 420 miles. The vessel was handsome and very clean, and the fare very moderate. I paid for the second cabin thirteen silver roubles, or twenty florins fifty kreutzers (£2 1s. 4d.) The only thing which did not please me in the Russian steamer, was the too great attention of the steward who, as I was told, pays for his office. All the travellers are compelled to take their meals with him, the poor deck passengers not excepted, who have often to pay him their last kopecs.

About afternoon we came to Feodosia (Caffa), which was formerly the largest and most important town in the Crimea, and was called the second Constantinople. It was at the height of its prosperity about the end of the fifteenth century, under the dominion of Genueser. Its population at that time is said to have been upwards of 200,000. It has now declined to a minor town, with 5,000 inhabitants.

Half-ruined fortification walls and towers of the time of Genueser remain, as well as a fine mosque, which has been turned into a Christian church by the Russians.

The town lies upon a large bay of the Black Sea, on the declivity of barren hills. Pretty gardens between the houses form the only vegetation to be seen.

28th September. We stopped this morning at Jalta, a very small village, containing 500 inhabitants, and a handsome church founded by the Prince Woronzoff. It is built in pure Gothic style, and stands upon a hill outside of the village. The country is again delightful here, and beautiful hills and mountains, partly covered with fine woods, partly rising in steep precipices, extend close to the sea-shore.

The steamer stayed twenty-four hours at Jalta. I took advantage of the time to make an excursion to Alupka, one of the estates of Prince Woronzoff, famous for a castle which is considered one of the curiosities of the Crimea. The road to it passed over low ranges of hills close to the sea through a true natural park, which had here and there been embellished by the help of art. The most elegant castles and country-houses belonging to the Russian nobles are seated between woods and groves, gardens and vineyards, in open spaces on hills and declivities. The whole prospect is so charming, that it appears as if prosperity, happiness, and peace, only reigned here.

The first villa which attracted me was that of Count Leo Potocki. The building is extremely tasteful. The gardens were laid out with art and sumptuousness. The situation is delightful, with an extensive view of the sea and neighbourhood.

A second magnificent building, which, however, is more remarkable for magnitude than beauty of construction, lies near the sea-shore. It resembles an ordinary square house with several stories; and, as I was informed, was built as a country bathing-place of the emperor, but had not yet been made use of. This castle is called Oriander.

Far handsomer than this palace was the charming country-house of Prince Mirzewsky. It is seated on a hill, in the centre of a magnificent park, and affords a delightful view of the mountains and sea. The principal front is Gothic.

The villa of Prince Gallizin is built entirely in the Gothic style. The pointed windows, and two towers of which, decorated with a cross, give to it the appearance of a church, and the beholder involuntarily looks for the town to which this gorgeous building belongs.

This place lies nearly at the extremity of the fine country. From here the trees are replaced by dwarf bushes, and finally by brambles; the velvety-green turf is succeeded by stony ground, and steep rocks rise behind, at the foot of which lie a quantity of fallen fragments.

Even here very pretty seats are to be seen; but they are entirely artificial, and want the charm of nature.

After travelling about thirteen wersti, the road winds round a stony hill, and the castle of Prince Woronzoff comes in sight in its entire extent. The appearance of it is not by any means so fine as I had imagined. The castle is built entirely of stone, of the same colour as the neighbouring rocks. If a large park surrounded the castle, it would stand out more prominently, and the beauty and magnificence of its architecture would be better shown. There is, indeed, a well laid out garden, but it is yet new and not very extensive. The head gardener, Herr Kebach (a German), is a master in his art; he well knows how to manage the naked barren land, so that it will bear not only the ordinary trees, plants, and flowers, but even the choicest exotic plants.

The castle is built in the Gothic style, and is full of towers, pinnacles, and buttresses, such as are seen in similar well preserved buildings of olden time. The principal front is turned towards the sea. Two lions, in Carrara marble, artistically sculptured, lie in comfortable ease at the top of the majestic flight of steps which lead from the castle far down to the sea-shore.

The interior arrangement of the castle reminded me of the "Arabian Nights;" every costly thing from all parts of the world, such as fine woods and choice works of art, is to be seen here in the greatest perfection and splendour. There are state apartments in Oriental, Chinese, Persian, and European styles; and, above all, a garden saloon, which is quite unique, for it not only contains the finest and rarest flowers but even the tallest trees. Palms, with their rich leafy crowns, extend to a great height, climbing plants cover the walls, and on all sides are flowers and blossoms. The most delightful odour diffused itself through the air, cushioned divans stood half-buried under the floating leaves; in fact, everything combined to produce the most magical impression upon the senses.

The owner of this fairy palace was unfortunately absent at a fête on a neighbouring estate. I had letters to him, and should have been glad to have made his acquaintance, as I had heard him spoken of here, both by rich and poor, as a most noble, just and generous man. I was, indeed, persuaded to wait his return, but I could not accept this offer, as I should have had to wait eight days for the

334

arrival of the next steamer, and my time was already very limited.

In the neighbourhood of the castle is a Tartar village, of which there are many in the Crimea. The houses are remarkable for their flat earth roofs, which are more used by the inhabitants than the interior of the huts; as the climate is mild and fine they pass the whole day at their work on the roofs, and at night sleep there. The dress of the men differs somewhat from that of the Russian peasants, the women dress in the Oriental fashion, and have their faces uncovered.

I never saw such admirably planted and clean vineyards as here. The grapes are very sweet, and of a good flavour; the wine light and good, and perfectly suited for making champagne, which indeed is sometimes done. I was told that more than a hundred kinds of grapes are grown in the gardens of Prince Woronzoff.

When I returned to Jalta, I was obliged to wait more than two hours, as the gentlemen with whom I was to go on board had not yet finished their carouse. At last, when they broke up, one of them, an officer of the steamer, was so much intoxicated that he could not walk. Two of his companions and the landlord dragged him to the shore. The jolly-boat of the steamer was indeed there, but the sailors refused to take us, as the jolly-boat was ordered for the captain. We were obliged to hire a boat, for which each had to pay twenty kopecs (8d.) The gentlemen knew that I did not speak Russian but they did not think I partially understood the language. I, however, overheard one of them say to the other "I have no change with me, let us leave the woman to pay." Upon this the other turned round to me, and said in French, "The share that you have to pay is twenty silver kopecs." These were gentlemen who made pretensions to honesty and honour.

29th September. Today we stopped at the strong and beautiful fortress Sewastopol. The works are partly situated at the entrance of the harbour, and partly in the harbour itself; they are executed in massive stone, and possess a number of towers and outworks which defend the entrance to the harbour. The harbour itself is almost entirely surrounded by hills, and is one of the safest and most excellent in the world. It can hold the largest fleets, and is so deep that the most gigantic men-of-war can lie at anchor close to the quays. Sluices, docks and quays have been constructed in unlimited splendour and magnificence. The whole of the works were not quite finished, and there was an unparalleled activity apparent. Thousands of men were busy on all sides. Among the workmen I was shown many of the captured Polish nobles who had been sent here as a punishment for their attempt, in 1831, to shake of the Russian yoke.

The works of the fortress and the barracks are so large that they will hold about 30,000 men.

The town itself is modern, and stands upon a range of barren hills. The most attractive among the buildings is the Greek church, as it stands quite alone on a hill, and is built in the style of a Grecian temple. The library is situated on the highest ground. There is also an open-columned hall near the club, with stone steps leading to the sea-shore, which serves as the most convenient passage to the town for those who land here. A Gothic monument to the memory of Captain Cozar, who distinguished himself greatly at the battle of Navarino, and was killed there, does not less excite the curiosity of the traveller. Like the church, it stands alone upon a hill.

The streets here, as in all the new Russian towns, are broad and clean.

30th September. Early in the morning we reached Odessa. The town looks very well from the sea. It stands high; and consequently many of the large and truly fine buildings can be seen at one glance. Among these are the Palace of Prince Woronzoff, the Exchange, the government offices, several large barracks, the quarantine buildings, and many fine private houses. Although the surrounding country is flat and barren, the number of gardens and avenues in the town give it a pleasant appearance. In the harbour was a perfect forest of masts. By far the greater number of ships do not lie here, but in the quarantine harbour. Most of the ships come from the Turkish shore, and are obliged to pass through a quarantine of fourteen days, whether they have illness on board or not.

Odessa, the chief town of the government of Cherson, is, from its situation on the Black Sea, and at the mouth of the Dniester and Dnieper, one of the most important places of commerce in South Russia. It contains 50,000 inhabitants, was founded in 1794, and declared a free port in 1817. A fine citadel entirely commands the harbour.

The Duke of Richelieu contributed most to the advancement of Odessa; for after having made several campaigns against his native country (France) in an emigrant corps, he went to Russia; and in 1803 was made governor-general of Cherson. He filled this post until 1814, during which time he brought the town to its present position. When he was appointed it contained scarcely 5,000 inhabitants. One of the finest streets bears the name of the duke, and several squares are also named in honour of him.

I remained only two days in Odessa. On the third I started by the steamer for Constantinople. I went through the town and suburbs in every direction. The finest part lies towards the sea, especially the boulevard, which is furnished with fine avenues of trees, and offers a delightful promenade; a life-size statue of the Duke Richelieu forms a fine ornament to it. Broad flights of stone steps lead from here down to the sea-shore; and in the background are rows of handsome palaces and houses. The most remarkable among them are the Government House, the Hotel St. Petersburgh, and the Palace of Prince Woronzoff, built in the Italian style, with a tasteful garden adjoining. At the opposite end of the boulevard is the Exchange, also built in the Italian style, and surrounded by a garden. Not far from this is the Academy of Arts, a rather mediocre one-story building. The Theatre, with a fine portico, promises much outside, but is nothing great within. Next to the theatre is the Palais Royal, which consists of a pretty garden, round which are ranged large handsome shops, filled with costly goods. Many articles are also hung out, but the arrangement is not near so tasteful as is the case in Vienna or Hamburgh.

Among the churches the Russian cathedral is the most striking. It has a lofty arched nave and a fine dome. The nave rests upon strong columns covered with brilliant white plaster, which looks like marble. The decorations of the churches with pictures, lamps, and lustres, etc., is rich but not artistic. This was the first church in which I found stoves, and really it was quite necessary that these should be used, the difference of temperature between this place and Jalta was very considerable for the short distance.

A second Russian church stands in the new bazaar; it has a large dome surrounded by four smaller ones, and has a very fine appearance from the exterior; inside it is small and plain.

The Catholic church, not yet quite finished, vies in point of architecture with the Russian cathedral.

The streets are all broad, handsome, and regular, it is almost impossible to lose your way in this town. In every street there are fine large houses, and this is the case even in the most remote parts as well.

In the interior of the town lies the so-called "crown garden," which is not, indeed, very large or handsome, but still affords some amusement, as great numbers of people assemble here on Sundays, and festivals, and a very good band of music plays here in summer under a tent; in winter the performances take place in a plain room.

The botanic garden, three wersti from the town, has few exotic plants, and is much neglected. The autumn changes, which I again saw here for the first time for some years, made a truly sad impression upon me. I could almost have envied the people who live in hot climates, although the heat is very troublesome.

The German language is understood by almost all but the lowest orders in Odessa.

On leaving the Russian dominions I had as much trouble with the passport regulations as on entering. The passport which was obtained on entering must be changed for another for which two silver roubles are paid. Besides this, the traveller's name has to be three times printed in the newspaper, so that if he has debts, his creditors may know of his departure. With these delays it takes at least eight days, frequently, however, two or three weeks to get away; it is not, however, necessary to wait for these forms, if the traveller provides security.

The Austrian Consul, Herr Gutenthal, answered for me, and I was thus able to bid adieu to Russia on the 2nd of October. That I did this with a light heart it is not necessary for me to assure my readers.

CHAPTER XXIV. CONSTANTINOPLE AND ATHENS.

*CONSTANTINOPLE—CHANGES—TWO FIRES—VOYAGE TO
GREECE—QUARANTINE AT ÆGINA—A DAY IN ATHENS—
CALAMACHI—THE ISTHMUS—PATRAS—CORFU.*

Little can be said of the passage from Odessa to Constantinople; we continued out at sea and did not land anywhere. The distance is 420 miles. The ship belonged to the Russian government, it was named Odessa, was of 260 horse power, and was handsome, clean, and neat.

In order that my parting with my dear friends, the Russians, might not be too much regretted, one of them was so good at the end of the passage as to behave in a manner that was far from polite. During the last night which was very mild and warm, I went out of the close cabin on to the deck, and placed myself not far from the compass-box, where I soon began to sleep, wrapt in my mantle. One of the sailors came, and giving me a kick with his foot, told me to leave the place. I thanked him quietly for the delicate way in which he expressed himself, and requesting him to leave me at peace, continued to sleep.

Among the passengers were six English sailors, who had taken a new ship to Odessa, and were returning home. I spoke with them several times, and had soon quite won them. As they perceived that I was without any companion, they asked me if I spoke enough Turkish to be able to get what I wanted from the ship's people and porters. On my answering that I did, they offered to manage everything for me if I would go on shore with them. I willingly accepted their offer.

As we approached land a customs' officer came on board to examine our luggage. In order to avoid delay I gave him some money. When we landed I wanted to pay, but the English sailors would not allow it; they said I had paid for the customs' officer, and it was therefore their time to pay for the boat. I saw that I should only have affronted them if I had pressed them further to receive the money. They settled with the porter for me, and we parted good friends. How different was the behaviour of these English sailors from that of the three well-bred Russian gentlemen at Jalta!

The passage into the Bosphorus, as well as the objects of interest in Constantinople, I have already described in my journey to the Holy Land. I went immediately to my good friend Mrs. Balbiani; but, to my regret, found that she was not in Constantinople; she had given up her hotel. I was recommended to the hotel "Aux Quatre Nations," kept by Madame Prust. She was a talkative French woman, who was always singing the praises of her housekeeping, servants,

338

cookery, etc., in which, however, none of the travellers agreed with her. She charged forty piasters (8s.), and put down a good round sum in the bill for servants' fees and such like.

Since my last stay here a handsome new wooden bridge had been erected over the Golden Horn, and the women did not seem to be so thickly veiled as on my first visit to Constantinople. Many of them wore such delicately woven veils that their faces could almost be seen through them: others had only the forehead and chin covered, and left their eyes, nose, and cheeks exposed.

The suburb of Pera looked very desolate. There had been a number of fires, which were increased by two during my stay; they were called "small," as by the first only a hundred and thirty shops, houses, and cottages, and by the second, only thirty were burned to the ground. They are accustomed to reckon the number destroyed by thousands.

The first fire broke out in the evening as we were seated at table. One of the guests offered to accompany me to see it, as he thought I should be interested by the sight if I had not seen such a one before. The scene of the fire was rather distant from our house, but we had scarcely gone a hundred steps when we found ourselves in a great crowd of people, who all carried paper lanterns, {330a} by which the streets were lighted. Every one was shouting and rushing wildly about; the inhabitants of the houses threw open their windows and inquired of the passers by the extent of the danger, and gazed with anxiety and trembling at the reflection of the flames in the sky. Every now and then sounded the shrill cry of "*Guarda! guarda!*" (take care) of the people, who carried small fire-engines {330b} and buckets of water on their shoulders, and knocked everything over that was in their way. Mounted and foot soldiers and watchmen rushed about, and Pashas rode down with their attendants to urge the people on in extinguishing the fire, and to render them assistance. Unfortunately almost all these labours are fruitless. The fire takes such hold of the wooden buildings painted with oil colours, and spreads with such incredible rapidity that it is stopped only by open spaces or gardens. One fire often destroys several thousand houses. The unfortunate inhabitants have scarce time to save themselves; those who live some distance off hastily pack their effects together and hold themselves prepared for flight at any moment. It may easily be supposed that thieves are not rare on such occasions, and it too often happens that the few things the poor people have saved are torn away from them in the bustle and confusion.

The second fire broke out in the following night. Every one had retired to sleep, but the fire-watch rushed through the street, knocking with his iron-mounted staff at the doors of the houses and waking the people. I sprang terrified out of bed, ran to the window, and saw in the direction of the fire a faint red light in the sky. In a few hours the noise and redness ceased. They have at last begun to build stone houses, not only in Pera but also in Constantinople.

I left Constantinople on the evening of the 7th of October, by the French

339

steamer *Scamander*, one hundred and sixty-horse power.

The passage from Constantinople to Smyrna, and through the Greek Archipelago is described in my journey to the Holy Land, and I therefore pass on at once to Greece.

I had been told, in Constantinople, that the quarantine was held in the Piræus (six English miles from Athens), and lasted only four days, as the state of health in Turkey was perfectly satisfactory. Instead of this, I learnt on the steamer that it was held at the island of Ægina (sixteen English miles from Piræus), and lasted twelve days, not on account of the plague but of the cholera. For the plague it lasts twenty days.

On the 10th of October we caught sight of the Grecian mainland. Sailing near the coast, we saw on the lofty prominence of a rock twelve large columns, the remains of the Temple of Minerva. Shortly afterwards we came near the hill on which the beautiful Acropolis stands. I gazed for a long time on all that was to be seen; the statues of the Grecian heroes, the history of the country came back to my mind; and I glowed with desire to set my foot on the land which, from my earliest childhood, had appeared to me, after Rome and Jerusalem, as the most interesting in the earth. How anxiously I sought for the new town of Athens—it stands upon the same spot as the old and famous one. Unfortunately, I did not see it, as it was hidden from us by a hill. We turned into the Piræus, on which a new town has also been built, but only stopped to deliver up our passports, and then sailed to Ægina.

It was already night when we arrived; a boat was quickly put out, and we were conveyed to the quay near the quarantine station. Neither the porters nor servants of this establishment were there to help us, and we were obliged to carry our own baggage to the building, where we were shown into empty rooms. We could not even get a light. I had fortunately a wax taper with me, which I cut into several pieces and gave to my fellow-passengers.

On the following morning I inquired about the regulations of the quarantine— they were very bad and very dear. A small room, quite empty, cost three drachmas (2s. 3d.) a-day; board, five drachmas (3s. 9d.); very small separate portions, sixty or seventy leptas (6d. or 7d.); the attendance, that is, the superintendence of the guardian, two drachmas a-day; the supply of water, fifteen leptas daily; the physician, a drachma; and another drachma on leaving, for which he inspects the whole party, and examines the state of their health. Several other things were to be had at a similar price, and every article of furniture has to be hired.

I cannot understand how it is that the government pays so little attention to institutions which are established for sanitary purposes and which the poor cannot avoid. They must suffer more privation here than at home; they cannot have any hot meals, for the landlord, who is not restricted in his prices, charges five or six times the value. Several artizans who had come by the vessel were put into the same room with a servant-girl. These people had no hot food the twelve days; they lived entirely upon bread, cheese, and dried figs. The girl, after a few days, begged me to let her come into my room, as the people had not behaved properly to her. In what a position the poor girl would have been placed if there had not happened to be a woman among the passengers, or if I had refused to receive her!

Are such arrangements worthy of a public institution? Why are there not a few rooms fitted up at the expense of government for the poor? Why cannot they have a plain hot meal once in the day for a moderate price? The poor surely suffer enough by not being able to earn anything for so long a time, without being deprived of their hard earnings in such a shameful manner!

On the second day the court-yard was opened, and we were permitted to walk about in an inclosed space a hundred and fifty paces wide, on the sea-shore. The view was very beautiful; the whole of the Cyclades lay before us: small, mountainous islands, mostly uninhabited and covered over with woods. Probably they were formerly a part of the mainland, and were separated by some violent convulsion of nature.

On the fourth day our range was extended, we were allowed to walk as far as the hills surrounding the lazaretto under the care of a guard. The remains of a temple stand upon these hills, fragments of a wall, and a very much decayed column. The latter, which consisted of a single piece of stone, was fluted, and, judging from the circumference, had been very high. These ruins are said to be those of the remarkably fine temple of Jupiter.

21st October. This was the day we were set at liberty. We had ordered a small vessel the evening before which was to take us to Athens early in the morning. But my fellow-travellers would insist upon first celebrating their freedom at a tavern, and from this reason it was 11 o'clock before we started. I availed myself of this time to look about the town and its environs. It is very small and contains no handsome buildings. The only remains of antiquity which I found were traces of the floor of a room in Mosaic work of coloured stones. From what I could see of the island of Ægina, it appeared extremely barren and naked, and it does not show any indications of having been once a flourishing seat of art and commerce.

Ægina is a Greek island, about two square miles in extent, it was formerly a separate state, and is said to have received the name of Ægina from the daughter of Æsop. It is supposed that the first money of Greece was coined in this island.

Our passage to the Piræus occupied a long time. There was not a breath of wind, and the sailors were obliged to row; we did not land at our destination until nearly 8 in the evening. We were first visited by the health-officer, who read through the certificates which we brought from the quarantine very leisurely. There was unfortunately nobody among us who was inclined to make it more understandable to him by a few drachmas. Of course we could not neglect going

341

to the police-office; but it was already closed, in consequence of which we dare not leave the town. I went into a large fine-looking coffee-house to look for night quarters. I was conducted to a room in which half of the window-panes were broken. The attendant said this was of no consequence, it was only necessary to close the shutters. In other respects the room looked very well but I had scarcely laid down on the bed when certain animals compelled me to take to flight. I laid down upon the sofa, which was no better. Lastly, I tried an easy chair, in which I passed the night, not in the most agreeable position.

I had already been told in Ægina of the great dirtiness and number of vermin prevalent in the Piræan inns, and had been warned against passing a night there; but what was to be done? for we could not venture to leave the town without permission of the police.

22nd October. The distance of the harbour of the Piræus from Athens is thirteen stadia, or six English miles. The road leads through olive-plantations and between barren hills. The Acropolis remains continually in sight; the town of Athens does not appear till afterwards. I had intended to remain eight days in Athens, in order to see all the monuments and remarkable places of the town and environs leisurely; but I had scarcely got out of the carriage when I heard the news of the breaking out of the Vienna revolution of October.

I had heard of the Paris revolution of the 24th February while in Bombay; that of March in Germany, at Baghdad; and the other political disturbances while at Tebris, Tiflis, and other places. No news had astonished me so much in my whole life as that from Vienna. My comfortable, peace-loving Austrians, and an overthrow of the government! I thought the statement so doubtful, that I could not give full credit to the verbal information of the Resident at Baghdad; he was obliged to show it to me in black and white in the newspaper to convince me. The affair of March so delighted and inspirited me that I felt proud of being an Austrian. The later occurrences of May, however, cooled my enthusiasm; and that of the 6th of October completely filled me with sadness and dejection. No overthrow of a state ever began so promisingly. It would have stood alone in history if the people had gone on in the spirit of the March movement; and then to end in such a way! I was so grieved and upset by the result of the 6th of October, that I lost all enjoyment of everything. Moreover, I knew my friends were in Vienna, and I had heard nothing from them. I should have hastened there immediately if there had been an opportunity of doing so; but I was obliged to wait till the next day, as the steamer did not start till then. I made arrangements to go by it, and then took a cicerone to show me all the objects of interest in the town, more for diversion than pleasure.

My fate had been very unfortunate; twelve days I had patiently endured being shut up in the lazaretto at Ægina, in order to be able to see the classic country, and now I was so anxious to leave it that I had neither rest nor peace.

Athens, the capital of the former State of Attica, is said to have been founded in the year 1300, fourteen hundred years before Christ, by Cecrops, from whom it then took the name of Cecropia, which in after-times was retained only by the castle: under Eriktonius the town was named "Athens." The original town stood upon a rock in the centre of a plain, which was afterwards covered with buildings; the upper part was called the "Acropolis," the lower the "Katopolis;" only a part of the fortress, the famous Acropolis, remains on the mountain, where the principal works of art of Athens stand. The principal feature was the temple of Minerva, or the Parthenon; even its ruins excite the astonishment of the world. The building is said to have been 215 feet long, ninety-seven feet broad, and seventy feet high; here stood the statue of Minerva, by Phidias. This masterly work was executed in gold and ivory; its height was forty-six feet, and it is said to have weighed more than 2000 pounds. Fifty-five columns of the entrance to the temple still remain, as well as parts of enormous blocks of marble which rest upon them, and belonged to the arches and roof.

This temple was destroyed by the Persians, and was again restored with greater beauty by Pericles, about 440 years after the birth of Christ.

There are some fine remains of the temples of Minerva and Neptune, and the extent of the amphitheatre can still be seen; there is but little of the theatre of Bacchus remaining.

Outside the Acropolis stands the temple of Theseus and that of Jupiter Olympus; the one on the north, the other on the south side. The former is in the Doric style, and is surrounded by thirty-six fine columns. On the *metope* are represented the deeds of Theseus in beautiful reliefs. The interior of the temple is full of fine sculptures, epitaphs, and other works in stone, most of which belong to the other temples, but are collected here. Outside the temple stand several marble seats which have been brought from the neighbouring Areopagus, the former place of assembly for the patricians. Of the Areopagus itself nothing more is to be seen than a chamber cut out of the rock, to which similarly cut steps lead.

Of the temple of Jupiter Olympus so much of the foundation-walls still remain as to show what its size was; there are also sixteen beautiful columns, fifty-eight feet in height. This temple, which was completed by Hadrian, is said to have exceeded in beauty and magnificence all the buildings of Athens. The exterior was decorated by one hundred and twenty fluted columns six feet in diameter and fifty-nine in height. The gold and ivory statue of Jupiter was, like that of Minerva, the production of the masterly hand of Phidias. All the temples and buildings were of pure white marble.

Not far from the Areopagus is the Pnyx, where the free people of Athens met in council. Of this nothing more remains than the rostrum, hewn in the rock, and the seat of the scribe. What feelings agitate the mind when it is remembered what men have stood there and spoke from that spot!

It was with sadness that I examined the cave near here where Socrates was imprisoned and poisoned. Above this memorable grotto stands a plain monument erected in memory of Philopapoe.

The Turks surrounded the Acropolis with a broad wall, in the building of which they made use of many fragments of columns and other remains of the most beautiful temples.

No remnants of antiquity are to be seen in the old town of Athens except the Tower of the Winds, or, as others call it, Diogenes' Lantern, a small temple in the form of an octagon, covered with fine sculpture; also the monument of Lysicrates. This consists of a pedestal, some columns, and a dome in the Corinthian style.

The chapel Maria Maggiore, is said to have been built by the Venetians, 700 years after Christ. Its greatest peculiarity is that it was the first Christian church in Athens.

The view of the whole country from the Acropolis is also very interesting; there can be seen the Hymetos, the Pentelikon, towards Eleusis, Marathon, Phylæ, and Dekelea, the harbour, the sea, and the course of the Ilissus.

Athens contains a considerable number of houses, most of which are, however, small and unimportant; the beautiful country-houses, on the contrary, surrounded by tasty gardens, have a very agreeable appearance.

The small observatory was built by Baron Sina, the well-known banker in Vienna, who is by birth a Greek.

The royal palace, which is of modern date, is built of brilliant white marble, in the form of a large quadrangle. On two sides, which occupy a large part of the breadth of the wings, under a peristyle, is a kind of small porch which rests upon pillars. The one approach is for the ministers, ambassadors, etc., the other for the royal family. With the exception of these two peristyles, the whole building is very tasteless, and has not the least ornament; the windows are in the ordinary form; and the high large walls appear so naked, bare, and flat, that even the dazzling white of the beautiful marble produces no effect; and it is only on a close approach that it can be seen what a costly material has been employed in the building.

I regretted having seen this palace, especially opposite to the Acropolis, on a spot which has made its works of art as classic as its heroes.

The palace is surrounded by a rather pretty though recently-formed garden. In the front stand a few palms, which have been brought from Syria, but they bear no fruit. The country is otherwise barren and naked.

The marble of which this palace is built, as well as the temples and other buildings on the Acropolis, is obtained from the quarries of the neighbouring mountain, Pentelikon, where the quantity of this beautiful stone is so great that

344

whole towns might be built of it.

It was Sunday, and the weather was very fine, {335} to which I was indebted for seeing all the fashionable world of Athens, and even the Court, in the open promenade. This place is a plain avenue, at the end of which a wooden pavilion is erected. It is not decorated by either lawns or flower-beds. The military bands play every Sunday from five to six. The King rides or drives with his Queen to this place to show himself to the people. This time he came in an open carriage with four horses, and stopped to hear several pieces of music. He was in Greek costume; the Queen wore an ordinary French dress.

The Greek or rather Albanian costume is one of the handsomest there is. The men wear full frocks, made of white perkal, which reach from the hips to the knees, buskins from the knee to the feet, and shoes generally of red leather. A close-fitting vest of coloured silk without arms, over a silk shirt, and over this another close-fitting spencer of fine red, blue, or brown cloth, which is fastened only at the waist by a few buttons or a narrow band, and lays open at the top. The sleeves of the spencer are slit up, and are either left loose or slightly held together by some cords round the wrists; the collar of the shirt is a little turned over. The vest and spencer are tastily ornamented with cords, tassels, spangles and buttons of gold, silver or silk, according to the means of the wearer. The material, colour and ornament of the Zaruchi correspond with those of the spencer and vest. A dagger is generally worn in the girdle, together with a pair of pistols. The head-dress is a red fez, with a blue tassel.

The Greek dress is, as far as I saw, less worn by the women, and even then much of its originality is lost. The principal part of the dress consists of a French garment, which is open at the breast, over this a close spencer is drawn on, which is also open, and the sleeves wide and rather shorter than those of the gown. The front edges of the gown and spencer are trimmed with gold lace. The women and girls wear on their head a very small fez, which is bound round with rose or other coloured crape.

24th October. I left Athens by the small steamer *Baron Kübeck*, seventy-horse power, and went as far as Calamachi (twenty-eight miles). Here I had to leave the ship and cross the Isthmus, three English miles broad. At Lutrachi we went on board another vessel.

During the passage to Calamachi, which lasts only a few hours, the little town of Megara is seen upon a barren hill.

Nothing is more unpleasant in travelling than changing the conveyance, especially when it is a good one, and you can only lose by doing so. We were in this situation. Herr Leitenberg was one of the best and most attentive of all captains that I had ever met with in my travels, and we were all sorry to have to leave him and his ship. Even in Calamachi, where we remained this day and the following, as the ship which was to carry us on from Lutrachi did not arrive, on account of

345

contrary winds, until the 25th, he attended to us with the greatest politeness.

The village of Calamachi offers but little of interest, the few houses have only been erected since the steamers plied, and the tolerably high mountains on which it lies are for the most part barren, or grown over with low brambles. We took several walks on the Isthmus, and ascended minor heights, from whence on one side is seen the gulf of Lepanto, and on the other the Ægean sea. In front of us stood the large mountain, Akrokorinth, rising high above all its companions. Its summit is embellished by a well-preserved fortification, which is called the remains of the Castle of Akrokorinth, and was used by the Turks in the last war as a fortress. The formerly world-famous city of Corinth, after which all the fittings of luxury and sumptuousness in the interior of palaces were named, and which gave the name to a distinct order of architecture, is reduced to a small town with scarcely a thousand inhabitants, and lies at the foot of the mountain, in the midst of fields and vineyards. It owes the whole of its present celebrity to its small dried grapes, called currants.

It is said that no town of Greece had so many beautiful statues of stone and marble as Corinth. It was upon this isthmus, which consists of a narrow ridge of mountains, and is covered with dense fig-groves, in which stood a beautiful temple of Neptune, were held the various Isthmian games.

How greatly a people or a country may degenerate! The Grecian people, at one time the first in the world, are now the furthest behind! I was told by everyone that in Greece it was neither safe to trust myself with a guide nor to wander about alone, as I had done in other countries; indeed, I was warned here in Calamachi not to go too far from the harbour, and to return before the dusk of the evening.

26th October. We did not start from Lutrachi until towards noon, by the steamer *Hellenos*, of one hundred and twenty-horse power.

We anchored for a few hours in the evening near Vostizza, the ancient Ægion, now an unimportant village, at the foot of a mountain.

27th October, Patras. That portion of Greece which I had already seen was neither rich in beauty, well cultivated, nor thickly inhabited. Here were, at least, plains and hills covered with meadows, fields, and vineyards. The town, on the Gulf of Lepanto, was formerly an important place of trade; and before the breaking out of the Greek revolution in 1821, contained 20,000 inhabitants; it has now only 7,000. The town is defended by three fortresses, one of which stands upon a hill, and two at the entrance of the harbour. The town is neither handsome nor clean, and the streets are narrow. The high mountains pleased me better; and their chain can be followed for a considerable distance.

I saw grapes here whose beauty and size induced me to buy some; but I found them so hard, dry, and tasteless, that I did not even venture to give them to a sailor, but threw them into the sea.

28th October. Corfu is the largest of the Ionian Islands, which formerly belonged to Greece, and lie at the entrance to the Adriatic sea. Corfu, the ancient Corcyra, has been subject to England since 1815.

The town of Corfu is situated in a more beautiful and fertile country than Patras, and is far larger. It contains 18,000 inhabitants. Adjoining the town are two romantic peaks of rock, with strong fortified works, upon which stand the telegraph and the lighthouse. Both are surrounded by artificial ditches, with draw-bridges leading across. The immediate environs of the town, as well as the whole island, are rich in delightful groves of olive and orange trees.

The town contains handsome houses and streets, with the exception of the bye-streets, which are remarkably crooked and not very clean. At the entrance of the town stands a large covered stone hall, in which on one side are the stalls of the butchers; on the other, those of the fishermen. In the open space in front are exposed the choicest vegetables and most beautiful fruits. The theatre presents a very pretty appearance; it would seem, from the sculptures upon it, to have been used for a church. The principal square is large and handsome; it is intersected by several avenues, and one side faces the sea. The palace of the English governor stands here; a fine building in the Grecian-Italian style.

The famous and much-visited church of St. Spiridion is but small; it contains many oil-paintings, some are good specimens of the old Italian School. In a small dark chapel at the furthest end of the church lies, in a silver sarcophagus, the body of St. Spiridion, who is held in great veneration by the Ionians. The chapel is always full of devotees who tenderly kiss the sarcophagus.

On the 29th of October we saw the low mountain-country of Dalmatia, and on the 30th I entered Trieste, whence I hastened on to Vienna the day following. I was obliged to pass several days in the greatest anxiety before the town, as it had been taken by storm on the last day of October and was not opened until the 4th of November. It was not until I had seen that all my relations were safe that I was able to return thanks with a grateful heart to the good Providence which, in all my dangers and troubles, had so remarkably protected and preserved me in health and strength. With equal gratitude I remembered those people who had treated me with such kindness, had so disinterestedly received me, and through whose help I had been enabled to overcome the frequent great hardships and difficulties I encountered.

From my readers I hope for a charitable judgment upon my book, which in simple language describes what I have experienced, seen and felt, and makes no higher pretension than that of being sincere and trustworthy.

NOTES.

{9} The sextant is a mathematical instrument by which the different degrees of longitude and latitude are determined, and the hour known. The chronometers also are set by it. In order to find the latitude the ship is in, an observation is taken at noon, but only when the sun shines. This last is absolutely necessary, since it is from the shadow cast upon the figures of the instrument that the reckoning is made. The longitude can be determined both morning and afternoon, as the sun, in this case, is not necessary.

{11} The heat does not require to be very great in order to melt the pitch in a ship's seams. I have seen it become soft, and form bladders, when the thermometer stood at 81.5 in the sun.

{12} Every four hours the state of the wind, how many miles the vessel has made, in fact, every occurrence, is noted down in the log with great exactitude. The captain is obliged to show this book to the owners of the ship at the conclusion of the voyage.

{13} Some years ago a sailor made an attempt to scale the Sugarloaf. He succeeded in attaining the summit, but never came down again. Most likely he made a false step and was precipitated into the sea.

{14} The worthy Lallemand family received her, a few days after her arrival into their house.

{23a} The princess was three weeks old.

{23b} Rockets and small fireworks are always let off at every religious festival, some before the church, and others at a short distance from it. The most ludicrous part of the affair is, that this is always done in open day.

{27} They are differently paid, according to what they can do. The usual hire of a maid-servant is from ten to twelve shillings per month; for a cook, twenty-four to forty; for a nurse, thirty-eight to forty; for a skilful labourer, fifty to seventy.

{34a} *Truppa* is a term used to designate ten mules driven by a negro; in most instances a number of truppas are joined together, and often make up teams or caravans of 100 or 200 mules. Everything in the Brazils is conveyed upon mules.

{34b} A cord, with a noose at the end; the native inhabitants of South America use it so skilfully that they catch the most savage animals with it.

{38} *Fazenda* is equivalent to our word "plantation."

{39} *Kabï* is African grass, which is planted all over the Brazils, as grass never grows there of its own accord. It is very high and reed-like.

{40} *Rost* (roaster) is employed to denote partly a strip of low brushwood, partly the place where a wood has stood previously to being burnt.

{42} All through Brazil, *carna secca* is one of the principal articles of food, both for whites and blacks. It comes from Buenos Ayres, and consists of beef cut into long, thin, broad stripes, salted and dried in the open air.

{47} Under the term "whites," are included not only those Europeans who have lately immigrated, but also the Portuguese, who have been settled in the country for centuries.

{50} This wholesome plant grows very commonly in the Brazils.

{53} In the southern hemisphere the seasons, as regards the months, are exactly the contrary to what they are in the northern. For instance, when it is winter on one side of the Equator it is summer on the other, etc.

{55} Maroon negroes are those negroes who have run away from their masters. They generally collect in large bands, and retire into the recesses of the virgin forests, whence, however, they often emerge to steal and plunder; their depredations are not unfrequently accompanied by murder.

{59} The Rio Plata is one of the largest rivers in Brazil.

{60} Other captains assured me that it was only possible for men-of-war to pass through the Straits of Magellan, as the passage requires a great number of hands. Every evening the ship must be brought to an anchor, and the crew must constantly be in readiness to trim or reef the sails, on account of the various winds which are always springing up.

{62} The glass sank in the day-time to 48° and 50°, and at night to 28° below Zero.

{73} All the Indians are Christians (Protestants), but I fear only in name.

{76} Elephantiasis, in this country, generally shows itself in the feet, and extends up as far as the calves of the legs. These portions of the body, when so affected, are greatly swollen, and covered with scurf and blotches, so that they really might be taken for those of an elephant.

{78} I purposely abstain from mentioning the names of any of the gentlemen at Tahiti, a piece of reserve which I think entitles me to their thanks.

{86} Up to the present period, Tahiti has produced nothing for exportation, and therefore all vessels have to clear out in ballast. The island is important to the French, as a port where their ships in the Pacific may stop and refit.

{91a} The expense of living at an hotel in Macao, Victoria, and Canton is from four to six dollars a-day (16s. to 24s.).

{91b} Carl Gützlaff was born on the 8th of July, 1803, at Pyritz, in Pomerania. As a boy he was distinguished for his piety and extraordinary talent. His parents

349

apprenticed him to a leather-seller. In this capacity he was noted for his industry, although he was far from contented with his position; and, in the year 1821, he found an opportunity of presenting a poem, in which he expressed his sentiments and wishes, to the King of Prussia. The king recognised the talent of the struggling youth, and opened to him a career in accordance with his inclination. In the year 1827 he proceeded as a missionary to Batavia, and, at a later period, to Bintang, where he applied himself with such assiduity to the study of Chinese, that in the space of two years he knew it well enough to preach in it. In December, 1831, he went to Macao, where he established a school for Chinese children, and commenced his translation of the Bible into Chinese. He founded, in conjunction with Morrison, a Society for the Diffusion of Useful Knowledge in China, and edited a monthly Chinese magazine, in which he endeavoured to interest the people upon history, geography, and literature. In 1832 and 1833 he penetrated as far as the province of Fo-Kien.

Gützlaff's Travels have made us acquainted with several very important facts connected with the different Chinese dialects, and are also of great worth to other scientific points of view. They are especially useful in enabling us to form a correct opinion as to the merits of the works that have lately appeared on China; and everyone must acknowledge his rare talent, must value his immovable fixedness of purpose, and must admire his zealous perseverance in the cause of science, and his unshaken belief in the principles of his religion. (Dr. Gützlaff died in November, 1851).

{93} All large vessels have two painted eyes let into the prow; with these, as the Chinese believe, they are better able to find their way.

{95} There is only one mail a month from Europe.

{101} When they copy a picture they divide it, like our own artists, into squares.

{102a} A *pikul* of raw opium is worth about 600 dollars (£120).

{102b} I had more especially reason to fear this latter circumstance, as the people had given out that on the 12th or 13th of August, at the latest, there would be a revolution, in which all the Europeans would lose their lives. My state of mind may easily be imagined, left, as I was, entirely alone with the Chinese servants.

{103} One of the ports which were opened to the English in 1842.

{104} His costume was composed of a wide over-garment reaching to the knees, and furnished with flowing arms, and, underneath this, trousers of white silk. The upper garment was made of brocade of very vivid colours and an extraordinary pattern. On his breast he wore two birds as marks of his rank, and a necklace of precious stones. His shoes, composed of black silk, were turned up into points at the extremities. On his head he wore a conical velvet hat with a gilt button.

{105} The reader must know that these animals are looked upon as particularly sacred.

{108} The town of Canton is nine miles in circumference. It is the residence of a Viceroy, and divided by walls into the Chinese and the Tartar town. The population of the town itself is reckoned at 400,000, while it is calculated that 60,000 persons live in the boats and schampans, and about 200,000 in the immediate vicinity. The number of Europeans settled here is about 200.

{110} The Chinese adopt white for mourning.

{112} Noble Chinese ladies pass a much more secluded life than Eastern women. They are allowed to visit one another very seldom, and that only in well-closed litters. They have neither public baths nor gardens in which they can meet.

{114} The leaves of this gathering are plucked with the greatest care by children and young people, who are provided with gloves and are bound to pick every leaf separately.

{116} 173 dollars the chief cabin, 117 the second (£34 12s. and £23 8s.)

{118} These steamers carry the mails, and make the voyage from Canton to Calcutta once a month, touching at Singapore on their way.

{120a} Horses cannot be bred here; they have all to be imported.

{120b} The East India Company, to which the island belongs, have a governor and English troops here.

{125} The mangostan is unanimously pronounced the finest fruit in the world.

{128} One of the four had been removed from the first cabin, because it was asserted that he was somewhat cracked, and did not always know what he said or did.

{150} The finest and most costly muslin is manufactured in the province of Dacca, and costs two rupees (4s.), or even two rupees and a half the ell.

{153} The *hurgila*, a kind of stork, that eats dead bodies, and is frequently to be seen near the rivers in India.

{158a} At the period of my visit there were about 782 of them.

{158b} Rajmahal was, in the seventeenth century, the capital of Bengal.

{160a} Monghyr is termed the Birmingham of India, on account of its extensive manufactories of cutlery and weapons. Its population is about 30,000 souls.

{160b} Patna is the capital of the province of "Bechar," and was once celebrated for the number of its Buddhist temples. Near Patna was situated the most famous town of ancient India, namely, "Parlibothra." Patna contains a great many cotton and a few opium factories.

{161} In all Indian, Mahomedan, and in fact all countries which are not Christian, it is a very difficult task to obtain anything like an exact calculation of the number of inhabitants, as nothing is more hateful to the population than such computations.

{162} I landed with two travellers at Patna, and rode on to Deinapore in the evening, where our steamer anchored for the night.

{170} If a Hindoo has no son, he adopts one of his relations, in order that he may fulfil the duties of a son at the funeral of his adoptive father.

{173} The dislike which the Hindoos evince towards the Europeans, is chiefly in consequence of the latter showing no honour to the cow, of their eating ox-flesh, and drinking brandy; and that they spit in their houses, and even in the temples, and wash their mouths with their fingers, etc. They call the Europeans "Parangi." This disrespect is said to make the Hindoos dislike the Christian religion.

{177} Many of the more recent Indian towns were built by the Mongolians, or were so much altered by them that they altogether lost their original character. India was conquered by the Mongolians as early as the tenth century.

{183} At the time of its greatest prosperity it had 2,000,000 inhabitants.

{185} Some writers describe this colossal crystal as being twenty-five feet long.

{190} If these two towers did belong to a mosque, why were they built of such different sizes?

{193} The cheprasses are servants of the English government. They wear red cloth scarfs, and a brass plate on the shoulders, with the name of the town to which they belong engraved upon it. Each of the higher English officials are allowed to have one or more of these people in their service. The people consider them much superior to the ordinary servants.

{200} Children are generally considered as impure until the ninth year, and are therefore not subject to the laws of their religion.

{204} The god Vishnu is represented as a tortoise.

{209} Although only the beginning of spring, the temperature rose during the day as high as 95° - 99° Fah.

{212a} Mundsch is the royal tutor, writer, or interpreter.

{212b} It is well known that saltpetre produces a considerable reduction of temperature.

{213} Indor lies 2,000 feet above the level of the sea.

{225} Monsoons are the periodical winds which blow during one-half the year from east to west, during the other half from west to east.

{226} The Black Town is that part of the town in which the poorer classes of inhabitants reside. That neither beauty nor cleanliness are to be sought there, is a matter of course.

{227} There are in all only 6,000 Parsees in the island of Bombay.

{228} And yet Bombay is the principal seat of the Fire-worshippers.

{268} This is an error: M. Botta made the first attempt to excavate the Ninevite remains at Khorsabad. Mr. Layard had, moreover, commenced his excavations before he received the countenance of the British Museum authorities. See "Nineveh—the Buried City of the East," one of the volumes of the "National Illustrated Library," for the rectification of this and other errors in Madame Pfeiffer's account.

{270} The manuscripts of the journey through Hindostan as far as Mósul miscarried for more than a year and a half. I gave them up as lost. This was the cause of the delay in the publication of my "Journey round the world."

{279} I had picked up enough of the language between here and Mósul to understand this much.

{287} Mela is the name of the Indian religious festivals at which thousands of people assemble. The missionaries frequently travel hundreds of miles to them in order to preach to the people.

{305} Tradition says that the country about Erivan is that part of the earth which was first of all peopled. Noah and his family dwelt here, both before and after the deluge; the Garden of Eden is also said to have been situated here. Erivan was formerly called Terva, and was the chief city of Armenia. Not far from Erivan lies the chief sacred relic of the Armenian Christians—the cloister Ecs-miazim. The church is simple in construction; the pillars, seventy-three feet high, consist of blocks of stone joined together. In the Treasury were, formerly, two of the nails with which Christ was crucified, the lance with which he was stabbed in the side, and, lastly, a seamless garment of Christ. It is asserted that in the centre of the church is the spot where Noah, after his delivery, erected an altar and offered sacrifice. Besides these, the church is in the possession of innumerable important relics.

{308} This is carried to such an extent that if a traveller has his horses already put to, and is in the carriage, and an officer arrives, the horses are taken off and given to the latter.

{309} Georgia was called Iberia by the ancients. Formerly, this country extended from Tauris and Erzerum, as far as the Tanais, and was called Albania. It is a country of mountains. The river Kurry, also called Cyrus, flows through the midst. On this river the famous conqueror of Persia, Cyrus, was exposed in his childhood. Tiflis was formerly one of the finest towns of Persia.

{312} His wives I dare not speak of, as the Mussulmen consider this an affront.

{314} The River Ribon, also called Rione, is considered to be one of the four

353

rivers of Paradise, and was known by the name of Pison. Its waters were formerly held sacred. On account of the number of trunks of trees, it is unnavigable for large ships.

{320a} The Circassians are so wild and warlike that no one dare venture into the interior of the country. Little is known of their habits, customs, or religion. Bordering on Circassia are the Atkans, who inhabit the coast country between Mingrelia and Circassia, and are also wild and given to plunder.

{320b} Large plains covered with short grass.

{321} Mithridates lived in Pantikapäum. The hill at Kertsch is called to this day "Mithridates' Seat." During the excavations in it, which have been made since 1832, many remains were found, such as funeral urns, implements of sacrifice, Grecian inscriptions, handsome figures, and groups.

{330a} Constantinople is not lighted—whoever goes out without a lantern is considered suspicious, and taken to the next watch-house.

{330b} The streets of Constantinople are narrow, full of holes, and uneven, so that carriages cannot be taken everywhere and people are obliged to manage with small fire-engines carried by four men.

{335} Here, where I arrived about four weeks after leaving Odessa, the sun appeared as hot as with us in July. The vegetation was greatly in want of rain, and the leaves were almost dying from the heat; while in Odessa they were already killed by the cold.

Made in the USA
Coppell, TX
02 March 2024

29652352R00197